ELEMENTS

OF

SYRIAC GRAMMAR

BY AN

INDUCTIVE METHOD

BY

ROBERT DICK WILSON, Ph.D.

PROFESSOR OF OLD TESTAMENT LANGUAGES AND HISTORY IN THE WESTERN
THEOLOGICAL SEMINARY, ALLEGHENY, PA.

WIPF & STOCK · Eugene, Oregon

Wipf and Stock Publishers
199 W 8th Ave, Suite 3
Eugene, OR 97401

Elements of Syriac Grammar by an Inductive Method
By Wilson, Robert Dick
ISBN 13: 978-1-5326-1275-6
Publication date 1/28/2016
Previously published by Charles Scribner's Sons, 1891

TO
PROFESSOR EDUARD SACHAU,
WHO HAS DONE SO MUCH FOR THE PROMOTION
OF SEMITIC STUDIES,
THIS BOOK IS AFFECTIONATELY DEDICATED
BY ONE OF HIS AMERICAN STUDENTS

PREFACE.

This Syriac grammar was undertaken six years ago at the suggestion of Professor W. R. Harper, Ph.D. It is designed to do in a measure for the Syriac language that which Professor Harper's text-books have done for the Hebrew. In the orthography and etymology the author has sought to draw his illustrative examples, as far as possible, from the chrestomathy published in his MANUAL OF SYRIAC. These are denoted by the page and line upon which they occur; thus, 2. 2. after an example shows that it is found on page 2, line 2, of the MANUAL. References to the Bible are to the Peshito version when not otherwise indicated.

In the syntax, the author has aimed to give two examples, at least, on which to base every rule, statement, or remark. It was his object to adduce one of these examples from the Peshito version and the other from some native classical source. It will be noted that Joshua the Stylite, in the edition of Professor W. Wright, Addai the Apostle, by Professor George Phillips, D.D., and the Spicilegium Syriacum, by W. Cureton, have been more frequently cited than any other original authorities. The reason for this was that they are all accessible to American or English students who may make use of the grammar. Indeed, it has been the author's hope that students, after they had mastered the MANUAL, would secure Joshua the Stylite, Addai the Apostle, and the Spicilegium Syriacum (the last of which was a text-book at Berlin some years ago), and continue their studies by reading these books in the unpointed text in which they have been published. The simplicity of the first, the intrinsic interest of the second, which centres around Abgar's letter to the Christ, and the variety of style and literature of the third, give wings to the student's zeal and further his rapid progress while making him unconscious of the labor of acquisition.

Thanks for aid in preparing the manuscript of this work are

due to Mrs. Ella Wilson Stewart, A.B. (Vassar), and to the Rev. W. O. Elterich, A.M.

The author has received inestimable assistance in regard to rules and examples from the grammars of Hoffmann, Hoffmann-Merx, Uhlemann, Phillips, Martin, and Agrell, but especially from those of Duval and Nöldeke, though he has throughout conscientiously worked up his material according to his own plan, and has enriched the store of illustrations by hundreds of new citations. The rules have been based upon the examples given, and it is hoped by the author that they are not merely more numerous, but better classified and more clearly defined than has ever before been accomplished in English.

The examples have been taken from accessible sources, denoted by the page and line, or by section, so that they can be readily confirmed. In the syntax, when the examples could not be verified, the grammar from which they have been taken has been noted.

The hope that this grammar would be a means of furthering the study of Syriac by American students, and of throwing fresh light upon the Sacred Scriptures, has encouraged the author, and, as he thinks, justified him in the publishing of this book.

The plates for the first sixty pages were made by Messrs. Tuttle, Moorhouse & Taylor, of New Haven, Conn.; those for the remainder by the firm of W. Drugulin, of Leipsic, Germany.

For convenience of cross reference, the order and arrangement of Professor Harper's "Elements" and "Syntax" have been followed as closely as practicable. Those who wish to compare the Syriac with the Hebrew can readily find where the two languages agree and differ by following the index of this volume (upon which much time and care have been expended in the effort to make it a full and accurate guide to the contents), and by comparing it with the indexes of Harper's or other Hebrew grammars.

In the citations, the following abbreviations occur:

A. A. or Ad. Ap. = Addai the Apostle ;
J. S. or Jos. Sty. = Joshua the Stylite ;
Spic. Syr. = Spicilegium Syriacum ;
Aphr. = Aphraates, by Professor W. Wright ;
Overbeck = S. Ephraemi Syri aliorumque opera selecta, by J. J. Overbeck.

TABLE OF CONTENTS.

Part First—Orthography.
1. The Alphabet.
2. Signs with two Sounds.
3. Pronunciation of Certain Signs.
4. Peculiarities of Form of Letters.
5. Classification of Letters.
6. Vowel Signs.
7. Vowel Sounds.
8. Diphthongs.
9. Unvowelled Consonants.
10. Rukhokh and Kushoy.
11. Linea Occultans.
12. Mehagyono and Marhetono.
13. Rebbuy.
14. Accent.
15. The Accents.
16. Syllables.
17. Kinds of Syllables.
18. Assimilation.
19. Occultation.
20. Addition.
21. Transposition.
22. Permutation.
23. Rejection.
24. Otiose Letters.
25. Quiescence.
26. Peculiarities of Gutturals.
27. Peculiarities of Wau and Yudh.
28. Quantity of Vowels.
29. Euphony of Vowels.
30. Loss of Vowels.
31. The Half-Vowel.
32. Shifting of Vowels.
33. New Vowels.

Part Second—Etymology.
34. Inseparable Particles.
35. Personal Pronouns.
36. Pronominal Suffixes.
37. Demonstrative Pronouns.
38. Relative and Possessive Pronouns.
39. The Interrogative Pronouns.
40. The Strong Verb.
41. Verb Stems.
42. General View of the Verb Stems.
43. The Pe‘al Perfect.
44. The Remaining Perfects.
45. The Pe‘al Imperfect.
46. Pe‘al Imperfects in A and E.
47. The Remaining Imperfects.
48. The Imperative.
49. The Infinitives.
50. The Participles.
51. The Verb with Suffixes.
52. Guttural Verbs.
53. Pê Nun Verbs.
54. Ê Ê Verbs.
55. Pê Olaph Verbs.
56. Ê Olaph Verbs.
57. Lomadh Olaph Guttural Verbs.
58. Pê Yudh Verbs.
59. Ê Wau Verbs.
60. Lomadh Olaph Verbs.
61. Lomadh Olaph Verbs with Suffixes.
62. Doubly Weak Verbs.
63. Quadriliterals.
64. Anomalous and Defective Verbs.
65. '*Ith* and *Layt*.
66. Inflection and Classification of Nouns.
67. Nouns with one Short Vowel.
68. Nouns with two Short Vowels.
69. Nouns with one Short and one Long Vowel.
70. Nouns with one Long and one Short Vowel.
71. Nouns with two Long Vowels.

TABLE OF CONTENTS.

72. Nouns with the Second Radical Doubled.
73. Nouns with one or more Radicals Doubled.
74. Nouns formed by Prefixes.
75. Nouns formed by Affixes.
76. Gender, Number, and State.
77. Nouns with Suffixes.
78. Declension.
79. First Declension of Masculines.
80. Second Declension of Masculines.
81. Third Declension of Masculines.
82. First Declension of Feminines.
83. Second Declension of Feminines.
84. Third Declension of Feminines.
85. Fourth Declension of Feminines.
86. Anomalies of Gender and Number.
87. Peculiar Anomalies of Nouns.
88. The Numerals.
89. The Particles.

Part Third—Syntax.

90. The Collective Noun.
91. Gender of Noun.
92. Number of Noun.
93. Determination.
94. Apposition.
95. The Nominative Absolute.
96. The Genitive.
97. The Genitive with d.
98. The Genitive with Prepositions.
99. The Adjective.
100. Comparative and Superlative.
101. The Personal Pronoun.
102. The Demonstrative Pronoun.
103. The Interrogative Pronoun.
104. The Relative Pronoun.
105. The Reflexive Pronoun.
106. The Possessive Pronoun.
107. The Indefinite Pronoun.
108. Uses of *Kul*.
109. Uses of *Medhem*.
110. Numerals.
111. The Verb.
112. The Perfect.
113. The Imperfect.
114. The Imperfect Continued.
115. The Imperative.
116. The Participle Active.
117. The Passive Participle.
118. Participles as Nouns.
119. The Infinitive Absolute.
120. The Infinitive Construct.
121. The Subject of the Verb.
122. Impersonal Verbs.
123. The Object of the Verb.
124. The Verb with Indirect Object.
125. The Verb with two or more Objects.
126. Passives, etc., with Objects.
127. Uses of *h'wo*.
128. Uses of *'Ith*.
129. *'ithidh* and other Auxiliaries.
130. Verbal and Nominal Sentences.
131. Simple Sentences.
132. The Interrogative Sentence.
133. Compound Sentences, Conjunctive.
134. Alternative and Adversative Sentences.
135. Complex Sentences.
136. Adjectival or Relative Sentences.
137. Adverbial Clauses or Sentences.
138. Conditional Sentences.

ELEMENTS OF SYRIAC.

ALPHABET.

Names of the Signs.	Jacobite. Unconnected (or final).	Jacobite. Connected to the right.	Jacobite. Connected to the left.	Jacobite. Connect. to the right and left.	Estrangelo.	Numerical Value.	REMARKS: English Equivalent of the sound.
Olaph			—	—		1	Spiritus lenis, *h* in *h*our.
Bêth						2	*b, bh.*
Gomal						3	*g, gh.*
Dolath			—	—		4	*d, dh.*
Hê			—	—		5	*h,* always as in *h*ome.
Wau			—	—		6	*w,* as in *w*o*ww*o*w.*
Zain			—	—		7	*z.*
Ḥêth						8	*ch,* as in lo*ch.*
Ṭêth						9	Emphatic *t.*
Yudh						10	*y,* as in *y*our.
Koph						20	*k* or *kh,* as in wor*kh*ouse.
Lomadh						30	*l.*
Mîm						40	*m.*
Nûn						50	*n.*
Semkath						60	*s.*
'Ê						70	Peculiar guttural.
Pê						80	*p, f.*
Ṣodhê			—	—		90	Like *ss* in hi*ss.*
Ḳoph						100	Guttural *k.*
Rîsch			—	—		200	*r.*
Shîn						300	Always *sh* as in *sh*ow.
Tau			—	—		400	*t, th.*

§ 1. The Syriac alphabet (see page 1) has twenty-two consonantal signs or letters. The first letter of the name of each sign represents its sound; e. g. ܒܝܬ "bêth" is the name of the sign, "b" is its sound; ܗܐ "hê" is the name, "h" is the sound.

§ 2. (1) (a) ܐܠܗܐ 'aloho' *God* (1:1); ܐܪܥܐ 'ar'o' *earth* (1:1).

(b) See last syllable in examples under (1) (a).

(c) ܕܠܝܘܪ dᵉlo'yor (1 Cor. 9:26); ܡܠܝܐ mᵉlo-yo' (1 Cor. 10:26); ܩܐܡ ḳo-yem (Matt. 13:1) (R. ܩܡ); ܫܐܠ sho-yel (Matt. 5:42) (R. ܫܐܠ); ܐܟܠ 'o-yel (Matt. 15:11) (R. ܐܟܠ).

(2) ܒܪܫܝܬ bᵉrîshith (1:1); ܚܫܘܟܐ ḥeshshukho' (1:2); ܬܘܗ ܘܒܘܗ tuh wᵉbhuh (1:1); ܐܦܝ 'ap-pay (1:2).

Some signs stand for two or more sounds.
(1) ܐ (Olaph) is generally—
 (a) a soft breathing, like *h* in "hour," or
 (b) quiescent in a preceding vowel; but sometimes it is
 (c) pronounced as Yudh, e. g. when preceded or followed by another Olaph, and in the active participle of verbs which have the middle radical Wau, Olaph, or doubled.

(2) ܒ ܓ ܕ ܟ ܦ ܬ with a point under them are aspirated; with a point above them they are unaspirated. See § 9.

§ 3. ܗܘ hu (21:5); ܠܗܘܢ lᵉhun (21:5); ܦܨܚܐ peṣ-ḥo' (21:8); ܪܘܚܗ ru-ḥeh (1:2); ܡܫܠܡ mash-lem (21:2); ܐܪܥܐ 'ar-'o' (1:1).

It is to be noted that ܗ is *always* pronounced like *h* in "home;" ܚ (ḥ), like *ch* in "loch," or German *ch* in "Rache;" ܫ (sh), like *sh* in "show;" and that ܥ is "produced by a smart compression of the upper part of the windpipe and forcible emission of the breath."

§ 4. 1. ܟܠܗ kulleh (5:9); ܐܟ akh (2:18); ܐܠܗܐ 'aloho' (1:1); ܥܠ 'al (1:2); ܫܡܝܐ shᵉmayo' (1:1); ܪܝܡ 'ᵉrîm (5:9); ܢܗܘܐ nehwê' (1:3); ܡܢ men (1:8); ܥܠ 'al (1:2); ܕܝܕܗ dîdha' (5:14).

2. (1) ܕܠܳܐ dᵉlo' (5:9); ܠܰܓ݂ܠܺܝܠܳܐ laghᵉlîlo' (24:5).

(2) ܐܰܠܳܗܳܐ (1:1); ܐܰܠܳܗܶܗ (23:14).

(3) ܫܐܶܠ (14:4).

3. (1) ܐܶܙܰܠ (23:12); ܐܰܪܥܳܐ (3:5).

(2) ܙܒܶܝܢ (23:1); ܟܳܗܢܶܝ (23:2).

(3) ܟܳܗܢܶܗ (23:7); ܟܳܗܢܺܝܢ (30:1).

(4) ܘܠܘܒܒܐ (24:2); ܘܩܘܡ (24:12).

(5) ܫܡܰܥܝ (23:8); ܐܬܝܩܘܢܝ (24:1).

(6) ܫܡܰܝܳܐ (24:16); ܘܢܶܬܟܠ (24:16); ܐܶܢܝ (24:17); ܫܡܰܥܝ (24:9).

4. ܐܰܪܥܳܐ (1:1); ܕܫܰܦܺܝܪ (1:4); ܡܰܝܳܐ (1:6); ܐܰܠܳܗܳܐ (1:1); ܗܘܳܬ (1:1); ܘܒܘܗܘ (1:2); ܢܘܗܪܐ (1:3); ܐܰܪܥܳܐ (1:13); ܨܰܦܪܳܐ (1:5); ܪܰܩܺܝܥܳܐ (1:6); ܨܦܪܐ (1:1); ܐܰܪܥܳܐ (1:1); ܝܳܬ (1:1); ܬܘܗ (1:1).

1. The five letters, Koph, Lomadh, Mim, Nun, and 'Ê, have peculiar forms at the end of words.

2. Lomadh before Olaph is perpendicular, like the latter, (1). Initial Olaph follows the slant of a succeeding Lomadh, (2); but medial Olaph remains perpendicular, (3). A medial Lomadh before a final Lomadh is written as in ܡܠܰܠ (Matt. 9:33).

3. To be carefully distinguished are,

(1) Olaph, ܐ, and Zain, ܙ;

(2) Bêth, ܒ, and Koph, ܟ;

(3) Dolath, ܕ, and Rîsh, ܪ;

(4) Wau, ܘ, and Koph, ܩ (Wau can be joined only to a letter which precedes, but Koph to a letter preceding or following);

(5) Yudh, ܝ, and Shin, ܫ; and

(6) Lomadh, ܠ, and 'Ê, ܥ, since they differ as to size only.

4. Olaph, Dolath, Hê, Wau, Zain, Ṣodhê, Rîsh, and Tau may be connected with the letter which precedes, but not with the letter which follows. The forms of Dolath (ܕ or ܕ), Rîsh (ܪ or ܪ), and Tau (ܬ or ܬ) are somewhat dissimilar in the two cases.

5. ܐ, ܝ, and ܘ are called vowel letters.

ܐ, ܗ, ܚ, and ܥ are called gutturals.

§ 5. Classification of Letters.

1.

Labials, ܒ ܘ ܡ ܦ

Dentals or Sibilants, ܐ ܣ ܙ ܬ

Linguals, ܪ ܕ ܢ ܠ ܛ

Palatals, ܝ ܟ ܓ ܨ

Gutturals, ܐ ܗ ܚ ܥ

Linguo-dental, ܨ

2.

Vowel letters, ܐ ܘ ܝ

1. According to their organic formation, consonants are classified as (1) Labials, (2) Dentals or Sibilants, (3) Linguals, (4) Palatals, (5) Gutturals, (6) Linguo-dentals.

2. The letters ܐ, ܘ, and ܝ were often used by the Syrians to express the long vowel sounds and diphthongs; and hence, they are called vowel-letters.

§ 6. Vowel Signs.

1. The vowel signs in use among the Jacobites, or Occidental Syrians, are the Greek letters Alpha, Epsilon, Eta, Omikron, and Upsilon, turned half over. They were introduced about 700 A. D., and represent the pronunciation of the Syriac at that time. They are ܲ (ă) Pethoḥo, ܳ (o) Zeḳofo, ܶ (e) Rebhoṣo, ܺ (î) Hebhoṣo, ܽ (u) 'Eṣoṣo.

[*Note.*—The Nestorians used a different system of vowel points.

̇ (ă) Pethâḥâ, e. g. ܡܚܕ (Ps. 1:2).

̣ (â) Zeḳâfâ, ܨܡ (Ps. 1:1).

̈ (ĕ, ĭ) Rebhâṣâ arrîḥâ, ܗܓ (Ps. 1:1).

̤ (ê) Rebhâṣâ karyâ, ܒܪ (Ps. 1:3).

̣ (î) Ḥebhâṣâ, ܡܢܝ (Ps. 1:5).

ܿ (u, û) 'Eṣâṣâ allîṣâ, ܘܐ (Ps. 1:4).

܂ (o, ô) 'Eṣâṣâ rewîḥâ ܐܡܚܕ (Ps. 1:2).

The later Jacobites combined the points with the Greek letter system. Among the Nestorians, ̣ (Zeḳâfâ) was pronounced like *a* in "father;"

among the Jacobites, its equivalent ܳ was pronounced like *o* in "note." The Jacobite Rebhoṣo and 'Eṣoṣo were separated into two signs and sounds among the Nestorians.]

2. The names of the vowels are of Syriac origin, and are derived from the position taken by the lips and teeth in their pronunciation. Pethoḥo means *opening*, the mouth being wide open when it is pronounced; Zeḳofo means *raising;* 'Eṣoṣo, *narrowing;* Rebhoṣo, *compression;* and Ḥebhoṣo, *depression.*

3. (1) ܐܠܗܐ 'aloho (1:1); ܫܡܝܐ sh'mayo (1:1); ܐܪܥܐ 'ar'o' (1:1).

(2) ܚܫܘܟܐ ḥeshshukho (1:2); ܦܨܚܐ peṣḥo (23:8); ܡܢ men (23:19); ܗܝܕܝܢ hoydên (24:2); ܓܝܪ gêr (24:3); ܥܢܐ 'onê (24:4); ܥܪܒܐ 'erbê (24:4).

(3) ܒܪܫܝܬ b'rîshîth (1:1); ܠܝ lî (23:2); ܕܝܠܬܟܝ dîyathîḳî (23:18); ܕܒܝܕܗ d'bhîdheh (23:13); ܪܘܚܗ ruḥeh (1:2); ܟܠܟܘܢ kull'khun (23:18).

(1) Pethoḥo was pronounced like *a* in "hat;"
Zeḳofo, like *o* in "note."

(2) Rebhoṣo was pronounced like *e* in "met." When followed by Yudh, it was pronounced like *ey* in "they;" as, also when followed by Olaph.

(3) Ḥebhoṣo was pronounced like *i* in "machine;"
'Êṣoṣo, like *oo* in "foot" or "fool."

4. ܕܨܡܚ (23:8); ܘܡܫܟ (23:17); ܫܢܝܐ (23:1); ܐܚܝܐ (23:7); ܘܡܫܠܟܘܢ (23:13); ܥܪܒܐ (24:4); ܕܚܝܘܬܐ (Rom. 8:2); ܐܢܫܐ (23:2); ܪܘܚܗ (1:2); ܗܘ (23:5).

All the vowels except 'Êṣoṣo may be written either above or below the line.

5. (1) ܐܬܝܢ (Acts 23:20); ܫܡܥܐ (23:3); ܕܝܢ (23:5); ܠܝ (23:2); ܗܘ (23:5).

(2) ܚܫܘܟܐ (1:2); ܠܠܝܐ (1:5); ܬܡܢ (2:11); ܥܡܟ (17:4); ܩܘܝܡܐ (17:14); ܫܒܘܩܬܗ (J. S. 11:19); ܐܠܗܐ (1:1).

Vowels may be written, (1) fully, i. e. with a homogeneous consonant, or (2) defectively.

'Êṣoṣo is always written fully, except in ܟܠ *all* and ܡܛܠ *on account of;* and sometimes it is written fully even in these instances.

Remark.—The homogeneous consonants, or vowel-letters (§ 4. 5), are ܐ , ܘ , and ܝ .

(1) Olaph was written for a final ô (coming from a final â, which it still is among the Nestorians) or ê (also for î derived from ê, e. g. ܢܐ among the Jacobites is nî).

(2) Olaph was written also for a medial â (or ô), ê (or î), e. g. ܦܐܪܢ Pêran (Jacobite, Pîran), ܣܐܢܝܢ sônîn (Jacobite, sânîn) (J. S. 18:5).

(3) Olaph was written for a final ă, and sometimes for a medial ă, in Greek words, e. g. ܕܘܓܡܐܛܐ δογματα.

(4) Yudh was written for î, and sometimes for medial ê, e. g. ܒܝܫ = bîsh, ܕܝܢ = dên.

(5) Yudh was written for the diphthong *ai*, e. g. ܒܝܬܐ baito.

(6) Wau was written everywhere for *u* (except in ܟܠ and ܡܛܠ) and also for Nestorian *o*.

(7) Wau was also written for the diphthong *au* (*aw*), e. g. ܠܘ lau.

(8) ܐܝ was found for î (ê); ܝܘ for îu or êu, e. g. ܟܐܝܢ = kîn (Mt. 1:19), ܐܬܚܢܝܘ Ethh'nîu (J. S. 3:11), ܢܫܡܠܝܘܗܝ n'shamlêu (J. S. 30:1).

(9) ܘ stands for long *o* in the exclamation ܐܘ *O!* (J. S. 20:17), but ܐܘ (J. S. 2:10) = ܐܘ *or.*

6. (1) ܡܠܟܐ (J. S. 7:11) = ܡܠܟܐ *king;* ܡܠܟܐ = ܡܠܟܐ *counsel;* ܐܣܪܐ = ܐܣܪܐ ; ܕܝܢܐ (J. S. 6:4) = ܕܝܢܐ ; ܗܘ (J. S. 8:16) = ܗܘ ; ܗܘ (J. S. 9:5) = ܗܘ ; ܫܡܪ (J. S, 23:20) = ܫܡܪ ; ܢܟܣܪ (J. S. 23:21) = ܢܟܣܪ ; ܢܘܚܐ (J. S. 4:11) = ܢܘܚܐ ; ܢܚܘܬܝܢ (J. S. 3:19) = ܢܚܘܬܝܢ .

(2) ܚܣܪܐ (J. S. 9:19) = ܚܣܪܐ ; ܚܣܪܗ (J. S. 2:11) = ܚܣܪܗ ; ܚܣܪܐ (S. S. 28:16) = ܚܣܪܐ ; ܡܢ = ܡܢ (or ܡܢ); ܡܢ (or ܡܢ) = ܡܢ ; ܗܢܘܢ (J. S. 8:3) = ܗܢܘܢ ; ܗܢܘܢ (J. S. 6:5) = ܗܢܘܢ ; ܡܢܝܢܐ (J. S. 9:4) = ܡܢܝܢܐ ; ܫܡܝܢܐ (J. S. 6:11) = ܫܡܝܢܐ ; ܗܝ (J. S. 6:9) = ܗܝ ; ܗܝ (J. S. 3:22) = ܗܝ .

(3) ܗܨܶܡ (J. S. 2:11) = ܗܨܰܡ ; ܨܠܝܟܐ (J. S. 4:18) = ܨܠܝܟܐ ;

ܐܡܚܝܟܡܐ (J. S. 10:2) = ܐܡܚܝܟܡܐ ; ܨܒܝ (S. S. 1:15) =

ܨܒܝܬ *thou art willing;* ܨܒܝ (J. S. 1:9) = ܨܒܝ ; ܨܒܝ =

ܨܒܝܬ (cf. ܣܝܡ J. S. 2:17) ; ܥܡܦ (J. S. 1:2) ; ܥܡܦ ; ܡܨܕܐ

(J. S. 1:1) = ܡܨܕܐ .

(1) In many manuscripts and books the vowels and forms are denoted by a system of diacritical points. See, for example, *Joshua the Stylite*, and the *Spicilegium Syriacum*.

(2) In general, it may be said that the point above a letter stands
 (a) for ă as distinguished from e, î, u, or the half-vowel;
 (b) for ô (â) as distinguished from all other vowels.

(3) Sometimes words have two points, both serving to differentiate the form; e. g. the 1st sing. has a point above, the 2d sing. a point below the line; but the 3d fem. sing. has a point above and one below.

Remark.—Many manuscripts vary their pointings; e. g. in *Joshua the Stylite* (18:9, *et al.*), we have ܥܒܕ = ܥܒܕ , because the Pe'al is usually marked in this way; whereas, elsewhere, the point is placed above, to denote the same form.

§ 7. Classification of Vowel Sounds.

1. (1) ܐܦܬ (1:2); ܟܠ (1:2);
ܦܢܝ (1:8); ܥܡܘܕܐ (1:13).
ܠܡܘܕܝܐ (1:5); ܡܚܟܝܡܢܐ (2:6).

(2) ܕܐ (1:1); ܗܘܐ (1:1); ܥܡ (1:11).
ܨܒܕ (1:7); ܪܟܬ (1:9); ܨܒܕܝ (22:1).
ܙܗܒܐ (1:1); ܡܕܒܪܢܐ (2:11); ܐܟܠ (2:16).
ܣܦܥܐ (1:2); ܕܣܘܨ (1:2); ܗܘ (22:5).

(3) ܒܪܐ b'ro' (1:1); ܫܡܝܐ sh'mayo (1:1).

1. As to quantity vowels are—
 (1) Short, ܲ ܲ ܲ
 (2) Long, ܲ ܲ ܲ ܲ ܲ
 (3) Half, not written, but pronounced like *e* in "below."

2. (1) ܩܛܰܠ ; ܩܰܛܶܠ ; ܩܽܘܕܫ *holiness;* ܢܰܚܡܶܕ *beloved.*

(2) ܩܳܛܶܠ (ܩܳܛܶܠ); ܟܢܳܦܳܐ *wing;* (ܫܡܰܝܳܐ 1:2).

(3) ܥܰܡܶܗ (1:7); ܥܰܝܢ *eye* (ܥܰܝܢܳܐ); ܕܺܝܢܳܐ *judgment;* ܢܽܘܗܪܳܐ (1:1); ܣܽܘܦ (ܣܳܘܦ *Nestorian*) *end* (ܣܰܘܦܳܐ); ܢܩܽܘܡ *he shall stand* (ܢܩܽܘܡ).

(4) ܐܰܠܦ *thousand;* ܐܶܥܛ (24:14); ܚܰܝܳܐ (24:5); ܩܽܘܫܛ (6:11); ܦܰܚܳܐ or ܦܰܚܳܐ *snare;* ܢܶܚܒ (Ps. 1:3).

2. As to origin, vowels are—

(1) Pure,		ă [ā],	(ĭ), ī,		ŭ, ū.	
(2) Obscured,	ō	(ā),	ĕ,		(o).	
(3) Contracted,			ê,	î,	(ô) û.	
(4) Heightened,	o	(ā)	ē,	ī.		

Note.—The letter in brackets is no longer found; the letters in parentheses are found in the Nestorian, but not in the Jacobite, or West Syriac. The Nestorians pronounced ◌ܶ (Rebhâṣâ arrîḥâ) sometimes as ĕ, sometimes as ĭ.

3. (1) ܡܰܠܟ, but ܡܰܠܟܳܐ *king;* ܩܛܰܠ *he killed*, but ܩܶܛܠܰܬ *she killed;* ܩܽܘܕܫ, but ܩܽܘܕܫܳܐ *holiness;* ܡܰܠܟܳܐ, but ܡܰܠܟܬܳܐ *queen.*

(2) (*a*) ܐܰܦ, ܐܰܦܳܐ *pure;* ܩܳܡ *he stood*, ܩܳܡܰܬ *she stood.*

(*b*) ܣܽܘܦ, ܣܰܘܦܳܐ *end;* ܥܰܝܢ, ܥܰܝܢܳܐ *eye.*

(*c*) ܕܰܟܝ *pure;* ܕܶܒܳܪܳܐ *wasp.*

(*d*) ܚܺܐܪܳܐ from ḥerro *free;* ܚܛܳܦܳܐ from ḥappo *violence.*

3. As to value in inflection, vowels are—

(1) *Changeable*, to wit: all half-vowels and all short vowels not in sharpened syllables, and heightened vowels.

(2) *Unchangeable*, to wit:

(*a*) Vowels long by nature or contraction, except (*b*), those derived from diphthongs.

(*c*) Short vowels in sharpened syllables, with a few exceptions (*d*).

§ 8. Diphthongs.

1. (1) ܡܘܨܥܐ (1:6); ܠܒܢܝܚܘܗܝ (23:7).
   (2) ܠܡܚܒܠܘܗܝ (6:13); ܐܒܪܟܘܗܝ (24:1); ܐܚܒܠܘܗܝ (26:7).
   (3) ܢܩܛܠܝܘܗܝ (Mt. 21:38); ܘܐܬܩܒܪܘ (25:10).
2. (1) ܐܦܝ (1:2); ܟܠܗܘܢ (25:1); ܕܚܬܝܬ (25:9).
   (2) ܚܙܝܗܝ (6:5); ܡܪܝܒܝ (25:12); ܗܝ (25:9).
   (3) ܪܒܘܝ *sign of plural.*

Waw and Yudh at the end of a syllable, after a heterogeneous vowel, form diphthongs. We have—

1. (1) Waw after *a*, pronounced like *ow* in "how."
   (2) ܘ pronounced ê-oo, or like Italian *eu* in "eufonia."
   (3) ܘ, like *ew* in "mew."
2. (1) ܝ, like the English adverb "ay."
   (2) ܝ, like *owi* in "owing."
   (3) ܘܝ, like *uoy* in "buoy," when you give the *o* the sound of *o* in "do."

§ 9. Unvowelled Consonants.

1. ܐܪܥܐ 'ar-'o' (1:1); ܢܘܗܪܐ nuh-ro' (1:3); ܪܡܫܐ ram-sho' (1:5).
2. Bᵉrîshîth bᵉrc' shᵉmayo' wᵉyoth (1:1).
3. ܘܦܪܫ (1:4); ܘܥܒܕ (1:7); ܕܠܬܚܬ (1:7).

Note.—ܚܕܘܬܐ *joy*; ܗܠܟܬܐ *ways*; ܚܟܡܬܐ *wisdom*; ܐܠܗܐ *God.*

In Syriac there is no sign to show that a consonant is without a vowel, or that it is to be pronounced with a quickly uttered *e* sound, or half-vowel. We have the facts, however, without the sign. See 1, 2.

3. The phenomena denoted in Hebrew by medial Shᵉwa occurred in Syriac also.

Note.—Consonants sometimes take a helping vowel. See § 32.

§ 10. Orthographic Signs. Rukhokh and Kushoy.

1. (1) ܢܶܣܰܒ݂ (1:1); ܒ݁ (1:1); ܫܳܡܕ݂ܐ (1:2); ܫܶܡ (1:6).

   (2) ܥܒ݂ܕ (1:2); ܚܳܨܶܕ݂ (1:7); ܚܰܝܠܫܐ (1:13); ܡܕ݂ܢܣܦ݂ܐ (1:2).

   (3) ܘܡܶܩܦ݂ܰܢ (1:4); ܟܠܕܘܢ̈ܐ ܣܦ݂ܝ̈ܕ݂ܐ (1:4); ܥܶܡܰܕ݂ (1:6).

2. (1) ܨܐ݇ (1:1); ܬܘܒ݂ (1:1); ܪܰܒ݁ܐ݇ (1:2); ܬܕ݂ܓ݁ܠܦ݂ܘܢ (1:10); ܚܶܣܛܐ (1:12); ܦܳܢ (2:12); ܚܰܒܪ (2:13).

   (2) ܐܦ݁ܬ݁ (1:2); ܢܶܨܡܕܐ (1:10); ܥܳܡܶܨ݁ܗ (3:12); ܡܰܟ݁ܕ݁ܦ݁ܘܣ (5:15); ܫܡܠܐ (25:6).

   (3) ܐܣ݁ܪ (2:18); ܚܰܡܠܦ݁ܘܢ (5:15); ܡܳܥܨ݂ܬܐ (2:6); ܐܦ݁ܗ ܬ݂ܟ݁ܶܗ (3:5).

   (4) ܐܳܙܻܠ (24:10); ܡܕ݂ܡ݁ܨܐ (24:17); ܪܰܩ݁ܐ݇ (24:1); ܘܡܨܶܡ (24:2).

1. Rukhokh (*softening*) is a point placed under the letters ܒ, ܓ, ܕ, ܟ, ܦ, and ܬ, to show that they are to be aspirated. It occurs whenever one of these letters is preceded either (1) by a full vowel, or (2) by a half-vowel.

   (3) It is to be noted, also, that these letters may be aspirated when the word immediately preceding them ends in a vowel.

2. Kushoy (*hardening*) is a point above the letters ܒ, ܓ, ܕ, ܟ, ܦ, and ܬ, to show that they are unaspirated. It occurs—

   (1) When the aspirates are not preceded by a vowel or half-vowel.

   (2) When they are preceded by a full vowel and are doubled.

   (3) After all diphthongs, except in ܐܽܘ.

   Note.—ܒܰܝܬܐ (3:8) and similar words are no exception, since the Yudh is doubled, and we read hay-y‘tho'.

   (4) We have no sign to denote the doubling in any but the aspirate letters. In many texts, it is omitted from them also.

§ 11. The Linea Occultans

1. ܥܣܰܩܬ (2:6); ܐܝܠܐ (5:10); ܚܰܝܠܫܘܢ (2:17); ܡܕ݂ܡ݁ܠܕܐ (11:2).

2. ܐܢ݇ܬܘܢ (2:17); ܐܢܐ (6:5); ܘܰܐܢ݇ܬܘܢ (22:2); ܐܣܢܬܢ (26:15); ܐܣܙܥ (26:19).

3. ܙܒܢ̈ܝ (21:7); ܐܡܪ̈ܘ (22:9); ܚܙܳܐ (22:11); ܟܬ̈ܒܘܗܝ (23:13); ܫܩܠ (23:16).

4. ܩܕܡ̈ܝ (Lk. 1:72); ܐܚܕ̈ܘܗܝ (John 15:4); ܟܣܦܐ (1 Cor. 11:2).

5. ܗܘܝ (1 Tim. 6:11); ܗܘܘ (1 Cor. 14:1); ܩܡ (Mt. 21:5).

R.—ܐܣܗܕ (Acts 23:11); ܐܥܕܝ (Mt. 21:21); ܐܥܕܟ (Heb. 13:17).

A line, called the *linea occultans*, is put under certain letters to show that, though written, they are not to be pronounced.

1. It occurs most commonly with an assimilated Nun or a silent Hê.
2. Olaph is occult when not preceded or followed by a vowel.
3. Waw and Yudh are never marked by the linea occultans, even when at the end of a word and not preceded by a vowel.
4. In ܐܬܕܟܪ *to remember*, 'Ê receives the linea occultans to show that it is to be pronounced like Olaph.
5. In ܗܘܘ *run*, and ܒܪܬ *daughter of*, rish has the linea occultans.

Remark.—In the Ethpe'el Imperative, a line occurs under the second radical among the Jacobites and over it among the Nestorians. This line has the force of Marhetono rather than of the Linea Occultans (cf. § 12. 2).

§ 12. Mehagyono and Marhetono.

1. ܐܒܓܡܠܬ (6:9); ܡܠܟܘܢܝ (2:3); ܚܟܡܬܐ *wisdom* (= ܚܟܡܬܐ); ܢܡܠܟܘܢ *they shall ask* (= ܢܡܠܟܘܢ).

2. (1) ܫܡܥܬ (2:15); ܦܠܓܘ *they have divided;* ܫܬ *six;* ܫܬܝܢ *sixty*.

(2) ܚܡ = ܚܡܝܫ (Kirsch, "Chrest.," p. 134); ܢ *fifty* (J. S. 21:20); ܐܘ (J. S. 1:1); ܐܘ (Kirsch, "Chrest.," p. 64:7).

1. **Mehagyono** is a sign placed under a letter to show that it is to be pronounced with a short vowel.

2. (1) **Marhetono** is a line placed above a letter to show that it is to be pronounced without a vowel.

(2) A diacritical line is used also to denote an abbreviation or a number. On the ܘ of the interjection ܐܘ we find either a line or the Greek Omega, to distinguish it from ܐܘ *or*.

Remark.—For Marhetono with the Imv. Ethpe'el, see § 11. *Rem.*

§ 13. Sign of the plural.

1. ܐܳܒ݂ (1:2); ܡܶܬ݂ܳܐ (1:3); ܡܶܬ݂ܓ݂ܰܡ݂ܠܳܐ (1:12); ܠܳܐܙܳܠ݂ܳܐ (2:3); ܟ݂ܡܰܬ݂ܳܐ (2:3).
2. ܩܳܐܙܳܐ (1:13); ܠܶܬ݂ܳܐ (2:2); ܚܳܙܳܐ (24:4).
3. ܡܳܟ݂ܰܬ݂ܳܐ (24:11); ܙܰܒ݂ (1:9).

1. Two points, called Rebbuy, are placed horizontally over a word to indicate that it is plural.

2. One of these points may coincide with the diacritical point of the Rîsh.

3. Rebbuy may stand with the dual also.

§ 14. Accent.

In modern Syriac, the accent is on the penult; the place of the accent in ancient Syriac is still in dispute. There follows a summary based on Duval:

1. The accent is generally on the penult.
2. The ultima receives it,
   (*a*) In monosyllables.
   (*b*) When it is a closed syllable with a long vowel.
   (*c*) When the first of two vowels is a helping vowel.
3. The antepenult never receives the accent, except when the second vowel is a helping vowel.

§ 15. The Accents.

An involved system of accents was used, especially for exegetical purposes, in commentaries on the Scriptures. According to Ewald, they were used, (1) to denote the relation of the parts of a chapter, (2) to denote the divisions of the sentences, (3) to denote the grammatical relations between words, (4) to denote the sentiment, or rhetorical characteristics of the sentence.

According to Bar Hebræus, the number of the accents was forty. In many manuscripts we have but two; a single dot, like our period, for short sentences, and four dots for longer. In the text of Walton's Polyglott, four dots are used for paragraphs, and one for shorter periods; while two are used to separate protasis and apodosis, dependent from principal sentences, and often the minor parts of subordinate sentences. Three dots are used to call special attention to what precedes. See Gen. 1:5,7; and Matt. 24:30,36,43,47.

§ **16.** Syllables.

1. ܐܰܠܳܗܳܐ 'a-lo-ho' (1:1); ܫܡܰܝܳܐ sh'ma-yo' (1:1); ܘܚܶܫܽܘܟ݂ܳܐ w'ḥesh-shu-kho' (1:2).

2. ܐܰܪܥܳܐ 'ar-'o' (1:1); ܗܘܳܬ݂ h'woth (1:1); ܘܪܽܘܚܶܗ (1:2).

Remark 1.—ܫܬܳܐ *six;* ܫܬܺܝܢ *sixty;* ܟܣܶܐ *covered;* ܬܠܳܬ݂ *three;* ܬܢܳܢ *here;* ܣܟܶܠܘ *they were foolish.*

Remark 2.—ܝܺܚܳܐ (15:8); ܝܺܫܽܘܥ (15:8); ܐܺܝܣܳܪܳܐ (17:15); ܐܺܝܬܰܝܟܽܘܢ (17:11).

1. A word has as many syllables as it has full vowels. A half-vowel does not constitute a syllable.

2. Every syllable must begin with a consonant. It may begin with two consonants, in which case the first takes a half-vowel.

Remark 1.—In ܫܬܳܐ and ܫܬܺܝܢ, and in later times in some other words, there is no half-vowel; e. g. ܫܬܳܐ = shto'.

Remark 2.—Words beginning with ܝ quiescing in ܺ are exceptions to this rule. According to some, they are to be pronounced, as they are sometimes written, with an Olaph before them. According to Bar Hebræus, ܝܺܕܰܥܬܳܐ is pronounced "īda'tho'" by the Jacobites, and "yida'-thâ'" by the Nestorians.

3. ܫܡܰܫܬ (15:7); ܬܶܫܟܚܽܘܢ (15:5); ܐܰܚܪܺܢ (16:11); ܩܳܐܡܺܝܢ (16:15); ܕܰܟ݂ܕܡܽܘܬܶܗ (1:7).

3. At the end of a syllable, two consonants may be pronounced, though more may be written.

§ **17.** Syllables.

1. ܐܰܠܳܗܳܐ (1:1); ܫܡܰܝܳܐ (1:1); ܬܗܽܘܡܳܐ (1:2).

2. ܝܳܬ݂ (1:1); ܗܘܳܬ݂ (1:1); ܡܫܰܒܚܳܬ݂ (1:6).

3. ܚܶܫܽܘܟ݂ܳܐ (1:2); ܐܰܦ̈ܝܳܐ (1:2); ܡܪܰܚܦܳܐ (1:4).

4. ܘܥܒܶܕ (1:7); ܕܰܒܬܚܶܝܬ (1:7); ܥܒܰܕܬܳܟ݂ *she made thee;* ܩܛܰܠܟܽܘܢ *he killed you;* ܡܰܠܟܰܝܟܽܘܢ *your kings;* ܓܰܪܒܳܐ *leper;* ܕܰܗܒܳܐ *gold;* ܡܶܠܚܳܐ

wing; ܛܰܝܒܽܘܬܳܐ *goodness;* ܣܒܰܪܬܳܐ *gospel;* ܢܶܫܡܬܳܐ *breath;* ܦܪܰܚܬܳܐ *bird;* ܫܰܪܒ̈ܳܬܳܐ *tribes.*

1. Syllables which end in a vowel are called open.

2. Syllables ending in a consonant are called closed.

3. A closed syllable whose last consonant is doubled is called sharpened.

4. A syllable ending in a short vowel followed by a consonant with a half-vowel is called half-open.

Note.—The syllable is half-open, (a) in the 3d fem. sing. Perf. before suffixes, (b) in the syllable before ܗܽܘܢ and ܟ݂ܽܘܢ when it does not end in a diphthong, (c) in many nouns, especially before the feminine ending.

§ **18.** Euphony of Consonants. *Assimilation.*

1. ܢܶܦܩܬܳܐ (R. נפק) (24:1); ܠܶܒܬܳܐ *brick* (11:3).

ܐܰܦ̈ܰܝ (1:2); ܐܰܢܗܰܪ *it shone* (Lk. 6:11); ܢܶܛܰܪ *he shall keep* (Lk. 11:21); ܡܰܦܩܳܢܳܐ (3:17); ܢܰܢܗܰܪ *let shine* (Mt. 5:16).

2. ܐܰܢܬܬܳܐ (5:5); ܐܰܢܬ (6:10); ܡܰܕܢܚܳܐ (15:9).

3. ܥܺܕܬܳܐ *church;* ܚܰܕܬܳܐ *new;* ܦܫܺܝܛܬܳܐ *simple;* ܐܶܬܕܢܺܝ *he assented;* ܐܶܬܛܰܝܰܒ *he prepared.*

Remark.—ܐܶܬܬܒܰܪ *it was broken;* ܘܕܕܳܡܶܐ *and that which was like.*

4. ܢܶܣܰܩ (Mt. 13:2); ܐܰܣܶܩ (Mt. 17:1).

1. At the end of a syllable, Nun is assimilated to the following consonant, which is then doubled.

Note.—Before ܗ this assimilation does not take place.

2. The Nun is sometimes written, though not pronounced. When not final, it then receives linea occultans.

3. When Taw is preceded or followed by Dolath or Teth, the first lingual is assimilated to the second, and written with or without the linea occultans.

R.—When one Taw or Dolath precedes another, both are unaspirated.

4. In the verb ܣܠܶܩ *to ascend*, where Semkath ends one syllable and Lomadh begins another, the Lomadh is assimilated to the Semkath; see § **65.** 8.

§ 19. Occultation.

1. (1) ܐܢܐ (2:17); ܐܢܐ (14:5; 22:14); ܐܣܝܐ (14:1).

   (2) ܒܠܕܒܒܝ *my enemy;* ܒܠܕܒܒܟܘܢ *your enemy.*

2. (1) *a.* ܫܦܝܪ ܗܘܐ (3:17); ܚܙܝܪ ܗܘܐ (5:9); ܟܘܡܪܐ ܗܘ ܗܘܐ *he was a priest* (Gen. 14:18).

   b. ܣܒܪ ܗܘܐ (25:7); ܐܡܪ ܗܘܐ (27:6).

   (2) ܣܒܪܬ (6:7); ܣܒܪ (28:7); ܣܒܪܘ (29:14).

   (3) ܐܣܪܘܗܝ (8:2); ܡܫܡܫܘܗܝ (11:8); ܬܠܡܝܕܘܗܝ (22:3); ܟܠܗܘܢ (22:13).

   (4) ܨܝܕܘܗܝ (22:12); ܐܢܘܗܝ (22:15).

   (5) ܪܗܘܡܐ *Rome;* ܪܗܘܡܝܐ (Eph. 3:12).

3. ܢܦܫܬܐ (1:12); ܚܛܗܐ (17:13); ܪܓܝܫܝܢ (11:16).

4. ܩܛܠܝܢ ܚܢܢ *we are killing.*

5. ܓܪܡ (Mt. 18:17); ܫܡܥ (Mt. 9:17); ܡܬܝ (Mk. 16:17).

6. ܐܢܬ (6:10); ܠܐܝܕܐ (5:9); ܡܚܪܒܕܐ (12:9); ܕܠܐܪܚܡ (32:14); ܐܟܟܪܐ (Lk. 12:16); ܨܒܝ (Acts 7:21); ܘܢܗܘܐ (1 Cor. 9:24).

7. ܐܘܐܚܪܝ (10:12); ܘܝܫܒܚ (10:15); ܡܬܥܒ ܐܣܘܬ (32:12).

Occultation occurs when a letter is written but not pronounced. It is generally denoted by the linea occultans. It occurs,

1. With Olaph, (1) at the beginning of a word when not followed by a vowel; (2) in the middle of a word when not preceded by a vowel.

2. With Hê, (1) In ܗܘܐ (*a*) after a predicate adjective, participle or noun, and (*b*) when an auxiliary verb.

   (2) In parts of ܝܗܒ *to give.*

   (3) In the 3d sing. masc. suffix.

   (4) In ܗܘ and ܗܝ when they are used for the verb *to be.*

   (5) In Greek words beginning with *Rho*, the *h* being written after the *r*, as in Latin.

16　ELEMENTS OF SYRIAC.　[§§ 20, 21.

3. When a letter is written twice to show the derivation of the word, the linea occultans being placed under the first.

4. With ܗܘ in ܗܘܐ when employed for the verb *to be*.

5. Sometimes with ܐ before ܙ.

6. Often with Nun, sometimes with Lomadh and Rîsh.

7. Occult ܘ and ܝ are never marked by the linea occultans. At the end of words they are occult whenever not preceded by a vowel.

§ 20. Addition.

1. ܐܘܓܣܛܐ (1:8); ܐܥܩܬ݀ (Mk. 13:19).

Rem. 1.—ܐܫܬܝܘ (23:18); ܐܣܛܕܝܐ *stadium;* ܐܫܬܐ *foundation.*

Rem. 2.—ܐܣܛܟܐ (1:5); ܐܬܡܨܝ (18:19).

An Olaph with a short vowel is sometimes put before an unvoweled consonant (Olaph prosthetic).

Rem. 1.—Before ܠ and foreign words beginning with ܣ the vowel is ܸ.

Rem. 2.—Before ܝ the prosthetic Olaph takes ܻ in which the ܝ quiesces.

2. ܐܝܠܟ (6:4); ܣܥܬܐ (from ܣܥܐ) (1 Tim. 4:16); ܟܪܙܐ (*r* inserted) (5:7); ܚܠܦ (R. ܚܠܦ) *he changed;* ܐܙܕܗܪܘ (ܗ inserted) (1 Cor. 7:29).

3. ܠܥܠܫܡ (Mk. 15:47); ܠܥܠ ܣܥܕ (Ex. 18:11 Hexaplar).

2. A letter is sometimes inserted in a word and strengthens it in the same way as the doubling of a radical.

3. In later times a Taw was added to the Ethpe'el of ê-Waw verbs, both being unaspirated.

§ 21. Transposition.

1. ܣܙܪ (1:13); ܐܙܕܗܪ (Mt. 11:19); ܐܣܬܟܠ (Mt. 16:12); ܠܚܝ (Heb. 10:23); ܐܬܗܦܟ (Lk. 9:36).

2. ܐܬܥܒܕ (Mt. 26:8; Spic. Syr. 40:14).

3. ܗܪܓܘ (1 Cor. 14:1).

[§ 22.] ELEMENTS OF SYRIAC. 17

Transposition occurs,

1. In the passives of the simple and intensive species when the first radical is a sibilant. Before ܐ the ܬ is changed into ܛ; before ܙ into ܕ. § 22. 4.

2. In the Ethpe'el of ܠ verbs.

3. In the Imperative of ܪܗܛ *to run*.

§ 22. Permutation.

1. (1) ܐܘܩܕ (Mt. 22:7); ܐܘܣܦ (5:3); ܐܣܒܗ (5:4); ܛܘܫ (R. 11ͅ) *to make unclean;* ܢܩܒܬ (23:8); ܐܟܬܒ (Ps. 5:3).

(2) ܐܬܬܣܝܡ (Mk. 15:47); ܐܬܬܣܝܡ (Mt. 25:10); ܐܬܬܣܪܚ (Did. 41:19). ܐܬܬܟܪܝ (Did. 3:3); ܐܬܬܢܣܒ (Ex. 2:23).

2. ܩܘܡ (Mt. 23:23); ܩܡ (32:21); ܩܐܡ ḳoyem (John 11:23); ܡܩܝܡܐ (Mt. 24:15); ܡܚܐܘܢܝ *they struck me* (Sym. Job 16:10).

Rem.—ܣܡܬ (J. S. 3:20); ܣܡܬ (J. S. 66:2); ܣܡܬ (J. S. 70:4; 77:12).

3. ܠܐܪܒ (Mt. 5:42); ܠܐܪܒ (Mt. 6:27); ܡܚܝܐ (1 Cor. 15:50); ܡܐܟܠܐ (Eccl. 9:4).

4. ܡܚܘܙܐ (1:13); ܐܙܕܒܢ (Mt. 9:17); ܐܙܕܟܝ (Lk. 24:7); ܐܙܕܡܢ (Mt. 11:19).

1. (1) In the causative of most verbs ܦ the first radical is changed to Waw; in ܐܬܐ *to come*, it is changed to Yudh. In some cases in verbs ܠ also, the Olaph is changed to Yudh.

(2) In the Ettaph'al of 'Ê Waw verbs, and in the Ethpe'el and Ethpa'al of a few Pê Olaph verbs, the Olaph is changed to Taw.

2. In all ܥ verbs, except ܩܘܡ and ܡܘܚ, the Waw is changed into Yudh. In the Part. active of ܥ verbs the Waw is changed to Yudh in pronunciation, though in the masc. sing. it is written with Olaph. In some verbs an Olaph is sometimes written where we generally have Waw.

Remark.—Four times in Joshua the Stylite, the Part. act. masc. sing. of an 'Ê Waw verb is written with a Yudh instead of an Olaph, in place of the second radical.

3. Yudh is changed to Olaph in the Pe'al Imperfect and Infinitive of verbs ܣܒ and sometimes in the verbal nouns of verbs ܥܒܕ.

4. In the passive conjugations of verbs beginning with ܙ or ܨ, transposition having first taken place, according to § 21. 1, Taw is changed to ܕ after ܙ and to ܛ after ܨ.

5. Hê is changed to Yudh in ܐܝܟܢ for ܐܝܟܢܐ (24:8; 1 Tim. 1:17); and perhaps 'Ê to Olaph in ܐܢܗܡ *lustful* ("Acta Martyrum," II. 361).

§ 23. Rejection.

1. (1) ܐܚܘ (Mt. 28:19); ܐܙܠ (11:1); ܐܬܢܣܒ (32:8); ܣܒ (23:9); ܣܒܪܬܐ (26:3); ܣܡܐ (Lk. 10:39).

(2) ܙܠ? (Prov. 3:6); ܗܒ (Mt. 5:42); ܬܒ (Mt. 22:44).

(3) ܣܒ (30:3); ܥܒܕ (Mt. 19:17).

(4) ܡܨܥܪܢܐ (Rom. 1:30); ܪܒܚܝܠܐ *president*.

1. Rejection may take place at the beginning of a word,
(1) With Olaph in the Imperative of Pê Olaph verbs, and often elsewhere when the Olaph is occult.
(2) With Yudh, in the Imperative of Pê Yudh verbs.
(3) With Nun, in the Imperative of Pê Nun verbs.
(4) With Mîm, in certain nouns formed from Pa'el Participles.

2. (1) ܐܥܪܩ (= ܐܐܥܪܩ) (Gen. 31:22); ܐܬܐ (Mt. 8:7); ܢܚܒ (Mt. 5:19); ܐܚܪ (Ps. 45:1); ܡܫܝܚܐ (25:17); ܥܡܡ (for ܥܐܡܡ) (16:14); ܥܕܝܬ (= ܥܕܐܝܬ) (Judges 11:25).

(2) ܚܕ (26:7); ܢܬܠܟܘܢ (25:15); ܟܡܚܕ (Mt. 6:5); ܥܠܬ (Jn. 5:21).

(3) ܠܘܛܬܐ (for ܠܘܐܛܬܐ) (James 3:6); ܠܘܛܬܐ (for ܠܘܐܛܬܐ) (Rom. 3:13); ܣܝ (for ܣܐܝ) (Ps. 45:3); ܐܗܦܟ (for ܐܗܦܐܟ) (24:1); ܫܡܥ (for ܫܡܐܥ) (Rev. 4:1).

(4) ܣܒܪܬܐ (for ܣܐܒܪܬܐ) (24:1); ܣܒܝ (Hex. Ruth 1:13); ܬܫܒܝܚ (Sym. Job 41:4); ܬܐܣܒ (Judges 6:18),

2. Rejection takes place in the middle of a word,—

(1) With Olaph, in the 1st sing. Imperfect Pe'al; and often, in the Imperfect and Participle of the Pa'el, and sometimes in the Ethpe'el, of Pê Olaph verbs. Olaph is sometimes rejected also from 'Ê Olaph derivatives.

(2) With Waw and Yudh, when they stand between two vowels, or between a half-vowel and a vowel; and sometimes elsewhere.

(3) In isolated instances, with Lomadh, Rish and Nun.

(4) With Taw, in the Ethpe'el, whenever three Taws would come together; and in a few nouns when two Taws would come together.

3. (1) ܣܓܝ (= ܣܓܝܐ) (28:14); ܘܐܬܢܣܒ (= ܘܐܬܢܣܒܘܢ) (6:3); ܢܟܠ (J. S. 26:13); ܘܐܬܦܬܚ (= ܘܐܬܦܬܚܘܢ) (6:1); ܐܬܦܢܝܘ (J. S. 15:10).

(2) ܐܦܬ (1:2); ܡܩܝܡܬܐ (1:12); ܦܐܪܐ (1:15); ܚܨܪܘ (23:7); ܢܥܬ (23:1); ܐܥܡܥܘ (23:2); ܡܢܨܒ (32:12).

(3) ܡܠܟܘ (Mt. 12:25); ܡܠܟܬܐ *queen;* ܬܘܪܝ (Ephr. 3:427); ܒܝ *house* (Mt. 12:25).

3. Rejection takes place at the end of a word,—

(1) Sometimes with Waw, in the 3d masc. plur.; and with Yudh, in the 3d fem. plur. of verbs. Olaph is sometimes rejected from ܣܓܝܐ *much.*

(2) The final Nun of verbs is generally rejected. The final Nun of nouns plural is always rejected in the emphatic and construct states.

(3) A final Taw is rejected from the feminine singular absolute of nouns; and in Mt. 12:25, from ܒܝܬܐ *house.*

4. (1) ܐܦܢ (= ܐܦ ܐܢ) (24:5); ܒܪܢܫ (= ܒܪ ܐܢܫ) (Mt. 12:12); ܒܬܪ (= ܒ ܐܬܪ) (24:4); ܡܣܬܒܪܝܢ (18:12); ܫܡܫܝܢ (= ܫܡܫܝܢ) (1 Thess. 3:3); ܫܪܝܪܐ (Lk. 4:36); ܗܢܘ (= ܗܢܐ ܗܘ) (23:17); ܡܛܠܗ (6:9); ܠܘ (= ܠܐ ܗܘ) (Mt. 13:27); ܗܟܢܐ (23:19); ܗܝܟ (= ܗܝܟ ܗܝ) (Judith 1:5).

20 ELEMENTS OF SYRIAC. [§ 24.

(2) ܡܷܬܩܛܠܳܢ ܢܷܬܩܛܠܳܢ

(3) ܐܰܩܒܽܘܪ *fountain;* ܫܒܰܥܣܰܪ *seventeen;* ܬܫܰܥܣܰܪ *nineteen.*

4. (1) Many compound words, or words which coalesce, drop one or more letters.

(2) The enclitic forms of the personal pronouns coalesce with Participles and adjectives, forming as it were, a new tense.

(3) When a number ending in 'Ê combines with ܥܣܰܪ *ten*, one 'Ê is dropped.

§ 24. Otiose Letters.

1. ܐܬܳܐ (1:12); ܐܡܳܐ (Mt. 19:29); ܐܒܥܳܐ (Mk. 1:23); ܐܩܳܐ (3 John:6); ܐܡܳܐ (14:15).

2. ܗܡܣܟܶܗ (6:2); ܡܪܰܘ (6:1); ܗܪܳܨ (6:1).

3. ܐܶܡܰܪܬ ܡܚܰܕ (32:12); ܐܚܰܕ (John 20:17); ܒܚܰܨܒܶܗ (6:9); ܫܠܶܡ (6:15); ܗܫܠܶܡܬܷܗ (6:14); ܐܒܰܗܝ (Mt. 2:6); ܟܰܬܒ (6:8); ܐܒܓܠܳܗ (6:9); ܬܡܗܟܠܢܝ (22:5); ܣܥܰܬ (13:3); ܡܪܰܥܕ (19:9).

Otiose letters are those which are neither quiescent in a previous vowel nor marked by the linea occultans, but yet are unpronounced. They are,

1. Olaph final when preceded by another Olaph.
2. Waw at the end of verbs, when not preceded by a vowel.
3. Yudh, in the 3d fem. plur. of verbs; in the 2d fem. sing. of verbs and pronouns; and in the pronominal suffixes of the 1st sing. (except when preceded by a vowel), 2d fem. sing., and of the 3d masc. sing. when it ends in Yudh.

§ 25. Quiescence.

1. (1) ܣܡܐܝܕ݂ (28:3); ܡܐܥܡ݂ (5:10); ܫܐܥܡ (2 Macc. 5:24).

   (2) ܢܡܐ݇ (James 1:6); ܡܐܝܕ݂ (Heb. 10:6); ܒܐܬ (1 Sam. 25:36); ܫܬܐܨܒ (Ezek. 16:27).

   (3) ܡܠܐܟܐ (32:2); ܐܝܐܫ (James 5:2); ܘܐܝܐܥܢ (28:1); ܥܬܐܥܢܐ (Hex. Jer. 10:19).

   (4) ܐܙܢ (18:17); ܥܟܕܐ (18:19); ܘܥܚܕܐ (18:17); ܥܢܐ (18:10); ܐܢܐܥ (1:1); ܩܕܥ (Rom. 16:1); ܥܣܡܠܐ (Rom. 16:3).

   Rem. 1.—ܐܥܢܘ (18:13); ܐܬܟܬܐ (18:15); ܨܐܩ (18:11); ܘܐܥܢ (1:6); ܘܐܟܢܐ (1:13); ܐܙܥܠܐ (1:8).

   Rem. 2.—ܘܐܟܠܐ (1:1); ܘܐܥܢ (1:3); ܘܐܢܥ (1:1); ܩܐܙܐ (1:13); ܘܥܕܐܐ (Rev. 5:9); ܘܐܣܦܬ (Lk. 2:1).

1. (1) At the end of a syllable Olaph loses its consonantal force and quiesces in the preceding vowel.

   (2) When Olaph with a vowel follows an unvoweled consonant, the vowel is usually thrown back on the preceding consonant, and the Olaph quiesces (cf. § 32. 3).

   (3) In the middle of a word, when Olaph should receive a half-vowel, it quiesces in a short full vowel given to the preceding consonant.

   (4) When a vowel-letter, Olaph always quiesces.

   Rem. 1.—The inseparable particles ܒ ܕ ܠ and ܘ draw back the vowel of the Olaph.

   Rem. 2.—Olaph may quiesce in any one of the vowels.

2. (1) ܚܣܘܐܐ (2 Pet. 3:9); ܚܣܘܕܐ (2 Pet. 1:2); ܚܘܕܐ (Acts 13:32); ܚܘܐܐ *inflammation* (Thes. Syr. 697).

   (2) ܣܡܐܬܐ (Heb. 12:20) ܣܡܐܬܐ ; ܣܥܐܬܐ (15:1); ܣܐܘܬܐ (2 Cor. 6:5).

   (3) ܬܘܣ (1:1); ܚܣ (1:2); ܫܡܕܛܐ (1:2).

2. (1) Waw quiesces at the end of a syllable after the homogeneous vowel ܘ݁.

(2) In the middle of a word, when it would have a half-vowel, it frequently quiesces in a ◌ֵ given to the preceding consonant.

(3) When a vowel-letter it always quiesces.

3. (1) ܐܘܥܕ (5:2); ܣܡܝܕ (18:19); ܠܡܨܬ (5:6); ܡܙ (11:10); ܚܝ (23:2).

(2) ܐܠܡܝ (23:14); ܐܠܘܣ (32:23); ܣܝܡܗܘܢ *their breast* (Thes. Syr. 1201).

(3) ܣܠܘ (26:3); ܣܘܗܪܐ (18:13); ܣܚܝܐ (18:7); ܣܟ (15:8); ܣܩ (15:9).

Rem. 1.—ܐܣܡܟܬ (1:5); ܐܡܗ (25:11); ܐܡܪܐ (17:15).

Rem. 2.—ܕܠܘ (14:3); ܣܕܘ (14:13); ܘܥܡܝܗܘܢ (17:1).

(4) ܡܥܣ (1:4); ܣܕܠ (1:7); ܙܥܪ (1:9); ܡܣܠܐ (1:10).

3. (1) At the end of a syllable, Yudh quiesces after the homogeneous vowel ◌ִ.

(2) In the middle of a word, when it would receive a half-vowel, it frequently quiesces in a ◌ִ given to the preceding consonant.

(3) At the beginning of a word, when it would have a half-vowel, it quiesces in ◌ִ.

Rem. 1.—This ◌ִ at the beginning of a word often takes prosthetic Olaph (§ 20. 1).

Rem. 2.—Prefixes draw the vowel to themselves, the Olaph prosthetic even being sometimes retained and quiescing.

(4) When a vowel-letter, Yudh quiesces in ◌ִ or ◌ֵ.

4. ܘܒܗܘܗ w‘bhuh (1:2); ܪܘܗܗ ruḥeh (1:2); ܬܘܗ tuh (1:1); ܓܢܣܘܗ gensoh (2:12).

4. Hê never quiesces in Syriac.

§ 26. Peculiarities of Gutturals.

1. (1) ܥܳܡܳܐ (Acts 20:1); ܐܰܥܶܡ (Acts 8:11); ܥܰܡ؟ (Acts 7:41); ܬܳܥܰܡܬ݂ (Lk. 12:3); ܥܰܡ؛ (Mt. 19:5); ܥܰ (Mt. 19:6).

(2) ܢܶܩܽܘܒ (Rom. 14:19); ܥܰܩ (Lk. 1:8); ܥܰܡܪܽܘ (2 Cor. 10:9); ܢ݂ܒ݂؟ (Heb. 11:34).

1. (1) Final gutturals and Rîsh prefer the vowel $\stackrel{\text{\textunderscore}}{}$
(2) Medial gutturals are treated like other letters.

2. (1) ܐܳܟ݂ܳܐ (1:1); ܐܰܢܐ (12:17); ܐܶܥܰܡ (13:6).

(2) ܡܰܠܟ݂ (Mt. 22:41); ܢܶܡܰܨ (23:8); ܐܰܠܶܟ݂ (Is. 16:6).

(3) ܥܳܡܳܐ (Acts 20:2); ܢܶܨܰܠ (Gen. 5:29); ܐܰܡܗܳܐ (Acts 4:36); ܐܶܬ݂ܟ݂ܳܕ݂ܳܗ (Judith 1:16); ܥܶܨܳܐ (Acts 10:14); ܐܶܨܛܰܗܰܝ (Rev. 17:4).

2. Olaph preserves its full consonantal force,—
(1) At the beginning of a word, when accompanied by a vowel.
(2) In the Pa'el and Ethpa'al of ܫܐܠ *to ask;* though in most verbs 'Ê-Olaph it is changed to Yudh. Cf. § 22. 1. (1).
(3) In a few verbs whose third radical is Olaph, as also in their derivatives.

Rem.—Cf. also §§ 19. 1; 20. 1; 22. 1; 23. 1. (1); 23. 2. (1); 23. 3. (1); 23. 4. (1); 24. 1; 25. 1.

3. In ܕ݂ܟ݂ܰܪ *to remember,* 'Ê is treated by the West Syrians as if it were Olaph.

4. For the peculiarities of Hê and Hêth, cf. §§ 19. 2, 4; 22. 5; 23. 4. (1), (2); 25. 4.

§ 27. Peculiarities of Waw and Yudh.

1. ܢܶܒ݂ܝܳܐ nᵉbhîyo (28:1); ܕ݂ܢܶܨܰܡܬ݁ܗ؟ (Lk. 1:70); ܕ݂ܢܶܨܳܐ؟ (25:18).

1. Yudh sometimes stands at once for a vowel-letter and a consonant.

2. For a connected view of the peculiarities of Waw, see §§ 19. 7; 22. 1, 2; 23. 2. (2), 3. (1); 24. 2; 25. 2.

3. For the peculiarities of Yudh, see §§ 19. 7; 22. 1, 2, 3; 23. 1. (2), 2. (2), 3. (1); 24. 3; 25. 3.

§ 28. Quantity of Vowels.

1. (1) ܫܽܡܥܶܬ݂ (1 Cor. 15:1); ܫܡܰܥܬܳܢ (John 15:16); ܐܶܫܬܰܡܥܰܬ݂

(2) ܐܳܒ݂ܪܰܟ݂ blessed; ܨܳܒ݂ܘܳܬ݂ (1 Cor. 7:36); ܢܰܦ݂ܫܳܐ (29:17);

ܐܳܒܰܕ݂ (Mt. 9:4); ܐܳܡܰܪ݂ (Mt. 24:15).

1. In closed syllables the vowel is generally short; but it is long,—
(1) Where the long vowel has arisen by contraction.
(2) Where the vowel is naturally long, and the syllable has become closed by the dropping of a short vowel.

2. (1) ܐܶܡܰܪ (27:6); ܐܶܟܰܠ *eaten*; ܐܶܨܰܕ (Lk. 1:59); ܐܶܟܽܘܠ (Acts 10:13).

(2) ܚܶܙܩܳܐ (Lk. 11:12); ܗܳܘܟܳܢ (Prov. 26:7); ܣܰܒܟܳܢܳܐ (1 Tim. 6:15).

(3) ܡܶܠܳܠܺܐ (32:2); ܡܶܫܩܳܠܺܐ (Lk. 14:21); ܕܶܣܩܳܐ (Ps. 25:19).

(4) ܗܳܘ݂ܐ݂ (4:8); ܥܶܣܺܝ (22:6); ܡܶܚܣܶܝܢ (1:7); ܐܶܒܟ݂ܳܗܶܢ (1:10); ܡܶܟܢܰܣܺܝ (1:11).

2. In open syllables the vowel is generally long; but a short vowel may stand in open syllables,—

(1) When it is necessary for the retention and pronunciation of an Olaph.
(2) Sometimes, like compound Sh'wa in Hebrew, to facilitate the pronunciation of a letter, especially of a guttural.
(3) In syllables which were originally closed.
(4) In half-open syllables.

3. (1) ܟܽܠܗ (2 Pet. 3:8); ܐܰܣ (8:4); ܟܠܰܝ (24:4); ܙܳܕܶܩ (7:11); ܢܶܒܛܰܐ (3:1); ܐܶܚܰܝ (3:3).

(2) ܣܰܪܳܝ (1:4) from parasha; ܙܰܩܺܝܥ (1:6) from raḳî'o';

ܡܢܰܗܪܺܝܢ (2:3) from manharîn; ܐܰܙܕܽܘܪ (2:5) from za'ûro;

ܬܶܫܠܛܽܘܢ (2:18) from neshlaṭun.

[§ 29.]   ELEMENTS OF SYRIAC.   25

(3) ܢܸܬܨܹܕ (Mk. 3:27); ܫܳܐܬܹܗ (Gen. 27:2); ܡܚܲܦܹܣ (John 19:24); ܬܡܲܗ (Mt. 9:30); ܢܦܲܩ (Mt. 13:2); ܟܦܸܢ (1:12); ܐܶܦܲܣ (1:14); ܣܶܡܳܠܳܢܝ̱ *she showed me;* ܚܶܪܡܳܐ 6;19); ܚܶܪܦܳܐ (3:15); ܚܽܘܪܳܐ (Mt. 1:18).

3. In other cases, where we would have a short vowel in an open syllable,—

(1) It is occasionally lengthened, especially after the fall of a guttural and in the feminine ending ܐ from ܬ.

(2) It is generally dropped, except where this cannot be done without injury to the form. So ܳ is always dropped, except in the Imperative Peʽal, and in a few nouns like ܕܺܐܳܠܐ *fawn.*

Remark.—The ܲ in such forms as ܨܲܠܲܚ and ܚܲܨܰܝ is anomalous.

(3) It is retained, the following radical being doubled,—

(a) Regularly after preformatives in ʽÊ doubled and Pê Nun verbs.
(b) In a few ʽÊ Olaph verbs.
(c) In the Peʽal Imperfect and Infinitive of ܢܣܲܒ and ܣܠܸܩ, the ܢ being dropped.
(d) In the 3d fem. sing. Perfect before suffixes.
(e) In some compound words.

§ 29. Euphony of Vowels.

1. (1) ܐܶܢܳܐ (1:1); ܐܘܿܣܡܳܐ (1:8); ܟܽܠ (1:2); ܐܳܦ (1:2); ܡܨܲܡܡܳܐ (1:10).

(2) ܐܚܨܲܪ (1:7); ܘܚܟܡܬܶܗ (1:10); ܐܟܚܶܓܠܡܳܐ (1:11); ܘܡܥܰܐ (4:8); ܣܚܠܳܐ *milk;* ܠܡܥܕܳܐ (4:2).

(3) ܐܚܕܳܐ (1:1); ܐܶܥܰܐ (28:19); ܐܳܥܶܡ (Mt. 3:3).

(4) ܗܘ ܡܚܠܦܳܐ (17:8); ܗܘ ܚܕܘܿܪ (17:9); ܐܶܠܟܽܘܢ *go ye* (32:10).

(5) ܠܡܣܥܰܐ (1:1); ܡܬܳܐ (1:3); ܡܠܬܳܐ (2:3); ܠܥܶܣܬܳܐ (Rev. 6:15); ܡܶܣܬܳܪܘܐ (Eph. 1:21).

(6) ܐܳܣܺܝܰܐ *Asia;* ܐܪܺܥܰܐ *Arabia;* ܐܕܢܰܐ *Adana;* ܐܪܰܐ ἄρα.

1. Short *a*, or Pethoḥo, is found,—
   (1) In closed syllables.
   (2) In half-open syllables, mostly after the inseparable prefixes.
   (3) In an open syllable caused by euphonic changes in the word.
   (4) In an open syllable caused by the coalescing of two words by the addition of a syllable.
   (5) In nominal plurals ending in ܹܐ or ܵܘ̈ܐ.
   (6) In an open syllable in many foreign words.

   2. (1) ܫܡܥܕܐ (1:2); ܚܘܝܟ (1:6); ܟܣܣܐ (1:14); ܡܢ̈ܪ (1:14); ܩܛܠܬ *she killed;* ܢܩܛܠ *he will kill;* ܐܡܪ (24:16).
   (2) ܐܚܖ (23:5); ܐܟܠ (6:1); ܐܡܪ (17:15); ܐܠ (24:17).
   (3) ܢܩܕܡ (= ܢܩܕܡ); ܩܛܠ̈ܢ (3 f. pl. Pa'el); ܐܚܬ (32:8).
   (4) ܛܠܦܐ (Mt. 4:5); ܪܛܒܐ *moisture;* ܚܢܩܐ (Mt. 7:16).
   (5) ܪܘܣܘ (1:2); ܚܙܝ (1:6); ܩܦܨ (1:12); ܐܟܕ (6:8).

2. Short *e* is generally obscured from an original *ă*. It is found,—
   (1) In closed syllables.
   (2) In an open syllable, when there is preservation of initial Olaph.
   (3) In an open syllable, arising from changes in the body of the word or from sufformatives.
   (4) Sometimes in half-open syllables.
   (5) The ܖ of the ultimate of such forms as are given in (5) are written with ܕ in East Syriac, perhaps because this syllable had originally the accent. See Nöldeke, *Syrische Grammatik,* § 47.

   3. (1) ܥܒܕ (1:4); ܕܗܒ (1:6); ܕܥܖ (1:9); ܡܛܥܡ (1:12); ܥܐܕܐ (1:13).
   (2) ܓܐܪܐ (from g e rro) *arrow;* ܢܦܐܫܐ *relaxation;* ܡܨܐܕܐ *snare.*

3. (1) Long *e* is formed by contraction, and is represented by ܝ or ܐ.
   (2) In East Syriac, we have a few cases of *e* long by compensation or position.

[§ 29.] ELEMENTS OF SYRIAC. 27

(14:16); ܨܶܦܝܳܐ *snare.*

ܟܶܟܡܳܐ (2:2); ܥܡܳܕܳܐ (Rom. 6:10).

4. ܰ is always long. It is written ܰ, ܰܝ, ܰܐ, ܝܰ, or ܰܘ. It is found,
(1) As formative in many nouns.
(2) As the vowel in which a ܝ at the beginning of a word quiesces.
(3) Heightened in an open syllable, especially before an Olaph which has become quiescent.
(4) Contracted from *ăy, iy, yi, iw,* and *wi.*

(2) ܟܳܠ *thousand;* ܐܰܚ (24:14); ܐܰܚܝ *my brother;* ܐܰܚܺܝܠܽܘ (2:16);

(3) ܡܢܳܬ (m'nawath) *portion;* ܒܽܨ (23:10); ܡܶܗܝܳܐ (25:3); ܥܰܡ

(1:6).

5. (1) When not final, ܳ generally represents an originally long *a.*
(2) In a few nouns, before certain suffixes (when the vowel was most probably heightened by the original accent; see Duval, § 157), and perhaps in the 3d sing. masc. Perf. of ܝ״ܠ verbs, it seems to have beeen heightened from an originally short *a.*
(3) In verbal forms and nouns derived from ܝ״ܠ and ܥ״ܘ verbs, ܳ often represents a contraction from *awa.*

(4) In a few cases, it was contracted from ܐ̈ or ܐ. In the absolute feminine singular, it was heightened in compensation for the elided Taw.

(5) In the emphatic state, the final ܐ is naturally long, being derived from the demonstrative particle ܗܳܐ. See Duval, § 259. *a.*

Remark.—In foreign words, ܳ is frequently followed by Waw, e. g. ܦܳܘܢܛܘܣ (1 Pet. 1:1).

6. (1) ܥܠܰܝܡܳܐ *youth* (form fu'ail); ܩܘܠܬܐ *vase* (form fu'ûl); ܬܶܟܬܒܘܢ (form neḳtulun); but ܟܬܘܒܘܢ *write;* ܥܘܙܠܐ *fawn.*

(2) ܩܘܪܒܢܐ (17:10); ܦܘܩܕܢܐ (18:2); ܐܘܪܚܐ (18:8); ܩܘܕܫܗ (18:14); ܬܫܡܫܘܢ (12:7); ܟܘܡܪܐ (12:15).

(3) ܪܘܚܐ (11:5); ܩܘܡ (11:1); ܬܪܟܘܢ (14:1); ܬܚܠܘܢ (14:1).

6. (1) Except in the Imperative Pe'al, and a few nouns, short *u* always falls away in an open syllable.

(2) In closed syllables, short *u* remains.

(3) When preceded or followed by Waw, short *u* becomes long *u.* See 7. (1).

7. (1) ܩܘܡ (11:1); ܪܘܚܐ (11:5); ܬܚܠܘܢ (14:1); ܬܪܟܘܢ (14:1).

(2) ܩܛܘܠ (25:17); ܣܘܦ *end* (emph. ܣܘܦܐ); ܬܘܪܬܐ *cow;* ܙܟܘܬܐ (13:4).

(3) ܬܫܡܫܬܐ (24:17); ܢܩܡܘܬܐ (Spic. Syr. 33:20); ܩܘܡ (Neh. 11:24).

(4) ܬܗܘܡܐ (1:2); ܚܫܘܟܐ (1:2); ܡܬܗܠܟܢܐ (3:8); ܗܘ (4:18); ܡܟܬܒܘܬܗ (24:2); ܬܡܠܟܘܢ (2:18).

7. (1) Long *u* comes by contraction from *wu*, or *uw*. See 6. (3).

(2) In a few cases, in West Syriac, by contraction from *aw* (East Syriac ܘ݁).

(3) In a few cases, it comes through *ô* from *â*.

(4) In many forms, it is long by nature.

§ **30.** Loss of Vowels.

1. ܟܬܒܬ (from kathabhath) *she wrote;* ܐܬܟܬܒ *it was written;* ܐܬܟܬܒ *be written;* ܐܥܝܪܬܗ *I awaked him;* ܢܐܠܕܘܢ *they shall bear;* ܒܝܫܬܐ *bad;* ܓܪܒܐ *leprous;* ܟܬܒܐ *writing;* ܕܡܟܐ *sleeping.*

2. (1) ܟܬܒ (from kathabha); ܟܬܒܬ ; ܟܬܒܬܘܢ ; ܟܬܒܘ ; ܟܬܒܢ ; ܟܬܒܢܢ .

(2) ܢܟܬܘܒ ; ܬܟܬܒܝܢ ; ܢܟܬܒܘܢ ; ܬܟܬܒܝ .

(3) ܟܬܘܒܝ ; ܟܬܘܒܘ ; ܟܬܘܒܝܢ ; ܟܬܘܒܘܢ ; ܟܬܘܒܝܢ .

(4) ܡܠܟ *king;* ܐܠܦ *thousand;* ܟܬܒ *writing;* ܒܝܫ *bad.*

(5) ܐܒܝ (24:14); ܒܢܝ (24:12); ܐܒܪܗܡ (24:1); ܠܐܪܥܗ (24:15); ܬܥܒܕܝ (6:9); ܐܠܗܝ (6:9); ܒܐܝܕܝ (6:14); ܥܒܕܝ (6:15); ܩܕܫܝ ܩܝܡܝ (Lk. 2:13); ܐܡܪܝ (Mt. 24:3); ܐܬܒܝܬܝ (John 4:52).

1. A vowel is frequently lost in the middle of a word.

2. A vowel is lost at the end of a word,—

(1) In all forms of the Perfect, except the 3d sing. fem.

(2) In all forms of the Imperfect.

(3) In all forms of the Imperative, except the 2d masc. sing.

(4) In the absolute of all nouns, adjectives, and participles.

(5) Final Yudh is written but not pronounced, in the suffix 1st sing. after consonants (but see § 31. *Rem.* 1); in the suffix 3d sing. masc.; in the 2d fem. sing.; and in a few other cases.

§ **31.** The Half-vowel.

1. ܒܪܐ (1:1); ܫܡܝܐ (1:1); ܟܠ (1:1); ܬܗܘܡܐ (1:2); ܡܪܚܦܐ (1:2); ܘܦܪܫ (1:4); ܠܟܢܫܝܢ (1:10); ܡܬܒܪܟ (1;13).

But ܫܬܐ *six;* ܫܬܝܢ *sixty.*

2. ܐܬܚܫܒ *meditate* (but ܐܬܚܫܒ *be accounted*); ܕܗܒܝ *my gold*; ܚܡܬܗܘܢ *their anger.*

3. ܡܠܟܬܐ (4:2); ܕܗܒܐ (4:9); ܕܥܒܕ (3:12); ܥܒܕܬܟܝ *she made thee* (but ܥܒܕܬܟܝ *I have made thee*).

1. Except in a few words, a half-vowel occurs with every unvoweled consonant which begins a syllable. This half-vowel does not constitute a separate syllable. It is equivalent to vocal Sh'wa in Hebrew.

2. In the Ethpa'al Imperative, and in certain other cases, it is found at the end of a syllable.

3. The half-vowel is found after a consonant which is medial, i. e. a consonant which, though not doubled, apparently closes one syllable and begins another.

Remark 1.—A short *e* was heard at the end of such words as ܓܒܪܝ *my man* and ܐܕܝ *my right.* See Duval, § 98.

Rem. 2.—The Participles of the four verbs ܥܒܕ *to make*, ܚܒܫ *to bind*, ܙܩܦ *to crucify*, and ܦܠܓ *to divide*, preserve the half-vowel and the aspiration of ܒ, ܓ and ܕ, e. g. ܥܒܕ. All other Participles lose it (cf. § 30. 1; and see Duval, § 127).

§ 32. Shifting of Vowels.

1. ܩܕܝܫ but ܩܘܕܫܐ *holiness*; ܟܬܒܬ from ܟܬܒܬ *I have written*; ܓܒܪ but ܓܒܪܐ *man*; ܟܬܘܒ *write*, but ܟܬܘܒܝܗ *write it*; ܢܩܛܠܘܗ (3:3); ܠܩܘܒܠܗ (1 Pet. 5:9).

2. ܥܓܠܬܐ for ܥܓܠܬܐ *heifer*; ܦܩܥܬܐ *plain*; ܡܫܘܚܬܐ *measure.*

3. ܟܐܘ for ܟܐܘ *they blamed*; ܟܐܒ for ܟܐܒ *he grieved*; ܢܟܐܒ for ܢܟܐܒ *he shall grieve.*

1. The vowel which follows a consonant sometimes passes before it.

2. In order to facilitate its pronunciation, a consonant frequently attracts to itself the vowel which precedes.

3. A vowel which follows an Olaph preceded by an unvoweled consonant is shifted to that consonant, the Olaph becoming quiescent. See § 25. 1. (2).

§ 33.] ELEMENTS OF SYRIAC. 31

§ 33. New Vowels.

1. ܐܙܠ (11:12); ܐܣܬܥܣܬ (12:13); ܐܢܐ (12:17); ܒܥܝ (15:9); ܐܙܠ (17:5); ܣܥܝܕܐ (18:7); ܐܚܪ (23:5); ܐܠܐ (24:10); ܐܣܪܗ (25:11).

2. ܚܙܘܗܝ (1:4); ܘܟܠܗ (1:7); ܚܙܐ (1:7).

3. ܐܙܠܝܢ (23:14); ܐܙܠܐܚܪ (Mt. 27:9); ܣܬܟܠܢ (16:10).

4. ܚܠܐ (Lk. 6:48); ܐܬܕܟܝ (Syr. Thes. 2504); ܐܬܕܟܝ *ear of corn.*

1. An unvoweled Olaph at the beginning of a word takes a short *a* or *e* to aid in its pronunciation; in the same circumstances, Yudh quiesces in *î*.

2. When three consonants would come together at the beginning of a word, a helping vowel, generally short *a*, is given to the first.

3. Often in the middle of a word, a helping vowel is added to a letter. This is regularly the case in the Ethpe'el of Pê-Yudh and Pê-Olaph verbs.

4. A vowel is frequently added in order to preserve the doubling of the preceding radical.

PART SECOND.—ETYMOLOGY.

§ **34.** Inseparable Particles.

1. ܕܲܢܥܡܹܕ (1:1); ܘܡ݂ܢ (1:1); ܠܚܕܘܗܝ (1:4); ܘܡܸܛܠ (1:4).

2. ܐܵܘܟܼܠܐ (1:1); ܘܒܐܟܼܠ (1:2); ܘܐܵܡܪ (1:6); ܕܐܘܡܢܐ (2:2); ܠܐܒܼܕܢܐ (5:4); ܘܒܐܒܼ (13:15).

3. ܘܗܘܐ (1:3); ܘܐܡܪ (1:3); ܘܡܸܛܠ (2:2); ܘܐܝܟܢܐ (2:3); ܘܐܥܨܝܢ (2:19).

Remark 1.—ܐܸܢ ܕ (3:9); ܕܐܘܡܢܐ (2:2).

Remark 2.—ܐܒܥܘ (Mt. 9:30); ܕܫܘܐ (John 21:18).

4. ܡܚܣܢܐ (1:5); ܘܥܕܢܐ (24:7); ܘܡܚܣܟܬܐ (24:11).

5. ܡܢܕܪܫ (24:7); ܡܢܚܠ (25:3); ܐܡܣܝ (Mt. 3:16); ܡܚܛ (Jn. 19:18).

The Inseparable Particles are the prepositions ܒ and ܠ, the conjunction ܘ, and the relative ܕ. They are always prefixed.

1. Before voweled consonants, they take a half-vowel.

2. When before Olaph, they draw the vowel of the Olaph to themselves, the Olaph quiescing. They are prefixed directly to words beginning with ܐ.

3. Before unvoweled consonants, they receive ܇.

Remark 1.—Before words which take a prosthetic Olaph, they take the vowel of the Olaph, the Olaph being either retained or dropped.

Remark 2.—When a vowel has been thrown back upon the first radical, the particle generally takes a vowel.

4. When more than one inseparable particle occur, every second one takes a vowel.

5. In a few compound words the Nun of the preposition ܡܢ is assimilated.

§ 35. The Personal Pronoun.

1. The following are the forms of the Personal Pronoun where used independently:

He	ܗܘ	They (m.)	ܗܢܘܢ
She	ܗܝ	They (f.)	ܗܢܝܢ
Thou (m.)	ܐܢܬ	Ye (m.)	ܐܢܬܘܢ
Thou (f.)	ܐܢܬܝ	Ye (f.)	ܐܢܬܝܢ
I	ܐܢܐ	We	ܚܢܢ

2. The following are the forms of the Personal Pronoun, where used as an enclitic subject:

ܩܛܠܢܐ or ܐܢܐ ܩܛܠ *I am killing.*

ܩܛܠܬ or ܐܢܬ ܩܛܠ *Thou* (m.) *art killing.*

ܩܛܠܬܝ or ܐܢܬܝ ܩܛܠܐ *Thou* (f.) *art killing.*

ܩܛܠܝܢܢ or ܚܢܢ ܩܛܠܝܢ *We are killing.*

ܚܢܢ ܩܛܠܢ *We* (f.) *are killing.*

ܩܛܠܝܬܘܢ or ܐܢܬܘܢ ܩܛܠܝܢ *Ye* (m.) *are killing.*

ܩܛܠܬܝܢ or ܐܢܬܝܢ ܩܛܠܢ *Ye* (f.) *are killing.*

Note.—The contracted forms from the participles of "ܠܐ" verbs are,

ܓܠܢܐ *I reveal.*   ܓܠܝܢܢ *We reveal.*

ܓܠܝܬ *Thou* (m.) *revealest.*   ܓܠܝܬܘܢ *Ye* (m.) *reveal.*

ܓܠܝܬܝ *Thou* (f.) *revealest.*

Remark 1.—These pronouns are used with adjectives also, e. g.—ܫܦܝܪܝܬܘܢ *ye are beautiful;* ܕܟܝܬ *thou art pure.*

Remark 2.—ܗܘܗܘ and ܗܝܗܝ often become ܗܘ and ܗܝ. See Mt. 11:14; Judith 1:5; but see also Col. 3:5.

§ 36. Pronominal Suffixes.

Tabular View.

		1. Possessive.		2. Objective.	
		After a Consonant.	After a Vowel.	After a Consonant.	After a Vowel.
SINGULAR.	3 m......	ܗ	ܝܗܝ	ܗ	ܝܗܝ, ܝܗܝ, or ܘܗܝ
	3 f......	ܗ̇	ܗ̇	ܗ̇	ܗ̇
	2 m......	ܟ	ܟ	ܟ	ܟ
	2 f......	ܟܝ	ܟܝ	ܟܝ	ܟܝ
	1 c......	ܝ	ܝ	ܢܝ	ܢܝ
PLURAL.	3 m......	ܗܘܢ	ܗܘܢ	—	—
	3 f......	ܗܝܢ	ܗܝܢ	—	—
	2 m......	ܟܘܢ	ܟܘܢ	ܟܘܢ	ܟܘܢ
	2 f......	ܟܝܢ	ܟܝܢ	ܟܝܢ	ܟܝܢ
	1 c......	ܢ	ܢ	ܢ	ܢ

1. The possessive suffixes are used with nouns; see § 77. The objective suffixes are used with verbs; see § 51.

2. Instead of a suffixed pronoun for the 3d plural after verbs, the enclitic pronouns ܐܢܘܢ and ܐܢܝܢ are used; see 2. 6; 2. 12; Lk. 24:11.

3. The inseparable preposition ܒ and ܠ are prefixed to the form of possessive pronominal suffixes which are used after consonants (*i. e.* the first column in the table). Before the first person singular they take the form ܒܝ, ܠܝ; *e. g.*, 2. 12; 16. 9; 16. 15; 19. 9; 17. 11; 23. 2.

§ 37. The Demonstrative Pronoun (see *Thes. Syr.*, p. 1023).

1. ܗܢ, ܗܢܐ *this* (m.); ܗܕܐ *this* (f.); ܗܠܝܢ *these* (m. or f.).

2. ܗܘ *that* (m.); ܗܝ *that* (f.); ܗܢܘܢ *those* (m.); ܗܢܝܢ *those* (f.).

3. ܗܢܘ ܦܓܪܝ *this is my body* (23:18); ܗܪܝܫ (John 2:11).

1. ܗܿܘ is found instead of ܗܿܘܐ.

2. The forms ܗܵܟܲܢ, ܗܵܟܸܢ are found occasionally instead of ܗܵܟܲܢܐ; and ܗܵܟܿܢ instead of ܗܵܟܢܐ.

3. *This is* is ܗܵܢܘ (contracted from ܗܵܢܐ ܗܘ; see § 23. 4. (1)), ܗܵܕܝܘ (hodoy) from ܗܿܘ ܗܿܕܐ.

§ 38. The Relative and Possessive Pronouns.

1. The Relative Pronoun is ܕ *who, which, that*. It has the same form in all genders, numbers, and cases. It is an inseparable particle, and is pointed according to § 34.

2. ܕ has been shortened from an original ܕܝ which is yet found in the possessive ܕܝܠ, compounded of ܕܝ *which* and ܠ *to*. It is used with the pronominal suffixes to express the independent possessive pronoun; e. g. ܕܝܠܝ *mine*; ܕܝܠܟ *thine*; ܕܝܠܗ *his*; ܕܝܠܢ *ours*.

§ 39. The Interrogative Pronouns.

1. ܡܲܢ *who?* ܡܵܢ, ܡܵܢܐ, ܡܢܐ *what?*
2. ܐܲܝܢܐ (m.), ܐܲܝܕܐ (f.), ܐܲܝܠܝܢ (m. or f. plural) *who? which? what?*

Remark 1. — ܡܲܢ is the Indefinite Interrogative for persons. It is not used as an adjective. See § 103. 1.

Remark 2. — ܡܵܢ is used for things. It is not used as an adjective.

Remark 3. — ܐܲܝܢܐ, ܐܲܝܕܐ and ܐܲܝܠܝܢ are generally used as Interrogative Adjectives, e. g., ܐܲܝܢܐ ܓܒܪܐ *which man?* But see § 103. 2. (1).

Remark 4. — *Who is?* is ܡܲܢܘ (from ܡܲܢ ܗܘ), ܡܲܢܝܘ. *What is?* is ܡܵܢܘ from ܡܵܢ ܗܘ.

36 ELEMENTS OF SYRIAC. [§§ 40, 41.

§ 40. The Strong Verb.

   (3) ܟܠ (26:3); ܢܣܰܒ (Lk. 22:17); ܗܘ (Gal. 4:14).

1. All words are derived from roots most of which have three letters or radicals. The third person singular masculine of the Perfect of the simple form (called Pᵉ‘al) is always given as the root, though in some weak verbs one of the radicals has disappeared from this form.

2. Verbs are called strong when the root contains no consonant which will cause a change in the vowels usually employed in a given inflection.

3. A verb is called weak when it contains a radical which modifies the vowels usually employed in a given inflection. Such verbs are,—

   (1) Those whose last radical is a guttural or Rîsh; and those any one of whose radicals is an Olaph.

   (2) Those whose first radical is Nun.

   (3) Those whose second and third radicals are alike.

   (4) Those any one of whose radicals was a Yudh or Waw.

§ 41. Verb Stems.

   (3) ܡܣܥܰܕ (Ps. 119:120); ܐܶܣܚܰܢ (Nahum 2:10).

4. ܐܶܬ݂ܦ݁ܶܫ (7:6); ܢܶܬ݂ܡܶܐ (24:5); ܐܶܬ݂ܡܶܐ (12:5); ܢܶܬ݂ܡܰܟ݁ܰܟ݂ (6:15);

ܐܶܬ݂ܩܪܺܝ (25:10); ܐܶܬ݂ܩܪܺܝܡ (*Thes. Syr.*, p. 120).

5. ܫܰܠܗܶܒ݂ (Rev. 1:15); ܐܶܫܬ݁ܰܡܰܫ (Rom. 10:3).

Rem. 1.—ܫܰܚܠܶܦ݂ (Acts 14:20); ܡܫܰܡܫܳܢܳܐ (Mt. 1:23).

Rem. 2.—ܐܰܢܶܦ݂ *to breathe,* ܐܶܬ݂ܐܰܢܰܦ݂ *id.*; ܩܪܶܒ݂ *to approach,* ܐܶܬ݂ܩܪܶܒ݂ *id.*

1. The simple verb-stem, called Pᵉ'al, has, for consonants, the three radical letters. In all strong verbs we have a half-vowel after the first radical and a short vowel after the second. This short vowel is, (1) in active verbs, usually *a;* (2) in stative verbs, usually *e;* (3) in two verbs, *u*.

2. The intensive verb-stem, called Pa'el, is formed by doubling the second radical, the vowel *a* being used with the first radical, and, except before gutturals and Rish, *e*, derived from *a*, after the second.

3. The causative verb-stem, called 'Aph'el, is formed by prefixing ܐ to the radical letters; the first radical being without a vowel, and the second having *e*, derived from *a*.

4. From each of these active stems a Reflexive or Passive is formed by prefixing ܐܶܬ݂ ; to wit,—from Pᵉ'al, the Ethpᵉ'el, with a half-vowel after the first radical and *e* after the second; from Pa'el, the Ethpa'al, with *a* after the first and second radicals; from 'Aph'el, the Ettaph'al, by changing the prefixed Olaph into Taw, and using *a* before the first and after the second radical.

5. Another form of the causative, called Shaph'el, is formed by prefixing *sha* instead of *'a*. Like other quadriliterals, the Shaph'el is inflected like the Pa'el (see § 63.). Its reflexive is Eshtaph'al.

Rem. 1.—According to some, there are sporadic cases of another stem, called Taph'el (see Merx-Hoffmann, *Gram. Syr.*, § 56. 1. A. end). Most of these are really denominative quadriliteral verbs (see § 63.). For similar forms in Hebrew see Olshausen's *Lehrbuch*, p. 56.

Rem. 2.—The signification of the stems is, in general, the same as that of the corresponding stems in Hebrew. It may be noted, however, that the Ethpᵉ'el of some intransitive verbs, and the Ethpa'al of some verbs whose Pa'el has a causative signification, have come to have the same sense as the Pᵉ'al.

§ 42. General View of the Verb-Stems.

	Original Form.	First Form.	Name.	Force.	Characteristic.
1.	ܩܛܰܒ݂	ܩܛܰܒ݂	Pᵉ'al.	Simple Root Meaning.	None.
2.	ܐܶܬܩܛܶܒ݂	ܐܶܬܩܛܶܒ݂	Ethpᵉ'el.	Passive or Reflexive of Simple Stem.	ܐܶ
3.	ܩܰܛܶܒ݂	ܩܰܛܶܒ݂	Pa'el.	Intensive Active.	Second Radical doubled, and always preceded by *a*.
4.	ܐܶܬܩܰܛܰܒ݂	ܐܶܬܩܰܛܰܒ݂	Ethpa'al.	Passive or Reflexive Intensive.	ܐܶ prefixed, and Second Radical doubled.
5.	ܐܰܩܛܶܒ݂	ܐܰܩܛܶܒ݂	Aph'el.	Causative Active.	ܐܰ
6.	ܐܶܬܬܰܩܛܰܒ݂	ܐܶܬܬܰܩܛܰܒ݂	Ettaph'al.	Passive or Reflexive Causative.	ܐܶܬܬ

Remarks.

1. The original penultimate *v* is changed to a half-vowel in the Pᵉ'al and Ethpᵉ'el.

2. The original ultimate *v* is changed to ܶ in the Pa'el, Aph'el and Ethpᵉ'el.

§ 43. The Pᵉ'al Perfect.

TABLE A.

1. *He wrote*............ܩܛܰܒ݂ = the simple verb-stem (§ 41. 1).

2. *She wrote*.........ܩܶܛܒܰܬ݂ = ܩܛܒ with ܰܬ݂ the usual fem. sign.

3. *Thou* (m.) *didst write* ܩܛܰܒܬ݂ = ܩܛܒ with ܬ݂ a fragment of the pronoun ܐܰܢܬ݂ *thou* (m.).

4. *Thou* (f.) *didst write* ܩܛܰܒܬܝ = ܩܛܒ with ܬܝ a fragment of the pronoun ܐܰܢܬܝ *thou* (f.).

5. *I wrote*............ܟܶܬܒܶܬ = ܟܬܰܒ with ܶܬ (compare תִּי).

6. *They* (m.) *wrote*......ܟܬܰܒܘ = ܟܬܰܒ with ܘ (not spoken) from earlier *ûna*.

7. *They* (f.) *wrote*......ܟܬܰܒ̈ܝ = ܟܬܰܒ with ܝ (not spoken) from earlier *îna*.

8. *Ye* (m.) *wrote*......ܟܬܰܒܬܽܘܢ = ܟܬܰܒ with ܬܽܘܢ a fragment of the pronoun ܐܰܢ̱ܬܽܘܢ

9. *Ye* (f.) *wrote*......ܟܬܰܒܬܶܝܢ = ܟܬܰܒ with ܬܶܝܢ a fragment of the pronoun ܐܰܢ̱ܬܶܝܢ

10. *We wrote*..........ܟܬܰܒܢ = ܟܬܰܒ with ܢ a fragment of the pronoun ܚܢܰܢ

TABLE B.

	Masculine Singular.	Feminine Singular.	Masculine Plural.	Feminine Plural.
Third Person,	ܟܬܰܒ	ܟܶܬܒ ܰܬ	ܟܬܰܒ ܘ	ܟܬܰܒ̈ ܝ
Second Person,	ܟܬܰܒ ܬ	ܟܬܰܒ ܬܝ	ܟܬܰܒ ܬܽܘܢ	ܟܬܰܒ ܬܶܝܢ
First Person,	ܟܶܬܒ ܶܬ		ܟܬܰܒ ܢ	

Remarks.

1. ܐܶܬܡܰܪ (6:9); ܚܣܰܪܘܗܝ (6:9); ܐܶܬܟܰܠܬ (6:9); ܚܣܰܪܘ (6:10).

2. ܢܶܦܩܰܬ (5:17); ܐܶܬܡܰܪ̈ܝ (Lk. 24:24); ܚܣܰܪܘܗܝ (6:9); ܝܺܕܰܥܬܶܝܢ (Gen. 31:6).

3. ܢܶܦܩܶܬ (5:17) (= ܢܶܦܩܶܬ = ܢܶܦܩܰܬ); ܐܶܬܟܠܶܬ (6:8) (= ܐܶܬܟܠܶܬ = ܐܶܬܟܰܠܬ).

4. ܦܰܪܚܝ (1:4); ܥܒܰܕܘ (6:2); ܚܣܰܪܘܗܝ (6:9); ܥܒܰܕܬܽܘܢ (26:13); ܩܪܰܒܝ (32:12).

5. ܐܶܙܰܠܢ (32:10); ܐܶܬܡܰܪܝ[ܢ] (Jos. Styl. 2:7); ܐܶܡܰܪ (for ܐܶܡܰܪܘ) (J. S. 4:10); ܢܶܦܠܬܝܢ (for ܢܶܦܠܬܝܢ) (Legends of St. Mary 26:20); ܩܪܳܒܬܽܘܢ (Acts 28:2); ܐܶܙܰܠܢ *we should go* (Lk. 9:13).

1. The pronominal fragments used in the inflection of the Perfect are always suffixed to the stem. To distinguish them from the pronominal suffixes (§ 36.) they may be called *sufformatives*.

2. We have distinct forms for both genders and both numbers in the second and third persons.

3. The vowel of the second radical is dropped in the 3d fem. and in the 1st com. sing., while the *a* of the first radical is obscured to *e*.

4. The sufformatives for person, gender and number, with the exception of the 3d fem. sing. and the 1st com. sing., are affixed directly and without causing any change in vocalization to the 3d m. sing., which may therefore, for convenience, be called the *first form* of the Perfect. This rule is true of all verbs, weak as well as strong, except the Lomadh Olaph verbs (§ 60.).

5. The third feminine plural sometimes ends in ܶܝ ; the third masculine plural sometimes ends in ܘ , and the first plural in ܢ (in Lk. 9:13 ܐܥܲܠܢ, from ܐܥܠ, is written, instead of ܐܥܠܢܢ, to avoid the three Nuns; cf. נָתַנּוּ). Sometimes, on the contrary, the third plural feminine, as well as masculine, was written just like the third masculine singular. According to Hoffmann (Merx, § 50. N. B., and § 59. I. (5)) a Yudh was sometimes added to the third feminine singular, e. g. ܦܶܩܕܰܬܝ . This is only a "signum graphicum fem. indicans," just as in the third feminine Imperfect (see § 45.).

Note 1. — The following summary of the endings of the Perfect in Syriac and Hebrew may be useful:

	3 m.	3 f.	2 m.	2 f.	1 c.	3 m.	3 f.	2 m.	2 f.	1 c.
		SINGULAR.				PLURAL.				
Syr.	—	ܰܬ	ܬ	ܬܝ	ܬ	ܘ (ܘܢ)	ܶܝ	ܬܘܢ	ܬܶܝܢ	ܢ or ܢܢ
Heb.	—	ָה	ָתָ	תְּ (תִּי)	תִּי	וּ (וּן)	—	תֶּם	תֶּן	נוּ

Note 2. — ܫܩܠ (Mt. 8:2); ܫܶܩܠܰܬ (Mt. 20:20); ܫܩܠܬ? (Mt. 25:25); ܢܣܒܬܘܢ (1 Cor. 11:17); ܫܩܠܘ (32:13); ܫܩܠܝ (32:22); ܢܣܒ (Acts 27:2); ܪܚܡܬܘܢ (John 16:27).

Verbs which have *e* in the *first form* (see § 43. Rem. 4.) retain it in all the forms derived from it; but in the 3d fem. and 1st sing. they are the same as verbs which have *a* in the *first form*.

§ 44. The Remaining Perfects.

	Ethpᵉ'el.	Pa'el.	Ethpa'al.	Aph'el.	Ettaph'al.
3 m. sing.	ܐܶܬܩܛܶܒ	ܩܰܛܶܒ	ܐܶܬܩܰܛܰܒ	ܐܰܩܛܶܒ	ܐܶܬܬܰܩܛܰܒ
3 f. sing.	ܐܶܬܩܛܒܰܬ	ܩܰܛܒܰܬ	ܐܶܬܩܰܛܒܰܬ	ܐܰܩܛܒܰܬ	ܐܶܬܬܰܩܛܒܰܬ
3 m. pl.	ܐܶܬܩܛܒܘ	ܩܰܛܒܘ	ܐܶܬܩܰܛܒܘ	ܐܰܩܛܒܘ	ܐܶܬܬܰܩܛܒܘ
1 sing.	ܐܶܬܩܛܒܶܬ	ܩܰܛܒܶܬ	ܐܶܬܩܰܛܒܶܬ	ܐܰܩܛܒܶܬ	ܐܶܬܬܰܩܛܒܶܬ

ܐܶܬܩܛܶܠ (12:5); ܐܶܬܕܒܰܪ (6:19); ܐܶܣܬܓܶܕ (Rev. 13:12); ܐܶܬܚܙܺܝ (32:18); ܐܰܪܝܡ (Rev. 11:18); ܐܰܘܪܶܒ (29:18); ܚܰܒܶܒ (7:3); ܐܶܫܬܰܟܚ (Gal. 4:12); ܩܰܛܶܠ (4:12); ܩܰܛܶܦ (Acts 23:30); ܩܰܛܪܘ (Acts 4:15); ܩܰܛܰܪ (Acts 15:24); ܐܶܬܩܰܛܰܠ (25:10); ܐܶܬܚܰܒܰܠ (Heb. 9:20); ܐܶܬܩܰܛܰܠ (Col. 4:10); ܐܶܬܰܕܒܰܪ (12:17); ܐܰܩܛܶܒ (6:1); ܐܰܣܗܶܕ (Lk. 20:23).

It will be noticed that all of these Perfects form all of their inflections on the analogy of the Perfect Pᵉ'al; *i. e.* the sufformatives for gender, number and person are in all cases, except the 3d fem. and 1st person singular, affixed directly to the 3d singular masculine, without causing any change in it. In the 3d singular feminine (and the 1st sing., which is formed like it) the only change in the last four stems is that the vowel of the second radical is changed to a half-vowel; in the Ethpᵉ'el the second radical loses its vowel and the first receives *a*.

Remark 1. — The Ethpᵉ'el 3d feminine singular and 1st common singular can be distinguished from those of the Ethpa'al only when the second or third radical is an aspirate and Kushoy and Rukhokh (§ 10.) are marked. It will be noted that in Ethpᵉ'el the second radical has Rukhokh, and the third, Kushoy; whereas in Ethpa'al the opposite is true.

Remark 2. — Notice the transposition of the Taw in the Ethpᵉ'el and Ethpa'al of verbs whose first radical is a sibilant, and the permutations of the Taw in those whose first radical is Zain or Sodhê (cf. §§ 21. 1; 22. 4).

§ 45. The Pᵉʿal Imperfect.

TABLE A.

1. *He will write*....... ܢܶܟܬܽܘܒ = ܟܬܽܘܒ with ܢܶ a pronom. prefix used to denote the 3d person.
2. *She will write*..... ܬܶܟܬܽܘܒ = ܟܬܽܘܒ with ܬ the usual fem. sign prefixed, and ܝ suffixed to distinguish it from the 2d masc. sing. Cf. § 43. Rem. 5.
3. *Thou* (m.) *wilt write* ܬܶܟܬܽܘܒ = ܟܬܽܘܒ with ܬܶ a fragment of ܐܰܢ݇ܬ *thou*, prefixed.
4. *Thou* (f.) *wilt write* ܬܶܟܬܒܺܝܢ = ܟܬܽܘܒ with ܬܶ prefixed, ܝܢ suffixed, and ܽܘ shortened and obscured to the half-vowel.
5. *I shall write*........ ܐܶܟܬܽܘܒ = ܟܬܽܘܒ with ܐܶ a fragment of ܐܶܢܳܐ *I* prefixed.
6. *They* (m.) *will write* ܢܶܟܬܒܽܘܢ = ܟܬܽܘܒ with ܢܶ prefixed for the 3d person, ܽܘܢ suffixed for the m. plural, and the vowel changed to a half-vowel.
7. *They* (f.) *will write*.. ܢܶܟܬܒܳܢ = ܟܬܽܘܒ as in the 3d m. pl., except that the ending is ܳܢ instead of ܽܘܢ
8. *Ye* (m.) *will write*.. ܬܶܟܬܒܽܘܢ = ܟܬܽܘܒ as in the 3d m. pl., except that we have ܬ prefixed instead of ܢ
9. *Ye* (f.) *will write*.... ܬܶܟܬܒܳܢ = ܟܬܽܘܒ as in the 3d f. pl., except that we have ܬ instead of ܢ prefixed.
10. *We shall write*...... ܢܶܟܬܽܘܒ = ܟܬܽܘܒ with ܢ a fragment of ܚܢܰܢ *we* prefixed.

TABLE B.

	Masculine Singular.	Feminine Singular.	Masculine Plural.	Feminine Plural.
Third Person,	ܢܶܩܛܽܘܠ	ܬܶܩܛܽܘܠ	ܢܶܩܛܠܽܘܢ	ܢܶܩܛܠܳܢ
Second Person,	ܬܶܩܛܽܘܠ	ܬܶܩܛܠܺܝܢ	ܬܶܩܛܠܽܘܢ	ܬܶܩܛܠܳܢ
First Person,	ܐܶܩܛܽܘܠ		ܢܶܩܛܽܘܠ	

Remarks.

1. The original stem is ܩܛܽܘܠ, the ܽܘ of which is changed to a half-vowel (*i. e.* volatilized) before sufformatives which begin with a vowel; *i. e.* ܛܠܺ, ܛܠܽ, ܛܠܳ.

2. The pronominal fragments employed in the inflection of the Imperfect are,—

Prefixes, ܢ, ܬ, ܬ, ܬ, ܐ ; ܢ, ܢ, ܬ, ܬ, ܢ

Affixes, —, ܝ, —, ܝܢ, — ; ܘܢ, ܢ, ܘܢ, ܢ, —

3. The ܶ of the preformative comes from an original *a*.

4. The preformatives and sufformatives of the Imperfect are the same for all stems, and for weak verbs as well as strong, except that the vowel of the preformative is sometimes other than ܶ.

5. Except the silent suffix ܝ, which is sometimes used with the 3d fem. sing., the five forms, ܢܶܩܛܽܘܠ, ܬܶܩܛܽܘܠ, ܬܶܩܛܽܘܠ, ܐܶܩܛܽܘܠ and ܢܶܩܛܽܘܠ differ merely in the consonant of the preformative; the other five forms always suffer the same changes in the root, *i. e.* ܬܶܩܛܠܺܝܢ, ܢܶܩܛܠܽܘܢ, ܬܶܩܛܠܽܘܢ, ܢܶܩܛܠܳܢ, ܬܶܩܛܠܳܢ.

6. The original forms of the Imperfect run,—nakṭulu, takṭulu, nakṭulûna, nakṭulâna. "De imperfecti formis notandum est vocales primitivas *ŭ* et *û* in *ŏ* et *ô* esse elatas, quorum loco serior aetas iterum *ŭ* et *û* pronunciavit, ita ut antiqui scribae et Nestoriani formas exhibeant ܢܶܩܛܠܽܘܢ et ܢܶܩܛܠܳܢ, recentiores vero Ja'ḳobitae et Maronitae ܢܶܩܛܠܽܘܢ et ܢܶܩܛܠܳܢ."—Merx-Hoffmann, *Gr. Syr.*, § 50. D.

§ 46. P^e'al Imperfects in A and E.
TABULAR VIEW.

	3 m. sg.	3 m. pl.
Imperfect with *u*,	ܢܶܩܛܽܘܠ	ܢܶܩܛܠܽܘܢ
Imperfect with *i*,	ܢܶܩܛܶܠ	"
Imperfect with *a*,	ܢܶܩܛܰܠ	"

1. ܢܶܚܨܽܘܕ (2:17); ܢܶܚܨܽܘܢ (Mt. 7:12); ܢܶܪܥܶܐ (Lk. 22:36); ܢܶܪܓܙܽܘܢ (Mt. 14:15); ܢܶܦܶܠ (for ܢܶܢܦܶܠ) (Mt. 5:29); ܢܶܦܠܽܘܢ (Mt. 24:29); ܢܶܦܶܩ (from ܢܦܩ) (Mt. 13:2); ܢܶܬܒܽܘܢ (Mt. 20:21); ܢܶܦܪ (from ܦܪܕ = פָּרַד) *he will err;* ܢܣܝܡ (from ܣܝܡ = שִׂים) (Mt. 19:13); ܢܶܓܶܕ (from ܢܓܕ) (John 12:32).

2. ܢܺܐܟܘܠ (Lk. 21:22); ܢܰܡܠܟܽܘܢ (Lk. 21:24); ܢܶܣܓܶܐ (Mt. 25:9); ܢܶܚܛܶܐ (Lk. 3:14); ܫܳܘܶܐ (Lk. 7:6); ܬܚܫܚܽܘܢ (Rom. 15:30); ܢܰܚܘܽܘܢ (2:18); ܢܶܫܡܰܥ (Mt. 18:17); ܢܶܫܡܥܽܘܢ (Mt. 13:15); ܢܶܥܒܶܕ (2:10).

3. ܠܡܶܥܒܰܕ (Mk. 10:48); ܢܶܥܒܕܽܘܢ (Mt. 20:31); ܢܶܪܥܶܐ (Mk. 8:22); ܢܶܪܥܽܘܢ (Mt. 14:36); ܢܶܫܬܶܐ (1 Cor. 4:25); ܢܶܫܡܰܥ (Jn. 4:23); ܢܶܣܓܶܐ (30:5).

 1. ܥܒܕ *to make* and ܙܒܢ *to buy* are the only strong verbs which have the Imperfect in ܶ ; but some weak verbs, mostly intransitives, form their Imperfect P^e'al in this manner; *e. g.* one Ê Ê, one Ê Yudh, one Pê Yudh, and a few Pê Nun verbs.

 2. Perfects in *e*, which are intransitive, have as a rule their Imperfect in *a;* as have also most intransitives in *a*, and most verbs whose second or third radical is a guttural.

 3. A few verbs having the Perfect in *e* have the Imperfect in *u*.

Note.—There were three Perfect stems, ܩܛܰܠ , ܩܛܶܠ , and ܩܛܽܘܠ (see § 41. 1.); and three Imperfect stems, ܢܶܩܛܰܠ , ܢܶܩܛܶܠ , and ܢܶܩܛܽܘܠ ; the *a* and *u* in each case being original, while the *e* has come from *i*.

§ 47. The Remaining Imperfects.

	Ethpᵉ'el.	Pa'el.	Ethpa'al.	Aph'el.	Ettaph'al.
3 m. sing.	ܢܶܬܩܛܶܠ	ܢܩܰܛܶܠ	ܢܶܬܩܰܛܰܠ	ܢܰܩܛܶܠ	ܢܶܬܰܩܛܰܠ
3 f. sing.	ܬܶܬܩܛܶܠ	ܬܩܰܛܶܠ	ܬܶܬܩܰܛܰܠ	ܬܰܩܛܶܠ	ܬܶܬܰܩܛܰܠ
3 m. pl.	ܢܶܬܩܛܠܽܘܢ	ܢܩܰܛܠܽܘܢ	ܢܶܬܩܰܛܠܽܘܢ	ܢܰܩܛܠܽܘܢ	ܢܶܬܰܩܛܠܽܘܢ
1 sing.	ܐܶܬܩܛܶܠ	ܐܩܰܛܶܠ	ܐܶܬܩܰܛܰܠ	ܐܰܩܛܶܠ	ܐܶܬܰܩܛܰܠ

ܢܶܙܕܩܶܦ (29:1); ܬܕܰܟܪ (6:11); ܢܶܬܡܰܠܠ (6:15); ܢܶܬܡܰܠܠܽܘܢ (1:10); ܬܬܰܪܓܡܽܘܢ (5:13); ܢܰܣܓܶܐ (2:9); ܢܶܬܝܗܶܒ (Mt. 25:29).

Rem. 1.—ܢܶܬܡܰܠܠܽܘܢ (1:10); ܬܬܰܪܓܡܽܘܢ (5:13); ܢܶܬܐܚܕܽܘܢ (2 Pet. 2:3).

It will be noticed that the preformatives and sufformatives of the derived stems are the same as those of the simple, or Pᵉ'al, stem (cf. § 45). What is said in § 45. Rem. 5, of the internal changes of the Pᵉ'al, is true also of the derived stems, *i. e.* the 3d fem. sing., the 2d masc. and the 1st com. sing. and plur. are the same, preformatives (and sufformative in the case of the 3d fem. sing.) excepted, as the 3d masc. sing. or *first form* of the Imperfect; and all other forms are the same, preformatives and sufformatives excepted, as the 3d masc. plural.

Rem. 1.—The 3d masc. plur., and the forms like it, of the Ethpᵉ'el and Ethpa'al, can only be distinguished in writing when the second or third radical is an aspirate. In the Ethpᵉ'el the second radical takes Rukhokh and the third Kushoy; whereas, in the Ethpᵉ'el the second takes Kushoy and the third Rukhokh; when neither the second nor the third radical is an aspirate the *usus loquendi* and the connection can alone determine whether the form be intensive or not.

Rem. 2.—In the Ettaph'al stem, whenever the preformative is a Taw, the other Taws are written as one, to avoid the occurrence of three Taws.

Rem. 3.—Notice the transposition and permutation before sibilants, according to §§ 21. 1; 22. 4.

Rem. 4.—The following table gives, (1) the preformatives of the different stems, (2) the vowel of the first radical, (3) the vowel of the second radical:

46 ELEMENTS OF SYRIAC. [§ 48.

	Pᵉ‘al.	Ethpᵉ‘el.	Pa‘el.	Ethpa‘al.	Aph‘el.	Ettaph‘al.
1.	ܢ	ܢܶ	ܢ	ܢܶ	ܢ	ܢܶܬ
2.	ܬ	ܬ	ܬ	ܬ	ܬ	ܬ
3.	ܝ (or ܐ)	ܝ	ܝ	ܝ	ܝ	ܝ

Rem. 5.—The various elements used as preformatives and sufformatives appear in the following table, the asterisks representing radicals:

He will.......   * * * ܢ   They (m.) will.. ܘܢ * * * ܢ
She will...... (ܬ) * * * ܝ   They (f.) will... ܢ̈ * * * ܢ
Thou (m.) wilt   * * * ܝ   Ye (m.) will.... ܘܢ * * * ܝ
Thou (f.) wilt.. ܝܢ * * * ܝ   Ye (f.) will...... ܢ̈ * * * ܝ
I shall........   * * * ܐ   We shall........   * * * ܢ

§ 48. The Imperatives.

	Imperfect.	Imperative 2 m. sg.	Imperative 2 f. sg.	Imperative 2 m. pl.	Imperative 2 f. pl.
Pᵉ‘al.	ܢܶܩܛܽܘܠ	ܩܛܽܘܠ	ܩܛܽܘܠܝ	ܩܛܽܘܠܘ(ܢ)	ܩܛܽܘܠ or ܩܛܽܘܠܶܢ
Pa‘el.	ܢܩܰܛܶܠ	ܩܰܛܶܠ	The endings for gender and number are the same for all the stems.		
Aph‘el.	ܢܰܩܛܶܠ	ܐܰܩܛܶܠ			
Ethpᵉ‘el.	ܢܶܬܩܛܶܠ	ܐܶܬܩܛܶܠ			
Ethpa‘al.	ܢܶܬܩܰܛܰܠ	ܐܶܬܩܰܛܰܠ or ܐܶܬܩܰܛܰܠ			
Ettaph‘al.	ܢܶܬܬܰܩܛܰܠ	ܐܶܬܬܰܩܛܰܠ			

1. ܩܨܘ݂ (31:13); ܡܲܟܸܠ (3:3); ܡܲܨܡܲܚ (30:13); ܚܣܲܪ (2 Tim. 4:5).

2. ܟܲܕܸܒ (33:3); ܐܲܚܪܸܡ (33:2); ܐܸܬܼܚܲܫܲܒ (Col. 3:18).

3. ܐܸܙܕܲܗܪ (31:17); ܐܸܬܼܡܲܥܕ (Col. 3:20).

The stem of the Imperative is the same as that of the Imperfect without the preformative; except in the Ethpᵉ'el and in one form of the Ethpa'al, where the original short *a* of the first radical is retained and the vowel of the second radical is dropped, its absence being often denoted by the linea occultans (see 3 above).

Note 1.—The Olaph of the Aph'el and of the passive stems, which is absorbed in the Imperfect, is retained in the Imperative.

Note 2.—The Imperative has no preformatives; the gender and number are denoted by sufformatives, which are, ܝ for the fem. sing.; ܘ or ܘܢ for the masc. plur.; ܝ or ܢ or ܝܢ for the fem. plural.

Note 3.—None of the sufformatives except ܘܢ and ܝܢ are pronounced.

§ 49. The Infinitives.

Pᵉ'al.	Ethpᵉ'el.	Pa'el.	Ethpa'al.	Aph'el.	Ettaph'al.
ܡܸܩܛܲܠ	ܡܸܬܼܩܛܵܠܘ	ܡܩܲܛܵܠܘ	ܡܸܬܼܩܲܛܵܠܘ	ܡܲܩܛܵܠܘ	ܡܸܬܲܩܛܵܠܘ

ܡܲܟܼܟܵܒܼܘ (2:6); ܡܸܨܦܲܗ (2:2); ܡܚܲܣܸܢ (3:13); ܡܲܠܕܘܿܕܼ (2:4); ܡܣܲܝܥܘ݂ (27:4); ܡܲܕܲܘܘܼܚ (1 Cor. 11:32).

1. The Infinitive of the Pᵉ'al is ܡܸܩܛܲܠ = ܩܛܲܠ + ܡ.

2. The Infinitives of the derived stems are all found by prefixing ܡ to the form used in the Imperfect, except that the vowel of the second radical is always ܵ and that the abstract ending ܘ is always suffixed. This ܘ becomes ܘܬ before pronominal suffixes. See § 85. Rem. 2.

§ 50. The Participles.

Pᵉ'al.	Ethpᵉ'el.	Pa'el.	Ethpa'al.	Aph'el.	Ettaph'al.
ܩܵܛܸܠ	ܡܸܬܼܩܛܸܠ	ܡܩܲܛܸܠ	ܡܸܬܼܩܲܛܲܠ	ܡܲܩܛܸܠ	ܡܸܬܲܩܛܲܠ
ܩܛܝܼܠ	—	ܡܩܲܛܲܠ	—	ܡܲܩܛܲܠ	—

48 ELEMENTS OF SYRIAC. [§ 51.

1. ܩܛܝܠ (1:6); ܐܣܝܪ (3:7); ܐܣܝܡ (3:4); ܪܫܝܡ (16:9); ܨܠܝܒ (Mt. 21:9); ܚܢܝܛ (Mk. 11:10).

2. ܡܚܢܛ (1:2); ܡܟܠܙܒ (2:3); ܡܚܬܡ (3:17); ܡܚܨܪ (16:9); ܡܩܛܪ (Lk. 24:51); ܡܒܪܟ (Lk. 1:42); ܡܚܝܠ (1:13); ܡܕܡܥ (7:8); ܡܕܥܟ (Mk. 9:20); ܡܨܠܐ (14:4); ܡܨܛܠܐ (14:4).

1. The Pe'al Active Participle is of the same form as the Hebrew קֹטֵל from an original ḳâtil. The Passive is of the form ḳătîl, just as in Biblical Aramaic, the ă becoming a half-vowel.

2. The Active Participles of the derived species are formed by prefixing ܡ to the first form of the Imperfect, the Nun having been elided. The Passive forms of Pa'el and Aph'el differ from the Active in the absolute masc. sing., where they have *a* instead of *e* (cf. the Arabic, where the Passive Participles are distinguished from the Active in like manner).

3. It will be noticed, in the above examples, that Participles are inflected like nouns.

§ 51. The Verb with Suffixes.

A. The following table gives a comparison between the Perfect Pe'al with and without suffixes:

	Form without Suffixes.	Form with Suffixes.	Form with "*her*."	Form with "*him*."
3 m. singular,	ܩܛܠ	ܩܛܠ	ܩܛܠܗ	ܩܛܠܗ
3 f. singular,	ܩܛܠܬ	ܩܛܠܬ	ܩܛܠܬܗ	ܩܛܠܬܗ
2 m. singular,	ܩܛܠܬ	ܩܛܠܬ	ܩܛܠܬܗ	ܩܛܠܬܝܗܝ
2 f. singular,	ܩܛܠܬܝ	ܩܛܠܬܝ	ܩܛܠܬܝܗ	ܩܛܠܬܝܗܝ
1 c. singular,	ܩܛܠܬ	ܩܛܠܬ	ܩܛܠܬܗ	ܩܛܠܬܗ

	Form without Suffixes.	Form with Suffixes.	Form with "*her*."	Form with "*him*."
3 m. plural,	ܩܰܛܠܘ	ܩܰܛܠܽܘ	ܩܰܛܠܽܘܗ	ܩܰܛܠܽܘܗܝ
3 m. plural,	ܩܰܛܠܘܢ	ܩܰܛܠܽܘܢܳܝ	ܩܰܛܠܽܘܢܳܗ	ܩܰܛܠܽܘܢܳܝܗܝ
3 f. plural,	ܩܛܰܠܝ̈	ܩܛܰܠܝ̈	ܩܛܰܠܳܗ	ܩܛܰܠܝ̈ܗܝ
3 f. plural,	ܩܰܛܠܶܝ̈	ܩܰܛܠܳܢܝ	ܩܰܛܠܳܢܳܗ	ܩܰܛܠܳܢܳܝܗܝ
2 m. plural,	ܩܰܛܶܠܬܘܢ	ܩܰܛܶܠܬܽܘܢܳܝ	ܩܰܛܶܠܬܽܘܢܳܗ	ܩܰܛܶܠܬܽܘܢܳܝܗܝ
2 f. plural,	ܩܰܛܶܠܬܶܝܢ	ܩܰܛܶܠܬܶܝܢ	ܩܰܛܶܠܬܶܝܢܳܗ	ܩܰܛܶܠܬܶܝܢܳܝܗܝ
1 c. plural,	ܩܰܛܶܠܢ	ܩܰܛܶܠܢܳܝ	ܩܰܛܶܠܢܳܗ	ܩܰܛܶܠܢܳܝܗܝ

B. The Perfect with Suffixes.

1. [ܩܰܛܠܝ̈ and ܩܰܛܠܶܝ̈ for ܩܛܰܠܝ̈ and ܩܰܛܠܳܢܝ] ܣܰܚܪܽܘܢܳܢܝ (Overbeck 137:9 (Nöl.)) ; ܚܰܨܡܽܘܢܳܝܗܝ (Nöl., *Gr.*, § 186.); ܢܰܚܬܽܘܢ (4:11); ܡܰܚܬܶܗ (25:12); ܢܰܚܪ (John 17:25); ܡܰܟܶܠܝ (Ps. 16:7); ܢܰܚܬܽܘܗܝ (25:19); ܐܰܣܪܘܗܝ (25:10); ܢܶܪܕܦܽܢܝ (Ps. 23:6); ܐܰܠܶܦܶܝܢ (Lk. 24:22).

Rem. 1.—ܠܳܐ ܐܰܫܟܚܽܘܗܝ *they did not find him* (Anal. Syr. 87:15 (Duv.)).

ܣܰܚܪܽܘܢܳܢܝ *they surrounded me* (Overbeck 137:9 (Nöl.)).

ܐܰܚܶܕܘܟ *they entrusted to thee* (Julianus 90:25 (Nöl.)).

ܚܰܨܡܽܘܢܳܝܗܝ *they made it* (Nöl., *Gr.*, § 186.).

Rem. 2.—ܠܚܶܨܟܘܢ *they oppressed you* (Judges 10:12).

ܕܰܠܚܽܘܟܘܢ *they troubled you* (Acts 15:24).

2. [ܩܛܠܟ or ܩܛܠܟ for ܩܛܠܟ [ܩܛܠܢܝ] ܚܲܣܚܦܬܼܢܝ (Lk. 10:40); ܢܲܓܕܘܼܢܝ (Ps. 69:2); ܐܲܚܕܲܬܼܢܝ (22:7); ܝܼܠܸܕܬܵܢܝ *thou hast borne me* (Jer. 2:27; see also Jer. 15:10); ܠܲܚܟܼܸܕܬܵܢܝ *thou hast deceived me* (?) (1 Sam. 19:17; see also Song of Songs 4:9).

Remark.—ܚܲܛܝܼܬܼܢܝ (Ps. 51:5); ܨܲܠܝܼܢܵܥܲܡ (Is. 51. 5; other reading for ܨܲܠܝܼܢܵܥܲܡ, Nöl., *Gr.*, § 186.), but ܚܲܣܚܦܬܼܢܝ (Lk. 10:40).

3. [ܩܛܠܗ for ܩܛܠܗ , ܛܠܟܗ ܩܛܠܟܗ for ܩܛܠܗ , 2 masc. sing. and plur. and 2d fem. plur. unchanged] ܚܲܣܚܦܬܵܗ (Ps. 22:1); ܝܲܓܪܘܼܗܝ (10:6); ܝܲܕܥܲܗ (John 17:25); ܚܲܣܚܦܘܼܗܝ (John 17:4); ܩܲܛܠܘܼܗܝ (6:7); ܐܲܣܲܪܬܘܼܢܵܝܗܝ (25:18); ܩܛܠܬܸܢܵܗ *ye* (f.) *have killed her.*

When the object of a verb is a pronoun other than the 3d plural it is suffixed directly to the verbal form, occasioning certain changes of termination and stem. For *them* the independent pronouns ܐܸܢܘܿܢ and ܐܸܢܹܝܢ are used, *e. g.* ܣܵܡ ܐܸܢܘܿܢ (2:6); ܐܸܢܘܿܢ ܡܸܣܟܸܢܗܿ (Lk. 24:11).

1. The forms ܬܹܗ and ܬܵܗ occur in the 3d masc. singular and plural.

Rem. 1.—The older and longer forms ܩܛܠܗܕ and ܩܛܠܗܡ occasionally are found.

Rem. 2.—The ending of the masculine plural is sometimes omitted before suffixes.

2. The old form ܩܲܛܠܲܬ (for an older ܩܲܛܠܲܬ) appears in the 3d fem. sing. and ܩܲܛܠܘܼܗܝ for ܩܲܛܠܝܼܗܝ in the 3d fem. sing.

3. The other forms, except the first person singular, remain unchanged. The first person singular takes the same form before suffixes as the 2d masc. sing., and is to be distinguished from it with the pronominal suffix for the 3d sing. masc. only; *e. g. I have killed him* = ܩܲܛܠܬܹܗ ; *thou hast killed him* = ܩܲܛܠܬܵܝܗܝ .

4. To forms ending in a vowel the suffixes are appended directly and without any change except in the case of the 3 m. sg. suffix (see 6. below).

5. To forms ending in a consonant the suffixes are appended by means of a union vowel or half-vowel, without any variation in the suffix except in the 3d sing. masc. (see 6. below). Before ܟ݂ܽܘܢ, ܟ݂ܶܡ the union vowel is always the half-vowel, except in the form ܩܛܰܠܢܳܟ݂ܽܘܢ, ܩܛܰܠܢܳܟ݂ܶܡ *we have killed you;* before ܟ݂ܝ *thee* (f.) the union vowel is always ܰ ; before ܗ̇ *her,* ܳܟ݂ *thee* (m.), ܢܝ *me,* and ܢ *us,* it is always ܳ except in the 3d sing. masc. and fem. before ܢܝ and ܢ where we have ܶ.

6. The 3 m. sg. suffix has the form ܗܝ with the 3 sg. m. and f. and with the 1 sg.; with the 3 pl. m. it has the form ܝܗܝ ; and elsewhere it has the form ܳܝܗܝ, except with the 2 f. sg. where it is ܺܝܘܗܝ.

C. Table giving the principal forms of the Imperfect with suffixes:

FORM WITHOUT SUFFIXES.
ܢܶܩܛܽܘܠ
ܢܶܩܛܠܽܘܢ

FORM WITH SUFFIXES,—SINGULAR.				
1st.	2d masc.	2d fem.	3d masc.	3d fem.
ܢܶܩܛܠܰܢܝ	ܢܶܩܛܠܳܟ݂	ܢܶܩܛܠܶܟ݂ܝ	ܢܶܩܛܠܺܝܘܗܝ or ܢܶܩܛܠܶܗ	ܢܶܩܛܠܺܗ̇
ܢܶܩܛܠܽܘܢܳܢܝ	ܢܶܩܛܠܽܘܢܳܟ݂	ܢܶܩܛܠܽܘܢܶܟ݂ܝ	ܢܶܩܛܠܽܘܢܳܝܗܝ ܢܶܩܛܠܽܘܢܳܗ̇	ܢܶܩܛܠܽܘܢܳܗ̇

FORM WITH SUFFIXES,—PLURAL.		
1st.	2d masc.	2d fem.
ܢܶܩܛܠܰܢ	ܢܶܩܛܠܟ݂ܽܘܢ	ܢܶܩܛܠܟ݂ܶܝܢ
ܢܶܩܛܠܽܘܢܳܢ	ܢܶܩܛܠܽܘܢܳܟ݂ܽܘܢ	ܢܶܩܛܠܽܘܢܳܟ݂ܶܝܢ

D. The Imperfect with Suffixes.

ܢܶܨܛܰܝܰܕ (8:10); ܢܶܚܨܕܳܢܝ (23:14); ܢܶܡܚܶܠܶܗ (23:12); ܢܳܒܶܝܗ (Ps. 16:1); ܢܶܡܚܶܕܳܢ̈ܝܗܝ ܢܶܡܚܶܕܶܝܗ̇ (23:3); ܐܶܥܒܕܳܟ (6:17); ܢܶܚܣܶܝܢܝ (4:11); ܢܶܡܚܶܕܳܢ̈ܝܗܝ (22:5); ܢܶܚܕܕܳܢܝ̈ܗܝ (31:14); ܐܶܣܝܥܶܝܗ̇ (25:17).

1. The only changes in the stem are in the forms ܢܶܩܛܘܠ, ܐܶܩܛܘܠ, ܐܶܩܛܘܠ, where the ܘ becomes a half-vowel.

2. With ܢܶܩܛܠ (from ܢܶܩܛܘܠ) and like forms, the suffixes and their union vowels are, —

ܢܝ, ܟ, ܟܝ, ܗܝ or ܝܗܝ, ܗ̇, ܢ, ܟܘܢ, ܟܝܢ.

3. With ܢܶܩܛܠܳܢ, ܢܶܩܛܠܝܢ, ܐܶܩܛܠܝܢ, ܐܶܩܛܠܝܢ and ܐܶܩܛܠܝܢ, the suffixes and union vowels are, —

ܢܝ, ܟ, ܟܝ, ܗܝ or ܝܗܝ, ܗ, ܢ, ܟܘܢ, ܟܝܢ.

4. The 2d masc. sing. has sometimes a second form before suffixes, to wit : ܢܶܩܛܠܰܝܟ, ܢܶܩܛܠܝܟ, ܐܶܩܛܠܝܟ.

E. The Imperative with Suffixes.

The following are the forms of the Imperative with Suffixes :

	2d masc. sing.	2d fem. sing.	2d masc. plur.	2d fem. plur.
1 sg. suff.	ܩܛܘܠܰܝܢܝ	ܩܛܘܠܝܢܝ	ܩܛܘܠܢܝ	ܩܛܘܠܳܢܝ
3 sg. m.	ܩܛܘܠܳܝܗܝ	ܩܛܘܠܝܗܝ	ܩܛܠܘܝܗܝ	ܩܛܘܠܳܝܗܝ
3 sg. f.	ܩܛܘܠܶܝܗ̇	ܩܛܘܠܝܗ̇	ܩܛܠܘܗ̇	ܩܛܘܠܳܝܗ̇
1 pl.	ܩܛܘܠܰܢ	ܩܛܘܠܝܢ	ܩܛܠܘܢ	ܩܛܘܠܳܢ

ܩܪܰܝܢܝ (Ps. 22:11); ܩܕܶܡܰܝܗܝ (3:3); ܐܰܣܠܶܡܰܝܗܝ (Ps. 2:11); ܢܰܚܶܬܳܝܗܝ (Ps. 22:23); ܐܶܩܪܝܗܝ (id.); ܐܶܠܝ ܐܶܠܝ (Ps. 28:9).

1. The 2d masc. sing. inserts ܝ before all suffixes.

2. The ـܟ of the 2d fem. sing. and the ܘ of the 2d masc. plur. become full vowels before suffixes.

3. The ـܝ of the 2d fem. plur. is dropped.

4. The long forms of the Imperative plural (i. e. ܩܛܘܠܘ and ܩܛܘܠܝܢ) are joined to the suffixes in the same way as the short form of the feminine plural.

F. The Infinitives and Participles with Suffixes.

1. The Infinitive P^e'al takes the suffixes of nouns without any change except the dropping of the second vowel before all save the suffix of the 1st sing. See § 81.

2. Occasionally the Infinitive P^e'al is joined to the 3d masc. and 3d fem. sing. suffixes by a Yudh after the analogy of the Imperfect; *e. g.* ܡܣܒܝܘܗܝ *to take him,* ܡܫܪܝܗ *to free her.* See Nöldeke, § 191.

3. The Infinitives of all the derived stems change the ending ܘ to ܘܬܐ and take the usual nominal suffixes. See § 85.

4. Participles take the nominal suffixes.

§ 52. Guttural Verbs.

ܫܡܥ (4:7); ܠܗ (32:1); ܚܨܕ (24:2); ܐܚܡܨ (5:1); ܢܙܥܩ (1:13); ܢܚܠܗ (Ps. 19:8); ܡܚܟܡ (Ps. 29:9); ܣܢܐ (= חָסַר) *to want;* ܠܒܐ *for* ܠܒܒ *he shall break;* ܐܠܗ (Luke 6:12); ܗܒܘ (Mk. 12:17).

1. Verbs whose first radical is a guttural, or Rîsh, are regular.

2. Verbs whose second radical is a guttural, or Rîsh, sometimes in East Syriac take *a* where we would expect *e*, *e. g.* ܛܚܢ (West Syriac ܛܚܢ) *to grind.*

3. When the third radical is a guttural (for verbs *tertiae Olaph*, see §§ 57, 60), or Rîsh, it changes an immediately preceding *e* into *a*.

Note 1.—In the Pa'el and Aph'el, this change of *e* into *a* causes the Participles Active and Passive to coincide.

Note 2.—In accordance with this rule, many intransitives, like ܣܢܐ, which would naturally have *e*, take *a* in the P^e'al Perfect.

4. In a few cases, when the third radical is a guttural, or Rîsh, ܘ of the Imperfect and Imperative is changed into *a*.

5. Verbs whose third radical is ܗ always receive *a* before it.

§ 53. Pê Nun Verbs.

1. ܣܲܒ݂ (Mt. 19:7); ܣܲܒ݂ (23:18); ܢܣܲܒ݂ (Acts 10:13); ܢܣܲܒ݂ (Mk. 9:21); ܦ݁ܘܿܩ (Mt. 21:21); ܢܦܘܿܩ (Mk. 16:11).

2. ܢܸܣܲܒ݂ (= ܢܸܢܣܲܒ݂) (Lk. 11:21); ܢܸܦ݁ܘܿܩ (Mt. 2:6); ܢܸܦ݁ܘܿܩ (Acts 16:18); ܢܸܦ݁ܠ݂ (Mt. 5:29); ܢܸܚܸܬ (Mt. 24:29); ܡܲܦܸܩ (Mt. 1:20); ܐܲܦܸ݁ܩ (Mt. 17:1); ܡܲܦܸܩ (Lk. 14:5); ܢܸܦ݁ܠ݂ (Mt. 5:31); ܐܸܬ݁ܬ݁ܢܝܼܚ (Heb. 4:8); ܥܪܘܿܩ (Jer. 6:8).

Pê Nun verbs are regular in the Ethpᵉ'el, Pa'el and Ethpa'al stems. In Pᵉ'al they are regular in the Perfect and in the Participles. But

1. In the Pᵉ'al Imperative the Nun is generally dropped.
2. In the Pᵉ'al Imperfect and Infinitive and in the Aph'el and Ettaph'al stems throughout, the Nun is generally assimilated. See § 18. In Pê Nun verbs which are also 'Ê 'Ê or 'Ê Waw, the Nun is firm. See § 62. 2.

§ 54. 'E 'E Verbs.
TABULAR VIEW.

	Pᵉ'al.	Aph'el.	Ethtaph'al.	Palpel.
Perfect,	ܥܲܪ	ܐܲܥܸܪ	ܐܸܬ݁ܬ݁ܥܲܪ	ܥܲܪܥܲܪ
Imperfect,	ܢܸܥܘܿܪ	ܢܲܥܸܪ	ܢܸܬ݁ܬ݁ܥܲܪ	ܢܥܲܪܥܲܪ
Imperative,	ܥܘܿܪ	ܐܲܥܸܪ	ܐܸܬ݁ܬ݁ܥܲܪ	ܥܲܪܥܲܪ
Part. Act.,	ܥܵܐܲܪ	ܡܲܥܸܪ	ܡܸܬ݁ܬ݁ܥܲܪ	ܡܥܲܪܥܲܪ
Part. Act.,	ܥܵܐܹܪ	ܡܲܥܸܪ	ܡܸܬ݁ܬ݁ܥܲܪ	ܡܥܲܪܥܲܪ
Part. Pass.,	ܥܝܼܪ	ܡܲܥܲܪ		ܡܥܲܪܥܲܪ

Remark. — The first three forms of the Pᵉ'al Perfect are, —

ܥܲܪ   ܥܸܪ   ܥܸܪܲܬ݂

The 3d masculine singular and plural of the Imperfect are, —

ܢܸܥܘܿܪ   ܢܸܥܪܘܿܢ

1. ܚܫ (Acts 1:3); ܪܓܬ (Acts 20:33); ܟܡܝܪ (Lk. 24:5); ܢܕܬܘܢ (Gal. 4:14); ܥܘܠ (Mt. 6:6); ܥܘܠܘ (Mt. 7:13).

2. ܢܥܘܠ (John 10:9); ܢܚܫ (Mt. 16:21); ܬܪܓ (Rom. 7:7); ܬܓܘܦ (Rom. 14:11); ܢܦܣ (John 19:24) [ܬܓܘܦ from ܬܓܦܘܦ, ܢܦܣ from ܢܦܣܣ]; ܐܓܢ (Lk. 1:35); ܐܥܠܘ (Mt. 9:31); ܢܡܟ (Mt. 23:12) [ܢܡܟ from ܢܡܟܟ].

3. ܪܐܛ [for ܪܛܛ] (Acts 16:29); ܚܐܫ (1 Pet. 2:23); ܚܫܝܢ (1 Cor. 12:26); ܪܓܝܐ (Gal. 5:17); ܪܓܝܢ (1 Cor. 10:6); but ܥܐܠܝܢ (Mt. 10:12); ܪܐܓܝܢ (Heb. 11:16); ܩܪܝܒ (John 19:42); ܚܫܝܫ (1 Cor. 4:4); ܟܦܝܦ (Rom. 11:10).

4. ܡܬܦܬܚ (Rev. 9:1); ܡܪܒܝܢܝܬܐ (1 Thes. 2:7); ܐܬܡܟܟ (Mt. 23:12); ܐܬܟܬܫ (2 Tim. 2:5); ܡܬܪܓܪܓ (Mt. 12:20); ܐܬܪܓܪܓܘ (Mt. 13:17); ܡܬܚܡܬܡ (Acts 17:16); ܐܬܒܗܬ (Phil. 1:20).

In verbs whose 2d and 3d radicals are identical the Ethpᵉʿel is regular.

1. In the Pᵉʿal Perfect and Imperative the second and third radicals are contracted into one, the vowel of the second radical being thrown back upon the first. When a syllable follows, the second and third radicals are written as one, but pronounced as two, *e. g.* reggath, noddᵉthun. The Pᵉʿal Perfect is the form given in the dictionary.

2. In the Pᵉʿal Imperfect and Infinitive, and in the Aphʿel and Ethpʿal stems throughout, the vowel of the second radical is thrown back upon the first, and the first radical is doubled and hardened.

3. *a.* The Part. Act. of Pᵉʿal in the first form, *i. e.* the 3d m. sg., is like the same form in Ê-Waw verbs,—the second radical is changed into Olaph, which is pronounced like Yudh (ܪܐܛ = royeth). See § 2. c. and § 59. 4.

b. But when additions for state, gender or number are made to the first form of the Participle, the Olaph is generally dropped, and the primitive second radical is doubled.

c. The Participle Passive of Pᵉʿal is regular.

4. In the intensive stem, though we have sometimes the regular forms, we usually have the Palpel and Ethpalpal. The stem of Palpel is formed by doubling the contracted Pᵉʿal, or simple stem. Palpel and Ethpalpal are inflected like Paʿel and Ethpaʿal.

§ 55. Pê Olaph Verbs.

1. ܐܶܚܰܕ݂ (27:6); ܐܶܣܽܘܬ݂ (32:9); ܐܶܚܬܽܘܢ (32:14); ܐܶܚܽܘܠ (Acts 10:13); ܐܶܚܰܕܬ݁; (23:17); ܐܶܚܰܕ݂ (Lk. 17:23); ܐ̱ܙܺܠ (Mt. 2:20); ܐܶܟ݂ܠ (23:6); ܐܰܚܬ݁ (32:10); ܐܶܡܰܪ (Mt. 3:3); ܐܶܡܰܪܺܝ (Acts 2:16); ܢܐܬܶܐ (32:8). See § 64. 4.

2. ܢܺܐܚܽܘܠ (4:13); ܐܶܬܐܟ݂ܶܠܝ (5:10); ܢܬܐܟܶܠ (5:12); ܐܶܬܐܡܰܪ (26:9); ܠܡܐܚܰܢ (32:11); ܡܳܐܟ݂ܶܠ (4:13); ܡܐܘܟ݂ܶܠ (23:10); ܐܶܟ݂ܽܘܠ (Phil. 2:19); ܐܶܬܐܟ݂ܶܠ (Mk. 14:14).

3. ܐܶܬ݁ܬ݁ܰܚܰܕ (28:1); ܐܶܬ݁ܐܰܒܰܕ (James 4:9); ܐܶܬܬܰܟܠܰܬ݂ (Mk. 5:26); ܐܶܬ݁ܬܟܶܠ (Acts 20:20); ܢܶܬܬܚܶܕ (Acts 4:18); ܐܶܬܬܣܰܪ (Mt. 25:10); ܠܡܶܬ݁ܬܰܥܰܟ (Rev. 18:15); ܐܶܬܬ݁ܰܣܰܪܬ݁ thou hast bound thyself (Jos. Styl. 2:13); ܐܶܬ݁ܬܟܰܪ (Mk. 25:16); ܐܳܬܶܐܚܶܕ (1:6).

4. ܐܶܙܰܠ (Mt. 22:7); ܐܰܣܰܪ (Mt. 21:33); ܢܶܠܐܶܡ (Thes. Syr. 126); ܡܶܣܠܰܡ (Acts 22:16); ܡܰܣܶܡ.

1. In Pê Olaph verbs, the Olaph receives a helping vowel in the P^e'al and Ethp^e'el stems. In the Ethp^e'el this vowel is thrown back upon the preceding Taw. See 3 below.

Note 1.—In the P^e'al Perfect this helping vowel is ܶ

Note 2.—In the P^e'al Imperative, with ܽ in the second syllable, the Olaph has ܶ; in the Imperative with ܰ the Olaph has ܽ; in the Imperative with ܶ the Olaph is dropped. § 23. 1. (1).

Note 3.—In the P^e'al Participle Passive the Olaph takes ܽ

2. In the P^e'al Imperfect and Infinitive of verbs which have ܰ in the second syllable of the Imperf. the vowel of the preformative is ܶ; in verbs which have ܽ in the second syllable of the Imperf., the preformative has generally ܳ. In either case the Olaph quiesces in the preceding vowel.

Note.—In the P^e'al Imperfect 1st sing. one Olaph falls out. § 23. 2. (1).

3. In Ethp^e'el, Ethpa'al, and in the Imperfect, Infinitive and Participles of the Pa'el, the vowel of the Olaph is thrown back upon the preceding consonant, and the Olaph quiesces.

Note 1.—In the 1st sing. Pa'el one Olaph is dropped and the form becomes ܐܟܶܠ (for ܐܐܟܶܠ).

Note 2.—In ܢܠܦ the Olaph of the Pa'el stem often falls away after preformatives.

Note 3.—In the Ethpe'el of ܐܚܕ *to seize*, and of some other verbs, and in the Ethpa'al of ܐܬܓܪ *to trade*, the Olaph is dropped and the Taw generally doubled. See § 22. 1. (2).

Note 4.—In West Syriac, when Olaph with a vowel is preceded by an inseparable particle, the particle takes the vowel and the Olaph quiesces. See § 34. 2.

4. In Aph'el, Shaph'el and their passives, Pê Olaph verbs pass over into the formation of verbs Pê Yudh. See § 58. 3. For ܐܘܣܦ compare §§ 58. 3. Note. (2), and 64. 4.

Remark.—ܥܗܕ *to remember* is treated in West Syriac as if it were a Pê Olaph verb; *e. g.* ܡܥܗܕܝܢ (1 Thes. 1:3); ܡܥܗܕܘ (1 Pet. 5:8).

§ 56. Ê Olaph Verbs.

1. ܫܐܠܬ (Lk. 1:40); ܡܐܢܬ (Heb. 3:10); ܟܐܒܬ (Thes. Syr. 438).

2. ܫܐܠ (31:6); ܫܐܠܬ (Heb. 10:6); ܫܐܠܢ (1 John 5:15); ܫܐܠܬܘܢ (John 16:24); ܫܐܒܬ (John 21:18); ܢܫܐܠ (James 1:6); ܢܬܐܣܐ (Heb. 12:13); ܫܐܠ (3 John 15); ܣܐܢ (Acts 12:8); ܡܫܐܠܢܐ (Lk. 14:18); ܡܫܐܠ (Jos. Styl. 3:15); ܐܒܐܫ (Acts 7:19); ܐܬܒܐܫ (22:8).

3. ܢܫܐܠܘܢ (Mt. 18:19); ܢܫܒܐܘܢ (Acts 7:6); ܡܛܐܒܝܢ (Lk. 6:33); ܢܫܐܠܝܘܗܝ (Mt. 7:9).

4. ܫܐܠ (Mt. 5:42); ܫܐܠܐ (Mt. 20:20); ܫܐܠܝܢ (Mt. 20:22); ܫܐܠ (Mt. 22:4); ܡܫܐܠ (Mt. 2:4); ܐܫܐܠ (Acts 25:26); ܢܬܡܫܘܢ (Rm. 6:19); ܐܬܡܫ (Ps. 5:3).

1. In Ê Olaph verbs, when Olaph ends a syllable it quiesces in the vowel preceding it.

2. When Olaph is preceded by a consonant, it throws back its vowel and quiesces in it.

3. When neither Olaph nor the consonant preceding it had a vowel, the helping vowel ◌̂ was given to the consonant preceding Olaph, and the latter quiesced.

Note.—This helping vowel was first given to the Olaph and then thrown back, as in 2 above.

4. The Participle Active Pᵉʿal and the Intensive stem throughout are regular.

Note.—For ܛܳܐܒ *to be good*, the Intensive in use is ܛܰܝܶܒ from ܛܺܝܒ. Compare § 59. 5.

§ 57. Lomadh Olaph Guttural Verbs.

ܢܰܙܟܰܐ (Rev. 22:11); ܒܰܝܰܐ (Acts 20:1); ܒܰܝܰܐܬ *she has consoled;* ܒܰܝܰܐܬ *thou hast consoled;* ܒܰܝܺܐܬ *I have consoled;* ܡܫܰܦܠܳܐ (Is. 2:12); ܬܰܪܰܐ *to teach;* ܐܶܬܦܰܝܰܐ *to be adorned;* ܐܶܬܛܰܢܦܢ (Job 18:3); ܒܰܝܰܐܘ (Acts 16:40); ܒܰܝܰܢ (2 Cor. 7:6); ܡܒܰܝܳܐܘ (Tit. 1:9); ܐܶܬܒܰܝܰܐܘ (Acts 15:31).

In a few verbs whose third radical is Olaph, the Olaph is treated throughout as a guttural, and the second vowel of the Paʿel is *a* instead of *e*. When the consonant preceding Olaph is unvoweled, it draws the vowel of the Olaph to itself, the Olaph quiescing. Most verbs originally of this class have come to be treated as Lomadh Olaph verbs. See § 60.

§ 58. Pê Yudh Verbs.

TABULAR VIEW.

	Pᵉʿal.	Ethpᵉʿel.	Aphʿel.	Eshtaphʿal.
Perfect,	ܝܺܪܶܬ	ܐܶܬܺܝܠܶܕ	ܐܰܘܠܶܕ	ܐܶܫܬܰܘܕܰܥ
Imperfect,	ܢܺܐܪܰܬ	ܢܶܬܺܝܠܶܕ	ܢܰܘܠܶܕ	ܢܶܫܬܰܘܕܰܥ
Imperative,	ܐܺܪܰܬ	ܐܶܬܺܝܠܶܕ	ܐܰܘܠܶܕ	ܐܶܫܬܰܘܕܰܥ
Infinitive,	ܡܺܐܪܰܬ	ܡܶܬܺܝܠܳܕܽܘ	ܡܰܘܠܳܕܽܘ	ܡܶܫܬܰܘܕܳܥܽܘ
Part. Act.,	ܝܳܪܶܬ	ܡܶܬܺܝܠܶܕ	ܡܰܘܠܶܕ	ܡܶܫܬܰܘܕܰܥ
Part. Pass.,	ܝܪܺܝܬ		ܡܰܘܠܰܕ	

Remark 1.—ܝܺܪܶܬ means *to inherit;* ܝܶܠܶܕ *to be born;* ܝܩܰܕ *to burn;* ܝܺܕܰܥ *to know.*

Remark 2.—The first three forms of the Perfect Pᵉʿal are, ܝܺܪܶܬ, ܝܺܪܬܰܬ, ܝܺܪܬܶܬ. The 3d sing. and 3d plur. masc. of the Imperf. are, ܢܺܐܪܰܬ, ܢܺܐܪܬܽܘܢ.

1. ܝܩܶܒ (15:9); ܐܶܬܝܠܶܕ (Mt. 2:1); ܝܰܩܪܽܘܢ (Acts 28:10); ܡܰܬܬܠܰܚܫܺܝܢ (Lk. 21:14); ܘܳܠܶܐ (25:15); ܘܰܠܶܕ (32:21); ܝܺܪܶܬ *to inherit;* ܝܩܰܕ *to burn;* ܝܺܕܰܥ *to know;* ܝܺܩܰܪ *to be heavy;* ܝܰܗܶܒ *to give;* ܕܰܥ *know;* ܬܶܒ *sit;* ܗܰܒ *give;* ܬܽܘܒ (24:10); ܐܶܬܝܠܶܕ (23:14).

2. ܡܳܐܬܠܕܳܐ (Rev. 12:2); ܡܳܐܪܬܳܐ (1 Cor. 15:50); ܬܶܐܠܕܺܝܢ (Lk. 1:31); ܢܺܐܪܬ (Mt. 19:29); ܡܰܘܬܶܒ (Rev. 3:21); ܢܬܶܒ (Mt. 13:2); ܡܶܬܝܰܕܰܥ (Mt. 13:11); ܢܶܕܰܥ (Mt. 9:30); ܐܺܐܪܰܬ (Mk. 10:17); ܐܶܬܪ (Phil. 3:8).

3. ܐܰܥܠܶܒܘܢ (1 Cor. 6:8); ܐܘܕܥܘ (Mt. 18:31); ܐܘܠܶܕ (Mt. 1:1); ܡܰܘܩܶܕ (Mt. 3:12); ܐܰܩܢܘܢ (Lk. 23:39); ܐܺܝܠܶܠܘ (James 5:1); ܚܰܘܕܰܥ (Rev. 1:1); ܐܰܫܬܰܘܕܰܥ (Acts 12:11).

4. ܝܰܩܰܪ (Mt. 15:4); ܡܝܰܩܰܪ (John 4:44); ܐܺܝܬܰܪ (Rom. 3:7); ܠܡܰܘܬܰܪ (2 Cor. 9:8); ܝܩܶܕ (Rev. 8:7); ܐܶܬܝܰܬܶܒ (Is. 44:26).

Remark.—ܐܶܝܩܳܐ (3:16).

1. Verbs whose first radical was originally Waw, change this Waw into Yudh, whenever it would begin a syllable. The only exceptions are ܘܳܠܶܐ *it is necessary,* and ܘܰܥܶܕ *to appoint.*

Rem. 1.—Pê Waw verbs take ̤ in the Pᵉʿal Perfect.

Rem. 2.—The Yudh, whenever it would stand with a half-vowel—

(1) Quiesces in Ḥebhoṣo at the beginning of a word, except in ܝܗܰܒ *to give.* See § 64. 7.

(2) Is dropped in the Imperative Pᵉ'al of ܝܕܥ *to know*, ܝܬܒ *to sit*, and ܝܗܒ *to give*.

(3) In the middle of a word, quiesces in Hebhoṣo, which is then thrown back upon the preceding consonant (§ 33. 3).

2. After the preformatives of the Pᵉ'al, the Waw, changed to Yudh, unites with the vowel of the preformative to form, in the East Syriac, *ē*, which in the West Syriac is further changed to *ī*. This *ī* is written mostly with an Olaph following, so that Pê Waw verbs come to have in the Imperfect, Imperative and Infinitive Pᵉ'al the same forms as Pê Olaph verbs which have *a* in the Imperfect (§ 55. 2). All Pê Waw verbs except ܝܬܒ *to sit* (see *Notes* below) and ܝܗܒ *to give* (see § 64.) have their Imperfect and Imperative in *a*.

Rem. 1.—ܝܕܥ *to know* and ܝܬܒ *to sit* lose their first radical after the preformatives of the Pᵉ'al, and by way of compensation double the first radical, hence becoming like Pê Nun Verbs.

Rem. 2.—In the first person singular of the Imperfect one Olaph is dropped, e. g. ܐܐܪܬ *I shall inherit*.

3. The Aph'el, Shaph'el and their reflexives, have Waw as the first radical even in verbs whose first radical was originally Yudh. The Aph'el, etc., of Pê Olaph verbs coincides with these in form (see § 55. 3).

Rem.—ܝܢܩ *to suck* has in the Aph'el ܐܝܢܩ, though ܐܘܢܩ is also found (see *Thes. Syr.*, p. 1608). ܐܝܠ *to howl* (from ܝܠ, not found in Pᵉ'al) is the only other exception to the rule. ܐܬܐ is from ܐܬܐ *to come* (see § 64. 4).

4. The Pa'el and Ethpa'al are regular.

Rem. 1.—Pê Yudh verbs often take prosthetic Olaph in those forms where the Yudh quiesces in Hebhoṣo.

Rem. 2.—Some Pê Olaph verbs pass over in certain forms into the Pê Yudh class, e. g. ܝܠܦ *to learn*, ܝܠܦ *to teach*, ܝܟܡ for ܐܟܡ *to be black*, ܝܪܟ for ܐܪܟ *to be long*.

§ 59. Ê Waw Verbs.

TABULAR VIEW.

	Peʿal.	Ethpeʿel or Ettaphʿal.	Aphʿel.	Paʿel.
Perfect,	ܩܡ	ܐܬܬܩܝܡ	ܐܩܝܡ	ܩܝܡ
Imperfect,	ܢܩܘܡ	ܢܬܬܩܝܡ	ܢܩܝܡ	ܢܩܝܡ
Imperative,	ܩܘܡ	ܐܬܬܩܝܡ	ܐܩܝܡ	ܩܝܡ
Infinitive,	ܡܩܡ	ܡܬܬܩܡܘ	ܡܩܡܘ	ܡܩܝܡܘ
Part. Act.,	ܩܐܡ	ܡܬܬܩܝܡ	ܡܩܝܡ	ܡܩܝܡ
Part. Pass.,	ܩܝܡ		ܡܩܡ	ܡܩܝܡ

Remark.—The first three forms of the Peʿal Perfect are ܩܡ, ܩܡܬ, ܩܡܬ. The 3d masc. sing. and plur. of the Imperf. are ܢܩܘܡ, ܢܩܘܡܘܢ.

1. ܩܡ (32:7); ܩܡܬ (Mt. 9:25); ܩܡܬ (Acts 24:20); ܡܬܘ (29:8); ܡܩܡ (19:12); ܡܩܡܘ (Mt. 3:9); ܡܬܬܩܡܘ (24:11); ܡܬܐܒ (Phil. 2:26).

2. ܩܘܡ (Mt. 2:13); ܩܘܡܘ (25:4); ܬܬܘܒ (17:16); ܢܬܬܘܢܘܢ (25:13).

3. ܫܝܡ (32:8); ܢܩܝܡ (25:14); ܐܩܝܡ (John 12:1); ܡܬܝܒܝܢ (30:1); ܡܩܝܡ (Mt. 12:11); ܐܩܝܡܘ (23:2); ܐܬܬܕܝܢܘ (24:16); ܡܬܬܕܝܢܝܢ (20:10).

4. ܩܐܡ (31:13); ܩܐܡܝܢ (27:3); ܐܐܠ (18:4).

5. ܢܩܝܡܘܢ (23:8); ܠܩܝܡܘܬܗ (23:5); ܩܝܡܘ (Acts 15:32); ܡܩܝܡܬܟܘܢ (Col. 2:13); ܢܩܝܡܘܢ (Rev. 3:4).

6. ܪܘܙ *to exult;* ܐܚܛܐ *to sin;* ܠܘܐ *to join;* ܚܘܪ *to be white;* ܗܘܐ *to be;* ܡܚܘܐ *to teach;* ܬܘܐ *to repent;* ܫܘܐ *to desire.*

Remark.—ܡܝܬ (Mt. 22:25); ܡܝܬܬ (Rom. 7:10); ܡܝܬܘ (Mt. 2:20).

1. Whenever in the regular verb the combinations *wă*, *wô* (from *wâ*) or *ʿwa* (from *awa*) would arise, they are contracted into *ô* (from *â*). This takes place in the Pᵉ'al Perfect (ḳʿwam = ḳôm), in the Pᵉ'al Infinitive (meḳwam = mᵉḳôm), in the Aph'el and Ethpᵉ'el and Ettaph'al Infinitives (maḳwomu = mᵉḳômu and methtaḳwômu = mettᵉḳômu), and in the Aph'el Pass. Part. (maḳwak = mᵉḳôm). See § 29. 5. (3).

2. Whenever *wu*, *ʿwu*, or *wᵉ* (from *wu*) would occur, they are changed into *û*. This change takes place in the Imperat. Pᵉ'al (ḳʿwum = ḳum), and in the Imperfect Pᵉ'al (neḳwum = nᵉḳum, nekwʿmûn = nᵉḳûmûn).

3. Whenever *we* (from *wi*), *ʿwe* (from *awa*) or *ʿwi* (from *awi*) would occur, the *w* is changed to *y* and contraction into *i* takes place. Throughout the Aph'el Perf., Imperf., Imperat. and Part. Act. *we* becomes *î* ('aḳîm = 'akwem); in the Pᵉ'al Part. Pass. *ʿwi* becomes *î* (ḳʿwîm = ḳîm); in the Ethpᵉ'el *ʿwe* becomes *î*, and the Taw is doubled and hardened (see § 19. 3). (Ethḳʿwem becomes Ettᵉḳîm, a half-vowel being inserted before the first radical.)

4. In the Part. Act. *owe* (*âwe*) becomes *oye*, the *y* in the first form, *i. e.* masc. sing., being written with Olaph (see § 2. (1) c), but elsewhere with Yudh, *e. g.* ܩܳܐܶܡ, ܩܳܝܡܳܐ, ܩܳܝܡܺܝܢ. Where the third radical is a guttural we find *oya*, as in ܫܳܐܶܠ (§ 26. 1. (1)). In Joshua the Stylite, p. 3, l. 20, we find ܩܳܝܡ written, instead of ܩܳܐܶܡ.

5. In the Pa'el and Ethpa'al *awwe* and *awwa* generally become *ayye*, *ayya*. Merx-Hoffmann, § 66. VI., mentions nineteen verbs which sometimes or always have Waw in the Pa'el or Ethpa'al. For ܩܰܝܶܡ see § 56. 4. Note.

6. Some verbs, mostly denominatives, are regularly conjugated. All verbs whose third letter is Olaph have the Waw firm.

Rem. 1.—The intransitive in *î* from *awi* is found in the Pᵉ'al Perfect of ܡܺܝܬ *to die.* Elsewhere it is like ܩܳܡ.

Rem. 2.—The only Ê-Yudh verb which differs in any respect from Ê-Waw verbs is ܝܺܕܥ, which has ܕܰܥ in the Pᵉ'al Imperative and ܢܶܕܰܥ in the Pᵉ'al Imperfect.

Rem. 3.—The preformatives of the Pᵉ'al and Aph'el sometimes take a short vowel, *e. g.* ܢܶܩܽܘܡ (Rom. 11:21). See Nöldeke, § 177. C.

§ 60. Lomadh Olaph Verbs.

TABULAR VIEW.

	Pe'al.	Ethpe'el.	Pa'el.	Aph'el.
Perfect,	ܪܡܳܐ	ܐܶܬܪܡܺܝ	ܪܰܡܺܝ	ܐܰܪܡܺܝ
Imperfect,	ܢܶܪܡܶܐ	ܢܶܬܪܡܶܐ	ܢܪܰܡܶܐ	ܢܰܪܡܶܐ
Imperative 2m. sg.,	ܪܡܺܝ	ܐܶܬܪܡܺܝ	ܪܰܡܳܐ	ܐܰܪܡܳܐ
2f. sg.,	ܪܡܳܝ	ܐܶܬܪܡܳܝ	ܪܰܡܳܝ	ܐܰܪܡܳܝ
2m. pl.,	ܪܡܰܘ	ܐܶܬܪܡܰܘ	ܪܰܡܰܘ	ܐܰܪܡܰܘ
2f. pl.,	ܪܡܳܝܶܝܢ	ܐܶܬܪܡܳܝܶܝܢ	ܪܰܡܳܝܶܝܢ	ܐܰܪܡܳܝܶܝܢ
Infinitive,	ܡܶܪܡܳܐ	ܡܶܬܪܡܳܝܽܘ	ܡܪܰܡܳܝܽܘ	ܡܰܪܡܳܝܽܘ
Part. Active.	ܪܳܡܶܐ	ܡܶܬܪܡܶܐ	ܡܪܰܡܶܐ	ܡܰܪܡܶܐ
Part. Passive,	ܪܡܺܝ		ܡܪܰܡܰܝ	ܡܰܪܡܰܝ

Remark.—The following forms are to be noted: Pe'al Perfect 3rd sg. fem. ܪܡܳܬ, 2nd sg. masc. ܪܡܰܝܬ, 1st sg. ܪܡܺܝܬ, 3rd masc. pl. ܪܡܺܘ, 3rd fem. pl. ܪܡܰܝ̈, 3rd sg. fem. Ethpe'el and in all other stems ends in ܝܰܬ, 1st sg. in ܝܬ, 3rd. fem. pl. in ܝ̈, all other forms being like those of the Pe'al. In the Imperfect, the sufformatives of all the stems are the same, *e. g.* 2nd sg. fem. ܬܶܪܡܶܝܢ, 3rd masc. pl. ܢܶܪܡܽܘܢ, 3rd fem. pl. ܢܶܪܡܝܳܢ.

1. ܒܪܳܐ (1:1); ܗܘܳܐ (1:1); ܚܙܰܝܬ (Acts 22:15); ܚܙܺܝܬ (6:5); ܗܘܰܘ (5:7); ܗ̈ܘܰܝ (30:19); ܗܘܰܝܬܝ (Mk. 5:34); ܫܰܡܠܺܝܬܽܘܢ (18:8); ܚܙܰܝܢ (Mt. 2:2); ܫ̈ܠܰܝ (Lk. 23:56).

2. ܚܙܶܐ (Lk. 23:8); ܚܳܙܶܝܬ (14:7); ܫܠܺܝܘ (Acts. 11:18); ܫ̈ܠܰܝ (Lk. 23:56); ܚܳܕܶܝܬ (Phil. 1:18); ܚܕܺܝܢ (2 Cor. 7:13); ܢܣܺܝܬ (Rev. 2:2); ܐܶܬܬܢܺܝܘ (27:11); ܐܰܪܡܺܝ (11:5); ܓܰܠܺܝ (12:13); ܫܰܕܺܝܘ (Mt. 8:33); ܐܶܬܕܰܟܺܝ (Mt. 8:3);

64 ELEMENTS OF SYRIAC. [§ 60.

ܐܢܨܝܼܢ (Lk. 17:14); ܐܙܕܡܢ (22:12); ܐܘܕܥܡܢ (11:11); ܐܬܝܼܡܝܼܒ (6:6);
ܐܬܛܫܝ (18:17); ܐܙܕܒܢ (30:15); ܐܬܣܝܼܡ (30:18).

3. ܢܗܘܐ (1:3); ܢܘܩܕ (11:11); ܐܣܛܐ (6:14); ܢܗܘܘܢ (2:3); ܢܣܒ (16:7);
ܕܥܒܕ (19:9); ܢܗܘܐ (18:3); ܬܥܒܕܘܢ (6:15); ܢܒܢܐ we will build. (16:5).

4. ܩܡ (11:10); ܡܟܟ (2:13); ܣܠܩܬ (32:8); ܐܥܒܕ (20:6); ܐܙܠܘ (Mt. 8:3); ܐܬܕܟܪ (Rev. 2:5); ܐܙܠܘ (Mt. 17:27); ܐܙܕܩܢ (John 21:6).

5. ܐܩܡ (17:3); ܬܥܒܕܢ (18:18); ܡܚܕܥܝܢ (20:19); ܡܣܒܐ (Mk. 14:17);
ܡܬܛܫܝ (29:3); ܡܬܚܫܒ (20:19); ܡܬܚܙܝܢ (20:19); ܡܚܕܬܐ (Lk. 23:2);
ܡܚܕܬ (Rom. 16:18); ܡܬܛܫܐ (19:10); ܡܕܡܚܡ (19:13); ܡܚܕܩܡ (Mt. 15:26); ܡܕܟܟܡ (Gal. 3:23); ܐܬܒܣܐ (13:1).

Lomadh Olaph verbs (not guttural, see § 57) are those in which an Olaph quiescent, or vowel letter, has taken the place in the 3rd sing. masc. Perf. P^eʿal of the original 3rd radical Waw, Yudh or Olaph.

1. *Awa, aya* or *a'a*, becomes *o* in the 3rd sing. masc. and fem. Perf. P^eʿal; *awi, ayi* or *a'i*, becomes *î* in the 1st pers. sing.; *awu, ayu* or *a'u*, becomes *aw* in the 3rd masc. plur.; *awy, ayy* or *a'y*, becomes *ay* in the 3rd fem. plur.; and *aw* or *a'* becomes *ay* in the 1st plur. and in the 2nd pers. throughout, *ay* remaining unchanged.

2. The P^eʿal Perf. of Intransitive verbs and the Perfect of all the derived stems of all verbs have ܝ in the 3rd sing. masc. and before all endings for gender and number and person except the 3rd fem. sing., which is regular (*i.e.* ܣܝܡܬ like ܩܛܠܬ).

Remark 1.—In the 3rd masc. plur. ܘ is the diphthong *iu*, see § 8. 1. (3).

Remark 2.—The 3rd fem. plur. of the derived stems is distinguished from the 3rd masc. sing. by Rebbuy § 13.

Remark 3.—The Taw of the 1st pers. sing. is aspirated, *e. g.* ܚܕܬܬ *ḥ^edhîth;* that of the 2nd pers. is unaspirated, *e. g.* ܢܣܝܬ *nassît*.

3. In all Imperfects, the 3rd sing. masc. and the forms like it (see § 45. Rem. 5), end in ܐ from *ay*, the 2nd fem. sing. ends in ܝܢ from *ayin*, the masc. plur. 2nd and 3rd pers. ends in ܘܢ, the preceding radical with its vowel being dropped; the fem. plur. 2nd and 3rd pers. is regular, the 3rd radical, however, being in every case Yudh. *e. g.* ܢܓܠܝܢ = ܢܓܠܘܢ.

4. In the first form of the Imperative, the original *ă* remains unchanged in the Ethpeʻel; in the Peʻal, *ay* is changed to ܘ; and in all the other species the last radical is dropped and the vowel heightened to *ô (â)*. The 2nd fem. sing. of all the stems ends in ܝ, see § 8. 2. (2). The 2nd masc. plur. ends in ܘ, the Yudh of the root having been dropped. The 2nd fem. plur. ends in ܝܢ.

Remark 1.—The Peʻal Imperat. 2nd masc. sing. of ܐܬܐ *to come* is ܬܐ, see § 64. 2. The same form from ܝܥܐ *to sprout*, ܝܡܐ *to swear*, and ܐܫܬܝ *to drink*, ends in ܝ.

Remark 2.—In the 2nd masc. plur., the long forms ܓܠܘ, ܒܢܘ are sometimes used; in the 2nd fem. plur. a short form in *ă* is sometimes found.

Remark 3.—The form ܐܙܕܠ is used in Lk. 9:38, 22:32, instead of the more usual Ethpeʻel Imperative. According to Bar Hebraeus ܐܬܡܚܝ was used for ܐܬܕܡܝ from ܡܚܐ *to strike* (see Duval p. 194). In some editions of the New Testament in Rev. 2:5, 15, 3:3, 19 ܐܬܬܘܒ is used instead of ܬܘܒ.

5. All participles end in ܐ except the Paʻel and Aphʻel passive which end in ܝ.

§ 61. Lomadh Olaph Verbs with Suffixes.

	Peʻal				Paʻel
	Form without suffixes.	Form with suffixes.	Form with "her"	Form with "him"	with "him".
Perfect,					
3. masc. sing.					
3. fem. sing.					
3. masc. plur.					
3. fem. plur.					
Imperfect,					
3. masc. sing.					
3. masc. plur.					

	Pe'al				Pa'el
	Form without suffixes.	Form with suffixes.	Form with "*her*".	Form with "*him*".	with "*her*".
Imperative,					
sing. masc.	ܓܠܺܝ	ܓܠܺܝ	ܓܠܺܝܗ̇	ܓܠܺܝܗ̱ܝ	ܓܰܠܳܝܗ̇
sing. fem.	ܓܠܳܝ	ܓܠܳܐܝ	ܓܠܳܐܝܗ̇	ܓܠܳܐܝܗ̱ܝ	ܓܰܠܳܐܝܗ̇
plur. masc.	ܓܠܰܘ	ܓܠܳܐܘܽ	ܓܠܳܐܘܗ̇	ܓܠܳܐܘܗ̱ܝ	ܓܰܠܳܐܘܗ̱ܝ
plur. fem.	ܓܠܶܝܶܝܢ	ܓܠܶܝܶܝܢ	ܓܠܶܝܢܳܗ̇	ܓܠܶܝܢܳܝܗ̱ܝ	ܓܰܠܶܝܢܳܝܗ̱ܝ

1. ܚܙܳܝܗ̇ (26:19); ܘܰܫܰܕܪܳܝܗ̱ܝ (15:8); ܐܰܘܫܶܕܪܳܢ (12:15); ܡܫܰܠܡܝܗ̱ܝ (25:11);
ܡܟܣܗ (30:12); ܒܢܳܢ (12:14); ܗܘܳܐܘܗ̱ܝ (12:9); ܘܐܰܘܫܕܳܐܘܢ (12:3);
ܢܶܫܬܳܐܘܢ (20:11).

2. ܐܰܫܩܺܝܘܗ̱ܝ (26:7); ܢܫܰܩܝܘܗ̱ܝ (27:15); ܢܫܰܩܶܐܟܘܢ (2 Cor. 3:1); ܢܦܰܨܶܝܢ (Rom. 7:24); ܢܶܚܙܳܘܢܳܝܗ̱ܝ (26:11); ܢܶܚܙܳܘܢܶܗ (14:2); ܢܶܚܙܳܘܢ (32:14); ܢܶܚܙܳܘܢܳܝܗ̱ܝ (Rev. 1:7); ܢܶܚܙܳܘܢܶܗ (Rom. 15:21).

3. ܦܨܳܢ (Mt. 6:13); ܦܨܳܢ (John. 12:27); ܚܙܳܐܘܗ̱ܝ (Heb. 3:1).

4. ܡܫܰܡܫܰܬܢ (Mt. 8:2); ܡܚܰܙܝܶܗ (Lk. 23:8).

1. The forms ending in a consonant suffer no change before suffixes. The suffixes are appended by means of the same union vowels as are employed with the same forms in the regular verb, see § 51. Of forms ending in a vowel, it may be remarked:—

(1). The 3rd sing. masc. Pe'al drops Olaph and appends the suffixes directly.

(2). The 3rd sing. masc. of the derived stems changes final ܝ to ܝ (*î* to *ey*) and appends the suffixes as in the regular verb, Yudh being treated as a radical.

(3). The 3rd masc. plur. appends the suffixes directly to the forms ܓܠܳܐܘܽ or ܓܠܰܘܽ.

(4). The 3rd fem. plur. takes the form ܓܠܰܝ, Yudh being treated as a consonant and the suffixes appended with their usual union vowels, see § 36.

2. The forms of the Imperfect which end in ܝܢ change this ending into ܘܢ to which the suffixes are appended directly. The forms of the Imperfect which end in a consonant are regular, see § 51. B.

3. The forms of the Imperative, that end in a vowel append the suffixes without any change, except that the Olaph of the masc. sing. Pa'el is dropped. The 2nd fem. plur. adds the suffixes by means of the customary union vowels, without any change in the perfect form, ܟܬܒ becomes ܟܬܒܝܢ and ܟܬܒ becomes ܟܬܒܘܢ or ܟܬܒܘܗܝ; the same as the 3rd masc. plur. of the Perfect.

Note. 3.—In the 2nd fem. sing. Imperat., the Yudh is sometimes omitted in writing *e. g.* Judith 10:16 ܫܡܥܘܢܝ instead of ܫܡܥܝܘܢܝ.

4. Infinitives and Participles are inflected like nouns, see § 81 ܡܟܬܒܘ and ܡܟܬܒܢܐ.

§ 62. Doubly Weak Verbs.

1. ܐܬܐ [R. ܐܬܐ] (2 Cor. 13:5); ܢܐܬܘܢ [R. ܐܬܐ] (Rev. 9:19); ܡܬܚܡ (Rev. 11:5); ܢܐܟܠ [R. ܐܟܠ] (John 16:20); ܐܟܠ (Mt. 11:17); ܡܫܚܝܢ [R. ܐܫܚ] (Mk. 6:13); ܢܐܬܐ [for ܢܐܬܐ] (John 4:47); ܐܬܝ (Mt. 8:13); ܐܬܬ (Mt. 25:11); ܐܙܠ (Mt. 27:33); ܢܐܙܠ (Mt. 10:13); ܐܡܝܕ (M. 14:11); ܡܚܕܐܘܗܝ (Mt. 5:25).

2. ܐܠܝܣ (Heb. 4:7); ܡܠܝܡܝܢ (30:1); ܬܡܬܝ (Mt. 25:5); ܐܠܝܣ (Acts 13:16); ܢܬܠܡ, *It will be abominable.* (R. נדד).

3. ܗܘܐ (Mt. 12:45); ܚܕܘܗܝ (Mt. 19:21); ܣܗܕ (Acts 1:3); ܡܚܣܡܐ (Heb. 9:16); ܩܘܐ (1 Tim. 4:2); ܠܟܬܐ (Tit. 3:13); ܕܐܡ (Rom. 1:11); ܣܒܥ (Mt. 15:32); ܪܘܐ (1 Thes. 5:7); ܚܣܢ (Lk. 20:35); ܡܚܕܐܘܗܝ (Mt. 5:25).

4. ܐܝܐ (Heb. 2:10); ܡܨܐ (Mt. 19:13); ܠܐܝܐ (Gal. 4:10); ܠܐܝܐ (Rom. 16:6); ܢܨܠܐ (Rev. 22:11).

5. ܐܢܬ [R. אנק], *thou sighest*; ܐܬܐܒܬ [R. אוב] (Is. 26:9), *I have desired*;

ܡܬܐܘܐ [R. אוח] (Mt. 5:25); ܡܬܝܐܒ [R. יאב] (Lk. 16:21) (ܡܬܝܐܒ id. Philox.).

1. Verbs Pê Nun and Lomadh Olaph, or Pê Olaph and Lomadh Olaph, partake everywhere of the peculiarities of both.

2. In verbs Pê Nun and Ê Waw, or Pê Nun and ÊÊ, the Nun everywhere remains as in the strong verb.

3. Verbs Ê Waw and Lomadh Olaph retain the Waw as consonant.

4. In verbs Ê Olaph and Lomadh Olaph, the Ê Olaph remains, but as usual its vowel is shifted to the preceding consonant and the Olaph quiesces according to the rule given in § 56.

5. Some further peculiarities of verbs one of whose radicals is Olaph may be seen above under 5.

§ 63. Quadriliterals.

1. ܫܘܕܥ (Rev. 1:1); ܬܪܝܢ (Acts 15:18); ܟܪܟܘܗܝ (Acts 14:20); ܐܫܒܗܪܐ (1 Cor. 1:25); ܡܬܪܣܝܢ (Mt. 6:26); ܫܡܠܝܗ (Acts 13:33); ܐܬܬܠܡܕ (Mt. 27:57); ܐܬܡܣܟܢ (2 Cor. 8:9); ܐܫܬܘܕܥ (Acts 12:11); ܡܬܦܪܟܣ (Mk. 9:20) *"wallowing"*.

2. ܡܬܕܝܘܢܝܢ (Mk. 1:32, [Philox.]) *possessed of demons.*

ܡܣܪܗܒ [R. ܪܗܒ] (Acts 20:16), *hastening.*

ܫܘܕܥ [R. ܝܕܥ] (Rev. 1:1), *to make known.*

ܣܝܒܪ [R. ܣܒܪ] (Heb. 12:2), *he endured.*

ܡܩܛܪܓ [from κατηγορέω] (John 5:45), *accusing.*

1. Quadriliteral verbs have the same inflection as the Paʿel and Ethpaʿal, the doubled middle radical being superseded by the 2nd and 3rd radicals of the quadriliteral.

2. Quadriliterals are mostly denominatives, intensives, or causatives.

§ 64. Anomalous and Defective Verbs.

1. ܐܙܠ *to go* has the Lomadh quiescent in the forms where the second radical is devoid of a vowel. The Imperative is ܙܠ. The Imperfect is regular *i. e.* ܢܐܙܠ.

2. ܐܫܬܝ *to drink* follows the conjugation of the Pe'al. The Imperative, however, is ܐܫܬܝ, see § 60. 4., Rem. 1. Imperf. ܢܫܬܐ, Part. Act. ܫܬܐ, Infin. ܡܫܬܐ. On the prosthetic Olaph, see § 20. 1, Rem. 1.

3. ܐܫܟܚ *to find*, like ܐܫܬܝ, follows the conjugation of the Pe'al, the Olaph being prosthetic, see § 20, Rem. 1, e. g. ܐܫܟܚ (Mt. 8:28), Imperat. ܐܫܟܚ, Part. Pass. ܫܟܝܚ (2 Pet. 1:8). The Part. Act., however, is ܡܫܟܚ (Mt. 26:8) and the Infin. ܡܫܟܚܘ. Some of these forms seem to be Aph'el with the *ă* changed to *ĕ* according to § 20, Rem. 1 and § 29. 2.

4. ܐܬܐ *to come* has ܬܐ, ܬܝ, ܬܘ, ܐܬܝܢ (see Mt. 28:6) in the Imperat. Pe'al. Imperf. ܢܐܬܐ, Part. Act. ܐܬܐ. Aphel ܐܝܬܝ see §§ 55. 4, 58. 3, Note, 62. 1.

5. ܗܘܐ *to be* when enclitic looses its ܗ e. g. ܡܨܝܐ ܗܘܐ (Mt. 2:22), see § 19. 2(1). In the Imperfect the Waw often falls away, e. g. ܢܗܐ (Gen. 9:15 [comp. וִיהִי]).

6. ܚܝܐ *to live* forms its Perf. and Imperat. and Part. Act. Pe'al like Lomadh Olaph verbs e. g. ܚܝܬ (Lk 2:36); ܚܝܘ (Rev. 20:4); ܚܝܝܢ (Rom. 6:13); ܚܝܘ ([Imperat.] Acts. 2:40); ܚܝ (Mt. 4:4). The Infinitive and Imperfect Pe'al and the Aph'el and Ettaph'al are formed as if from an *ĒĒ* root, e. g. ܢܚܐ (Nestorian. ܢܚܐ from ܢܚܣܐ as ܢܣܒ from ܢܣܡܟ or ܢܦܩ from ܢܛܥܡ, see § 54. 2), ܢܚܐ (Mt. 9:18); ܢܚܐ (Rom. 10:1); (ܢܚܘܢ is found in 1 Tim. 2:4, ܢܚܘܢ is found in 1 Thess. 2:16); ܡܚܐ (Mk. 10:26) is the usual form of the Infin. though ܡܚܐ and ܡܚܝܐ are found. Examples of the Aph'el are: ܐܚܝ (30:4); ܐܚܝ (John 5:21); ܐܚܝܬ (30:4); ܐܚܝ (Lk. 23:37); ܢܚܐ (Mt. 16:25); ܢܚܐ (1 Cor. 7:16).

7. In the Perfect of ܝܗܒ *to give* the ܗ receives linea occultans, § 11:1, whenever the ܒ is without a vowel, e. g. ܝܗܒ (28:7); ܝܗܒ (Mt. 15:36); but ܝܗܒܬ (Mk. 6:28); ܝܗܒܬ (28:2). In the Imperat. the Yudh is dropped, see § 23. 1(2), e. g. ܗܒ (Mt. 5:42); ܗܒ (John 4:7); ܗܒܘ (Mt. 10:8); ܗܒܝ (Mt. 25:8). The Participles are ܝܗܒ (Mt. 13:23) and ܝܗܒ (Mt. 13:11). The Imperfect and Infinitive are formed from ܢܬܠ, which is used nowhere else e. g. ܢܬܠ (Mt. 5:31); ܢܬܠ (Mt. 7:11). The Ethpiel is ܐܬܝܗܒ (32:23).

8. ܣܠܩ *to ascend*, in forms where ܣ ends one syllable and Lomadh

begins another, has the Lomadh assimilated to the Semkath, § 18. 4 ܬܫܦ [for ܢܫܟܚ] (Mt. 13:2); ܐܫܡ [for ܐܫܟܚ] (Mt. 17:1). In the Imperative Pe'al the Lomadh is dropped, see § 23. 2(3), e. g. ܫܡ [for ܫܟܚ] (Rev. 4:1), ܫܡܘ (John 7:8).

9. ܘܠܐ *it behooves*, ܠܐ *it is well*, ܙܕܩ *it is right* are used only in the Part. Act. Pe'al in the sense of a present intransitive, e. g. ܘܠܐ (25:15); ܠܐ (Mt. 3:15): ܙܕܩ (Lk. 24:46). Compare § 122.

10. The 3rd fem. Perf. and Imperf. Pe'al of ܟܪܐ is used impersonally; compare § 122, e. g. ܟܪܝܬ ܠܝܘܢܢ (14:7) *it grieved Jonah*, ܬܟܪܐ ye shall grieve (John 16:20). The participles are used in a like sense, the active as a present or future, the passive as a present or with ܗܘܐ as a past, e. g. ܟܪܝܐ ܠܗ (John. 16:22); ܟܪܝܐ (28:12); ܟܕ ܟܪܝܐ ܠܗ (Mk. 3:5).

11. As in ܟܪܐ, so in ܡܠܐ *to grieve* or *be weary*, the 3rd fem. is everywhere used impersonally in the Pe'al, e. g. ܡܠܬܟܘܢ (Heb. 3:7); ܠܐ ܬܡܠܐ ܠܟܘܢ (Heb. 12:3); ܠܐ ܡܠܐ ܠܝ (Phil. 3:1). Compare § 122.

§ 65. ܐܝܬ and ܠܝܬ.

1.
ܐܝܬܝ	"I am"	ܐܝܬܝܢ	"We are"
ܐܝܬܝܟ	"Thou art"	ܐܝܬܝܟܘܢ	"You are"
ܐܝܬܝܟܝ	"Thou (f.) art"	ܐܝܬܝܟܝܢ	"You (f.) are"
ܐܝܬܘܗܝ	"He is"	ܐܝܬܝܗܘܢ	"They are"
ܐܝܬܝܗ	"She is"	ܐܝܬܝܗܝܢ	"They (f.) are".

2. ܐܝܬ (Mt. 3:9); ܐܝܬܝܟܘܢ (2 Pet. 1:3); ܐܝܬܘܗܝ (Mt. 6:30); ܐܝܬܘܗܝ ܗܘܐ (Mt. 3:4); ܠܝܬ (Mt. 13:13); ܠܝܬ ܗܘܐ (Lk. 2:7); ܐܝܬܝ (Acts 22:3); ܐܝܬܝܗܘܢ (Mt. 4:18); ܠܐ ܐܝܬܘܗܝ (Spic. Syr. 9:9).

ܐܝܬ (Heb. יֵשׁ) is really a noun meaning "existence"; but in usage it has passed over into the class of verbs. It takes pronominal suffixes like a plural noun; but like a verb may be used also with separate pronouns or with nouns. It sometimes stands uninflected with enclitic ܗܘܐ. With ܠܐ "not", it may be written separately, as in John 12:8; but generally it coalesces with ܠܐ and forms ܠܝܬ. See § 128.

§ 66.]   ELEMENTS OF SYRIAC.   71

§ 66. The Inflection and Classification of Nouns.

A. INFLECTION.

1. (1) ܢܘܗܪܐ (1:3) from ܢܗܪ to shine.

   ܚܫܘܟܐ (1:2) from ܚܫܟ to be dark.

   (2) ܐܒܗܘܬܐ fatherhood, from ܐܒܐ father.

2. (1) ܫܡܫܐ (2:15); ܝܡܐ (1:1).

   (2) ܩܛܠܐ (1:12); ܐܘܠܕܐ (2:3).

   ܡܕܒܪܢܝ (2:3).

3. (1) ܐܚܬ (1:2); ܬܩܠܐ (2:18).

   ܡܕܝܢܬܐ (1:6); ܪܚܝܡ (3:1).

   (2) ܢܨܝܚܐ (1:10); ܐܘܠܕܐ (2:3).

4.   ܡܚܐ (6:2); ܚܘܐ (1:2).

   ܩܕܫܝ (5:11); ܟܠܠܬܟ (5:15).

The inflection of nouns includes:—

1. The formation of the noun-stems (1) from the root or (2) from other nouns.

2. The addition of affixes for (1) gender and (2) number.

3. The changes of stem and terminations in the formation of the states (1) conctruct and (2) emphatic.

4. The addition of pronominal suffixes.

B. CLASSIFICATION.

1. (1) ܪܡܫܐ evening; ܥܣܒܐ herb; ܩܘܕܫܐ holiness.

   (2) ܕܗܒܐ gold; ܓܪܒܐ leprous; ܩܠܐ voice.

   (3) ܩܪܒܐ war; ܡܫܝܚܐ Messiah; ܥܠܝܡܐ youth.

   (4) ܥܠܡܐ world; ܩܐܡ standing; ܬܪܥܐ doorkeeper.

   (5) ܩܛܘܠܐ murderer; ܐܚܕܐ slough; ܩܨܨܬܐ abbreviation.

2. (1) ܨܦܪ bird; ܩܦܣܐ bolt.

   (2) ܡܠܚܐ sailor; ܢܨܝ quarrelsome; ܐܘܠܨ labour.

(3) ܠܶܫܳܢܳܐ *tongue;* ܐܶܓܳܪܳܐ *roof;* ܥܶܩܳܪܳܐ *root.*

(4) ܐܘܟܳܡ *black;* ܫܘܐܳܠܐ *question;* ܙܘܘܳܓܐ *marriage.*

(5) ܐܰܒܺܝܕ *lost;* ܡܰܟܺܝܟ *humble;* ܪܰܚܺܝܩ *far.*

(6) ܢܳܚܳܐ *at rest;* ܐܰܬܘܢܳܐ *furnace;* ܫܰܒܛܳܐ *sceptre.*

(7) ܚܶܫܘܟ *dark;* ܕܶܒܘܪܳܐ *bee.*

(8) ܡܓܺܕܠܳܐ *mantelet;* ܣܰܟܠܺܝܠܳܐ *idle;* ܦܶܬܳܐ *altar.*

3. (1) ܡܰܕܢܚܳܐ *east;* ܡܰܪܕܘܬܳܐ *correction;* ܡܰܬܩܳܠܳܐ *weight.*

(2) ܬܰܠܡܺܝܕܳܐ *scholar;* ܬܶܫܡܶܫܬܳܐ *service;* ܬܰܟܬܘܫܳܐ *combat.*

(3) ܐܘܪܳܝܬܳܐ *divine law;* ܐܘܪܕܥܳܐ *frog;* ܢܘܪܒܳܐ *shoot.*

4. (1) ܦܘܩܕܳܢܳܐ *commandment;* ܣܶܦܪܳܢܳܐ *little book.*

(2) ܢܘܪܳܢܳܐ *fiery;* ܣܰܠܘܳܝ *quail;* ܚܠܘܨܝܳܐ *robbery.*

(3) ܫܰܛܝܘܬܳܐ *folly;* ܢܘܢܳܝܐ *little fish.*

Nouns are differentiated by internal or external means. The internal means are 1. vowels, 2. doubling of radicals.

1. Those formed by vowels may be divided into those which had originally.

(1) one short vowel *a*, *i*, or *u*.

(2) two short vowels.

(3) one short and one long vowel.

(4) one long and one short vowel.

(5) two long vowels.

2. Those formed by doubling are such as double the second [(1)—(7)] or third radical (8). These may be subdivided according to their vowels.

3. Nouns formed by external changes may be formed by preformatives, the most usual of which are Mim and Tau or

4. By sufformatives, the most usual of which are Nun, Yudh and Waw.

§ 67. Nouns with one originally short vowel.

1. (1) ܪܡܫܐ (ܐܰܡܫܰܐ) *evening;* ܡܠܟ *king;* ܓܒܪ *man;* ܨܠܡ *image* but ܚܩܠܐ *field;* ܨܦܪ *morning;* ܬܪܥܐ *door.*

   (2) ܥܣܒܐ *herb;* ܣܐܡܐ *silver;* ܪܓܠ (ܐܪܓܠܐ) *foot.*

   (3) ܩܘܕܫܐ *holiness;* ܒܘܪܟ *knee;* ܫܘܚܕܐ (ܫܘܚܕܐ) *bribe.*

2. (1) ܐܪܥ *earth;* ܐܠܦ *ship;* ܤܘܦܐ (R. ܐܣܦ) *end;* ܫܓܐ (for ܫܓܐ) *many.*

   (2) ܝܪܚ *month;* ܝܠܕ *child;* ܫܢܬܐ *sleep;* ܨܦܬܐ *care;* ܝܕܥܬܐ *knowledge.*

   (3) ܢܦܫ *soul;* ܢܘܛܦܐ (R. ܢܛܦ) *drop;* ܢܫܡܬܐ (R. ܢܫܡ) *breath.*

   (4) ܕܘܐ *grief;* ܒܝܫ (R. באש) *evil.*

   (5) ܣܘܦ *end;* ܝܘܡ *day;* ܪܘܚ *spirit;* ܢܘܪ *fire.*

   ܥܝܢ *eye;* ܕܝܢ *judgment;* ܒܝܬ *house.*

   (6) ܐܦ (R. ܐܢܦ) *face;* ܓܒ (ܓܢܒ) *side.*

   (7) ܥܡ *people;* ܐܡ *mother;* ܛܠ *dew;* ܚܝܠܐ *strength.*

   (8) ܢܝܚ *rest;* ܚܙܘܐ *appearance;* ܚܕܘܬܐ *joy;* ܟܣܝܐ *covering;* ܕܡܘܬܐ *likeness.*

3. ܡܠܟܬܐ *queen;* ܢܨܒܬܐ *plant;* ܥܓܠܬܐ *calf;* ܕܘܢܒܬܐ *tail.*

   ܢܘܫܩܬܐ *kiss;* ܡܫܘܚܬܐ *measure.*

1. The vowel $\breve{}$ occurs in the absolute and construct singular of most words of this class which had originally $\acute{}$, except in those whose third radical is a guttural or Rish. These nouns correspond to the *Segholates* in Hebrew and like them are divided into three classes:—the *a* class, the *i* class and the *u* class.

2. When the root contains one or more weak radicals, certain changes occur:—

   (1) When the first radical is an Olaph it takes a helping vowel, except in ܐܠܦܐ when it is dropped. When the third radical is an Olaph it throws back its vowel upon the preceding radical and quiesces.

   (2) When the first radical is a Yudh, it quiesces in $\breve{}$, or is dropped. Waw occurs as the first radical only in ܘܥܕܐ *consultation.*

   (3) Nouns from Pê Nun roots are usually regular. A few, however, drop the Nun.

(4) Nouns from Ê Olaph roots throw back the vowel and quiesce. The Olaph may even be changed to Yudh as in ܒܝܫ.

(5) Nouns from Ê Waw and Ê Yudh roots have the following changes:—*wu* and *uw* become *û*; *iw*, *iy*, *yi* and *wi* become *î*; *aw* remains unchanged (except in ܬܘܪܬܐ *cow*), but *wa* becomes ܘ in ܡܘܬܒ and ܡܘܦܩ (and in Nestorian in ܗܘܢ *understanding*, ܓܘܢ *color*, which, however, in Jacobite are ܗܘܢ and ܓܘܢ); *ay* remains unchanged, (except perhaps in ܒܝܥܬܐ *egg*), but *ya* becomes ܝ in ܒܝܬ *house*, (ܥܝܢ *eye*), or ̈ as in ܥܝܢ *eye*.

(6) Nun, when the middle radical, is sometimes assimilated.

(7) In Ê doubled roots, the 2nd and 3rd radicals are contracted into one and the vowel of the second radical is thrown back upon the first.

(8) ܫܠܝܐ *rest* is the only word from a Lomadh Olaph root which preserves the absolute or construct state; the emphatic state is regular.

ܚܙܘܐ *appearance*, ܚܕܘܐ *joy* and ܫܠܘܐ *rest* are the only masculine nouns of this class that have Waw as the third radical.

The third radical has disappeared in ܬܕܐ *breast* and in ܦܐܪܐ *fruit*.

3. Feminine nouns are formed by affixing the feminine ending to the primary forms, the vowel either remaining with the second or being thrown back upon the first radical.

§ 68. Nouns with two short formative vowels.

1. ܕܗܒܐ (זָהָב) *gold;* ܚܠܒܐ (חָלָב).

ܟܢܦܐ (כָּנָף) *wing.*

2. ܕܩܢ (זָקֵן) *old;* ܐܩܢ *time.*

ܓܡܠ (גָּמָל) *camel.*

3. ܓܪܒ (גָּרֵב) *leprous.*

ܚܕܬ (חָדָשׁ) *new;* ܫܦܠ (שָׁפֵל) *low;* ܥܩܪ (עָקָר) *sterile.*

4. ܢܫܡܬܐ (נְשָׁמָה) *breath;* ܫܦܠܬܐ (שִׁפְלָה) *low;* ܚܪܒܬܐ (חֲרֵבָה) *waste.*

ܟܦܢܬܐ (כָּפָן) *hungry;* ܚܒܪܬܐ (חֲבֵרָה) *companion.*

ܢܗܡܬܐ (נְהָמָה) *roar;* ܥܢܒܬܐ (עֵנָב) *grapes.*

5. ܩܠܐ (ל ק)=kăwălâ, *voice.*

ܣܐܒ=să'ăbh, *elder.*

ܣܐܒܬܐ=să'ăbheṯhâ, *old woman.*

ܣܘܢܩܬܐ=(ܣܘܢܩܘܬܐ) *need.*

ܛܡܐܐ=(טָמֵא) *unclean.*

ܕܟܝܐ *clean;* ܩܫܝܐ *hard.*

ܕܟܝܬܐ *clean;* ܩܫܝܬܐ *hard.*

ܒܥܘܬܐ=baʿăwăthâ (*awa* contracted) *request.*

ܣܘܪܬܐ *smell.*

ܨܐܬܐ (for ܨܐܐܬܐ) *dirt.*

ܥܠܠܬܐ *produce.*

Almost all traces of these nouns have disappeared, having for the most part come to coïncide with the last class. We can still distinguish them (1) in some words which have an aspirate as third radical, and (2) in those which, not being Ê or Lomadh guttural, have in the absolute and construct singular ܶ under the second radical.

3. Adjectives with but one vowel remaining in the absolute may also be safely put in this class.

4. Feminines of this class are often of the same form as those of the first class.

5. Examples of nouns of this class from roots with one or more weak radical may be seen under number 5 above. It will be noted, (1) that awa or a'a becomes ô; (2) that ܶ remains with forms of this class when third radical is guttural Olaph (compare § 57); (3) that îy final becomes ܐ̈, but when not final ܝ; (4) that nouns from Ê doubled roots are regular.

§ **69.** Nouns with one short and one long formative vowel.

1. ܟܬܒ (כְּתָב) *writing;* ܩܪܒ (קְרָב) *war;* ܥܒܕ (עֲבָד) *work.*

2. ܚܡܪ (חֲמוֹר) *ass;* ܐܢܫ (אֱנוֹשׁ) *man;* ܐܠܗܐ (אֱלָהּ) *god.*

3. ܫܠܡ (שָׁלוֹם) *peace;* ܬܠܬ (שָׁלוֹשׁ) *three.*

4. ܩܛܝܠ (קָטִיל) *killed;* ܐܡܝܪ *said;* ܐܒܝܠ *sad, ascetic.*

ܝܠܝܕ *born;* ܓܙܝܙ *shorn;* ܣܝܡ *set;* ܣܝܡ *placed.*

ܣܢܝܐ *hated;* ܐܣܝܪ (אֲסִיר) *prisoner;* ܝܡܝܢܐ (יָמִין) *right hand.*

ܡܫܝܚܐ (מָשִׁיחַ) *Messiah;* ܢܒܝܐ (נָבִיא) *prophet;* ܟܠܝܠܐ *crown.*

ܣܦܝܢܬܐ (סְפִינָה) *ship;* ܚܙܝܪܬܐ (חֲזִיר) *swine;* ܒܥܝܪܐ (בְּעִיר) *beast.*

5. ܣܢܘܐܐ (שְׂנִיאָה) *hated;* ܫܡܘܥܬܐ (שְׁמוּעָה) *heard i. e. report.*

ܓܢܘܒܬܐ (גְּנוּבָה) *stolen i. e. theft;* ܒܬܘܠܬܐ (בְּתוּלָה) *virgin.*

ܠܒܘܫܐ (לְבוּשׁ) *clothing;* ܩܒܘܪܬܐ (קְבוּרָה) *sepulchre.*

9. ܥܠܝܡܐ (غُلَيِّم) *youth;* ܥܘܙܠܐ (غُزَيِّل) *fawn;* ܚܙܝܪܐ *pig.*

The short vowel, except when preceded by Olaph, is dropped and the consonant is pronounced with a half-vowel, which may originally have been *a*, *i*, or *u*. Nouns of the form ḳuṭail are diminutives; those of the form ḳaṭîl are usually passive participles Pe'al; a few of the form ḳaṭûl (קָטוּל) have the meaning of a passive participle.

§ 70. Nouns with one long and one short formative vowel.

1. ܥܠܡ (עוֹלָם) *world;* ܚܬܡ (חוֹתָם) *signet.*

2. ܩܛܠ (קוֹטֵל) *killing;* ܨܦܪܐ *bird;* ܬܒܪ (שֹׁבֵר) *breaking.*

ܩܐܡ *standing;* ܣܢܐܐ (=ܣܢܝܐ) *hater;* ܓܠܐ (גֹּלֶה) *revealing.*

ܪܬܬ (ܪܬܬ) *trembling.*

3. ܬܪܥܐ (שׁוֹעֵר) *doorkeeper;* ܥܓܠܬܐ (עֲגָלָה) *waggon.*

ܙܢܝܬܐ (זוֹנָה) *harlot;* ܩܪܝܬܐ (קוֹרָה) *beam;* ܟܗܢܐ (כֹּהֵן) *preast.*

1. There are but two nouns with *a* certainly after the second radical.

2. Nouns of the form ḳâṭil are used as the active participles of verbs, and to denote the agent; and, in a few sporadic cases, in other senses.

§ 71. Nouns with two long vowels.

1. ḳâṭûl ܩܛܘܠܐ *murderer;* ܛܠܘܡܐ *oppressor;* ܐܟܘܠܐ *eater;* ܝܪܘܪܐ *jackal;* ܦܬܘܪܐ *table.*

2. ḳâṭîl ܢܘܠܐ *weaver's beam;* ܪܣܝܣܬܐ *gush of rain;* ܚܛܝܛܬܐ *club;* ܐܫܝܦܐ *slough;* ܦܣܝܩܬܐ *abbreviation.*

1. From every active participle, Nomina Agentis can be formed after the form ḳâtûl (Compare in Arabic جَاسُوس *spy*). Certain other nouns also take this form.

2. There are a few nouns of the form ḳâtîl.

§ 72. Nouns with the second radical doubled.

1. ܨܶܦܪ *bird*; ܚܶܠܳܠܳܐ *halm*; ܣܽܘܟܪܳܐ *bolt*; ܣܶܒܶܠܬܳܐ *ladder*.

ܐܶܕܪܳܐ *threshing-floor*; ܣܰܟܪܳܐ *shield*; ܩܽܘܦܕܳܐ *hedgehog*.

2. (1) ă—â ḳăttâl ܡܰܠܳܚܳܐ (מַלָּח) *sailor*; ܓܰܢܳܒܳܐ (גַּנָּב) *thief*.

ܚܰܪܳܫܳܐ *magician*; ܨܰܠܳܝܳܐ *praying*; ܣܰܩܠܳܐ *pernicious*; ܕܰܝܳܢܳܐ (דַּיָּן) *judge*;

ܐܰܟܳܪܳܐ (=אִכָּר) *farmer*.

(2) ĭ—â ḳĭttâl ܣܶܬܪܳܐ *veil*; ܐܶܓܳܪܳܐ *roof*.

(3) ŭ—â ḳŭttâl ܫܽܘܐܳܠܳܐ *question*; ܐܽܘܡܳܢܳܐ *artist*; ܣܽܘܟܳܠܳܐ *perception*; ܐܽܘܟܳܡܳܐ *black*; ܫܽܘܥܳܐ *yellow*.

(4) ă—î ḳăttîl ܝܰܬܺܝܒ *sitting*; ܐܰܒܺܝܕ *lost*.

ܪܰܟܺܝܟ *soft*; ܣܰܓܺܝ *many*.

(5) ă—û ḳăttûl ܣܰܚܺܘܪ *reclining restfully*.

ܚܽܘܛܪܳܐ *staff*; ܐܰܬܽܘܢܳܐ *stove*.

(6) ĭ—û ḳĭttûl ܕܶܒܽܘܪܳܐ *wasp*.

ܚܶܫܽܘܟܳܐ *darkness*.

After the norm of 2 (3), a *nomen actionis* can be formed from the intensive species of any verb. Of the form (4) are many verbal adjectives, especially such as serve for participles of intransitive verbs.

§ 73. Nouns with one or more radicals reduplicated.

1. NOUNS WITH THE THIRD RADICAL REDUPLICATED.

These are few in number. They are such as

ܦܬܰܟܪܳܐ *idol altar*; ܕܰܚܢܳܐ *millet*; ܐܰܙܕܰܗܪܳܐ *splendor*; ܦܰܪܬܽܘܬܳܐ *crumb*.

ܚܶܕܥܳܝܳܐ *appearance*; ܟܰܠܕܳܪܳܐ *bandrol*; ܡܰܢܕܰܠܳܐ *mantelet*.

ܡܰܨܛܰܠܳܐ *idle*; ܥܰܪܙܺܝܪ *ferocious*.

78   ELEMENTS OF SYRIAC.   [§ 74.

2. NOUNS WITH TWO RADICALS REDUPLICATED.

ܟ݂ܰܪܟ݂ܪܳܐ *threshing instrument;* ܩܰܡܩܡܳܐ *bug;* ܢܳܡܳܢܳܐ *milleped.*

ܥܰܠܥܳܠܳܐ *storm;* ܩܰܡܨܳܨܳܐ *locust;* ܓܰܪܓܪܬܳܐ (=gargarto) *throat.*

ܟܰܘܟ݂ܰܒ݂ (=kabkab) *star;* ܪܰܘܪܒ݂ܝܢ (=rabrᵉbhin) *many.*

ܡܟܰܠܠܟ݂ܡ *perfect;* ܣܰܚܠܳܠܳܐ *ivy;* ܙܰܠܙܰܠܺܝܬܳܐ *spark.*

§ 74. Nouns formed by Prefixes.

1. ܐܰܒ݂ܘܒ݂ܳܐ (נבב) *flute;* ܐܰܓ݁ܪܬܳܐ *manuscript;* ܬܢܳܢܳܐ *smoke;* ܥܘܪܕܥܳܐ *frog.*

2. (1) ă—ă ܡܰܫܟ݁ܢܳܐ (=מִשְׁכָּן) *tabernacle;* ܡܰܪܒ݁ܥܳܐ *womb.*
   ܡܩܰܒ݁ܠܳܐ (=מְקַבֵּל) *acceptance;* ܡܰܪܟ݁ܒ݂ܬܳܐ (=מֶרְכָּבָה) *chariot.*
   ܡܰܕ݁ܥ (from ܝܕܥ) *knowledge;* ܡܰܘܗܰܒ݂ܬܳܐ (from ܝܗܒ) *gift.*
   ܡܰܫܬ݁ܝܳܐ (=מִשְׁתֶּה) *drink;* ܡܰܬ݂ܩܠܳܐ (from ܬܩܠ) *balance.*
   ܡܰܥܠܬܳܐ (=ܡܰܥܠܟ݂ܬܳܐ) *entrance;* ܡܰܓ݁ܢܳܐ (from ܡܰܓܢܳܢܳܐ abs. ܡܰܓ݁ܢ) *shield.*
   ܡܰܩܡܳܐ (=ܡܰܩܡܥ) *standing place.*

   (2) ă—ĭ ܡܰܟ݂ܬ݁ܡܳܐ *broom;* ܡܰܒ݁ܘܥܳܐ (=מַעְיָן) *spring.*
   ܡܨܺܝܕܬܳܐ (מִצְרְדָא) *net.*

   (3) ă—ŭ ܡܶܐܟ݂ܘܠܬܳܐ *food;* ܡܶܫܬ݁ܘܕܥܳܐ *acquaintance.*

   (4) ă—â ܡܰܬ݂ܩܳܠܳܐ (=מִשְׁקוֹל) *weight;* ܡܰܣܳܪܳܐ (מַסּוֹר) *saw;* ܡܰܘܠܳܕ݂ܳܐ *birth.*

   (5) ă—û ܡܰܒ݁ܘܥܳܐ (=מַבּוּעַ) *spring;* ܡܰܦ݁ܘܚܳܐ (=מַפֵּחַ) *bellows.*
   ܡܰܟ݂ܫܘܠܳܐ (מִכְשׁוֹל) *stumbling block.*

   (6) ĭ—ă ܡܚܺܝܕܳܐ *web.*

   (7) ĭ—â ܡܚܰܫܢܳܐ *pawn;* ܡܕ݂ܺܝܪܳܐ *dwelling.*

   (8) ŭ—ă ܡܘܰܕ݂ܠܳܐ *spindle* (=مِغْزَل).

   (9) â—ŭ ܡܳܙܘܢܳܐ *food;* ܡܳܕܺܝܢܬܳܐ *city.*

3. (1) ă—â ܬܰܘܬܳܒ݂ܳܐ *settler* (R. ܝܬܒ *to dwell*).
   (2) ă—î ܬܰܠܡܺܝܕ݂ܳܐ (תַּלְמִיד) *scholar;* ܬܰܟ݂ܪܺܝܬܳܐ *help.*

(3) ă—û ܬܫܘܚܠܦܐ *exchange;* ܬܡܢܘܪܐ *flattery.*

(4) ă—ă ܬܟܫܦܬܐ *supplication;* ܬܟܣܝܬܐ *clothing.*

(5) ă—ĭ ܬܒܗܬܬܐ *shame;* ܬܘܣܦܬܐ *addition.*

(6) ă—û ܬܫܪܝܘܬܐ *skeleton;* ܬܪܥܘܬܐ *reconciliation.*

(7) ĭ—ŭ ܬܫܒܘܚܬܐ *praise;* ܬܕܡܘܪܬܐ *wonder.*

(8) ĭ—ă ܬܫܪܝܬܐ *camp.*

The participles of all the derived species and the infinitives of all the species are formed by prefixing ܡ. Nouns with the prefix ܬ are mostly abstracts and are formed generally from the intensive species or from the Aphʿel.

§ 75. Nouns formed by means of affixes.

The most common of these affixes are ܢ, ܘܢ, ܢ, ܘܣ ܣ, ܝ, ܝ ܝ, ܝܐ, ܝܬ and ܘܬ.

1. (1) ܡܢܗܪܢܐ *enlightener;* ܡܢܣܝܢܐ *tempter.*

(2) ܐܪܥܢܝ (from ܐܪܥܐ) *earthy;* ܡܠܠܢܝ (from ܡܠܠ) *talkative.*

ܫܡܝܢܝ (from ܫܡܝܐ) *heavenly.*

(3) ܡܘܬܢܐ *pest;* ܦܘܩܕܢܐ *command;* ܒܢܝܢܐ *building.*

ܪܢܝܢܐ *thought.*

2. ܒܪܘܢܐ *little son;* ܟܬܒܘܢ *little book;* ܐܠܦܘܢܝܬܐ *small ship;* ܡܕܝܢܬܘܢܝܬܐ *village* (Compare יְשֻׁרוּן): ܢܣܝܘܢܐ *temptation;* ܓܠܝܘܢܐ *revelation.*

3. ܨܦܪܝܐ *early morning;* ܫܘܦܝܢܐ *file.*

4. ܢܘܢܘܣܐ *little fish;* ܥܠܝܡܘܣܐ *little boy;* ܥܠܝܡܘܣܬܐ *little girl.*

ܩܠܬܝܣܬܐ *a small water pot.*

5. ܢܘܪܢܝܐ *fiery;* ܡܠܟܝܐ *royal;* ܥܪܛܠܝܐ *naked;* ܝܗܘܕܝܐ *Jew.*

ܐܡܗܝܐ *motherly;* ܫܡܗܝܐ *nominal.*

6. ܣܠܘܝܬ *quail* (Ex. 16:12); ܫܘܚܠܬ *error* (Lev. 5:18); ܛܘܫܝܬ *secret* (Eph. 5:12) § 86. 6.

7. ܐܣܘܪܝܐ *binding;* ܗܦܘܟܝܐ *overturn;* ܚܛܘܦܝܐ *robbery.*

ܕܒܘܪܝܬܐ *bee;* ܣܢܘܢܝܬܐ *swallow;* ܪܫܝܬܐ *beginning.*

8. ܡܠܟܘܬܐ (מַלְכוּת) *kingdom;* ܛܒܘܬܐ *goodness;* ܐܒܗܘܬܐ *fatherhood;* ܕܟܝܘܬܐ *purity* (Bib. Aram. דכי); ܣܥܘܕܬܐ *meal* (=sârᵉwuthâ); ܒܥܘܬܐ *request* (Bib. Aram. בָּעוּ); ܕܡܘܬܐ (דְמוּת) *likeness.*

1. Nouns with the affix ܘ may be formed from all participles of the derived species and from *nomina agentis,* 1(1). Added to many nouns it forms adjectives, 1(2). It forms, also, many abstract nouns and names of things, 1(3).

2. Nouns with the ending ܘ݊, ܝ݊, ܘܢ or ܝܢ are generally diminutives see 2., 3. and 4.

3. Nouns with the ending ܝ generally form relative adjectives.

4. Nouns with the ending ܘܬ are abstract and can be formed from any noun.

§ 76. Gender, Number and State.

	Sing.		Plur.	
	masc.	fem.	masc.	fem.
Abs.	ܚܟܝܡ	ܚܟܝܡܐ	ܚܟܝܡܝܢ	ܚܟܝܡܢ
Cons.	ܚܟܝܡ	ܚܟܝܡܬ	ܚܟܝܡܝ	ܚܟܝܡܬ
Emph.	ܚܟܝܡܐ	ܚܟܝܡܬܐ	ܚܟܝܡܐ	ܚܟܝܡܬܐ

1. *a.* ܚܣܝܪ (1:4); ܡܚܣܪ (Mt. 21:5); ܐܢܬ (Mt. 19:3); ܢܚܡܬܢ (1 Cor. 9:21.)

   b. ܡܟܝܟ (Heb. 7:1); ܥܟܣ (Rom. 11:34); ܚܪ (Mt. 10:3).

   c. ܢܕܝܕܐ (1:3); ܠܚܘܡܐ (1:2); ܟܠܗ (1:1).

2. *a.* ܪܘܙܐ (15:3); ܟܐܠܐ (11:4); ܡܣܛܐ (1:2); ܡܢܬܐ *part;* ܡܚܠܩܬܐ (Mt. 12:25); ܟܣܝܬܐ *covering;* ܚܨ (Ined. Syr. 18:1); ܪܝܫܝܬܐ (John 1:1).

   b. ܡܓܕܠ (1:6); ܪܒܝܬܐ *usury;* ܙܟܘܬܐ *victory.*

   ܪܚܡܬܐ (2:18); ܡܟܝܕܗ (5:12); ܪܟܕܝ (13:4); ܚܨܦ (12:14); ܐܪܙܗ (26:2).

§ 76.]   ELEMENTS OF SYRIAC.   81

c. ܡܚܚܕܪ̈ܐ (Mt. 20:22); ܘܚܕܐ (Mk. 16:12); ܡܨܡܐ (1:10); ܩܘܣܐ (2:9).

3. a. ܚܢܦܟܡܝ (5:7); ܡܥܢܝ (Mt. 26:2); ܘܩܒܝ (Mt. 5:11).

b. ܐܩܦ (1:3); ܢܕܠܦ (2:18); ܐܡܟܠ (5:10).

c. ܩܐܘ (1:13); ܐܡܟܢܐ (3:15).

4. a. ܥܨܝ (Heb. 6:18); ܪܟܝ (Eph. 6:18); ܡܚܘ̈ܐ (Tit. 3:8); ܚܬܡ (Mt. 12:45).

b. ܨܠܐ (Lk. 23:23); ܢܦܦܘ (John 21:17); ܫܦܘܗ (Mt. 15:8); ܚܨܡ (1 Thess. 3:7).

c. ܐܙܘܐ (2:3); ܡܩܡܟܐ (2:3); ܩܡܠܢܬܐ (7:2).

5. ܬܪܝ (13:8); ܬܪܣܝܢ (5:7); ܬܪܝܢ (1:9); ܟܠܬܝ (Mk. 6:27).

The Syriac noun has two genders,—masculine and feminine; two numbers,—singular and plural; and three states,—the absolute, the construct and the emphatic or definite.

Remark 1.—The emphatic or definite state is everywhere denoted by the ending ܐ.

Remark 2.—For the changes of nouns in construction with pronominal suffixes, see the declension § 79 sq.

1. The absolute and construct singular masculine have no particular indication; the emphatic is formed by appending ܐ to the root. For the changes thus occasioned in the root, see the declensions § 79 sq.

2. The sign of the feminine gender is an appended Taw. This feminine ending has a twofold treatment.

(1) It is dropped in the fem. sing. and the vowel ̊ heightened to ܐ, except in a few nouns like ܡܢܬ *part* and ܪܫܝܬ *beginning*.

(2) In the construct it is retained; as also, before pronominal suffixes and the sign of the emphatic state.

3. The ending of the absolute plural masculine is ܝܼܢ; of the construct ܝܼ; of the emphatic ܐ (from ܝܐ).

4. The ending of the absolute plural feminine is ܢ; of the construct ܬ; of the emphatic ܬܐ.

5. Remains of a dual appear in the words for *two* and *two hundred*. In construction they take the same form as the plural.

L

ELEMENTS OF SYRIAC. [§ 77

§ 77. Nouns with Suffixes.

	Masc. sing.	Masc. plur.	Fem. sing.	Fem. plur.
Abs.				
Const.				
Emph.				
Sing. 1. c.				
2. m.				
2. f.				
3. m.				
3. f.				
Plur. 1. c.				
2. m.				
2. f.				
3. m.				
3. f.				

4. ܐܘܪܚܬܗܘܢ (14:5); ܐܘܪܚܬܝ (Heb. 3:10); ܐܘܪܚܬܗ (Acts 13:10); ܐܓܪܬܟܘܢ (Jam. 5:4).

5. ܠܪܓܠܝܗܘܢ (28:17); ܡܫܟܢܬܗ (28:14); ܡܪܥܝܬܝ (13:4); ܒܝܬܗ (13:9); ܠܬܠܡܝܕܝܗ (14:14).

6. ܟܘܪܣܝܗ (13:15); ܟܘܪܣܝܗ (Acts 2:30); ܟܘܪܣܝ (Acts 7:49); ܚܣܝܟ (Acts 2:27); ܛܠܝܝ (Lk. 7:7).

For a tabular view of the pronominal suffixes with nouns, see § 36. The form of the noun before suffixes is in general the same as the form of the noun before the emphatic ending ܐ. It is to be noted, however, that

1. The masculine plural has the suffixes appended directly to the diphtong ܝ̈, causing ܝ instead of *ayi* with the 1st sing. suffix; ܘܗܝ instead of *ayhu* with the 3rd masc. sing.; and ܝܗ instead of *ayah* with the 3rd fem. sing.

2. The feminine singular inserts a helping vowel before the grave suffixes ܗܘܢ, ܗܝܢ, ܟܘܢ, ܟܝܢ and before the ܝ of the 1st sing.

3. The dual takes the plural form before suffixes, (see 5 above and § 76.5).

4. Some prepositions take the plural form before suffixes.

5. Nouns which end in ܝܐ in the emphatic sing. retain this ܝ before the suffixes of the 2nd and 3rd sing. and of the 1st plur. ܟܘܪܣܝܐ *throne*, ܡܫܪܝܐ *camp*, and ܡܫܬܝܐ *drink* have forms like ܟܘܪܣܝ with the 1st sing. suffix; other nouns have ܝܝ like ܛܠܝܝ *my boy*. (Nestorian ܛܠܝܝ). Before the grave suffixes, *i. e.* those of the 2nd and 3rd plural, the Jacobites have with ܟܘܪܣܝܐ &c the form ܟܘܪܣܝܗܘܢ (the Nestorians ܟܘܪܣܝܗܘܢ); with other nouns, both dialects have ܝܗܘܢ.

6. Short adjectives and participles, like ܚܣܝܐ, can either retain or drop the Yudh before suffixes, *e. g.* ܚܣܝܘܗܝ or ܚܣܝܘܗܝ *his saints*; but substantives have always the shorter form, *e. g.* ܡܥܘܗܝ *his bowels.*

7. Collectives, which have no plural, take the suffixes of the sing. nouns and are marked with Rebbuy; but ܐܢܫܐ, abs. ܐܢܫܝܢ, takes the plural form, and ܩܘܪܝܐ *cities* has either the sing. or the plur. form *e. g.* ܩܘܪܝܗ or ܩܘܪܝܗ.

§ 78. Declension of Nouns.

For purposes of inflection masculine nouns may be divided into three classes or declensions; feminine nouns, into four, as follows:

I. Masculine Nouns.

1. Those which have but one vowel in the absolute singular and that movable. This includes most nouns which had originally one or two short vowels.
2. Those which have one or more vowels all immovable.
3. Those which have at least two vowels,—the vowel of the ultimate being movable and that of the penult immovable.

II. Feminine Nouns.

1. Those in which the vowel before the ending is movable.
2. Those in which the vowel of the penult is immovable, but which have a vowel inserted before the emphatic singular ending and before the construct singular with suffixes.
3. Those in which all the vowels of the first form, *i. e.*, of the absolute singular, are immovable and which do not insert a helping vowel.
4. Those whose first form ends in ܘ or ܝ or which insert a Yudh in the plural.

§ 79. First Declension of Masculines.

A.

	malk (*king*).	zedk (*righteousness*).	kudsh (*holiness*).	karakh (*city*).
Abs. sing.	ܡܠܟ	ܙܕܩ	ܩܘܕܫ	ܟܪܟ
Cons. sing.	ܡܠܟ	ܙܕܩ	ܩܘܕܫ	ܟܪܟ
Emph. sing.	ܡܠܟܐ	ܙܕܩܐ	ܩܘܕܫܐ	ܟܪܟܐ
Const. sing. with ܗ "*his*".	ܡܠܟܗ	ܙܕܩܗ	ܩܘܕܫܗ	ܟܪܟܗ
Abs. plur.	ܡܠܟܝܢ	ܙܕܩܝܢ	ܩܘܕܫܝܢ	ܟܪܟܝܢ
Const. plur.	ܡܠܟܝ	ܙܕܩܝ	ܩܘܕܫܝ	ܟܪܟܝ
Emph. plur.	ܡ̈ܠܟܐ	ܙܕ̈ܩܐ	ܩܘܕ̈ܫܐ	ܟܪ̈ܟܐ
Const. plur. with "*his*".	ܡܠܟܘܗܝ	ܙܕܩܘܗܝ	ܩܘܕܫܘܗܝ	ܟܪܟܘܗܝ

It will be seen that this declension includes nouns which had originally one or two short vowels.

Remark 1.—Forms Pê Olaph like ܐܓܪ *hire* and ܐܠܦ *ship,* come under this class.—The first vowel being merely a helping vowel § 33(1).

Remark 2.—Forms Pê Yudh like ܝܪܚ *month* are also in the class, the ܶ being a helping vowel § 33(1).

Remark 3.—Forms like ܕܗܒ and ܩܪܒ which had originally two short vowels, have come in inflection to coincide with Segholates in almost all respects. It will be noted that they preserve the half-vowel before the aspirate *e. g.* dăhebhâ not dăh-bâ.—Comp. שִׁבְכָה.

B.

	yawm (*day*).	ʿayn (*eye*).	ṭaby (*gazelle*).	kanay (*cane*).	kashiy (*hard*).
Abs. sing.	ܝܘܡ	ܥܝܢ			ܩܫܐ
Cons. sing.	ܝܘܡ	ܥܝܢ			
Emph. sing.	ܝܘܡܐ	ܥܝܢܐ	ܛܒܝܐ	ܩܢܝܐ	ܩܫܝܐ
Abs. plur.	ܝܘܡܝܢ	ܥܝܢܝܢ	ܛܒܝܢ	ܩܢܝܢ	ܩܫܝܢ
Cons. plur.	ܝܘܡܝ	ܥܝܢܝ	ܛܒܝ	ܩܢܝ	ܩܫܝ
Emph. plur.	ܝܘܡܐ	ܥܝܢܐ	ܛܒܝܐ	ܩܢܝܐ	ܩܫܝܐ

1. Ê Waw and Ê Yudh segholates of the *a* class contract *aw* into û (Nestorian ȯ) and *ay* into î (Nestorian ê) in the absolute and construct singular.

2. Lomadh Olaph segholates with the exception of ܛܠܐ are found in the singular only in the emphatic state. In the plural the form ܛܒܝܢ becomes ܛܒܝܢ but instead of ܛܒܝܐ we find ܛܒܝܐ as if from nouns which have two short vowels. The same is true of most nouns of this kind; we find, however, ܨܪܝܐ *rents* and ܩܪܝܐ *colds.*

3. Lomadh Olaph nouns which have originally two short vowels, have in the plural the same forms as nouns which had one short vowel, *e. g.* ܩܰܢܝܳܐ *cane,* in table above.

4. But adjectives from Lomadh Olaph roots differ from the nouns in having forms like ܥܰܡܡܺܝ̈, instead of ܥܰܡܡܺܝ in the plural absolute (compare עֲנִיִּים) and like ܥܰܡܡܰܝ̈ in the plural construct.

Remark 1.—Segholates of the *i* and *u* classes from Ê Waw and Ê Yudh verbs come under declension two *e. g.* ܕܺܝܢ, and ܐܘܿܢ.

Remark 2.—Segholates from Ê Olaph, Ê Nun, and ÊÊ verbs come under the third declension, *e. g.* ܪܺܫ *head* (R. ראש); ܓܐܘܿ *well*; ܐܟܳܐ *oppression* (R. ܗܕܐ); ܟܰܡ *people* (R. עמם).

Remark 3.—Nouns like ܩܳܠ *voice* (from kăwălô) and ܣܳܒ *old* (from ܣܐܒ) which had originally two short vowels come under the third declension.

Remark 4.—With consonantal Olaph as the third Radical, we have ܛܰܡܐܳ, ܛܰܡܐܺܝ̈ *unclean*. The vowel of the Olaph being thrown back and the Olaph quiescing. See § 24(1).

§ 80. Second Declension of Masculines.

	rabb (*many*).	kawal (*voice*).	gannobh (*thief*).	kărâbh (*war*).	dîn (*judgment*).	malkây (*royal*).
Abs. sing.	ܪܰܒ	ܩܳܠ	ܓܰܢܳܒ	ܩܪܳܒ	ܕܺܝܢ	ܡܰܠܟܰܝ
Cons. sing.	ܪܰܒ	ܩܳܠ	ܓܰܢܳܒ	ܩܪܳܒ	ܕܺܝܢ	ܡܰܠܟܰܝ
Emph. sing.	ܪܰܒܳܐ	ܩܳܠܳܐ	ܓܰܢܳܒܳܐ	ܩܪܳܒܳܐ	ܕܺܝܢܳܐ	ܡܰܠܟܳܝܳܐ
Abs. plur.	ܪܰܒܺܝܢ	ܩܳܠܺܝܢ	ܓܰܢܳܒܺܝܢ	ܩܪܳܒܺܝܢ	ܕܺܝܢܺܝܢ	ܡܰܠܟܳܝܺܝܢ
Cons. plur.	ܪܰܒܰܝ	ܩܳܠܰܝ	ܓܰܢܳܒܰܝ	ܩܪܳܒܰܝ	ܕܺܝܢܰܝ	ܡܰܠܟܳܝܰܝ
Emph. plur.	ܪܰܒܶܐ	ܩܳܠܶܐ	ܓܰܢܳܒܶܐ	ܩܪܳܒܶܐ	ܕܺܝܢܶܐ	ܡܰܠܟܳܝܶܐ

Remark 1.—ܥܰܡ *people* and ܝܰܡ *sea* are inflected like ܪܶܫ, except that in the plural we have the forms ܥܰܡܡܺܝܢ, ܥܰܡܡܶܐ, ܝܰܡܡܺܝܢ, ܝܰܡܡܶܐ. Compare הֲרָרֵי from הַר.

Remark 2.—The *i* and *u* class segholates from Ê Waw and Ê Yudh verbs come under this declension; as also, ÊÊ and Ê Nun segholates, *e. g.* ܪܽܘܚ *spirit,* ܪܺܝܚ *smell,* ܐܰܦܶܐ (R. אנף) *face,* ܠܶܒܳܐ (R. לבב) *heart.*

Remark 3.—Nouns from Ê Waw and Ê Olaph roots which had originally two short ă vowels belong to this declension, *e. g.* ܩܳܠ *voice* from kăwălâ, ܛܳܒ *good* from tawabhâ, ܣܳܒ *old* from sa'abhâ.

Remark 4.—Here are to be found all nouns which had originally a short vowel in the penult, and a long one in the ultimate, *e. g.* ܩܪܳܒ *war;* ܣܺܝܡ *put;* ܓܙܺܝܙܳܐ *shorn;* ܥܠܰܝܡܽܘܬܳܐ *youth;* ܪܚܺܝܡܳܐ *beloved.*

Remark 5.—Here are to be classed all nouns which have a naturally long vowel or a closed syllable in the penult and a naturally long vowel in the ultimate, *e. g.* ܩܳܛܽܘܠܳܐ *murderer;* ܐܰܓܡܳܐ *swamp;* ܡܰܠܳܚ *sailor;* ܙܰܟܳܝ *victorious;* ܠܶܫܳܢ *tongue;* ܫܽܘܐܳܠܳܐ *question;* ܩܰܪܺܝܒ *near;* ܝܰܠܽܘܕ *child;* ܚܰܡܽܘܨ *sour;* ܚܶܫܽܘܟ *darkness;* ܡܰܬܩܽܘܠܳܐ *weight;* ܡܰܒܽܘܥܳܐ *fountain;* ܥܶܠܺܝܬܳܐ, *roof-story, building;* ܡܶܣܟܺܢ *poor;* ܡܕܺܝܢܬܳܐ *city;* ܬܽܘܥܕܳܪܳܐ *help;* ܬܰܡܠܽܘܩܳܐ *flattery;* ܬܰܘܬܳܒܳܐ *settler;* ܥܽܘܪܕܥܳܐ *frog;* ܡܰܘܬܳܢܳܐ *pest* (and all nouns ending in ܘܢ ܘܬ etc.)

§ 81. Third Declension of Masculines.

	sâhidh (*witness*)	'emmar (*lamb*).	madbaḥ (*altar*).	shâthăy (*drinking*).	mashtăy (*banquet*).	maḥzăy (*vision*).
Abs. sing.	ܣܳܗܶܕ	ܐܶܡܰܪ	ܡܰܕܒܰܚ	ܫܳܬܶܐ	ܡܰܫܬܝ	ܡܰܚܙܳܐ
Cons. Sing.	ܣܳܗܶܕ	ܐܶܡܰܪ	ܡܰܕܒܰܚ	ܫܳܬܶܐ	ܡܰܫܬܝ	ܡܰܚܙܳܐ
Emph. Sing.	ܣܳܗܕܳܐ	ܐܶܡܪܳܐ	ܡܰܕܒܚܳܐ	ܫܳܬܝܳܐ	ܡܰܫܬܝܳܐ	ܡܰܚܙܝܳܐ
Abs. plur.	ܣܳܗܕܺܝܢ	ܐܶܡܪܺܝܢ	ܡܰܕܒܚܺܝܢ	ܫܳܬܶܝܢ	ܡܰܫܬܶܝܢ	ܡܰܚܙܶܝܢ
Cons. plur.	ܣܳܗܕܰܝ	ܐܶܡܪܰܝ	ܡܰܕܒܚܰܝ	ܫܳܬܰܝ	ܡܰܫܬܰܝ	ܡܰܚܙܰܝ
Emph. plur.	ܣܳܗܕܶܐ	ܐܶܡܪܶܐ	ܡܰܕܒܚܶܐ	ܫܳܬܝܶܐ	ܡܰܫܬܝܶܐ	ܡܰܚܙܝܶܐ

Here belong nouns of the forms ܩܶܛܠ, ܩܛܳܠ, ܩܰܛܠ, ܩܰܛܶܠ, ܩܛܽܘܠ, ܡܰܩܛܠ, ܡܶܩܛܳܠ, ܡܰܩܛܰܠ, ܡܰܩܛܽܘܠ, ܡܰܩܛܠܽܘܠ etc.

Remark.—Some Syriac grammarians give an absolute singular form ܪܕܽܘܦ for ܪܕܽܘܦܝܳܐ ܪܕܽܘ̈ܦܝܳܐ *persecution.* This would place it in this declension, and also nouns like it such as ܚܛܽܘܦܝܳܐ *rapine;* ܛܠܽܘܡܝܳܐ *oppression;* ܚܒܽܘܩܝܳܐ *embrace.*

§ 82. First Declension of Feminines.

	hăbhrăth (*companion*).	ʽĕghlăth (*calf*).	mŭshhâth (*measure*).	yădhʽăth (*science*).	tălyăth (*girl*).	mahwăth (*blow*).
Abs. sing.	ܚܰܒܪܳܐ	ܥܶܓܠܳܐ	ܡܫܽܘܚܳܐ	ܝܰܕܥܳܐ	ܛܰܠܝܳܐ	ܡܰܚܘܳܐ
Cons. sing.	ܚܰܒܪܰܬ	ܥܶܓܠܰܬ	ܡܫܽܘܚܰܬ	ܝܰܕܥܰܬ	ܛܰܠܝܰܬ	ܡܰܚܘܰܬ
Emph. sing.	ܚܰܒܪܬܳܐ	ܥܶܓܠܬܳܐ	ܡܫܽܘܚܬܳܐ	ܝܺܕܰܥܬܳܐ	ܛܠܺܝܬܳܐ	ܡܰܚܘܬܳܐ
Abs. sing.	ܚܰܒܪ̈ܳܢ	ܥܶܓ̈ܠܳܢ	ܡܫܽܘ̈ܚܳܢ	ܝܰܕ̈ܥܳܢ	ܛܰܠ̈ܝܳܢ	ܡܰܚ̈ܘܳܢ
Cons. plur.	ܚܰܒܪ̈ܳܬ	ܥܶܓ̈ܠܳܬ	ܡܫܽܘ̈ܚܳܬ	ܝܰܕ̈ܥܳܬ	ܛܰܠ̈ܝܳܬ	ܡܰܚ̈ܘܳܬ
Emph. plur.	ܚܰܒܪ̈ܳܬܳܐ	ܥܶܓ̈ܠܳܬܳܐ	ܡܫܽܘ̈ܚܳܬܳܐ	ܝܰܕ̈ܥܳܬܳܐ	ܛܰܠ̈ܝܳܬܳܐ	ܡܰܚ̈ܘܳܬܳܐ

These are nouns which had originally in the masculine one or two short vowels.

Remark 1.—In Pê Yudh nouns like ܝܰܕܥܳܐ, the Yudh quiesces in when it would otherwise have a half-vowel.

Remark 2.—In Ê Waw nouns the diphthong passes over into ܘ in the emphatic singular and in the singular with suffixes, *e. g.* ܬܰܘܪܬܳܐ *cow*; ܟܢܽܘܫܬܳܐ *collection.*

Remark 3.—In segholate feminines from Lomadh Olaph roots the Yudh quiesces in its homogeneous vowel in the emphatic singular and before suffixes. Generally, this causes the preceding consonant to lose its vowel, *e. g.* ܛܠܺܝܬܳܐ. For exceptions, see § 85.

Remark 4.—Like ܛܠܝܬܐ are ܕܟܝܬܐ *pure* and ܩܫܝܬܐ *hard*, and, in general, participles and adjectives of the form ܩܫܝܐ, ܕܟܝܐ.

Remark 5.—Instead of ܡܚܘܬܐ, some give the abs. sing. as ܡܚܘ, making it like ܪܒܘ Declension IV. ܣܚܘܬܐ *bath* is in the singular like ܡܚܘܬܐ, but in the plural it has ܣܚܘܢܬܐ.

Remark 6.—Feminine nouns in ܝܬܐ from masculines in ܝ or ܘܝ are inflected like ܛܠܝܬܐ, except that the vowels of the penult remain firm. So also, feminine nouns in ܬܐ from masculines of the form ḳâtûl, *e. g.* ܡܠܟܘܢܝܬܐ *little queen;* ܚܒܘܠܝܬܐ *perishable things.*

Remark 7.—Nouns like ܥܩܬܐ *affliction* from ʿăwăḳâ have in the construct ܥܩܬ, emphatic ܥܩܬܐ.

§ 83. Second Declension of Feminines.

	'armalăth (*widow*).	zĕdhḳăth (*alms*).	ʿâgilăth (*carriage*).	hăywăth (*animal*).	ṣûḥyăth (*opprobrium*).	shânĭyăth (*foolish*).
Abs. sing.	ܐܪܡܠܐ	ܙܕܩܐ	ܥܓܠܐ	ܚܝܘܐ	ܨܘܚܝܐ	ܫܢܝܐ
Cons. sing.	ܐܪܡܠܬ	ܙܕܩܬ	ܥܓܠܬ	ܚܝܘܬ	ܨܘܚܝܬ	ܫܢܝܬ
Emph. sing.	ܐܪܡܠܬܐ	ܙܕܩܬܐ	ܥܓܠܬܐ	ܚܝܘܬܐ	ܨܘܚܝܬܐ	ܫܢܝܬܐ
Abs. sing.	ܐܪܡܠܢ	ܙܕܩܢ	ܥܓܠܢ	ܚܝܘܢ	ܨܘܚܝܢ	ܫܢܝܢ
Cons. sing.	ܐܪܡܠܬ	ܙܕܩܬ	ܥܓܠܬ	ܚܝܘܬ	ܨܘܚܝܬ	ܫܢܝܬ
Emph. sing.	ܐܪܡܠܬܐ	ܙܕܩܬܐ	ܥܓܠܬܐ	ܚܝܘܬܐ	ܨܘܚܝܬܐ	ܫܢܝܬܐ

It should be noticed that the only change in these nouns is the insertion of a helping vowel before the ending of the emphatic singular and before the pronominal suffixes with the singular.

Remark 1.—Active Participles from Lomadh Olaph verbs, and nouns like them, change the Yudh into the homogeneous vowel in the emphatic singular and in the singular before suffixes.

Remark 2.—Like ܣܺܝܡܳܐ is ܚܰܕܽܘܬܳܐ *joy*, perhaps, also, ܡܢܳܬܳܐ *part.* Like ܪܳܘܡܳܐ, are ܐܽܘܟܠܳܐ *lamentation;* ܩܽܘܒܥܳܐ *cap;* ܩܽܘܒܰܚ *chant;* ܩܽܘܪܝܳܐ *city;* ܬܽܘܢܳܝܳܐ *recital.* For other nouns of this kind, see § 85. 3.

§ 84. Third Declension of Feminines.

	bathûlăth (*virgin*).	zăddîkăth (*righteous*).	sâhĭdăth (*witness*).
Abs. sing.	ܒܬܘܠܳܐ	ܐܙܕܝܩܳܐ	ܣܳܗܕܳܐ
Cons. sing.	ܒܬܘܠܰܬ	ܐܙܕܝܩܰܬ	ܣܳܗܕܰܬ
Emph. sing.	ܒܬܘܠܬܳܐ	ܐܙܕܝܩܬܳܐ	ܣܳܗܕܬܳܐ
Abs. plur.	ܒܬܘܠܳܢ	ܐܙܕܝܩܳܢ	ܣܳܗܕܳܢ
Cons. plur.	ܒܬܘܠܳܬ	ܐܙܕܝܩܳܬ	ܣܳܗܕܳܬ
Emph. sing.	ܒܬܘܠܳܬܳܐ	ܐܙܕܝܩܳܬܳܐ	ܣܳܗܕܳܬܳܐ

No changes take place in this declension, the endings for gender, number and state being affixed directly to the noun stem.

§ 85. Fourth Declension of Feminines.

	săbhwâth (thing).	băryâth (creature).	ṣalawath (?) (prayer).	kârĭyîth (beam).	mălăkûth (kingdom).
Abs. sing.	ܣܒ݂ܘܳܬ݂	ܒܪܝܳܬ݂	?	ܩܳܪܝܺܬ݂	ܡܰܠܟܽܘܬ݂
Cons. sing.	ܣܒ݂ܘܰܬ݂	ܒܪܝܰܬ݂	?	ܩܳܪܝܰܬ݂	ܡܰܠܟܽܘܬ݂
Emph. sing.	ܣܒ݂ܘܬ݂ܳܐ	ܒܪܝܬ݂ܳܐ	ܨܠܽܘܬ݂ܳܐ	ܩܳܪܝܺܬ݂ܳܐ	ܡܰܠܟܽܘܬ݂ܳܐ
Abs. plur.	ܣܒ݂ܘܳܢ	ܒܪܝܳܢ	ܨܠܘܳܢ	ܩܳܪܝܳܢ	ܡܰܠܟܘܳܢ
Cons. plur.	ܣܒ݂ܘܳܬ݂	ܒܪܝܳܬ݂	ܨܠܘܳܬ݂	ܩܳܪܝܳܬ݂	ܡܰܠܟܘܳܬ݂
Emph. plur.	ܣܒ݂ܘܳܬ݂ܳܐ	ܒܪܝܳܬ݂ܳܐ	ܨܠܘܳܬ݂ܳܐ	ܩܳܪܝܳܬ݂ܳܐ	ܡܰܠܟܘܳܬ݂ܳܐ

All nouns of this declension end in ܘ or ܝ in the abs. sing. except nouns like ܨܠܽܘ which, however, in the plural are formed like ܩܳܪܝ.

1. Like ܣܒ݂ܘ is ܕܡܘ *likeness*.
2. Like ܒܪܝ are ܓܒܺܝܬ݂ܳܐ *choice*; ܐܰܠܝܬ݂ܳܐ *fat tail of a sheep*; ܥܠܶܩܬ݂ܳܐ שִׁלְיָה *embryo*, ܓܶܒܬ݂ܳܐ *side*.
3. Like ܨܠܽܘ are ܫܳܩܐ *leg* and ܣܪܳܐ *sawdust*.
4. Like ܩܳܪܝ are all nouns of two or more syllables ending in ܝ such as ܟܣܳܝܬ݂ *covering*; ܪܶܒܝܬ݂ *interest*; ܡܰܪܕܝܬ݂ *gait*.
5. Like ܡܰܠܟܽܘ are most nouns of two or more syllables ending in ܘ such as ܒܳܥܽܘ *request*, ܣܳܗܕܽܘ *testimony*.

Remark 1.—ܐܰܣܝܽܘܬ݂ܳܐ *healing* has in the plural ܐܰܣܘܳܬ݂ܳܐ see Lk. 13:32. ܡܕܰܒܪܳܢܽܘܬ݂ܳܐ *government* has in the plural ܡܕܰܒܪܳܢܘܳܬ݂ܳܐ. ܓܰܒܪܽܘܬ݂ܳܐ *manhood* has for plural ܓܰܒܪܘܳܬ݂ܳܐ *wonders* Acts 5:12. ܝܳܪܬܽܘܬ݂ܳܐ *inheritance*; ܣܳܗܕܽܘܬ݂ܳܐ *testimony*, and ܦܶܠܓܽܘܬ݂ܳܐ *half*, have in the plural beside the regular forms ܦܵܐܪ̈ܶܐ, ܣܰܘ̈ܩܶܐ, the forms ܦܳܐܟ̈ܐ, ܣܰܘ̈ܩܐ.

Rem. 2.—The Infinitives of the derived stems end in ܘ in the absolute and in ܘ in the construct state, see § 49. 2.

§ 86. Anomalies of Gender or Number or State.

1. Some masculine nouns form plurals from a lengthened form in ܶܐ.

ܐܳܐܪ *fruit;* ܐܰܢ̈ܐ or ܐܰܐ̈.

ܒܣܰܪ *flesh;* ܒܶܣܪ̈ܐ or ܒܣܪ̈ܐ.

ܒܶܣܡܐ *incense;* ܒܶܣ̈ܡܢܐ or ܒܣ̈ܡܐ.

ܓܢܣ *genus;* ܓܢ̈ܣܢܐ or ܓܢ̈ܣܐ.

ܚܡܪܐ *wine;* ܚܡܪ̈ܢܐ.

ܡܫܚܐ *ointment;* ܡܫ̈ܚܢܐ.

ܪܝܚܐ *odour;* ܪܝ̈ܚܢܐ or ܪܝ̈ܚܐ.

ܪܰܒܝ *teacher;* ܪܒ̈ܝ *teachers.*

ܪܘܪ̈ܒܢܐ *magnates.*

ܣܡܐ *medicine;* ܣ̈ܡܢܐ.

ܫܠܝܛܐ *prefect;* ܫ̈ܠܝܛܢܐ or ܫ̈ܠܝܛܐ.

Note.—So also the feminine ܐ̱ܚܪܬܐ *other,* pl. ܐ̱ܚܪ̈ܢܝܬܐ, adding ܬ according to 4 below.

2. Some masculine substantives form their plural with the ending ܘܳܬܐ *e. g.*

(1) ܐܰܬܪܐ *place;* ܐܰܬܪ̈ܘܬܐ (ܐܰܬܪ̈ܐ)

ܚܝܠܐ *power;* ܚ̈ܝܠܘܬܐ or ܚ̈ܝܠܐ.

ܠܒܐ *heart;* ܠܒ̈ܘܬܐ.

ܢܗܪܐ *river;* ܢܗܪ̈ܘܬܐ.

(2) Many in ܐ form their plural in this manner, *e. g.*

ܐܰܪܝܐ *lion;* ܐܰܪ̈ܝܘܬܐ.

§ 86.] ELEMENTS OF SYRIAC.

ܬܕܳܐ *breast;* ܬܕܘ̈ܬܳܐ.
ܚܘܝܳܐ *serpent;* ܚܘܘ̈ܬܳܐ.
ܟܘܪܣܝܳܐ *throne;* ܟܘܪܣܘ̈ܬܳܐ.
ܠܠܝܳܐ *night;* ܠܝ̈ܠܘܬܳܐ.
ܣܘܣܝܳܐ *horse;* ܣܘܣܘ̈ܬܳܐ.

So also the substantive participles in ܝܳܐ *e. g.* ܪܳܥܝܳܐ *shepherd;* ܐܳܣܝܳܐ *physician;* ܡܳܪܝܳܐ *Lord.*

Note.—Many words of Greek origin, especially feminine, form their plurals with the same ending, *e. g.* ܦܠܰܛܝ̈ܳܬܳܐ=plural of πλατεῖα, ܐܣܛܕܝܘܢ, στάδιον plural=ܐܣܛܕܝ̈ܘܬܳܐ.

3. Some feminine nouns form their plural in ܘܳܬܳܐ.

ܐܶܡܬܳܐ *people;* ܐܶܡܘ̈ܬܳܐ.
ܐܶܫܬܳܐ *wall;* ܐܶܫܘ̈ܬܳܐ generally ܐܶܫ̈ܐ.
ܐܳܬܳܐ *sign;* ܐܳܬܘ̈ܬܳܐ.
ܐܶܫܬܳܐ *fever;* ܐܶܫܘ̈ܬܳܐ.
ܢܘܪܳܐ *fire;* ܢܘܪܘ̈ܬܳܐ.
ܣܶܦܬܳܐ *lip;* ܣܶܦܘ̈ܬܳܐ.

4. Some feminines, especially diminutives in ܝܬܳܐ, form their plurals in ܝ̈ܳܬܳܐ *e. g.*

ܕܘܟܬܳܐ *place;* ܕܘܟ̈ܝܳܬܳܐ.
ܟܘܬܝܢܳܐ *tunic;* ܟܘܬܝ̈ܢܝܳܬܳܐ.
ܕܪܬܝܬܳܐ *little court;* ܕܪܬܝ̈ܳܬܳܐ.

5. Some feminine nouns which in the singular have ܬܳܐ (âthâ from awăthâ) have ܘܳܬܳܐ in the plural *e. g.*

ܡܢܳܬܳܐ (מְנָת) *part;* ܡܢ̈ܘܳܬܳܐ; ܟܪܥܳܐ *thumb;* ܕܶܒܚܳܐ *sacrifice;* ܚܒܪܳܐ *fellow.*

But some of these are treated as if the ܬ belonged to the stem, *e. g.* ܒܥܘܬܳܐ *request;* ܒܥ̈ܘܳܬܳܐ *see* 9 *below.*

94   ELEMENTS OF SYRIAC.   [§ 86.

6. Feminine nouns in ܳܐ, § 75. 6, are indeclinable, e. g.

ܛܽܘܥܝܰܝ error; ܐ̱ܪܳܙܳܐ secret; ܣܰܠܘܰܝ quail; ܙܢܳܐ condition.

7. Many nouns of feminine gender have in the singular no feminine ending, but take one in the plural.

ܐܽܘܪܚܳܐ way;   ܐܰܪܥܳܐ earth;   ܓܽܘܫܡܳܐ body;   ܓܰܒܳܐ side;

ܚܰܩܠܳܐ field;   ܢܰܦܫܳܐ soul;   ܟܰܬܦܳܐ shoulder;   ܥܰܪܣܳܐ bed.

8. Some feminine nouns, having originally the sense of a *nomen unitatis*, have the feminine form in the singular but the masculine in the plural. Duval gives a list of sixty-four such nouns, in § 270. Among those occurring most frequently are:

ܐܰܡܬܳܐ ell; ܐܰܡܺܝ̈ܢ.	ܓܠܺܝܡܬܳܐ mantle; ܓܠܺܝ̈ܡܶܐ.
ܒܰܥܬܳܐ egg; ܒܶܥ̈ܶܐ.	ܡܶܠܬܳܐ word; ܡܶܠ̈ܶܐ.
ܓܰܢܬܳܐ garden; ܓܰܢ̈ܶܐ.	ܥܶܢܒܬܳܐ grape; ܥܶܢ̈ܒܶܐ.
ܕܶܡܥܬܳܐ tear; ܕܶܡ̈ܥܶܐ.	ܩܨܳܬܳܐ lot; ܩܶܨ̈ܶܐ.
ܚܶܛܬܳܐ wheat; ܚܶܛ̈ܶܐ.	ܫܰܒܬܳܐ sabbath; ܫܰܒ̈ܶܐ.
ܢܽܘܩܬܳܐ drop; ܢܽܘܩ̈ܶܐ.	ܫܳܥܬܳܐ hour; ܫܳܥ̈ܶܐ.

9. Some nouns have treated the ܬ of the fem. sing. as a radical and have their plurals as if masculine, e. g.

ܒܶܙܬܳܐ booty; ܒܶܙ̈ܳܬܳܐ.	ܡܰܕܰܐܬܳܐ tribute; ܡܰܕܰܐ̈ܬܳܐ.
ܒܳܥܽܘܬܳܐ request; ܒܳܥ̈ܘܳܬܳܐ.	ܕܶܒܚܬܳܐ sacrifice; ܕܶܒܚ̈ܳܬܳܐ.
ܓܥܳܬܳܐ cry; ܓܥ̈ܳܬܳܐ.	ܨܶܦܬܳܐ care; ܨܶܦ̈ܳܬܳܐ.
ܚܙܳܬܳܐ view; ܚܙ̈ܳܬܳܐ.	ܩܥܳܬܳܐ cry; ܩܥ̈ܳܬܳܐ.

10. Some nouns are masculine in form but feminine in gender, e. g. ܒܺܪܳܐ well; ܒܽܘܪܟܳܐ knee. (See full list in Nöld. § 84.)

11. Some nouns have two plurals, sometimes the same, sometimes different in meaning. (See Duval § 272) e. g.

ܥܰܝܢܳܐ eye, spring;	ܥܰܝܢ̈ܶܐ eyes;	ܥܰܝܢ̈ܳܬܳܐ springs.
ܐܶܕܢܳܐ ear;	ܐܶܕܢ̈ܶܐ ears;	ܐܶܕܢ̈ܳܬܳܐ handles.
ܐܺܝܕܳܐ hand;	ܐܺܝܕ̈ܶܐ hands;	ܐܺܝܕ̈ܳܘܳܬܳܐ handles.

ܪܘܚܐ *wind, spirit;* ܪܘܚܶܐ *winds;* ܪܘܚܳܬܐ *spirits.*

ܕܰܝܪܐ *dwelling;* ܕܰܝܪܶܐ *dwellings;* ܕܰܝܪܳܬܐ *convents.*

ܪܰܒܐ *great;* ܪܰܒܶܐ or ܪܰܘܪܒܶܐ *great;* ܪܰܒܰܝ *masters;* ܪܰܘܪܒܳܢܐ *magnates.*

12. Some nouns are of common gender, *e. g.*

ܒܥܺܝܪܐ *cattle;* ܕܰܝܪܐ *dwelling;* ܣܰܝܦܐ *sword;* ܣܰܗܪܐ *moon;*

ܫܶܡܫܐ *sun;* ܪܩܺܝܥܐ *firmament;* ܫܡܰܝܐ *heaven;* ܪܘܚܐ *wind.*

13. Before the feminine ending, many nouns insert a Yudh.

(1) Words ending in ܶ or ܳ, *e. g* ܩܳܛܶܠ *murdering,* f. ܩܳܛܠܳܝܬܐ; ܡܰܠܟܘܢܐ *little king;* ܡܰܠܟܘܢܺܝܬܐ *little queen.*

(2) Probably nouns of the form ḳâṭûl *e. g.* ܩܳܛܘܠܐ *murderer,* ܩܳܛܘܠܬܐ; ܚܳܠܘܦܳܝܬܐ *transitory things.*

(3) The adjective ܙܥܘܪ *small,* anywhere except in the emphatic singular which is ܙܥܘܪܬܐ.

14. A few nouns insert Hê before the plural ending, *e. g.* ܐܰܒܳܗܶܐ or ܐܰܒܳܗܳܬܐ *fathers,* sing. ܐܰܒܐ; ܐܶܢܕܳܗܳܬܐ *handles,* sing. ܐܺܝܕܐ *hand;* ܚܡܳܗܶܐ *fathers in law,* sing. ܚܡܐ; ܫܡܳܗܶܐ or ܫܡܳܗܳܬܐ from ܫܡܐ *name;* ܐܶܡܗܶܐ or ܐܶܡܗܳܬܐ *mothers* from ܐܶܡܐ; ܐܶܣܢܳܬܐ *anvils,* sing. ܐܶܣܢܐ.

15. Nouns which had a letter assimilated, or dropped, in the singular, often preserve it in the plural, *e. g.* ܓܦܶܢ *vine* ܓܦܰܢܬܐ; ܓܒܶܢ *cheese* ܓܒܶܢܬܐ; ܠܒܶܢ *brick* ܠܒܶܢܬܐ; ܚܳܬ *sister* ܐܰܚܘܳܬܐ; ܝܰܡ *sea* ܝܰܡܡܳܬܐ; ܥܰܡ *people,* ܥܰܡܡܳܢܐ.

16. The original emphatic plural ending ܝܢ is still preserved in a few nouns, *e. g.* ܒܢܰܝܐ *sons;* ܡܰܝܐ *water;* ܫܡܰܝܐ *heaven;* ܫܢܰܝܐ *years;* ܐܺܝܕܰܝܐ *hands;* ܐܶܢܝ *kinds;* ܬܕܰܝܐ *breasts;* ܐܰܦܰܝ *curtains;* ܕܡܰܝܐ *price;* ܐܰܠܦܰܝ *thousands,*

17. Some nouns have but one state.

(1) Feminine nouns in ܰܝ are always in the absolute state, *e. g.* ܣܰܠܘܰܝ *quail;* ܥܰܕܰܝ *contract.*

(2) Some which have Waw for the third radical are used in the emphatic state only, *e. g.* ܫܰܠܘܐ *cessation;* ܙܺܝܘܐ *splendor.*

§ 87. Peculiar Anomalies of Nouns.

1. ܐܰܒܐ *father;* ܐܰܚܐ *brother* and ܚܡܐ *father in law,* have the forms ܐܰܒ, ܐܰܚ, ܚܡ before suffixes, except before the 1st sing. suffix where they

have ܐܒ, ܐܚ, ܚܡ. The plural are ܐ̈ܒܗܐ, ܐ̈ܚܗܐ or ܐ̈ܚܘܬܐ, and ܚ̈ܡܘܗܐ, *see* § 86. 14.

2. ܐܝܕܐ (for יְדָא § 24. 3, Note 1) *hand;* in construction with ܒ or ܠ, ܡܢ, elsewhere ܐܝܕ. Plur. ܐܝ̈ܕܝܐ, ܐܝ̈ܕܐ or in a figurative sense ܐܝ̈ܕܘܬܐ, *see* § 86. 14.

3. ܐܘܡܬܐ *nation, see* § 86. 3.

4. ܐܚܪܢܐ, pl. ܐܚܪ̈ܢܝܢ *other, see* § 86. 1, Note.

5. ܐܠܦ *thousand;* ܐܠܦܐ, Pl. ܐܠ̈ܦܝܢ, ܐܠ̈ܦܐ.

6. ܐܡܐ, ܐܡܬܐ *anvil;* Pl. ܐܡܗ̈ܬܐ § 86. 14.

7. ܐܡܐ *mother;* Pl. ܐܡܗ̈ܬܐ or ܐܡܗ̈ܐ § 86. 14.

8. ܐܢܬܬܐ *woman;* Pl. ܢܫ̈ܐ.

9. ܐܦ̈ܝܢ *face;* (R. אנף) singular in use ܦܐܬܐ (Heb. פֵּאָה).

10. ܒܪ *son;* ܒܪܗ *his son;* ܒܪܟܘܢ *your son;* Pl. ܒ̈ܢܝܢ, ܒ̈ܢܝܐ, ܒ̈ܢܝ.

11. ܒܪܬܐ *daughter,* cons. ܒܪܬ; ܒܪܬܝ *my daughter;* ܒܪܬܟ *thy daughter;* Pl. ܒ̈ܢܢ, ܒ̈ܢܬ, ܒ̈ܢܬܐ.

12. ܒܝܬܐ *house* (Mt. 12. 25 ܒܝܬ), cons. ܒܝܬ; ܒܝܬܗ *his house;* Pl. ܒ̈ܬܐ.

13. ܕܡ, ܕܡܐ *blood;* ܕܡܝ *my blood;* ܕܡܟ *thy blood,* Pl. ܕ̈ܡܐ.

14. ܙܢܐ *kind,* cons. ܙܢ (Nestorian ܙܢ); Pl. ܙ̈ܢܝܢ, ܙ̈ܢܝܐ, ܙ̈ܢܝ.

15. ܚܕܬ *new* ܚܕܬܐ, Pl. ܚ̈ܕܬܐ. Fem. sing. ܚܕܬܐ, Pl. ܚ̈ܕܬܬܐ, § 17. 3.

16. ܚܬܐ *sister;* ܚܬܝ *my sister,* Pl. ܐܚ̈ܘܬܐ; § 86. 3.

17. ܚܕܝܐ *breast,* Pl. ܚ̈ܕܘܬܐ § 86. 2 but also ܚ̈ܕܝܐ ܚܕܝܗܘܢ *their breasts* Lk. 23. 48.

18. ܛܠܝܐ, f. ܛܠܝܬܐ *young* forms the plural ܛ̈ܠܝܐ ܛ̈ܠܝܢ ܛ̈ܠܝܬܐ as also in the meaning *"servant";* but when it means *"boy", „girl",* it forms the plural ܛܠ̈ܝܐ, ܛܠ̈ܝܢ f. ܛܠ̈ܝܬܐ.

19. ܠܠܝܐ or ܠܝܠܝܐ *night* (abs. ܠܠܝܐ or ܠܠܐ) Pl. ܠܠ̈ܘܬܐ.

20. ܡܐܐ *hundred. Nomen unitatis* ܡܐܬܐ, ܡܐܬܝܢ 200, ܡܐ̈ܘܬܐ (for ܡܐ̈ܐܬܐ) *hundreds.*

21. ܡܘܡܬܐ *oath* (R. ܝܡܐ), Pl. ܡܘ̈ܡܬܐ.

22. ܡܝܐ *water* abs. ܡܝܢ cons. ܡ̈ܝ. With suff. ܡܝ *my water,* ܡܝܟ or ܡ̈ܝܟ *thy water* &c.

23. ܡܳܪܝܳܐ or ܡܳܪܳܐ *lord*, cons. ܡܳܪܳܐ, ܡܳܪܝ *my lord;* ܡܳܪܗܽܘܢ *their lord*, Pl. ܡܳܪ̈ܰܘܳܬܳܐ or ܡܳܪ̈ܶܐ, abs. ܡܳܪ̈ܰܘܳܢ, cons. ܡܳܪ̈ܰܘܳܬ, (ܡܳܪ̈ܰܘܳܬܳܐ is also used). Fem. ܡܳܪܬܳܐ, ܡܳܪܰܬ, ܡܳܪ̈ܬܳܐ.

24. ܣܶܦܬܳܐ *lip;* ܣܶܦ̈ܘܳܬܳܐ, ܣܶܦ̈ܘܳܬ, ܣܶܦ̈ܘܳܬܳܐ § 86. 3.

25. ܩܰܛܽܘܬܳܐ *cucumber*, Pl. ܩܰܛ̈ܽܘܝܢܳܐ Num. 11. 5, ܩܰܛ̈ܽܘܝܢ, Also ܩܰܛ̈ܽܘܬܳܐ.

26. ܡܕܺܝܢ݈ܬܳܐ *city;* abs. ܡܕܺܝܢܳܐ, cons. ܡܕܺܝܢܰܬ or ܡܕܺܝܢܰܬ, Pl. ܡܕܺ̈ܝܢܳܐ, constr. ܡܕܺ̈ܝܢܳܬ. Pl. with suff. ܡܕܺ̈ܝܢܳܬܗܽܘܢ or ܡܕܺ̈ܝܢܳܬܟ. Other plurals ܡܕܺ̈ܝܢܳܬܳܐ and ܡܕܺ̈ܝܢܰܘܣ (this last is an imitation of the Greek. So also ܓܰ̈ܢܰܘܣ *gardens*). ܡܕܺܝܢܳܐ is a collective, *see* § 90. 1.

27. ܪܰܒ *great*, f. ܪܰܒܬܳܐ, Pl. ܪܰܘܪ̈ܒܺܝܢ (for ܪܰܒܪ̈ܒܺܝܢ). But in the sense of "*magnates*", the plural is ܪܰܘܪ̈ܒܳܢܶܐ, f. ܪܰܘܪ̈ܒܳܢܝܳܬܳܐ; in the sense of "*teachers*", it is ܪ̈ܰܒܳܢܶܐ, In certain constructions ܪ̈ܰܒܰܝ is used, *e. g.* ܪ̈ܰܒܰܝ ܡܳܘܬ݂ܳܢܶܐ (27:14), ܪ̈ܰܒܰܝ ܡܕܺܝܢܬܳܐ (Gal. 4:2).

28. ܫܡܰܝܳܐ *heaven;* ܫܡܰܝܳܢ, ܫܡܰ̈ܝܳܐ, ܫܡܰܝܟ. According to some, when ܫܡܰ̈ܝܳܐ has rebbuy, it means *heavens, e. g.* Mk. 1:10, Acts 7:56. According to form, it is always plural.

29. ܫܡܳܐ *name;* cons. ܫܶܡ, ܫܡܳܟ *thy name.* Pl. ܫܡܳܗ̈ܶܝܢ, § 86. 14 or ܫܡܳܗ̈ܳܬܳܐ.

30. ܫܰܢ݈ܬܳܐ *year;* abs. ܫܢܳܐ, cons. ܫܢܰܬ. Pl. ܫܢܰ̈ܝܳܐ, ܫܢܺ̈ܝܢ, ܫܢܰ̈ܝ (ܒܢܰ̈ܝ ܫܢܰ̈ܝ Gal. 2:14 sons of my years, *i. e.* my contemporaries).

31. ܫܶܬ *foundation*, whose plural is ܐܶܫܬܳܐܣܳܬܳܐ, is cons. of ܐܶܫܬܳܐܣܳܐ. The Olaph is prosthetic, *see* § 19. 1.

32. ܬܕܳܐ *breast*, Pl. ܬܕܰ̈ܝܢ, ܬܕ̈ܰܝܳܐ, ܬܕܰ̈ܝܗܽܘܢ (Rev. 1:13).

§ 88. The Numerals.

I. THE CARDINALS.

A.

	masc.	fem.		masc.	fem.
1	ܚܰܕ	ܚܕܳܐ	6	ܫܬܳܐ (ܐܶܫܬܳܐ)	ܫܶܬ
2	ܬܪܶܝܢ	ܬܰܪ̈ܬܶܝܢ	7	ܫܰܒܥܳܐ	ܫܒܰܥ
3	ܬܠܳܬܳܐ	ܬܠܳܬ	8	ܬܡܳܢܝܳܐ	ܬܡܳܢܶܐ
4	ܐܰܪܒܥܳܐ	ܐܰܪܒܰܥ	9	ܬܶܫܥܳܐ	ܬܫܰܥ
5	ܚܰܡܫܳܐ	ܚܰܡܶܫ	10	ܥܶܣܪܳܐ	ܥܣܰܪ

B.

	masc.	fem.		masc.	fem.
11	ܚܕܥܣܪ	ܚܕܥܣܪܐ	15	ܚܡܫܬܥܣܪ	ܚܡܫܥܣܪܐ
12	ܬܪܥܣܪ	ܬܪܬܥܣܪܐ	16	ܫܬܬܥܣܪ	ܫܬܥܣܪܐ
13	ܬܠܬܥܣܪ	ܬܠܬܥܣܪܐ	17	ܫܒܥܣܪ	ܫܒܥܣܪܐ
14	ܐܪܒܥܣܪ	ܐܪܒܥܣܪܐ	18	ܬܡܢܬܥܣܪ	ܬܡܢܥܣܪܐ
			19	ܬܫܥܣܪ	ܬܫܥܣܪܐ

C.

20	ܥܣܪܝܢ	50	ܚܡܫܝܢ	80	ܬܡܢܝܢ	200	ܡܐܬܝܢ (ܡܐܬܝܢ)
30	ܬܠܬܝܢ	60	ܫܬܝܢ	90	ܬܫܥܝܢ	300	ܬܠܬܡܐܐ
40	ܐܪܒܥܝܢ	70	ܫܒܥܝܢ	100	ܡܐܐ	1000	ܐܠܦ

10000 ܪܒܘ.

Remark 1.—For the Masculine from fourteen to nineteen, forms with a ܬ inserted may be used, *e. g.*

ܐܪܒܥܬܥܣܪ or ܐܪܒܬܥܣܪ *fourteen;* ܚܡܫܬܥܣܪ *fifteen;* ܫܬܬܥܣܪ *sixteen;* ܫܒܥܬܥܣܪ or ܫܒܬܥܣܪ *seventeen;* ܬܡܢܬܥܣܪ *eighteen;* ܬܫܥܬܥܣܪ or ܬܫܬܥܣܪ *nineteen.*

Remark 2.—The emphatic form ܬܪܥܣܪܬܐ *"the twelve"* is used of the twelve apostles. *E. g.* 25:5; John. 20:24.

Remark 3.—We sometimes find the construct in ܬ, *e. g.*

ܥܣܪܬ ܡܕܝܢܬܐ *Decapolis* (Mt. 4:25).

ܐܪܒܥܬ ܪ̈ܘܚܐ *four winds* (Mt. 24:31).

ܕܐܪܒܥܬ ܪ̈ܓܠܝܗܘܢ *quadrupeds* (Acts 10:12).

Remark 4.—We find the emphatic forms ܐܪܒܥܬܐ, ܚܡܫܬܐ, ܫܒܥܬܐ, ܬܫܥܬܐ and ܥܣܪܬܐ, used to denote the day of the month, *e. g.*

ܒܥܣܪܬܐ ܒܗ ܒܝܪܚܐ (Lev. 16:29; Num. 29:7).

Remark 5.—The Absolute state of masculine numbers from one to fifteen, when preceded by the preposition ܒ means „*on the first*", „*second*" &c, *e. g.*

ܒܫܒܥܣܪ ܝܘܡܝܢ ܒܝܪܚܐ (Gen. 7:11).

ܒܚܕ ܒܫܒܐ (John. 20:1).

Remark 6.—For the numerals with suffixes, the following examples will suffice to show the forms:—

ܬܪܝܗܘܢ *both of them* (5:7). ܬܪܬܝܗܝܢ *both of them* (f.).

ܬܠܬܝܗܘܢ (1 John. 5:7).

ܐܪܒܥܬܝܗܝܢ (Mk. 13:27).

ܫܒܥܬܝܗܘܢ (Mt. 22:26).

It will be seen that they take a fem. plur. form before suffixes, except ܬܪܝܢ and ܬܪܬܝܢ which though dual take a masc. plur. form before suffixes.

II. THE ORDINALS.

Except ܩܕܡܝܐ, (f.) ܩܕܡܝܬܐ *first* and ܬܪܝܢܐ, (f.) ܬܪܝܢܝܬܐ *second*, the ordinals are formed from the radicals of the cardinals by appending ܐ and inserting ܝ after the second radical, *e. g.* ܬܠܝܬܝܐ (Rev. 6:5); ܪܒܝܥܝܐ (Rev. 6:7).

Remark 1.—Occasionally ܥܣܪܝܢܝܐ *the 20th;* ܪܒܘܬܢܝܐ *the* 10000*th* and the ordinals of the other cardinals, except of ܡܐܐ 100 and ܐܠܦ 1000, are found.

Remark 2.—By appending ܐܝܬ to the ordinals, adverbs denoting order may be formed, *e. g.* ܬܠܝܬܐܝܬ *in the 3rd place.* ܘܬ and ܬ are also thus appended, *e. g.* ܩܕܡܝܬ *at first;* ܐܚܪܝܬ *at last;* ܬܠܝܬܝܘܬ *for the third time.*

Remark 3.—From the radicals of the cardinals from 3 to 9 fractional numbers may be formed by inserting ܘ after the first radical, *e. g.* ܬܘܠܬܐ *one third;* ܪܘܒܥܐ *one fourth.*

§ 89. Particles.

A. ADVERBS.

1. ܩܠܝܠ (24:13); ܫܦܝܪ (25:14); ܛܒ (28:14); ܬܘܒ (3:9); ܫܪܝܪܬ (26:5); ܩܕܡܝܬ (Acts 11:26).

2. ܡܢ ܩܘܕܡ (Lk. 1:2); ܡܢ ܫܠܝܐ (Mk. 9:8); ܒܛܘܫܝܐ (Mk. 4.22); ܡܢ ܗܫܐ (23:19).

3. ܫܘܝܐܝܬ (Acts 11:17); ܫܪܝܪܐܝܬ (Mt. 14:33); ܒܛܘܫܝܐܝܬ (Mt. 1:19).

4. ܐܝܟܐ (23:5); ܐܝܟܢܐ (23:7); ܠܡܢܐ (23:11); ܟܕ (23:5); ܗܫܐ (23:19); ܗܪܟ (24:2); ܠܐ (25:18); ܐܝܢ (Mt. 11:9).

5. ܘ *and;* ܐܘ *or;* ܐܦ *also;* ܐܢ *if;* ܕ *that;* ܥܕܡ *until;* ܡܢ=μέν; ܓܝܪ=γάρ.

1. Some masculine nouns in the absolute state and some feminines in the construct state are used as adverbs.

2. A phrase formed by a preposition with its noun may be used as an adverb.

3. Many adverbs are formed by appending ܐܝܬ to adjectives.

4. There are many proper adverbs, simple and compound, especially adverbs of place, time, affirmation, negation, hypothesis, comparison and interrogation.

5. The conjunctions are mostly adverbs. The relative ܕ is employed as a conjunction either alone or after a particle.

B. PREPOSITIONS.

1. ܥܕܡ *until;* ܒܝܬ *between;* ܥܠ *upon;* ܡܢ *from;* ܥܡ *with.*

2. ܠܩܕܡ *in the sight of;* ܠܥܠ *above;* ܡܢ ܒܬܪ *after;* ܡܢ ܒܠܥܕ *without.*

3. ܠܘܬܟܘܢ (23:7); ܒܬܪܗ (Mt. 4:20); ܒܣܬܪܗ (Lk. 7:38); ܩܕܡܝ (John. 1:15); ܥܠܝܟ (Mt. 4:6); ܥܠܘܗܝ (14:14).

Prepositions are simple (1) or compound (2). They are mostly the construct of nouns. With suffixes some take the sing. others the plural construct form.

Remark 1.—For the inseparable prepositions, *see* § 34.

Remark 2.—For the prepositions with suffixes, *see* §§ 36. 3, 77. 4.

Remark 3.—Special peculiarities belong to the following prepositions.

1. ܐܝܟ *as, like,* takes the form ܐܟܘܬ before suffixes, *e. g.* ܐܟܘܬܟܘܢ (John. 8:55).

2. ܒܝܬ *between,* with suffixes takes a plur. cons. masculine or feminine, *e. g.* ܒܝܢܝ (Mt. 18:15); ܒܝܢܬܗܘܢ (Mt. 20:26).

3. ܒܠܚܘܕ *only,* takes pronominal suffixes like a plural noun ܒܠܚܘܕܘܗܝ (Mt. 4:10). So also ܠܚܘܕ, *e. g.* ܠܚܘܕܝܗ (John. 8:9).

4. ܠܘܩܒܠ *before,* with suffixes appended by means of a vowel becomes ܠܩܘܒܠ § 31. 1, but before others remains unchanged, *e. g.* ܠܩܘܒܠܗ (Mt. 14:24); ܠܘܩܒܠܟܘܢ (Mt. 21:2).

5. ܠܒܝܬ with suffixes usually becomes ܠܒܝ̈ܬ, *e. g.* ܠܒܝ̈ܬܗܘܢ (Lk. 5:25).

6. ܡܛܠ takes the fem. plur. form before suffixes, *e. g.* ܡܛܠܬܝ (Mt. 5:11); ܡܛܠܬܟܘܢ (Phil. 2:19).

C. ܝܬ.

ܝܬ, the sign of the direct object (=Targ. יָת, Heb. אֵת), is found only in about a dozen places in the Old Testament in the Peshito version, *e. g.* Gen. 1:1.

SYNTAX.

§ 90. The Noun Used Collectively.

1. ܒܥܝܪܐ *cattle* (Gen. 2:20); ܒܩܪܐ *a herd of cattle* (Mt. 8:30).

ܥܢܐ *flock* (John. 10:12); ܪܚܫܐ *reptiles* (Gen. 1:24).

ܪܟܫܐ *horses* (Rev. 9:7); ܩܘܪܝܐ *villages* (Mt. 14:15).

2. ܦܪܚܬܐ (Mt. 6:26) *birds* [*i. e.* the genus, *bird*], (Rev. 18:2=*bird*); ܦܪ̈ܚܬܐ (Jam. 3:7) *birds;* ܫܘܫܢܬܐ *the lily, a lily,* ܫܘܫܢ̈ܐ *the lilies* (Mt. 6:28).

3. ܥܡܐ *the people* (Mt. 4:16); ܥܡ̈ܡܐ (Mt. 12:18) *peoples.*

ܩܝܣܐ *wood;* ܩܝ̈ܣܐ *timber.*

ܚܛܬܐ *wheat;* ܚܛ̈ܐ *wheat corn.*

ܩܰܡܨܳܐ *locusts* (Ex. 10:12); ܩܰܡ̈ܨܶܐ (Mt. 3:4; Rev. 9:7).

ܠܰܚܡܳܐ *bread* (Mt. 4:3); ܚܰܡܫܳܐ ܠܰܚܡܺ̈ܝܢ *loaves* (Mt. 14:19).

4. *a.* ܒܩܪܐ ܕܚܙܝܪܐ—ܒܩܪܐ (Mt. 8:30); ܥܰܡܳܐ ܕܝܳܬܶܒ—ܚܙܳܐ (Mt. 4:16).

b. ܚܘܽܪܘ ܒܦܳܪܰܚܬܳܐ ܕܫܡܰܝܳܐ ܕܠܳܐ ܙܳܪܥܺܝܢ (Mt. 6:26); ܐܶܬܳܬ ܦܳܪܰܚܬܳܐ (Mt. 13:4).

Collective nouns are those that are singular in form but plural in sense.

1. Collective nouns which have no plural are usually marked by Rebbuy, § 13.

2. Some nouns in the singular may denote either a collective or an individual idea; and in the plural, a number of individuals.

3. Many nouns in the singular are collective, even when Rebbuy is not employed; the plural denoting either a number of individuals, or a number of collectives.

4. Collective nouns have verbs and adjectives either in the singular or plural. Compare § 121. 2.

Remark 1.—Those nouns which are always collective have a different word to denote the individual, *e. g.* ܥܳܢܳܐ *flock* (John 10:3), but ܠܥܶܪ̈ܒܰܘܗܝ *his sheep* id. ܪ̈ܰܟܫܳܐ *horses;* ܣܘܣܝܳܐ *horse* (Rev. 6:2).

Remark 2.—ܐ̱ܢܳܫܳܐ in the emphatic state is used as a singular in the phrase ܒܰܪܐ̱ܢܳܫܳܐ (also written ܒܰܪܢܳܫܳܐ Mt. 15:20) *man* (Mt. 12:12); ܐ̱ܢܳܫ means "*some one*", *e. g.* Mt. 28:35; ܐ̱ܢܳܫܺܝܢ ܐ̱ܢܳܫ̈ܐ means "*some*", *e. g.* ܘܢܶܦܩܽܘ ܐ̱ܢܳܫ̈ܐ (John. 4:30; Mt. 27:47).

§ 91. Gender of Nouns.

1. ܐ̱ܢܳܫ *man;* ܒܰܪ *son;* ܒܶܣܰܪ *flesh.*

2. (1) ܐܶܡܳܐ *mother;* ܐܰܬܳܢܳܐ *she-ass;* ܣܘܣܝܳܬܳܐ *mare.*

ܦܪܺܝܣܩܺܠܳܐ *Priscilla;* ܓܰܡܠܳܐ *camel;* ܚܡܳܪܳܐ *ass.*

(2) *a.* ܐܶܠܦܳܐ *ship;* ܥܶܠܥܳܐ *rib.*

ܕܶܒܽܘܪܬܳܐ *bee;* ܥܶܕܪܳܐ *herd;* ܓܽܘܕܳܐ *troup.*

b. ܫܽܘܫܰܢܬܳܐ *lily;* ܛܠܘܦܚܳܐ *lentil.*

c. ܐܶܕܢܳܐ *ear;* ܐܺܝܕܳܐ *hand;* ܟܰܦܳܐ *palm;* ܟܰܬܦܳܐ *shoulder.*

ܟܶܢܦܳܐ *wing.*

(3) ܐܶܠܦܳܐ *ship;* ܟܰܟܪܳܐ *talent.*

§ 91.] ELEMENTS OF SYRIAC. 103

ܥܢܳܐ *burden;* ܫܘܦܢܳܐ *handful;* ܓܝܓܠܳܐ *wheel.*

ܥܪܣܳܐ *bed;* ܪܚܝܳܐ *millstone;* ܣܟܝܢܳܐ *knife.*

ܪܘܡܚܳܐ *lance;* ܟܘܬܝܢܳܐ *tunic.*

(4) ܢܘܪܳܐ *fire;* ܟܐܦܳܐ *stone.*

ܡܕܒܪܳܐ *desert;* ܬܝܡܢܳܐ *south;* ܥܢܢܳܐ *cloud.*

ܥܠܥܳܠܐ *tempest;* ܟܝܡܳܐ *pleiades;* ܢܦܫܳܐ *soul.*

ܢܫܡܬܳܐ *breath;* ܪܘܚܳܐ *spirit.*

ܫܡܫܳܐ *sun;* ܪܩܝܥܳܐ *firmament.*

(5) ܢܝܢܘܐ (Jon. 3:3); ܒܝܬܠܚܡ (Mt. 2:6); ܐܳܠܦ *Olaph.*

1. The names of male beings and most nouns without a distinct feminine ending are masculine.

2. Under feminine nouns are included:—

(1) All denoting feminine beings.

Remark—ܓܡܠܐ *camel* and ܚܡܪܐ *ass,* when they denote males, are masculine.

(2) *a.* Many words which do not denote feminine beings but which have feminine endings.

b. Especially names of vegetables.

c. Members of the body.

(3) Names of vessels, weights, measures, articles of furniture, utensiles, instruments and clothing.

(4) Names of the elements, of natural phenomena and objects of spirit, matter and place.

(5) Names of countries, cities and towns and the names of the letters of the alphabet.

3. (1) ܝܘܡܐ (Gen. 1:5); ܛܒ *good;* ܒܝܫ *bad* (Mt. 27:23); ܛܒܬܐ *the good;* ܒܝܫܬܐ (Mt. 6:34).

(2) ܛܒܬܐ *bona;* ܗܠܝܢ *these;* ܒܝܫܬܐ ܗܠܝܢ ܟܠܗܝܢ (2 Cor. 5:10); *omnia haecce mala.*

4. ܒܥܠܕܒܒܘܬܐ *enmity* (Luk. 23:12) is feminine; ܒܥܠܕܒܒܐ *enemy* (Mt. 13:28) is masculine.

3. The neuter is expressed in Syriac only in the Interrogative pronoun, *i. e.* ܡܐ, ܡܢ, ܡܢܘ=*what?* ܡܢ=*who?*

(1) In the singular either a masculine or feminine form may take its place.

(2) In the plural, the feminine is always used for it.

4. The gender of compound nouns is indicated by the second noun.

Remark—This rule is sometimes violated as in Acts 16:26 ܫܶܬܐܣ̈ܐ is masculine plural from ܐܶܣܳܐ f. *wall.*

5. Plural nouns whatever their ending follow the gender of the singular, *e. g.* ܟܠܝܠ̈ܬܐ and ܢܗܪ̈ܘܬܐ are masculine because their singular is masculine. ܡ̈ܠܐ and ܫ̈ܢܝܐ from the singulars ܡܶܠܬܳܐ and ܫܰܢ̱ܬܳܐ are feminine.

6. Nouns used figuratively are often given the gender of the things which they represent, *e. g.* ܡܶܠܬܳܐ *word,* when used for the Logos, (John. 1:1), is masculine, elsewhere, feminine. ܚܰܝܽܘܬ ܝܰܡܳܐ (Rev. 13:1) is masculine though each noun is feminine.

§ 92. Number.

1. (1) ܡܢܗܪ̈ܝܢ (Gen. 1:15); ܢܗ̈ܝܪܐ (Gen. 1:14); ܐܦ̈ܝ (Gen. 1:2); ܫ̈ܢܝܐ (Gen. 1:14); ܬܫܡܫ̈ܬܐ.

(2) ܥܢ̈ܐ *flock;* ܣܘܓ̈ܐܐ *many;* ܫܪ̈ܟܐ *the rest.*

(3) ܒܕܘܟܐ ܕܘܟܐ (Mt. 24:7) *in every place;* ܕܝܢܪ ܕܝܢܪ (Mt. 20:9) *a penny each;* ܟܘܪܗܢ ܟܘܪܗܢ (Mk. 2:17) *various deseases;* ܒܐܬܪ ܐܬܪ (Spic. Syr. 13:17) *in different places;* ܐܢܫ ܐܢܫ (Acts 10:23) *some;* ܡܕܡ ܡܕܡ (Spic. Syr. 2:27) *whatsoever, anything.*

(4) ܬܪ̈ܝܢ ܐܕܡ *two Adams;* ܬܪ̈ܝܢ ܢܘܢ *two Nuns;* ܚܡܫܐ ܓܪ *five gers.*

2. (1) ܡ̈ܝܐ *water;* ܫܡ̈ܝܐ *heaven;* ܐܦ̈ܐ *face.*

(2) ܚܐܪܘܬܐ (Rom. 8:2) *liberty;* ܚ̈ܝܐ (John. 1:4) *life;* ܪ̈ܚܡܐ (Rom. 1:31) *compassion.*

3. ܬܠܬܐ ܝܘܡ̈ܝܢ (Mt. 26:61) but ܟܠܗܘܢ ܝܘܡ̈ܬܐ (Mt. 28:20).

4. ܡܘܡܐ ܐ̱ܢܐ ܒܡܪܘܬܗ *I swear by the Lord* (Michaelis Chrest. 30).

5. (1) ܫܶܬܐܣ̈ܐ *foundations* (Lk. 6:48) [sing. ܫܶܬܐܣܬܳܐ]; ܒܥܠܕܒ̈ܒܐ *enemies* (Rom. 5:10).

(2) *a.* ܒܝܬ ܩܒܘܪ̈ܐ *tombs* (Mt. 27:52); ܒܝܬ ܡܫܩ̈ܝܢ (Lk. 12:18).

b. ܒܢܝ̈ ܡܠܟܗ *his counsellors* (Acts 25:12).

c. ܪ̈ܒܝ ܟܗܢ̈ܐ *chief priests* (Mt. 27:1).

6. ܪܚܡܐ *womb;* ܪ̈ܚܡܐ *compassion.*

1. The plural idea is denoted in one of four ways.

(1) By means of the plural affixes, § 76. 3, 4.

(2) By means of words which have a collective signification, *see* § 90.

(3) By the repetition of a word without a connective.

(4) In the case of proper names, most of the letters of the alphabet, and the particle ܝܬ, by the numerals.

2. In a few words the plural termination is employed for the designation of ideas which are singular; especially is this the case

(1) To denote portions of space.

(2) To denote abstract ideas.

3. Some nouns have a plural of paucity, *i. e.* a plural to denote that from two to ten of a thing are meant.

4. The plural of majesty occurs only in the Hebrew word for *Lord, e. g.* ܐܕܘܢܝ (Did. 82:15).

5. Compound ideas form their plural either by pluralizing the second or the first or both. When the word is a true compound, the second part only is pluralized.

6. The plural form of certain nouns often conveys a shade of meaning different from the singular.

7. The feminine plural of a noun is sometimes used in a different sense from the masculine plural, *see* § 86. 11.

§ 93. Determination.

I.

1. (1) *a.* ܒܟܠ ܒܝ̈ܫܢ *in all evils* (Prov. 5:14); but ܠܟܠ ܡܗܝܡ̈ܢܐ *to all believers* (Aphr. 202:1).

b. ܗܠܝܢ ܬܪ̈ܬܝܢ ܦܘܩܕ̈ܢܝܢ *these two commandments* (Mt. 22:40).

c. ܟܡܐ ܐܣܦܪ̈ܝܕܝܢ *how many baskets?* (Mt. 16:10); ܒܐܝܢܐ ܫܘܠܛܢܐ *by what authority?* (Mt. 21:23); ܐܝܢܐ ܬܫܢܝܩܐ *what torment?* (Spic.

Syr. 40:20). But ܒܚܕ ܩܠܐ *with one voice* (Acts 19:34); ܟܡܐ ܢܦܩܬܐ *how much expense* (Jos. Styl. 15:18); ܐܝܢܐ ܦܘܩܕܢܐ *which commandment?* (Mt. 22:36).

(2) ܦܬܓܡ ܟܬܒ *the Scripture-text;* ܐܠܗ ܒܪܢܫ *the Theanthropos.*

(3) ܕܝܢܪ ܕܝܢܪ *to every one a penny.*

(4) ܣܠܘܝ *the quail;* ܛܘܥܝܝ *the error;* ܛܘܫܝܝ *the secret.*

2. (1) ܡܘܬܐ *death;* ܐܪܝܐ *lion;* ܬܘܪܐ *bull;* ܚܘܡܐ *heat;* ܡܘܩܡܐ *situation.*

(2) ܠܐ ܟܣܦܐ (Is. 55:1) *without money;* ܠܐ ܪܚܡܢܐ (Rom. 1:31) *unmerciful;* ܕܠܐ ܚܛܝܬܗ (John. 8:1) *without sin;* ܕܠܐ ܟܣܦ (Ex. 21:11); ܠܐ ܬܘܩܠܬܐ *without offence* (Didasc. 14:19); ܕܠܐ ܡܕܒܪܢܐ *without a guide* (Sp. Syr. 43:4).

Nouns were originally made definite by putting them in the emphatic state; but in almost all cases the emphatic and absolute states have come to loose all distinction as to definiteness, so that:

1. Nouns in the *absolute* state are often definite.

(1) *a.* After ܟܠ *all.*

b. With numerals.

c. With ܟܡܐ *how much? how many?* and ܐܝܢܐ *which? what?*

(2) In some compound words, which are definite, the absolute state always occurs in the second noun.

(3) A noun repeated in a distributive sense is generally in the absolute state, *see* § 92. 1, (3).

(4) In nouns where the emphatic state is not fouud, the absolute serves for both, *see* § 86. 6.

2. Nouns in the emphatic state are often indefinite.

(1) All nouns which have lost the absolute state may be indefinite in the emphatic which has taken its place.

(2) In negative expressions the noun though indefinite is often in the emphatic state.

Remark—In most of the above cases the other state, if found, would be equally proper.

II.

1. (1) ܡܲܠܸܠ ܗܘ ܚܲܪܫܵܐ *the mute man spake* (Mt. 9:33).

   ܣܵܡܲܬ݂ ܗܝ ܬܲܪܬܹܝܢ *she placed the second* (Addai the Ap. 14:10);

   ܗܵܢܘܿܢ ܕܹܝܢ ܐ̱ܢܵܫܵܐ ܕܐܸܟܲܠܘ *but the men who ate* (Mt. 14:21). (See also John. 18:16, 4:49.)

   (2) ܘܗܵܐ ܟܵܘܟܒ݂ܵܐ ܗܘ ܕܲܚܙܵܘ *and behold the star that they saw* (Mt. 2:9).

   ܐܵܚܝ ܗܘ ܕܐܝܼܬ݂ ܗܘܵܐ ܥܲܡܝ *the brother who was with me* (Joshua the Sty. 29:15). (See also John. 5:9.)

   (3) ܘܗܘ ܡܸܠܬ݂ܵܐ *and the word* (John. 1:1); ܘܗܵܢܘܿܢ ܬܲܠܡܝܼܕ݂ܵܘ̈ܗܝ *and the disciples* (Mt. 14:19); ܘܠܵܐ ܗܘ ܩܝܼܬ݂ܵܪܵܐ ܝܕ݂ܲܥ *and the cithara knew not* (Sp. Syr. 4:17).

   (4) ܘܗܵܕ݂ܹܐ ܗܘܲܝܬ ܨܵܒܹܐ ܐܲܢ̱ܬ *and this thou art wishing* (J. S. 7:22).

   ܗܵܢܘܿܢ ܗܵܠܹܝܢ (Ad. Ap. 10:20); ܗܵܢܘܿܢ ܗܵܠܹܝܢ ܐ̱ܢܵܫܵܐ *these men* (Sp. Syr. 9:4).

2. ܐܲܙܒ̈ܢܝܼܢ ܣܲܓܝܼ̈ܐܵܢ *many times* (Mk. 9:22); ܡܸܢ ܫܸܠܝܵܐ *suddenly* (Lk. 2:13).

To avoid the ambiguity arising from the emphatic state's losing its power of determination, nouns were often made definite by the personal or demonstrative pronoun.

(1) The demonstrative might precede its noun.
(2) The demonstrative might follow its noun.
(3) The personal pronoun preceded its noun.
(4) ܗܘ might be put before the demonstrative pronoun in order to make it emphatic.

2. The absolute state is yet used in cases which are necessarily indefinite, especially in adverbial phrases.

3. (1) ܚܸܙܘܵܐ ܫܲܪܝܼܪܵܐ *the true vision* (Sp. Syr. 22:6).

   ܠܥܲܡܵܐ ܢܘܼܟ݂ܪܵܝ *to a strange people* (Ex. 21:8); ܠܒ݂ܘܼܫܵܐ ܪܲܟܝܼܟ݂ܵܐ *soft raiment* (Mt. 11:8); ܐܵܬ̈ܘܵܬ݂ܵܐ ܣܲܓܝܼ̈ܐܵܬ݂ܵܐ *many miracles* (John. 11:47); ܪܘܼܚܹ̈ܐ ܐ̱ܚܪܵܢܝܵܬ݂ܵܐ *other spirits* (Lk. 11:26).

Rem. 1.—ܬܪܬܝܢ ܢܫܝܢ ܝܩܝܪ̈ܬܐ *two women of rank* (J. S. 70:10).

ܣܗܕ̈ܐ ܫܪܝܪ̈ܐ *true witnesses* (Aphr. 461:3).

Rem. 2.—ܫܒܥܐ ܪ̈ܘܚܝܢ ܐܚܪ̈ܢܝܢ *seven other spirits* (Mt. 12:45). (See Mt. 28:12, Gen. 41:18, Acts 9:43, 17:4.) ܕܗܒܐ ܠܐ ܐܟܢ *not a little gold* (J. S. 37:5).

Rem. 3.—ܛܘܥܝܝ ܐܚܪܝܬܐ *the second error* (Mt. 27:64); ܛܘܥܝܝ ܡܚܒܠܢܝܬܐ *the destructive error* (Ad. Ap. 22:5).

(2) *a.* ܐܝܕܥܬ ܕܝܢ (Gen. 3:11); ܡܝܐ ܕܓܢܝܒܝܢ ܚܠܝܢ *stolen waters are sweet* (Prov. 9:17). (See also, Gen. 1:2, 1:6, Mt. 12:34); ܟܐܒ̈ܐ ܕܢܦܫ̈ܬܢ ܣܓܝ̈ܐܝܢ ܗܘܘ *the diseases of our souls were many* (J. S. 21:4) (See also, 21:8, 17.) ܗܕܡ̈ܐ ܢܛܝܪܝܢ ܗܘܘ *the limbs were kept* (J. S. 22:18).

b. ܐܥܒܕܝܗܘܢ ܗܘܘ ܓܝܪ ܒܝܫ̈ܬܐ ܣܢܝ̈ܬܐ *for their deeds were evil* (John 3:19); ܐܢܬܘܢ ܕܒܝܫ̈ܐ ܐܢܬܘܢ *Ye, who are evil* (Mt. 7:11). (See also, Mt. 12:34, Lk. 1:42, 11:13, 16:11); ܗܘܘ ܡܛܝܒܝܢ *Be ye ready* (Lk. 12:40); ܡܗܝܡ̈ܢܐ ܐܢܘܢ ܙܥܘܪ̈ܝܢ *the believers are few* (Ad. Ap. 9:17); ܕܫܪܝܪ̈ܝܢ ܐܢܘܢ *that they are true* (Sp. Syr. 18:7).

4. ܢܗܪܐ (Gen. 1:18); ܐܣܝܪܐ (J. S. 65:20); ܐܢܐ (J. S. 67:13); ܠܒܕ (=לְבַד); ܐܐܪ ἀήρ.

3. (1) Attributive adjectives usually follow the determination of their nouns.

Rem. 1.—The noun is sometimes in the absolute and the adjective in the emphatic state.

Rem. 2.—The noun is sometimes in the emphatic and the adjective in the absolute state.

Rem. 3.—Nouns found in the absolute state only may have adjectives in the emphatic state.

(2) *a.* A predicate noun, adjective, or participle, is commonly put in the absolute state.

b. But the predicate is sometimes put in the emphatic, especially if it is a substantive or if it is an adjective or participle taken as a substantive.

4. Pronouns are always determinate. Infinitives, the names of months, and most foreign words are indeterminate in form, even when determinate in sense. ܫܒܐ when used in connection with a numeral for a day of the week is unchangeabls, *e. g.* ܚܕ ܒܫܒܐ *Sunday* (Mt. 28:1); ܒܫܒܘܥ ܐܪܒܥܐ ܒܫܒܐ *Wednesday* (J. S. 62:2).

§ 94. Apposition.

1. ܫܡܥܘܢ ܩܢܢܝܐ (Mt. 10:4); ܪܘܚܐ ܡܥܪܒܝܐ *the west-wind* (Ex 10:19); ܢܘܗܪܐ ܦܪܙܠ (J. S. 84:7); ܕܢܒܬܐ ܐܘܕܐ ܡܥܫܢܬܐ *tails, burning firebrands* (Is. 7:4); ܫܥܕܢܐ ܩܒܐ ܒܚܡܫܡܐܐ ܢܘܡܝܢ *chickpeas were* 500 *numia a kab* (J. S. 34:20).
2. ܡܐܐ ܡܟܘܪܝܢ ܡܫܚܐ *a hundred measures of oil* (Lk. 16:6). ܚܡܫܐ ܛܥܢܝܢ ܙܘܙܐ *five loads of silver coin* (J. S. 10:21).
3. ܛܒ ܛܒ *very good* (Kirsch Chrest. p. 130:12); ܒܝܫ ܒܝܫ *very lad* (S. S. 23:14, Mt. 4:24); ܚܕ ܚܕ *one by one* (John. 8:9, J. S. 77:2); ܒܐܪܥܐ ܕܒܥܠܕܒܒܘܗܝ ܒܐܪܥܐ ܕܡܘܐܒ *in the land of his enemies, in the land of Moab.*
4. ܗܘ ܩܕܡ ܦܨܝܗ ܩܕܡܝܐ *he was the first to save him* (J. S. 3:1). ܐܫܬܐܪ ܗܘܐ ܗܡܢ ܦܨܝܐ *Haman remained, as an escaped one* (Aphr. 52:15); ܗܘ ܚܘܝ ܩܕܡܝܐ ܪܥܝܢܐ ܫܦܝܪܐ *he first showed good will* (J. S. 23:17); ܘܗܢܘܢ ܕܐܣܬܒܪܘ ܩܕܡܝܐ (=lit.) *and they who first had the gospel preached [to them].* (Heb. 4:6)
5. ܣܓܝܐܢ ܨܒܘܬܐ *many things* (Sp. Syr. 6:6); ܐܪܥܐ ܣܓܝܐܐ *much earth* (Mk. 4:5); ܒܘܝܐܐ ܩܠܝܠ *a little consolation* (J. S. 32:10); ܩܠܝܠ ܢܘܗܪܐ *the little light* (J. S. 31:15).

Rem. 1.—ܛܘܪܐ ܕܙܝܬܐ *the mount of Olives* (Mt. 21:1); ܛܘܪ ܙܝܬܐ *id* (Mt. 26:30); ܒܐܪܚܣ ܐܪܙ (J. S. 65:20).

Rem. 2.—ܬܠܬܐ ܩܘܢܝܩܣܝܢ ܕܣܥܪܐ *three measures of barley* (Rev. 6:6); ܩܒܐ ܕܦܣܬܩܐ *a kab of beans* (J. S. 34:20).

1. The first noun denotes a person or thing, the second defines it.

2. The second denotes the principal idea, the first defining its measure, weight &c.

3. The second noun is a repetition of the first for emphasis, distribution, or multiplication (*see* § 92. 1. (3); or the first word in a clause is repeated in order to add a new idea to it.

4. We meet occasionally with constructions similar to the Greek predicative, or modal accusative.

5. ܣܓܝ *many;* ܩܠܝܠ *little* and ܐܚܪܢ *other,* often stand before their noun; as also do other adjectives occasionally, *see* § 99. 1, *Rem.* 1.

Rem. 1.—Names of places and times are frequently connected by ܕ, or may be in simple construction, *see* § 96. A. B. The construction with ܕ is really a kind of apposition.

Rem. 2.—The thing contained may be connected with the thing containing by means of ܕ.

6. (1) ܗܕܐ ܟܠܗ ܒܘܝܐܐ *all this consolation* (J S 42. 14).

ܠܟܠܗ ܚܝܠܗ *all his army* (J. S. 88. 9).

ܒܟܠܗ ܐܪܥܐ *in all the land* (Lk. 4:25).

(2) ܫܕܝܗܝ ܟܣܦܐ *he cast the silver* (Mt. 27:5). (So Mt. 14:10, 26:51).

ܟܕ ܐܡܪܗ ܗܢܐ ܦܬܓܡܐ . *when he told this word* (Aphr. 520:18).

(3) ܢܒܛܠܝܗ ܠܪܚܡܘܬܐ *he should destroy the friendship* (Ined. Syr. 8:16).

ܦܨܝܗ ܝܘܢܬܢ ܠܕܘܝܕ *Jonathan delivered David* (J. S. 2:18). (*See also* 12:9, 21:6).

(4) ܕܢܫܠܡܝܗ ܠܗ ܠܡܕܝܢܬܐ *that he would deliver the city* (J. S. 56:1).

6. (1) The second noun may be in apposition with the pronominal suffix of the first. So especially after ܟܠ meaning „*all the*".

(2) The noun may be in apposition with the pronominal suffix of the verb.

(3) The noun in apposition with the pronominal suffix of a verb is generally preceded by ܠ.

(4) Occasionally, we find a pronoun and a noun each preceded by by ܠ and both in apposition with the pronominal suffix of the verb.

§ 95. The Nominative Absolute.

1. ܓܒܪܐ ܓܝܪ ܡܐ ܕܐܬܗܦܟ ܡܢ ܛܘܥܝܝ ܩܠܝܠ ܡܬܩܒܠ ܠܗ *For when a man has been turned from the little error, there is received by him etc.* (Sp. Syr. 22:3). (lit. *For a man when etc.*); ܟܐܦܐ ܕܐܣܠܝܘ ܒܢܝܐ ܗܝ ܗܘܬ ܠܪܝܫ ܙܘܝܬܐ *The stone which the builders rejected, it has become the head of the corner* (Mt. 21:42). (See also Mt. 4:10); ܐܦ ܠܢ ܓܝܪ ܐܣܬܒܪܢ (*lit.=*) *For we, also, we have been preached the gospel* (Heb. 4:2).

2. (1) ܣܒܪ ܕܐܫܟܚ ܐܬܪܐ ܠܗ *he hoped that he had found the time* (J. S. 18:12); ܡܪܘܕܐ ܠܐ ܝܕܥܝܢ ܠܗ *rebellion, they know it not* (Aphr. 177 ult.); ܕܡܗ ܕܡܝܠܟ ܠܩܘܗ ܠܗ ܟܠܒܐ *his own blood, the dogs licked it up* (Aphr. 183:16).

(2) ܘܠܝ ܦܩܕܢܝ ܡܪܝܐ *and me, the Lord commanded me* (Deut. 4:14). ܠܐܠܝܐ ܪܕܦܬܗ ܐܝܙܒܠ *Elijah, Jezebel persecuted him* (Aphr. 123:18).

(3) ܠܝܫܘܥ ܡܢܐ ܐܥܒܕ ܠܗ *to Jesus what shall I do to him?* (Math. 27:22). ܠܩܘܣܛܢܛܝܢܘܣ ܥܒܕܗ ܠܗ ܐܪܟܐ ܪܒܐ *Constantine he made a general* (J. S. 45:8). (See also 91:5).

3. ܙܝܢܗ ܩܠܝܠ ܗܘ ܡܢ ܕܝܠܢ *his weapon, it is weaker than ours* (Aphr. 137:21); ܐܒܘܢ ܕܝܠܢ ܐܒܪܗܡ ܗܘ *Our father Abraham is he* (John. 8:39). (See also Heb. 3:4, Aphr. 7:2, 14:10, Mt. 26:48). ܕܡܒܪܟ ܡܒܪܟ ܗܘ *he that blesses, blessed is he* (Did. 4:14); ܟܠ ܕ— ܗܘ ܗܘ ܫܡܗ *all that &c. that is its name* (Gen. 2:19).

4. (1) ܥܠ ܗܝܡܢܘܬܗ ܕܗܒܝܠ ܐܬܩܒܠ ܩܘܪܒܢܗ *For on account of Abel's faith, his gift was accepted* (Aphr. 18:4). (See also 63:17, 449:15).

112   ELEMENTS OF SYRIAC.   [§ 95.

ܐܘ ܐܢܬ ܐܡܪ ܥܠܐ ܠܡܪܦܝܢ ܠܟܕܗܘܢ ܨܡܝܟܕܘܬܐ *if they shall speak evil against a man falsely* (Did. 14:14).

(2) ܐܝܟܕܟܢܬ ܘܡܟܪܙ ܗܘܝܬ ܠܟܘܢ ܗܟܢܐ ܐܬܕܒܪܬ *according to all which I was preaching to you, so have I conducted myself* (Ad. Ap. 41:3).

(3) ܥܪܒܐ ܕܐܒܕ ܡܢ ܟܠܗ ܓܙܪܐ ܗܘ ܗܘ ܕܥܠܘܗܝ ܝܨܦ ܪܥܝܐ *the sheep, which from the whole flock was lost, for it does the shepherd care* (Aphr. 142:10).

Rem. ܥܠ ܝܫܘܥ ܬܘܒ ܗܟܢܐ ܟܬܝܒ *concerning Jesus it is further so written* (Aphr. 112:9).

5. ܡܫܝܚܐ ܗܐ ܐܬܬܒܪ ܩܪܢܬܗ ܕܕܟܪܐ ܐܢܘܢ *now are the ram's horns broken* (Aphr. 83:20); ܘܡܚܘܬܗ ܕܗܘ ܕܠܐ ܒܗܬ ܐܬܐܣܝܬ *and the wound of him who is not ashamed is healed* (Aphr. 136:3). (So Aphr. 449:15).

6. ܘܗܕܐ ܗܝ ܕܨܒܐ ܐܢܬ ܕܬܐܠܦ *and thou wishest to learn this very thing* (J. S. 7:22); ܗܢܐ ܕܝܢ ܡܕܡ ܕܣܢܐ ܠܐ ܚܨܝܡ ܠܗ *but this one, nothing despicable has been done by him* (Lk. 23:41); ܐܢܬ ܡܢ ܐܢܬ *thou—who art thou?* (John. 1:19); ܐܢܐ ܕܝܢ ܐܡܪ ܐܢܐ ܠܟܘܢ ܗܕܐ *but I, I say this to you* (Ded. 1:23); ܐܢܬ ܒܪܟܝܗܝ ܠܡܫܡܥܗ *do thou bless him* (Did. 2:13); ܚܢܢ ܢܦܝܣܝܘܗܝ ܠܗ *we will persuade him* (Mt. 25:14).

A noun or pronoun, called the Nominative Absolute, is often put for emphasis at the beginning of a sentence, its grammatical position and case being assumed generally by a pronoun agreeing with it in gender and number. Sometimes the noun, or pronoun, to be emphasized, is itself repeated.

1. The logical subject of the sentence may be put first.

2. The logical object may be put first: (1) the noun without, the pronoun with Lomadh; (2) the noun with Lomadh, the pronoun suffixed to the verb; (3) both with Lomadh.

3. The logical subject is often resumed by ܗܘ or ܗܝ, especially when the latter is equivalent to the copula.

4. The nominative absolute is often the logical object of a preposition,

(1) expressed, or (2) understood. The object is emphasized when the demonstrative pronoun is used after the preposition instead of the pronominal suffix, see (3).

Remark—The preposition may be used before the noun placed first in the sentence as well as before the pronoun, which assumes the usual grammatical position of the noun.

5. The nominative absolute is often the logical genitive after a noun, its grammatical place being assumed by a pronominal suffix.

6. The same rules that are true of the noun are true also of the pronoun when in the nominative absolute.

§ 96. The Genitive.

The Genitive relative may be expressed:
  I. By the construct state.
  II. By means of the relative pronoun ܕ.
  III. By means of the pronominal suffix and the relative pronoun ܕ.
  IV. By means of the preposition ܠ.

I. Construction or Annexion.

1. *a.* ܒܥܠܙܒܘܒ *Beelzebub* (Mt. 13:28); ܒܪܢܫܐ *son of man* (John. 2:25); ܒܓܠܝܬܐ *openly* (Bar Heb. Sch. Mor. 1:23); ܡܣܒܪ ܚܫܒܐ *suspicion* (1 Tim. 6:4); ܡܫܟܒܝ ܥܡ ܕܟܪܐ *sodomites* (Dit. 1:21).

b. ܬܪܝܨܘܬ ܫܘܒܚܐ *orthodoxy;* ܒܪ ܬܫܡܫܬܐ συλλειτουργος *Athan.* (Fest. Lett. 25:7); ܫܦܝܪܝ ܚܫܐ εὐπαθοῦντες (Ps. 91:15 Hex.[Nöl.]).

2. *a.* ܒܝܬ ܡܠܟܘܬܐ *palace* (Bar Heb. Sch. Mor. 1:14); ܦܐܪܝ ܡܪܪܐ *bitter fruits;* ܡܕܝܢܬ ܡܠܟܘܬܐ *capital city* (J. S. 12.2); ܛܘܪ ܙܝܬܐ *mount of Olives* (Mt. 26:30); ܒܥܠ ܡܠܟܐ *counsellor* (Rom. 11:34).

b. ܚܣܝܪܝ ܪܥܝܢܐ *wanting of mind* (Gal. 3:1); ܥܒܕܐ ܙܒܝܢ ܟܣܦܐ *a slave bought for silver* (Ex. 12:44); ܟܪܝܗܬ ܚܘܒܐ *sick of love* (Song of Songs 2:5).

Rem. ܫܦܝܪܬ ܒܚܙܘܐ *beautiful in countenance* (Gen. 12:11); ܡܫܠܛ ܒܢܦܫܗ *ruling over himself* (Sp. Syr. 19:8).

3. ܡܢ ܡܕܢܚܗ ܦܪܕܝܣܐ *from the east of Paradise* (Gen. 3:24); ܒܡܥܪܒܝ ܫܡܫܐ *at sunrise* (Mk. 1:32); ܣܓܝܐܢ ܐܪܡܠܬܐ *many widows* (Lk. 4:25); ܩܠܝܠ ܝܘܡܬܐ *a few days* (John. 2:12); ܒܝܕ ܢܒܝܐ *through the prophet* (Mt. 27:9); ܩܕܡ ܟܢܫܐ *before the assembly* (Mt. 27:24); ܒܫܡ ܐܒܐ *in the name of the father* (Mt. 28:19); ܒܝܘܡܬ (J. S. 2:15).

4. (1) ܡܠܟ ܫܠܝܡ *king of Salem* (Gen. 14:18); ܚܛܗܝܗܘܢ *their sins* (Gen. 18:20); ܐܢܬܬ ܚܒܪܗ *the wife of his neighbor* (Did. 1:19); ܢܦܫܟ *thy soul* (J. S. 2:17); ܚܟܡܬܗ *his wisdom* (J. S. 4:8).

(2) ܕܚܠܬ ܐܠܗܐ *fear of God* (Acts 9:31); ܒܪܚܡܬ ܫܠܡܐ *for the love of peace* (J. S. 90:5); ܕܚܠܬܗ *fear of him* (Sp. Syr. 2:25); ܪܚܡܬ ܟܣܦܐ *the love of silver* (1 Tim. 6:10); ܥܠܬ ܪܚܡܬܗ ܒܠܒܗ *the love for her entered his heart* (Sind. 4:10).

Rem. 1.—ܥܠܬ ܡܢ ܚܘܒܠܢܐ *now the cause of the destruction* (Ephr. II. 124:3 [Nöld.]); ܓܢܒܪ ܗܘܐ ܚܝܠܗ *he was a hero of strength* (Judges 11:1).

Rem. 2.—ܟܬܒܐ ܟܬܝܒܝ ܩܕܡܐܝܬ *βιβλία ἀναγεγράμμενα* (James of Edessa Z. D. M. G. XXXII, p. 488.9); ܚܝܝ ܒܝܫܐܝܬ *living miserably* (Jul. 112:13 [Nöld.]); ܪܚܡܬ ܠܐܠܗܐ *God-loving* (J. S. 1:1).

Rem. 3.—ܒܝܪܚ ܚܙܝܪܢ ܘܠܬܡܘܙ *in the month of Haziron and of Tammuz* (J. S. 40:10).

The genitive relation, called construction or annexion, is denoted by a noun in the construct state (*see* § 76), followed by a noun in the emphatic state. The following varieties may be noted.

1. Where two, or more, words form together but one idea, as (*a*) in compound words, and (*b*) in translations of a single Greek word.

2. Where the first word has a main idea which the second limits as to quality, origin, possession, designation &c. The first may be (*a*) a noun, or (*b*) an adjective:

Rem.—A preposition may come between the adjective and the noun.

3. Where the second noun has the main idea, which the first limits as to time, place, quantity, manner &c. Many compound prepositions are used in this construction.

4. Where two words have distinct ideas of equal value, we have (*a*) the subjective genitive, (*b*) the objective genitive.

Rem. 1.—A particle, or enclitic verb, occasionally comes between the two nouns in construction.

Rem. 2.—A participle may be in construction with an adverb, or with a governed noun preceded by ܠ.

Rem. 3.—A noun in the construct may have two nouns after it. Generally, however, in such cases the relative ܕ is employed.

§ 97 A.

II. The Genitive with ܕ.

1. ܢܒܝ̈ܐ ܕܕܓܠܘܬܐ ψευδοπροφῆται (Mt. 24:24).

2. ܡܠܟܘܬܐ ܕܫܡܝܐ *the kingdom of heaven* (Mt. 13:11); ܒܐܪܥܐ ܕܟܠܕܝܐ *in the land of the Chaldeans* (Julianos 6:1); ܛܘܪܐ ܕܙܝܬܐ *the mount of Olives* (Mt. 21:1); ܪܘܚܐ ܕܩܘܕܫܐ *the Holy spirit* (Mt. 28:19); ܥܕܥܕܐ ܕܦܨܚܐ *the Passover* (John. 13:1); (Mt. 2:1).

3. ܫܢܝ̈ܐ ܕܫܬܐ ܐܠܦ̈ܝܢ 6000 *years* (Aphr. 36:20); ܩܒܐ ܕܚ̈ܛܐ *a kab of beans* (J. S. 34:20).

4. ܫܘܒܚܐ ܕܐܠܗܐ *the glory of God* (John. 11:4); ܐܘܪܚܐ ܕܚܛܝ̈ܐ *in the way of sinners* (Mt. 5:10); ܢܦܩ̈ܬܐ ܕܒܢܝܢܐ *expenditures for the building* (J. S. 81:18); ܡܛܠ ܚܠܝܠܘܬܐ ܕܦܓܪܝܗܘܢ *on account of the leanness of their bodies* (J. S. 37:1); ܐܘܪܚܐ ܕܐܝܠܢܐ *the way to the tree* (Gen. 3:24).

Rem. 1.—ܒܙܒܢܐ ܕܫܘܠܡܐ ܕܚܝܘܗܝ *at the time of the end of his life* (J. S. 91:15), ܐܘܠܨܢܐ ܕܩܡܨܐ ܘܕܟܦܢܐ ܘܕܡܘܬܢܐ *afflictions of locusts and famine and pestilence* (J. S. 40:16). See, also, J. S. 92:11; Did. 1:5. ܬܘܠܕܬܐ ܕܫܡܝܐ ܘܕܐܪܥܐ (Gen. 2:4). See, also, Gen. 30:37; Mt. 26:28. ܟܬܒܟ ܕܚܝܐ *thy book of life* (Ps. 69:28); ܚܛܝܬܐ ܕܝܠܝ ܘܕܐܒܗܝ *my sin and that of my fathers* (Legends of St. Mary [Ms.] p. 9:1); ܡܠܐ ܕܡܪܢ ܘܕܡܫܝܚܗ *the words of our Lord and of his Messiah* (J. S. 46:7); ܚܫܐ ܕܢܦܫܗ ܘܕܦܓܪܐ *sufferings of his soul and of the body* (Overbeck 175:26).

Rem. 2.—ܟܠ ܒܣܪ ܕܚܝܘܬܐ *any flesh of an animal* (Sp. Syr. 7:26); ܡܢ ܟܠ ܫܘܠܛܢܐ ܕܪܗܘܡܝܘܬܐ *from all the power of Rome* (Did. 75:6); ܐܬܝܠܕ ܕܠܐ ܙܘܘܓܐ *born without marriage* (Overbeck [Nöld. § 206]).

Rem. 3.—ܐܣܛܘܐ ܕܫܠܝܡܘܢ *Solomon's porch* (John. 10:23); ܒܝܬ ܠܚܡ ܕܝܗܘܕܐ *Bethlehem Judah* (Mt. 2:1); ܛܘܥܝܝ ܕܥܘܬܪܐ *the deceitfulness of riches* (Mt. 13:22).

Rem. 4.—ܥܠܬܐ ܡܕܡ ܕܡܘܬܐ *any cause whatsoever of death* (Ad. Ap. 12:13); ܕܝܘܠܦܢܐ ܐܠܗܝܐ ܚܬܡܐ ܗܘ ܕܪܥܝܢܐ *because the divine teaching is the seal of the mind* (Sp. Eph. Syr. Overbeck p. 22:6).

By means of the relative ܕ, all the varieties of the genitive mentioned under I. may be expressed, ܕ being in apposition with the noun preceding it, and in construction with that which follows.

Rem. 1.—The construction with ܕ is usual where there are two or more genitives. Where two or more genitives are dependent on one noun, the first may be in construction, the second with ܕ, though usually both, or all, have ܕ.

Rem. 2.—The first noun is occasionally found in the absolute state, or even the construct.

§ 97b.]   ELEMENTS OF SYRIAC.   117

Rem. 3.—This is the construction used with foreign and indeclinable nouns, *see* § 86. 6.

Rem. 4.—Sometimes a word comes between the first noun and the relative, *see* B. Rem. 2.

§ 97 B.

III. The Genitive relation denoted by the pronominal suffix and ܕ.

ܒܠܒܗ ܕܐܪܥܐ *in the heart of the earth* (Mt. 12:40).

ܥܒܕܘܗܝ ܕܡܫܝܚܐ *the works of Messiah* [lit. *The works of him who is Messiah*] (Mt. 11:2).

ܚܣܕܗ ܕܡܫܝܚܐ *the reproach of Christ* (Heb. 11:26).

ܕܚܠܬܗ ܕܡܪܝܐ *the fear of the Lord* (Did. 1:8).

Rem. 1.—ܐܕܢܗ ܕܝܡܝܢܐ *his right ear;* ܡܠܟܘܬܗ ܕܠܥܠܡ *his eternal kingdom* (Did. 1:5).

Rem. 2.—ܕܚܠܬܗ ܓܝܪ ܕܐܠܗܐ *for the fear of God* (Sp. Syr. 2:26); ܐܒܐ ܗܘ ܓܝܪ ܕܝܬܡܐ *for he was the father of the orphans* (Overbeck 207:19); ܐܢ ܒܪܗ ܐܢܬ ܕܐܠܗܐ *if thou be the son of God* (Mt. 27:40); ܘܡܫܘܬܦܐ ܗܘ ܬܘܒ ܕܐܒܝܠܐ *and he was, moreover, a companion of the sorrowing* (Ov. 207:2); ܗܢܐ ܗܘ ܒܪܗ ܗܘ ܕܐܠܗܐ *this was the son of God* (Mt. 27:55).

Rem. 3.—ܡܛܠܗܢܐ ܕܗܢܐ *because of this* (J. S. 11:19). (But Sp. Syr. 2:11 ܡܛܠ ܕܗܢܐ).

Rem. 4.—ܒܟܠܗ ܐܪܥܐ *in all the earth* (Lk. 4:25); ܚܝܠܗ ܟܠܗ *his whole army* (J. S. 10:12); ܟܠܗ ܕܗܝܡܢܘܬܢ *of our whole faith* (Aphr. 6:16).

When the second noun is determinate, the first often takes a pronominal suffix, agreeing in gender and number with the second noun. The second noun is really in apposition with the pronominal suffix of the first.

Rem. 1.—When the clause with ܕ is an adjective clause, limiting the noun and not the pronominal suffix, it is treated as a nominal sentence, of which ܕ is the subject and the noun, substantive or adjective, is the predicate. If this predicate is an adjective, it is in the absolute state and agrees with its antecedent in gender and number, see § 79. 2.

Rem. 2.—One, or two words, especially particles, pronouns, enclitic copulas may come between the pronominal suffix and the relative, see A, Rem. 4.

Rem. 3.—A preposition may take this construction.

Rem. 4.—ܟܠ *all*, takes the pronominal suffix agreeing in gender and number with the following noun. The noun, however, is put in direct apposition with the suffix, ܕ being omitted.

§ 98.
IV. Genitive with Prepositions.

1. ܗܘܬ ܒܢܫܐ ܕܐܝܬܝܗܝܢ ܠܡܠܟܐ *she was among the women belonging to the king of the Huns* (J. S. 19:6); ܟܘܒܫܐ ܠܪ̈ܓܠܝܟ *a stool for thy feet* (Acts 2:35); ܡܣܝܡ ܠܗ *composed by him* (J. S. 51:18); ܠܕܘܝܕ *by David* (Ps. 3 heading).

Rem.—ܓܡܘܪܐ ܠܗܝܡܢܘܬܢ *finisher of our faith* (Heb. 12:2); ܙܟܘܬܐ ܠܩܘܣܛܢܛܝܢܘܦܘܠܝܣ *the conquest of Constantinople* (Kirsch, Chrest. 136:1).

2. ܐܚܕ ܚܡܫܐ ܡܢ ܪܝܫܢܝܗܘܢ *he seized five of their chiefs* (J. S. 82:22); ܚܕ ܡܢ ܐܣܛܪ̈ܛܝܓܐ *one of the generals* (J. S. 59:13); ܬܪܝܢ ܡܢܟܘܢ *two of you* (Mt. 18:19).

1. The genitive of possession and of the author may be expressed by the preposition ܠ.

Rem.—Verbal and some other nouns govern another noun in the accusative, the construction being equivalent to our genitive relation.

2. The partitive genitive is expressed by means of the preposition ܡܢ.

§ 99. The Adjective.

1. ܢܗܝ̈ܪܐ ܪܘܪ̈ܒܐ *great lights* (Gen. 1:16); ܬܫܒ̈ܚܬܐ ܪܘܪ̈ܒܬܐ *great praises* (J. S. 1:5); ܢܘܗܪܐ ܪܒܐ *great light* (Gen. 1:16); ܒܗܬܬܐ ܪܒܬܐ *great shame* (J. S. 1:6); ܪܘܚܐ ܪܒܬܐ *great wind* (Jon. 1:4); ܐܬܘ̈ܬܐ ܪܘܪ̈ܒܬܐ *great signs* (Mt. 24:24); ܪܘܚܐ ܛܥܝܬܐ *an erring spirit* (Is. 19:14); ܪܘܚ̈ܐ ܛܥܝ̈ܬܐ *erring spirits* (1 Tim. 4:1).

Rem. 1.—ܡܬܠܐ ܐܚܪܢܐ *another parable* (Mt. 13:24); ܣܓ̈ܝ ܨܒܘ̈ܬܐ *many things* (Sp. Syr. 6:6); ܙܒܢܐ ܩܠܝܠ *a little time* (Rev. 12:12); ܫܡ ܩܕܡܝܐ (Gen. 5:7); ܫܬܐܣܬܐ ܩܕܡܝܬܐ *the first foundation* (Sp. Syr. 49:29); ܕܝܢ ܣܪܓܝܣ ܡܝܬܪܐ *now the excellent Sergius;* ܡܪܝܡ ܩܕܝܫܬܐ *holy Mary* (Aphr. 180:2); ܝܥܩܘܒ ܕܝܢ ܡܝܩܪܐ *now the honored Jacob.*

Rem. 2.—ܗܠܝܢ ܬܠܬܐ ܟܐ̈ܢܐ ܐܕܫ̈ܝܐ *these three righteous men* (Aphr. 454:3); ܝܘܡܐ ܚܕ *day one* (Gen. 1:5); ܫܒܥ ܬܘܪ̈ܬܐ ܦܛܝ̈ܡܬܐ *seven fat kine* (Gen. 41:18).

Rem. 3.—ܟܢܫܐ ܣܓܝܐܐ ܥܡܗ *a great company with him* (Mt. 26:47); ܚܠܦ ܗܢܐ ܛܒܬܐ ܗܝ *for this is a good thing* (Sp. Syr. 1:20); ܪܘܚܗ ܩܕܝܫܐ *his Holy spirit* (Did. 1:6); ܨܒܝܢܟ ܚܝܠܬܢܐ *thy energetic will* (J. S. 2:1).

Rem. 4.—ܕܡܗ ܕܟܝܐ ܘܝܩܝܪܐ *his pure and precious blood* (Did. 1:7); ܫܘܥܝ̈ܬܐ ܟܪ̈ܝܬܐ ܘܡܠܢ̈ܝܬܐ *sad and melancholy tales* (J. S. 5:9).

2. ܕܛܒ *that it was good* (Gen. 1:3); ܪܘܚܗ ܕܐܠܗܐ ܡܪܚܦܐ *the spirit of God was brooding* (Gen. 1:2); ܘܚܘܝܐ ܚܪܥ ܗܘܐ *and the serpent was cunning* (Gen. 3:1); ܟܠ ܕܛܒ *anything that was good* (J. S. 2:17); ܕܛܒܢ *that they are true* (J. S. 5:12); ܐܝܠܝܢ ܕܩܪܝܢ ܐܘ ܫܡܥܝܢ *those that read or hear* (J. S. 5:12).

Rem. 1.—ܐܢܐ ܡܗܝܡܢ *I believe* (John. 9:38); ܬܟܝܠ ܐܢܐ *I rely* (J. S. 4:2).

Rem. 2.—ܡܬܦܬܚܢ ܥܝܢܝܟܘܢ *your eyes shall be opened* (Gen. 3:5); ܡܬܒܠܥ ܢܘܗܪܗܘܢ ܒܙܝܘܗ ܕܫܡܫܐ *absorbed is their light in the splendor of the sun* (Aph. 434:21).

Rem. 3.—ܕܣܡܝܐ ܗܘܐ *who had been blind* (John. 9:13); ܟܐܢܐ ܚܢܢ *we are upright* (Gen. 42:11); ܫܪܝܪܐܝܬ ܗܢܘ ܫܠܝܚܐ *truly this is the apostle* (Addai Apost. 34:8).

1. The adjective, or participle, when used in an attributive sense, follows the noun which it modifies and agrees with it in gender, number and state.

Rem. 1.—The adjectives ܐܚܪܢܐ *other*, ܣܓܝ *much*, ܩܠܝܠ *little*, *few*, often precede their nouns; as, also, do other adjectives occasionally, especially words of praise or blame.

Rem. 2.—Occasionally, the noun and adjective do not agree as to state.

Rem. 3.—One, or more words, may occur between the noun and its adjective. The pronominal suffix occurs regularly between the noun and adjective.

Rem. 4.—More than one adjective may limit the same noun.

2. When the adjective or participle is predicative, it agrees with its antecedent in gender and number, but is generally in the absolute state. It usually follow the subject noun. But:—

Rem. 1.—The predicate precedes the plural pronoun which becomes enclitic.

Rem. 2.—Sometimes when emphatic the predicate precedes the subject noun.

Rem. 3.—When the definiteness of the predicate is to be emphasized, it is put in the emphatic state. The predicate is emphatic also in nouns which have no absolute state. § 86. 17 (2).

§ 100. Comparative and Superlative.

1. ܚܪܝܡ ܡܢ ܟܠܗ ܚܝܘܬܐ *subtler than any beast* (Gen. 3:1).

ܝܬܝܪ ܡܢ ܢܦܫܝ ܐܚܒܬܢܝ *more than thyself thou hast loved me* (J. S. 2:14).

ܝܬܝܪ ܡܢ ܬܪܬܥܣܪܐ ܪܒܘܢ ܓܒܪܝܢ *more than* 120000 *men* (Jon. 4:11).

ܣܲܓܝܼܐܝܼܢ ܐܸܢܘܿܢ ܗܵܠܹܝܢ ܡܸܢ ܗܵܠܹܝܢ *more are these than those* (J. S. 80:4).

ܣܓܸܕܘ ܠܲܒܪܝܼܬܵܐ ܝܲܬܝܼܪ ܡܸܢ ܕܲܠܒܵܪܘܿܝܵܗ̇ *they worshipped the creatures more than their Creator* (Rom. 1:25).

Rem. 1.—ܪܵܘܪܒ ܠܝܼ *too great for me* (J. S. 3:8).

ܛܠܸܐ ܗܘܵܐ ܡܸܢ ܚܛܵܗܹܐ *too young for sins* (Aphr. 221:12).

Rem. 2.—ܣܐܸܒ ܡܸܢ ܕܲܠܡܵܘܠܵܕܘܼ *too old to beget* (Sp. Syr. 11:8).

ܪܲܒ ܥܵܘܠܵܐ ܡܸܢ ܕܲܠܡܸܫܒܲܩ *too great to forgive* (Gen. 4:13).

ܦܲܩܵܚ ܠܝܼ ܕܐܹܡܘܼܬ ܝܲܬܝܼܪ ܡܸܢ ܕܲܐܚܸܐ *it is much better for me to die than to live* (Jon. 4:3).

Rem. 3.—ܚܘܲܪܘ ܡܸܢ ܚܲܠܒܵܐ *they are whiter than milk* (Lam. 4:7).

ܘܲܕܟܝܼܘ ܡܸܢ ܬܲܠܓܵܐ *they are purer than snow* (Lam. 4:7).

Rem. 4.—ܠܨܘܿܪ ܘܲܠܨܲܝܕܵܢ ܢܸܗܘܹܐ ܢܝܼܚ ܒܝܵܘܡܵܐ ܕܕܝܼܢܵܐ ܐܵܘ ܠܟ݂ܘܿܢ *It will be more tolerable for Tyre et Sidon in the day of judgment than for you* (Mt. 11:22).

ܦܲܩܵܚ ܗ̱ܘ ܠܡܸܡܲܬ ܡܸܢ ܟܲܦܢܵܐ ܐܵܘ ܥܲܡܠܵܐ ܣܲܓܝܼܐܵܐ ܠܡܲܚܫܵܟ݂ܘܼ ܢܲܦ̮ܫܵܐ *It is better to die of hunger than by much food to obscure the soul* (Anal. syr. 7:2). ܦܲܩܵܚ ܠܡܸܡܲܬ—ܘܠܵܐ ܠܡܹܐܒܲܕ *It is better to die &c. rather than to perish* (J. S. 65:12).

Rem. 5.—ܡܫܲܡܫܵܢܵܘܗܝ ܣܲܓܝܼܐܝܼܢ ܡܸܢ ܡܸܢܝܵܢܵܐ *his servants are innummerable* (St. Ephrem on Dan. 7:10). (See Duval § 366 g.)

2. (1) ܗܵܢܵܘ ܦܘܼܩܕܵܢܵܐ ܪܲܒܵܐ ܩܲܕܡܵܝܵܐ *this is the greatest and the first commandment* (Mt. 22:38); ܙܥܘܿܪ—ܪܲܒ *least—greatest* (Mt. 5:19); ܐܸܢܵܐ ܐ̱ܢܵܐ ܐܚܪܵܝܵܐ ܕܲܫܠܝܼܚܹܐ *I am least of the apostles* (1 Cor. 15:9); ܡܝܲܬܪܵܐ ܕܓܲܒܪܹܐ *most excellent of men* (J. S. 1:1).

(2) ܐܲܝܢܵܐ ܦܘܼܩܕܵܢܵܐ ܪܲܒ ܒܢܵܡܘܿܣܵܐ *which commandment is greatest in the law?* (Mt. 22:36); ܙܥܘܿܪܬܵܐ ܒܡܲܠܟܹ̈ܐ ܕܲܝܗܘܼܕܵܐ *least among the kings of Judah* (Mt. 2:6).

(3) ܪܰܒܳܐ ܡܶܢ ܟܽܠ ܡܰܚܘ̈ܳܢ *the greatest of all plagues* (Eph. 1:204c); ܐܢ̱ܬ ܗ̄ܝ ܪܫܝܥܐ ܘܒܝܫ ܡܢ ܟܠܗܘܢ ܒܢܝ̈ܢܫܐ *Thou art the most wicked and the worst of men* (Act. Martyr. 223).

(4) *a.* ܡܰܠܟܳܐ ܕܡܰܠ̈ܟܶܐ *king of kings* (Rev. 17:14); ܥܒܶܕ ܥܰܒܕܺܝܢ *servant of servants* (Gen. 9:25); ܩܽܘܕܫ ܩܽܘܕ̈ܫܶܐ *holy of holies* (Ex. 26:33).

b. ܚܺܐܪܽܘܬܳܐ ܡܚܰܪܰܪܬܳܐ *perfect liberty* (Anal. syr. 49:21).

(5) ܪܺܝܫ ܡܰܠܰܐ̈ܟܶܐ *archangel* (1 Thess. 4:16); ܪܺܝܫ ܚܰܕܘܳܬܝ *my chief joy,* (Song of Songs 4:14); ܪܰܒܬܳܐ ܠܰܐܠܳܗܳܐ *exceeding great* (Jon. 3:3); ܛܽܘܪ̈ܶܐ ܕܰܐܠܳܗܳܐ *mighty mountains* (Ps. 36:6).

1. The comparative of adjectives is expressed by the simple adjective with ܡܶܢ. The comparative idea may be strengthened by the use of such adjectives as ܛܳܒ, ܣܰܓܺܝ and ܝܰܬܺܝܪ.

Rem. 1.—ܡܶܢ may sometimes be translated by "*too*".

Rem. 2.—ܡܶܢ in the sense of "*too*" or "*than*" is frequently used before an infinitive with the relative § 120. 1 (6).

Rem. 3.—ܡܶܢ is sometimes used in a comparative sense after verbs.

Rem. 4.—ܐܘ and ܘ are sometimes used instead of ܡܶܢ.

Rem. 5.—The construct state of an adjective is occasionally found before ܡܶܢ.

2. The superlative degree may be expressed:

(1) By a determinate noun *i. e.* a noun in the emphatic or construct state.

(2) By means of the preposition ܒ.

(3) By means of ܡܶܢ ܟܽܠ.

(4) *a.* By means of a noun in the singular in the genitive relation with the same noun in the plural; or (*b*) by means of a noun limited by an adjective from the same root.

(5) By means of ܪܺܝܫ *chief;* and *perhaps,* in a few cases, by means of ܐܰܠܳܗܳܐ *God.*

§ 101. The Personal Pronoun.

A. AS SUBJECT OR COPULA.

1. (1) ܢܳܛܽܘܪܶܗ ܐ̱ܢܳܐ ܕܰܐܚܝ *am I my brother's keeper?* (Gen. 4:9).

ܙܰܟܳܝ ܐ̱ܢܳܐ *I am guiltless* (Job. 33:9).

ܐܢܬ ܐܠܗܐ *thou art God* (Addai 3 ult.).

ܥܡܟ ܚܢܢ *thy people are we* (Aphr. 448:9).

Rem.—ܡܫܐܠ ܐܢܐ *I ask* (Eph. 3:13)

ܚܝܒ ܗܘ *he is a debtor* (Gal. 5:3).

(2) ܐܦ ܐܢܬܘܢ ܬܚܘܢ *ye shall live also* (John. 14:19).

ܗܘ ܢܕܘܫ ܪܫܟ *he shall bruise thy head* (Gen. 3:15).

ܘܗܘ ܐܬܬܚܕ *and he himself was taken* (Jos. St. 10:12).

ܗܘ ܕܝܢ ܕܘܝܕ *now Ḳawid himself* (Jos. Sty. 19:4). (See also Rom. 14:9; Ephes. 4:20; Acts 19:15; Lk. 3:14; Spic. Syr. 1:7).

(3) ܢܦܩ ܣܝܚܘܢ ܠܐܘܪܥܢ ܗܘ ܘܟܠܗ ܥܡܗ *Sihon went out to meet us, he and all his people* (Deut. 2:32); ܕܬܦܠ ܐܢܬ ܘܝܗܘܕܐ ܥܡܟ *that thou shouldest fall thou and Judah with thee* (2 King 14:10). (See also Deut. 5:14, 12:7; Gen. 6:18, 13:1).

2. (1) ܚܢܢ ܕܝܢ ܐܡܪܝܢܢ *but we say* (Jos. Sty. 42:19).

ܘܐܢܬܘܢ ܒܝ ܐܢܬܘܢ ܘܐܢܐ ܥܡܟܘܢ ܐܢܐ *and ye are in me and I am in you* (John. 14:20).

ܐܦ ܐܢܬ ܡܢܗܘܢ ܐܢܬ *thou art one of them* (Matt. 27:73).

Rem. 1.—ܐܢ ܕܬܐܠܦ ܗܘ ܨܒܝܬ *If to learn thou art willing* (Spic. Syr. 1:15).

ܡܛܠ ܗܠܝܢ ܚܛܐ ܗܘ ܫܠܝܡܐ ܡܠܟܐ *because of these things Solomon sinned* (Neh. 15:26).

ܘܐܢ ܗܕܐ ܗܝ ܡܠܬܐ *and if this word* (Spic. Syr. 2:5).

ܗܘܐ ܡܠܠ *he has spoken* (Aphr. 5:1).

ܐܠܐ ܢܡܘܣܐ ܗܘ ܡܩܝܡܝܢܢ *but the law we are establishing* (Rom. 3.31).

Note.—ܗܕܐ ܗܘ ܕܢܥܒܕ *this to do* (Jos. Sty. 3:32).

ܘܟܕ ܐܬܐ ܗܘ ܗܢܐ ܠܐܢܛܝܘܟܝܐ *when this one came to Antioch* (Jos. Sty. 13:1). (See also Jos. Sty. 12:11, 7:22).

Rem. 2.—ܗܝ ܗܝ ܨܥܪ *that is Zoar* (Gen. 14:8).

ܒܩܘܪܝܬ ܓܢܒܪܐ ܗܝ ܗܝ ܚܒܪܘܢ *in the city of giants i. e. Hebron* (Gen. 23:2).

ܥܣܘ ܗܘܝܘ ܐܕܘܡ *Esau i. e. Edom* (Gen. 36:19; Comp. 36:43).

Note.—ܩܕܡ ܢܕܘܒܥܠ ܕܗܘ ܓܕܥܘܢ *Nedubaal, that is Gideon rose up early* (Jud. 7:1).

2. (2) ܐܢܐ ܗܘ ܝܫܘܥ *I am Jesus* (Acts 22:8).

ܐܢ ܐܢܬ ܗܘ ܡܫܝܚܐ *Art thou the Christ* (Luke 22:67).

A. The personal pronoun may be used separately (*compare* § 95:1).

1. (1) As the subject of a nominal sentence.

Rem.—The pronoun often coalesces with the preceding participle or adjective, *see* § 35. 2.

(2) In verbal sentences to emphasize the subject. It may then often be translated by "*self*".

(3) If a second subject follows the verb the subject contained in the verbal form is emphasized by the corresponding personal pronoun.

2. It is used as a kind of copula, *see* § 130. 1 (2).

(1) Agreeing in person, number and gender with the subject.

Rem. 1.—(*comp.* § 95. 4) Here belongs the use of ܗܘ without agreement of gender or number for the putting of special emphasis upon the word which precedes it.

Note.—Sometimes the pronoun precedes the word. It is then equivalent to the article.

Rem. 2.—ܗܝ ܗܝ denotes "*that is*", "*id est*".

Note.—ܕܗܘ also is sometimes used for "*that is*".

(2) Agreeing in number and gender only with the subject.

B. AS SUFFIX.

1. (1) ܕܢܫܠܡܘܢܗ *that they should deliver it* (Jos. St. 56:1).

ܒܪܝܗܝ *created he him* (Gen. 1:27).

ܫܕܪܗ *he sent it* (Ad. 1:3).

ܚܙܐܘܗܝ *they saw him* (Ad. 2:10).

ܚܘܝܐ ܐܛܥܝܢܝ *the serpent beguiled me* (Gen. 3:13).

ܬܫܘܦܝܘܗܝ *thou shalt bruise him* (Gen. 3:15).

Rem. 1.—ܒܪܐ ܐܢܘܢ *created he them* (Gen. 1:27).

ܒܪܟ ܐܢܘܢ *he blessed them* (Gen. 1:28); ܠܐ ܡܩܒܠ ܐܢܐ ܠܗܘܢ *I will not accept them* (Mal. 1:13).

Rem. 2.—ܫܕܝܗܝ ܠܟܣܦܐ *he cast the silver* (Matt. 27:5).

ܦܣܩܗ ܠܐܕܢܗ ܕܐܠܘܣ *he cut off the ear of Illus* (Jos. St. 12:9).

ܦܩܕ ܗܘܐ ܐܢܘܢ ܠܬܠܡܝܕܐ *he had commanded the disciples* (Acts 1:2).

ܟܬܒܬ ܐܢܝܢ ܠܬܫܥܝܬܐ *I have written these narratives* (Jos. St. 20:17).

Rem. 3.—ܕܡܦܩܕ ܐܢܐ ܠܟ ܐܝܕܐ ܘܒܪܟ ܘܒܪ ܒܪܟ *which I am commanding thee and thy son and thy son's son* (Deut. 6:2).

Rem. 4.—ܩܕܡܝ ܗܘ *and he was before me* (John. 1:15).

ܐܙܠܘ ܗܘܘ ܒܬܪܗ *they went after her* (John. 11:31).

ܡܫܟܚ ܐܢܐ ܓܝܪ ܠܘܬ ܐܒܝ *and I go to my father* (Ad. 4:15; Acts 5:39; Acts 12:19, 10:26, 12:15; Rom. 1:22).

(2) ܬܐܟܠܝܘܗܝ *thou mayest eat of it* (Gen. 3:17).

ܡܢܘ ܚܘܝܟ *who showed thee* (Gen. 3:11).

2. (1) a. ܒܨܠܡܗ *in his image* (Gen. 1:27).

ܘܒܝܬ ܙܪܥܟ ܠܙܪܥܗ *and between thy seed and her seed* (Gen. 3:15).

ܚܝܝܟ *thy life* (Gen. 3:17).

b. ܠܕܘܟܪܢܝ *for a memorial of me* (Lk. 22:19).

ܕܚܠܬܗ *fear before him* (Ex. 20:20).

Rem. 1.—ܠܚܡܐ ܕܣܘܢܩܢܢ *our necessary bread* (Mt. 6:11; Mk. 16:14);

ܡܢ ܐܘܪܚܬܟܝ ܕܙܢܝܘܬܐ *from thy whorish ways* (Ezech. 16:27).

Rem. 2.—ܒܛܘܪܗ ܩܕܝܫܐ *in his holy mount* (Ps. 87:1).

ܒܪܗ ܒܘܟܪܐ *her first born son* (Mt. 1:25, so also Mt. 3:17).

ܚܐܪܘܬܢ ܙܟܝܬܐ *our prevailing freedom* (Overbeck 21:20).

3. (1) ܒܗ ܒܫܪܒܐ ܗܢܐ *with this history* (Jos. Sty. 8:7).

ܒܗ ܒܫܘܠܛܢܗܘܢ *under their government* (Jos. Sty. 8:15).

ܒܗܘܢ ܕܝܢ ܒܝܘܡܬܐ ܗܢܘܢ *Now in those days* (Mat. 3:1).

(2) *a.* ܘܒܗ ܒܫܥܬܐ *and in the same hour* (Acts 3:7; Mt. 26:74), ܒܗ ܒܡܠܬܐ *through the same word* (Overbeck 21:20); ܒܗ ܒܐܬܪܐ *in the same place* (Luk. 2:8); ܠܗ ܠܡܠܬܐ *the same word* (Matt. 26:44); ܦܓܥ ܒܗ ܒܐܝܠܘܣ *he met Illus* (Jos. Sty. 12:6).

b. ܕܠܐ ܝܕܥ ܐܢܐ ܠܗ ܠܓܒܪܐ *I know not the man* (Mat. 26:74). ܕܠܐ ܐܢܫ ܢܩܛܘܠ ܠܗܘܢ ܠܐܝܠܝܢ ܕܡܫܕܪ ܐܢܐ *no man shall kill those whom I send*; ܠܗ ܠܡܫܬܘܬܐ *to the feast.*

Rem.—ܡܢܗ ܡܢ ܐܠܦܐ *from the ship* (Acts 27:3).

ܥܡܗ ܥܡ ܡܫܝܚܐ *with Christ* (Rom. 6:8).

ܥܠܘܗܝ ܥܠ ܗܕܐ *on account of this* (Acts 9:21).

ܥܠܘܗܝ ܥܠ ܟܐܦܐ *over the stone* (Aphr. 6 ult.)

B. The pronominal suffixes are substituted for the independent pronoun in all oblique cases; except in the case of the third plural after verbs, where the enclitics ܐܢܘܢ and ܐܢܝܢ are used.

1. With verbs.

(1) The pronominal suffix is generally the direct object.

Rem. 1.—The 3rd person plural after verbs is either the independent personal pronoun or the pronominal suffix after Lomadh.

Rem. 2.—The pronominal suffix is often used after a verb to determine its object.

Rem. 3.—When a second object follows, the independent personal pronoun may be used to strengthen the suffix.

Rem. 4.—Preceded by ܠ, it forms the socalled ethical dative, which can rarely be translated into English. *See* § 124:5.

(2) Sometimes it is the indirect object.

2. With nouns.

(1) The pronominal suffix may be treated as a genitive (*see* §§ 96:98):

a. subjective when it is equivalent to an adjective or possessive pronoun.

b. objective.

§ 102.]   ELEMENTS OF SYRIAC.   127

Rem. 1.—In the genitive relation the pronoun is usually attached to the last noun, but sometimes to the first.

Rem. 2.—With adjectives, the pronominal suffix is attached to the noun.

3. With prepositions.

(1) The pronominal suffix is used with the preposition where the noun following it is definite.

(2) When ܒ and ܠ are used with a suffix they are repeated before the noun. In this construction

a. the suffix with ܒ sometimes denotes *"the same"*, though generally it has the force of the definite article merely, *see also* § 107. 9.

b. the suffix with ܠ often has the sense of the definite article.

Rem.—The preposition ܡܢ with the pronominal suffix sometimes occurs before the same preposition followed by its noun.

ܠܘܬ and ܥܡ are used in the same way.

§ 102. The Demonstrative Pronoun.

1. ܗܢܐ ܒܙܒܢܐ *at this time* (Jos. Sty. 2:3).

   ܐܬܘܬܐ ܗܠܝܢ *these signs* (Jos. Sty. 3:17).

   ܡܛܠ ܕܗܕܐ ܡܠܬܐ *on account of this word* (Spic. Syr. 20).

   ܡܛܠ ܗܠܝܢ ܣܘܥܪܢܐ *on account of these deeds* (Spic. Syr. 6:2).

   ܒܗܢܐ ܙܒܢܐ *this time* (5:4).

2. ܗܘܫܥ ܗܢܘ ܡܪܝܐ ܦܪܘܩܐ *Hosea, that is "the Lord is Saviour"* (Bar Heb. Sch. M. 1:7).

   ܗܢܘ ܦܓܪܝ *this is my body* (Matt. 26:26). *See* § 36:3.

3. ܗܘ ܕܒܠܚܘܕ ܗܘ ܕܦܩܝܕ ܠܗܘܢ ܕܢܥܒܕܘܢ *that that alone which was commanded them should they do* (Spic. Syr. 3:15).

   ܗܘ ܕܝܢܐ ܕܥܠܡܐ ܕܥܬܝܕ *the judgement of the world to come* (Jos. Sty. 6:4).

   ܙܒܢܐ ܗܘ ܕܣܝܡ ܒܡܕܥܗ ܗܘ ܕܠܐ ܛܥܐ *until the time decreed in His unerring knowledge* (Jos. Sty. 6:8). (*So* Jon. 4:49; Matt. 14:21 and Jos. Sty. 49:64, 5:16, 29:6).

Rem.—ܡܠܝܢ ܗܠܝܢ *these our words* (Aphr. 299:2).

ܒܝܕܥܬܗ ܗܘ ܕܠܐ ܛܥܝܐ *in his knowledge that which is unerring* (Jos. Sty. 6:8, 1:27).

4. ܠܘܩܒܠ ܗܕܐ ܕܝܠܟ *in comparison with this of thine* (Jos. Sty. 2:19).

ܗܢܐ ܕܝܠܟ *this of thine* (Sim. Stylites 331, Nöld.).

5. ܒܫܘܠܡܗ ܕܗܕܐ *at the end of it* (Addai 16:1).

ܡܛܠܬܗ ܕܗܕܐ *on account of this* (Jos. Sty. 11:19).

ܥܠ ܐܦܝ ܗܕܐ *for the sake of this* (Jos. Sty. 8:18).

6. ܒܗ ܒܝܪܚܐ ܗܢܐ *in the same month* (Jos. Sty. 58:6).

ܘܗܘ ܗܘ ܝܘܡܐ *and the same day* (John. 5:9).

ܗܝ ܗܝ ܡܕܝܢܬܐ *the same city* (Bar Heb. Sch. M. 1:13).

ܗܘ ܗܢܐ *the same* (Spic. Syr. 22:18).

7. ܕܗܘ ܕܐܫܬܡܥ *of him who has obeyed* (Spic. Syr. 5:2).

ܗܢܘܢ ܕܥܠܝܗܘܢ *those upon whom* (Spic. Syr. 12:2).

ܗܠܝܢ ܕܒܗܝܢ ܦܩܕܬ ܠܝ *those in which thou hast commanded me* (Jos. Sty. 1:2); ܗܘ ܕܡܫܠܡ ܠܝ *he who shall betray me* (Matt. 26:46); ܐܠܐ ܗܘ ܕܐܦ ܡܢ ܚܫܐ ܡܚܪܪ ܗܘܐ *but he who has been delivered from sufferings* (Overbeck 175:26).

Of the demonstrative pronoun it may be remarked.

1. As an adjective it may be placed either before or after its substantive.

2. Before the personal enclitic pronoun it generally coalesces into ܗܢܘ (ܗܢܐ ܗܘ)=*that is, this is*, see § 37. 3.

3. It is sometimes used like ܗܘ for distinction or emphasis, or as an article.

Rem.—A demonstrative may limit a noun in construction with pronominal suffix.

4. The demonstrative may be in construction with a personal pronoun.

5. The demonstrative may be used as a genitive.

6. "The same" is generally expressed by the demonstrative pronoun preceded by the personal pronoun. *See* § 107:9.

7. The demonstrative is used before the relative in the sense of "that which", "he who" &c. *See* § 104. 2, *Rem.* 1.

§ 103. The Interrogative Pronoun.

1. (1) ܡܰܢ ܗ݈ܝ ܐܶܡܝ ܘܡܰܢ ܐܶܢܘܢ ܐܰܚܰܝ *who is my mother and who are my brethren?* (Matt. 12:48). ܕܡܳܢܐ ܫܠܳܡܐ ܗ݈ܢܐ *what is this salutation?* (Luke 1:29). ܡܰܢܘ ܗܘ ܕܰܡܫܰܡܶܫ ܗܘܐ *who would be he that ministered?* (Spic. Syr. 3:24).
   (2) ܒܰܪ̇ܬ ܡܰܢ ܐܰܢ݈ܬܝ *whose daughter art thou?* (Gen. 24:23).
   (3) ܡܳܢܐ ܐܳܡܪܝܢ ܗܘܰܝܬܘܢ *what were you saying?* (Spic. 1:5).
   (4) ܒܡܳܢܐ ܚܛܰܘ *in what have they sinned?* (Jos. St. 40·3).
   (5) ܡܛܠ ܡܰܢ *on account of whom* (Jonah 1:7).
   ܡܶܛܠܡܳܢܐ *on account of what* (Jon. 1:8).

Rem. 1.—ܡܐ ܩܰܛܝܢ ܬܰܪܥܐ *how strait is the gate* (Matt. 7:14). ܡܐ ܠܢ ܠܳܟ *what is that to us?* (Matt. 27:4). ܡܐ ܠܝ ܘܠܶܟܝ *what have I to do with thee?* (John. 2:4).

Rem. 2.—ܡܰܢ ܫܡܳܟ܂ ܐܳܡܰܪ ܠܶܗ ܠܶܓܝܘܢ *what is thy name? He saith to him Legion* (Lk. 8:30). (See also, Ex. 3:13; Jud. 13:17).

Rem. 3.—ܡܳܢܐ ܡܰܠܝܗ ܣܳܛܳܢܐ ܠܠܶܒܳܟ *what Satan hath filled thy heart?* (Barh. I. p. 184, l. 24 [Duv.]). ܡܳܢܐ ܐܶܢܘܢ ܡܰܠܟܶܐ ܗܳܠܶܝܢ *who are those kings?* (Chrest. Knös. p. 80 vers 10 [Duv.]).

Rem. 4.—ܘܡܰܢ ܗܘ ܕܥܰܒܕܳܗ *of him whosoever had done it* (Jos. Sty. 76:17).

1. ܡܰܢ *"who?"*, ܡܰܢܘ (ܡܰܢ ܗܘ) *"who is?"*, ܡܰܢ, ܡܳܢܐ, ܡܐ *"what?"*, ܡܳܢܰܘ *"what is?"* are used substantively and may stand:—
(1) As subject.
(2) As genetive.
(3) As object direct.
(4) As object indirect.
(5) After prepositions.

Rem. 1.—ܡܐ sometimes means *"how"*. It is used also in certain idiomatic phrases.

Rem. 2.—ܡܳܢ is equivalent to our "*what*" in the phrase ܡܳܢ ܫܡܳܟ "*what is thy name?*".

Rem. 3.—ܡܶܕܶܡ is in a few instances used as an adjective, and occasionally for persons.

Rem. 4.—ܡܰܢ ܕ or ܡܳܢ ܕ may denote "*whoever*", ܡܳܐ ܕ *whatsoever*. See § 107. 7 (4).

2. (1) ܥܰܡ ܡܰܢܽܘ ܐܶܬܟܪܺܝ ܠܶܗ *with whom was he grieved?* (Heb. 3:17); ܐܰܝܢܽܘ ܓܶܝܪ ܣܰܒܪܰܢ *for what is our hope?* (1 Thess. 2:19); ܐܰܝܢܳܐ ܡܶܢܗܽܘܢ ܢܶܦܽܘܩ ܩܰܕܡܳܝܳܐ *which of them should go out first?* (Jos. Sty. 26:1, see also 3:7).

(2) ܒܰܐܝܢܳܐ ܫܽܘܠܛܳܢ *by what authority?* (Matt. 21:23).

ܕܶܐܝܕܳܐ ܐܢ̄ܬܽܘܢ ܪܽܘܚ *of what spirit ye are* (Luke 9:55, see also Rev. 3:5); ܡܶܢ ܐܰܝܢܳܐ ܐܺܝܬ ܥܰܡܳܐ *from what people art thou?* (Jon 1:8).

(3) ܐܰܝܠܶܝܢ ܕܡܶܢ ܚܰܝܠܝ ܥܰܡܺܝܩܳܢ *those things which are too hard for* (*i. e. above*) *my strength* (Jos. Sty. 3:13).

ܫܰܒܩܢܳܗ̇ ܠܐܰܝܕܳܐ ܕܗܘܳܐ *we surrendered to that which was* (Acts 27:15).

Rem.—ܡܨܰܠܶܝܢ ܥܰܠ ܐܰܝܢܳܐ ܕܡܶܬܦܢܶܐ ܠܘܳܬܝ *praying against* (*him*) *who is turned unto me* (Mal. 3:5).

(4) ܕܐܰܝܟ ܐܰܝܠܶܝܢ ܘܳܠܶܐ ܠܟܽܘܢ ܕܬܶܗܘܽܘܢ *what manner of persons ought ye to be?* (2 Heb. 3:11).

2. ܐܰܝܢܳܐ, ܐܰܝܕܳܐ, ܐܰܝܠܶܝܢ, "*who?*", "*which?*", "*what?*" may be used:—

(1) Independently or substantively.

(2) As an adjective.

Rem.—The personal pronoun sometimes comes between the adjective and the noun.

(3) In connection with ܕ to denote "*he who*". In this sense it is sometimes preceded by the demonstrative. Compare 1, Rem. 4.

Rem.—"*he who*", "*that which*" &c. are occasionally denoted by the interrogative alone. In such cases, the whole interrogative sentence is a substantive clause. § 135.

(4) ܐܰܝܟ ܐܰܝܢܳܐ means "*qualis*", "*what manner of?*"

§ 104. The Relative Pronoun.

1. (1) ܕܒܝܬ ܐܝܠܘܣ *they of the house of Illus* (Jos. St. 14:12).

ܐܝܠܢܐ ܕܡܬܩܪܐ ܕܝܕܥܬܐ *the tree which is called that of knowledge.*

ܕܩܣܪ ܠܩܣܪ *the things of Caesar to Caesar* (Mt. 22:21).

(2) ܕܡܪܢ ܚܢܢ *we are the Lord's* (Rom. 14:8).

ܗܢܘܢ ܕܣܡܠܐ *those who are the left's* (Spic. Syr. 12:6; 1 Cor. 3:23; John. 1:52).

(3) ܕܐܝܢܐ ܡܢܗܘܢ ܬܗܘܐ ܐܢܬܬܐ *whose wife shall she be of them* (Mk. 12:23; Gen. 32:17; Mt. 22:20).

(4) ܕܝܠܗܘܢ ܗܝ ܕܐܝܠܝܢ ܕܩܪܝܢ *it is their part that* (*namely*) *of those who read* (Jos. St. 5:12).

ܕܠܒܘܫܐ ܘܕܡܐܢܐ *such as clothes and utensils* (Jos. St. 35:4).

2. ܕܒܪ ܠܠܝܐ ܣܠܩ *which* (masc. sg.) *went up in a night* (Jon. 4:10).

ܕܠܐ ܝܕܥܝܢ *who* (masc. pl.) *know not.*

Rem.—ܕܣܝܡ ܗܘܐ ܒܗ *wherein was put* (Matt. 28:6).

ܕܠܐ ܠܐܝܬ ܒܗ *on which* (sg.) *thou hast not labored* (Jon. 4:10).

ܕܪܓܙ ܥܠܝܗܘܢ ܡܪܝܐ *against whom the Lord has raged* (Mal. 1:4).

ܕܡܒܥܝܢ ܐܢܬܘܢ ܠܗ *whom ye seek* (Mal. 3:1).

2. (1) See § 102. 7.

(2) ܕܗܘ ܗܘܐ ܪܝܫܐ ܕܓܙܪܬܐ *who was the chief of the island* (Acts 28:7).

ܕܗܢܘܢ ܥܒܕܘ ܢܦܫܗܘܢ ܡܗܝܡܢܐ *who have made themselves faithful* (Matt. 19:12).

Rem.—ܕܝܬܒ *he who sitteth* (Ps. II, 4).

ܕܥܡܗ *those who were with him* (Matt. 27:54).

ܕܡܩܪܒ *he who offers* (Mal. 2:12).

ܕܦܠܚܘ *those who served* (Mal. 3:18).

3. ܝܨܦܝܢ ܗܘܘ ܕܢܦܩܬܗܘܢ *they took charge of their expenses* (Jos. St. 38:12).

ܠܐ ܗܟܝܠ ܬܐܨܦܘܢ ܕܡܚܪ *do not then take thought for the morrow* (Matt. 6:34).

Rem.—ܨܦܝܬ ܗܘܝܬ ܕܝܠܝ *thou didst take care of me* (Jos. St. 3:10).

ܗܘ ܓܝܪ ܡܚܪ ܢܐܨܦ ܕܝܠܗ *for the morrow will take thought for itself* (Matt. 6:34).

4. ܒܗ ܒܐܬܪܐ ܕܫܪܝܢ ܗܘܘ ܬܡܢ *in the same place where they were abiding* (Lk. 2:8).

ܢܦܩ ܡܢ ܡܠܝܛܝܢܐ ܕܬܡܢ ܡܣܬܐ ܗܘܐ *he set out from Melitine where he had been wintering* (Jos. Sty. 64:20).

5. ܕܐܝܟ ܗܕܐ ܗܟܝܠ ܐܬܐ *such a sign also* (Jos. Sty. 41:7).

ܐܘܠܨܢܐ ܕܐܝܟ ܗܠܝܢ *such oppressions* (Jos. Sty. 4:17).

Rem.—ܐܝܟ ܕܣܗܕܘܬܐ *by way of witness* (Jos. Sty. 1:3).

6. ܡܛܠ ܨܒܘܬܐ ܐܝܕܐ ܗܝ *on account of anything whatsoever* (Jos. Sty. 16).

ܟܠ ܐܝܢܐ ܕܗܘ ܩܒܪܐ *any old grave no matter what* (Jes. Sty. 39:10).

7. ܕܚܘܝ ܘܩܪܐ ܘܩܪܒܗ *who showed and called and made him to approach.* (L'omelia di Giac. di Sarug. 504.)

The Syriac relative pronoun ܕ was originally a demonstrative being equivalent to the Hebrew זֶה, זוּ which are also used sometimes as relative pronouns, *e. g.* Ps. 74:2; Ex. 15:13.

1. ܕ is still used as a demonstrative.

(1) In phrases which correspond to the Greek article with the genitive.

(2) In phrases which correspond to the Greek predicate or possessive genitive.

(3) In the genitive construction mentioned in § 97 A, especially noteworthy is such a use before the interrogative.

(4) Sometimes it introduces an appositional or epexegetical phrase.

Note.—ܕܗܘ also may be used in this sense, see § 101 A, Rem. 2. Note.

2. It is used as a relative pronoun for all numbers, genders, cases. See § 38. 1.

Rem.—The oblique cases are expressed, as in English, by means of prepositions, which follow with a pronominal suffix agreeing with the antecedent of the relative.

(1) *That which* is usually expressed by the demonstrative followed by the relative, see § 102. 7.

(2) For emphasis sake the relative is followed by the personal pronoun.

Rem.—The relative alone sometimes stands for *"he who"*.

3. ܗܘܐ and ܐܝܬ in the sense of *"to have"* and ܝܨܦ *"to take charge of"*, *"to have care of"*, *"to take thought for"*, take after them a noun preceded by ܠ.

Rem.—ܕܠ may also be used after ܝܨܦ.

4. After nouns of place, the relative is usually followed by the adverb ܬܡܢ.

5. ܐܝܟ܂ followed by the relative pronoun means *"such"*.

Rem.—ܐܝܟ ܂ followed by ܠ means *"by way of"*.

6. ܕ preceded by the interrogative and followed by the demonstrative pronoun means *"whatsoever"*, *"no matter what"*.

7. More than one verb may be used after one relative.

8. It is used as a relative conjunction, especially in the senses *"that"* and *"because"*, see §§ 135, 136, 137.

§ 105. The Reflexive Pronoun.

1. ܐܙܕܪܥܬ *have I conducted myself* (Ad. 41:4).

ܠܚܡܣܢܘ *to confirm thyself* (Spic. Syr. 43:11).

ܥܕܠܝܗܘܢ ܨܥܢ *laying their blame on time* (Spic. Syr. 44:7).

ܠܡܬܚܒܪܘ *to associate themselves* (Ad. 31:6).

2. ܥܗܕܝܢ ܕܟܠܗܘܢ ܚܛܗܝܗܘܢ *reminding themselves of their sins* (Aphr. 223:19).

ܗܝ ܠܗ ܚܒܠܬ *she harmed herself* (Ephr. III. 2c.)

ܐܫܠܡ ܗܘ *he delivered himself* (Jos. Sty. 71:1).

ܡܢܗ ܕܝܠܗ *on his part* (Jos. Sty. 62:6).

3. ܦܨܝ ܢܦܫܟ *save thyself* (Matt. 27:40, see also 27:5).

ܚܠܩܐ ܡܢܘܗܝ ܠܐ ܐܝܬܘܗܝ *fate itself does not exist* (Spic. Syr. 9:9).

ܗܘ ܥܡ ܢܦܫܗ *it disagrees with itself* (Overbeck's Eph. 45:6).

ܡܢ ܨܒܘܬ ܢܦܫܗ *of himself* (John. 7:18).

ܐܢ ܠܐ ܬܕܥܝ ܢܦܫܟܝ *if thou thyself know not* (Song of Songs 1:8).

ܘܓܚܟܬ ܣܪܐ ܒܢܦܫܗ *and Sarah laughed within herself* (Gen. 18:12).

ܦܪܫ ܢܦܫܗ *he distinguished himself* (Spic. Syr. 4:1 [Duv.]). See also Lk. 2:17; 11:17.

The reflexive pronoun is expressed :—
1. Generally by the reflexive species of the verb.
2. By the personal and possessive pronoun.
3. By such words as ܢܦܫܐ "*soul*", ܩܢܘܡܐ "*person*", ܐܝܬܐ "*existence*", ܪܥܝܢܐ "*mind*", ܠܒܐ "*heart*", and similar words.

§ 106. The Possessive Pronoun.

1. ܕܕܝܠܟ ܗܝ ܡܠܟܘܬܐ *because thine is the kingdom* (Matt. 6:13).

ܕܝܠܢ ܕܝܢ *for our part* (Spic. Syr. 2:9.)

ܘܢܩܝܡܘܢ ܥܠܘܗܝ ܡܠܟܐ ܡܢ ܕܝܠܗܘܢ *and to set up over it a king of their own* (Jos. Sty. 17:23).

Rem. 1.— ܙܒܢܐ ܕܝܠܝ *my time* (John. 7:8).

ܘܣܡ ܩܒܘܬܐ ܩܕܡ ܒܝܪܬܐ ܕܝܠܗ *and he placed a box in front of his palace* (Jos. Sty. 24:1).

Rem. 2.— ܒܥܝܢܝ ܕܝܠܟ *in thine own eyes* (Lk. 6:42).

ܠܫܘܒܚܐ ܕܝܠܗ *to his own glory* (Rom. 3:7).

Rem. 3.— ܛܒܬܐ ܕܝܢ ܕܝܠܗ ܗܝ ܕܓܒܪܐ *for the good is the man's own* (Spic. Syr. 6:11).

ܐܦܝܣܩܦܐ ܕܝܠܗ ܕܡܕܝܢܬܐ *the city's own bishop* (Jos. Sty. 29:4).

ܒܝܪܚ ܐܒ ܕܝܠܗ ܕܫܢܬܐ ܗܕܐ *in the month Ab of this same year* (Jos. 28:1).

Rem. 4.—ܢܗܘܘܢ ܠܝ *they shall be mine* (Mal. 3:17).

1. The independent or absolute possessive is rendered by ܕܝܠ followed by the suffix of the person.

Rem. 1.—ܕܝܠ is composed of ܕ (primarily ܕܝ) and ܠ, and hence ܕܠܝ=what is to me, what I have. Hence ܕܝܠ can be used instead of the possessive adjective pronoun.

Rem. 2.—The independent possessive may be added for emphasis to a substantive or a possessive pronoun.

Rem. 3.—ܕܝܠ is sometimes used to emphasize the substantive which is usually subjoined with ܕ.

Rem. 4.—The preposition Lomadh with the pronominal suffix is also used to denote possession.

§ 107. The Indefinite Pronoun.

1. ܐܡܪ ܕܝܢ ܠܗ ܐܢܫ *then one said to him* (Matt. 12:47).

ܐܢܫ ܠܐ ܐܚܒܠ ܬܡܢ *it wounded no one there* (Jos. Sty. 25:17).

2. ܚܕ ܚܕ *every one* (Mk. 14:19; Matt. 26:22).

ܐܢܫ *every man* (Cor. 3:8, 7:2).

ܟܠ ܢܦܫ *every soul* (Rom. 13:1).

ܚܕ ܟܠ *every one* (Anal. Syr. 49:6 [Dur.]).

ܚܕ ܚܕ ܟܠ *every one* (Eph. 5:33).

ܐܢܫ ܟܠ *every one* (Lk. 14:33).

ܒܚܕ ܚܕ ܡܢ ܗܕܡܝܗܘܢ *in every one of their limbs* (Jos. Sty. 21:24).

Rem.—ܠܨܦܪܐ *every morning* (Am. 4:4); ܒܟܠܝܘܡ *each day* (Jer. 37:21).

3. ܚܕ ܡܢ ܚܕ *one from another* (Matt. 25:32).

ܚܕ ܒܚܕ *one on another* (John. 13:22).

ܪܓܠܐ ܚܕ ܕܚܕ *one another's feet* (John. 13:14).

ܚܕ݂ܳܕ݂ܶܐ *one another* (Luke. 23:12, 4:36).

ܢܰܫܶܩܘ ܚܕ݂ܳܕ݂ܶܐ *they kissed each other* (Bern. Ch. 47:12).

4. ܢܦܰܩܘ ܡܶܢ ܐ̱ܢܳܫ *some went out* (Jos. Sty. 60:12).

ܐܶܢ ܡܶܢ ܣܰܘܟ݁ܶܐ *if some of the branches* (Rom. 11:17).

ܡܶܢܗܘܢ *some of them* (Bern. Ch. 144:7; Rom. 3:3; Mk. 2:5).

ܐ̱ܢܳܫ ܕ݁ܐܳܡܪܺܝܢ *some say* (John. 9:9).

ܐܢܳܫ ܐܢܳܫ *some* (Phil. 1:15).

5. (1) ܐܢܳܫܺܝܢ ܡܶܢܗܘܢ ܡܶܬ݂ܛܦܺܝܣܺܝܢ ܗܘܰܘ ... ܘܐ̱ܚܪ̈ܳܢܶܐ ܠܐ *some of them were persuaded ... and others not* (Acts 28:24).

(2) ܐ̱ܢܳܫ ܕ݁ܐܳܡܪܺܝܢ ܕ݁ܡܽܘܫܶܐ ܐ̱ܚܪ̈ܳܢܶܐ ܕ݁ܶܝܢ ܐܺܠܺܝܳܐ *some said: it is John; but others, it is Elias* (Matt. 16:14).

(3) ܐܢܳܫ ܐܢܳܫ ܡܶܢ ܣܶܢܶܐܬ݂ܳܐ ܐ̱ܚܪ̈ܳܢܶܐ ܕ݁ܶܝܢ ܒ݁ܨܶܒ݂ܝܳܢܳܐ ܛܳܒ݂ܳܐ *some out of envy, but others in good will* (Phil. 1:15); ܗܘܰܘ ܡܡܰܝܶܩܺܝܢ ܐ̱ܚܪ̈ܳܢܶܐ ܕ݁ܶܝܢ ܐܳܡܪܺܝܢ ܗܘܰܘ *some mocked but others said* (Acts 17:32).

6. (1) ܠܚܰܕ݂ ܢܶܣܢܶܐ ܘܰܠܐ̱ܚܪܺܢܳܐ ܢܰܚܶܒ݂ *the one he hates and the other he loves* (Matt. 6:24).

(2) ܐ̱ܚܪܺܝܢ ܗܘ ܙܳܪܰܥ ܘܐ̱ܚܪܺܝܢ ܚܳܨܶܕ݂ *one soweth and another reapeth* (John. 4:37).

(3) ܗܳܠܶܝܢ ܒ݁ܡܰܪܟ݁ܒ݂ܳܬ݂ܳܐ ܘܗܳܠܶܝܢ ܒ݁ܪ̈ܰܟ݂ܫܳܐ *some trust in chariots and others in horses* (Ps. 20:7).

7. (1) ܟ݁ܽܠ ܕ݁ܫܳܡܰܥ *whosoever heareth* (Matt. 13:19; Spic. Syr. 4:2).

(2) ܟ݁ܽܠ ܐܰܝܢܳܐ ܕ݁ܐܺܝܬ݂ ܠܶܗ *everyone who has* (1 John. 3:3).

(3) ܐܰܝܢܳܐ ܕ݁ܰܡܗܰܝܡܶܢ *everyone who believeth* (Mk. 16:16).

(4) ܡܰܢ ܕ݁ܐܺܝܬ݂ ܠܶܗ ܐܶܕ݂ܢ̈ܶܐ *whosoever has ears* (Mk. 7:16; Mal. 1:14).

8. (1) ܡܶܕ݁ܶܡ ܕ݁ܰܢܡܰܠܶܠ *in whatsoever he shall speak* (Acts 3:22).

(2) ܡܶܕ݁ܶܡ ܕ݁ܐܳܡܰܪ ܐ̱ܢܳܐ *whatsoever I say* (Matt. 10:27).

(3) ܟ݁ܽܠ ܡܶܕ݁ܶܡ ܕ݁ܐܺܝܬ݂ ܗ̱ܘܳܐ *whatsoever was in the midst of it* (Jos. Sty. 29.3).

Rem.—ܡܛܠ ܥܠܬܐ ܐܝܕܐ ܕܗܝ *on account of anything whatsoever* (Jos. Sty. 80:16).

ܟܠ ܐܝܢܐ ܕܗܘ ܩܒܪܐ ܥܬܝܩܐ *any old grave whatsoever* (Jos. Sty. 39:10).

9. ܗܢܝܢ ܐܝܟ ܗܢܝܢ ܕܒܚܐ ܡܩܪܒܝܢ ܗܘܘ *they were bringing the same sacrifices* (Heb. 10:1).

ܡܛܠ ܐܝܬ ܠܢ ܗܝ ܐܝܟ ܗܝ ܪܘܚܐ *since we have the same spirit* (Festal Letter of Athan. 7:17).

The indefinite pronouns are expressed:—

1. *One, a certain one,* by ܚܕ, or ܐܢܫ.

2. *Every, every one,* by ܚܕ, or ܟܠ followed by ܚܕ, ܐܢܫ or some similar word.

Rem.—The plural, or the repetition of the noun, or sometimes even the singular, denotes distribution, see § 92. 1*c*.

3. *One another, each other,* by ܚܕ̈ܕܐ; but when a preposition, or the relative ܕ, comes before *another*, by ܚܕ followed by ܚܕ with the appropriate preposition, or ܕ.

4. *Some,* by ܚܕ ܚܪ̈ܢܐ or ܡܢ partitive.

5. *Some—others,* by ܐܢܫ̈ܝܢ or ܐܝܬ ܕ followed by ܐܚܪ̈ܢܐ; or by repetition of the word ܐܢܫ; or by a combination of the words for *some* mentioned under 4.

6. *The one—the other,* by ܚܕ—ܚܪܢܐ, ܚܪܢܐ—ܚܪܢܐ and ܗܠܝܢ—ܘܗܠܝܢ.

7. 8. *Whoever, whosoever,* by ܟܠ ܕ, ܟܠ ܐܝܢܐ ܕ, ܐܝܢܐ ܕ, ܡܢ ܕ; *whatever, whatsoever,* by ܟܠܡܕܡ ܕ, ܡܕܡ ܕ, ܟܠ ܡܕܡ ܕ.

Rem.—ܕܗܘ or ܕܗܝ may generalize any indefinite pronoun.

9. *The same* is expressed by two demonstrative pronouns of like gender and number, separated by ܐܝܟ *as.* See also § 102. 6.

§ 108. Uses of ܟܠ.

1. (1) ܡܪܐ ܕܟܠ *Lord of all* (Spic. Syr. 27:24).

ܐܫܠܡ ܟܠ ܒܐܝܕܘ̈ܗܝ *he gave all over into his hands* (Aphr. 123:2).

(2) ܡܣܓܕ ܡܢ ܟܠܐ *worshipped of all* (Ephr. III. 532*c*).

(3) ܟܠ ܕܒܥܝܢ ܠܗ *all who were seeking him* (Aphr. 198:10).

(4) ܟܠܗ ܐܪܥܐ ܕܥܪܒܝܐ *in all the country of the Arabs* (Spic. Syr. 16 ult.).

ܟܠܗ ܡܕܝܢܬܐ *the whole city* (Jos. Sty. 37:2).

ܟܠܗܘܢ ܝܘܡܬܐ *always* (Matt. 28:20).

2. See § 107:7.8.

3. ܟܠ ܫܘܠܛܢܐ *all power* (Matt. 28:18).

ܟܠ ܦܢܝܢ *all quarters* (Jos. Sty. 30:12).

4. ܟܠ ܐܡܬܝ *always when* (Kirsch. Chrest. 171:15; 1 Cor. 11:25).

ܟܠ ܟܠܗ *quite all* (Kirsch. Chrest. p. 129:18; Acts 22:20).

1. ܟܠ may be used as a substantive
(1) In the absolute state.
(2) Occasionally in the emphatic state.
(3) Before the relative pronoun.
(4) In apposition with a noun in the sense of *"all the"*, *"the whole"*.
2. It may be used as an indefinite pronoun.
3. As an adjective it is used in the sense of *"every"* or *"all"*.
4. As an adverb in the sense of *"always"*, *"quite"*, *"just"*.

§ 109. Uses of ܡܕܡ.

1. (1) ܡܕܡ ܕܢܘܕܥ *to make known anything* (Jos. Sty. 24:2).

ܠܝܬ ܗܘܐ ܒܗ ܡܕܡ ܕܩܐܡ *there was nothing in it that was standing* (Jos. Sty. 30:2).

ܡܕܡ ܠܐ ܚܛܝܬ *nothing have I sinned* (Acts 25:10).

ܒܡܕܡ ܐܚܪܝܢ *in anything else* (Jos. Sty. 50:4).

(2) ܠܒܘܫܐ ܐܝܬ ܠܗ ܕܡܕܡ ܡܕܡ *he had clothes of different kind* (Jos. Sty. 56:7)

ܗܘ ܡܕܡ ܡܕܡ *that anything whatsoever* (Spic. Syr. 2 ult.)

(3) ܡܕܡ ܕܐܝܬܘܗܝ *whatsoever is* (Spic. Syr. 22:10).

ܡܶܕܶܡ ܕܳܐܡܰܪ ܐ̱ܢܳܐ ܠܟܽܘܢ *whatsoever I say to you* (Mk. 13:37).

(4) ܗܰܘ ܡܶܕܶܡ ܕ *of whatsoever* (Spic. Syr. 10 ult.).

ܗܳܠܶܝܢ ܡܶܕܶܡ ܕܡܶܬܦܰܩܕܺܝܢ ܐܢ̱ܬܘܢ *whatsoever ye are commanded* (Spic. Syr. 1:7)

ܗܰܘ ܡܶܕܶܡ ܕܙܳܪܰܥ ܐܰܢ̱ܬ *whatsoever thou sowest* (1 Cor. 15:39).

2. (1) ܘܠܳܐ ܐܶܫܟܰܚܘ ܡܶܕܶܡ ܕܢܶܥܬܳܐ ܣܰܢܝܳܐ *and they found not any evil accusation* (Acts 25:18).

ܡܶܕܶܡ ܚܪܺܢܳܐ ܣܘܽܥܪܳܢܳܐ *any other work* (Add. Aph. 32:15).

ܐܶܚܕܳܐ ܡܶܕܶܡ *any enmity* (Matt. 5:23).

(2) ܕܠܳܐ ܣܰܡܳܐ ܕܡܶܕܶܡ *without medicin of any kind* (Add. 7:10).

The pronominal and adjective indefinite for things is ܡܶܕܶܡ. It is used
1. As a pronoun:
(1) In the sense of *"anything"*.
(2) When repeated, in the sense of *"anything whatsoever"*.
(3) Before ܕ, in the sense of *"whatsoever"*.
(4) It may be emphasized by the demonstrative.
2. As an adjective:
(1) Absolutely before or after its noun in the sense of *"any"*.
(2) Preceded by ܕ, forming an adjective clause, see § 136.

§ 110. Numerals.

A. CARDINALS.

1. (1) ܡܳܐܐ ܫܢܺܝ̈ܢ *a hundred years* (Jul. 220:23).

ܐܰܪܒܥܳܐ ܡܕܰܝ̈ ܚܶܛ̈ܐ *four modii of wheat* (Jos. Sty. 33:18).

ܥܶܣܪܺܝܢ ܘܚܰܕ ܝܰܘܡܳܐ *twentyone days* (Aphr. 56:21).

Rem.—ܥܶܣܪܺܝܢ ܐܰܠܦ̈ܝܢ *twenty thousand* (Jos. Sty. 75:12).

ܬܠܳܬ ܡܳܐܐ *three hundred* (Jos. Sty. 34:21).

ܚܰܡܫܺܝܢ ܘܐܰܪܒܥܳܐ ܐܰܠܦ̈ܝܢ ܘܐܰܪܒܰܥܡܳܐܐ *fifty and four thousand and four hundred.*

(2) ܐܬܘ̈ܬܐ ܬܠܬ *three signs* (Jos. Sty. 32:12).

ܫܪ̈ܒܬܐ ܐܪܒܥܣܪܐ *fourteen generations* (Matt. 1:17).

Rem.—ܫܢܝ̈ܢ ܐܪܒܥܝܢ ܘܚܕܐ *forty-one years* (Aphr. 466:17).

(3) ܠܝܛܪ̈ܐ ܕܕܗܒܐ ܡܐܐ ܘܐܪܒܥܝܢ *a hundred and forty pounds of gold* (Jos. Sty. 26:11, see also 34:21).

ܡܐܐ ܘܚܡܫܝܢ ܐܠܦܝ̈ܢ ܘܐܪܒܥ ܡܐܐ ܘܚܡܫܝܢ *one hundred and fifty one thousand and four hundred and fifty* (Num. 2:16).

(4) ܫܒܥܐ ܐܠܦܝ̈ܢ *seven thousand* (Num. 3:20).

ܫܬܐ ܐܠܦܝ̈ܢ ܫܢܝ̈ܢ *six thousand years* (Aphr. 36:20).

ܡܐܬܝܢ ܐܠܦܝ̈ܢ ܟܪ̈ܣܛܝܢܐ *two hundred thousand Christians* (Jul. 83:8).

(5) ܗܐ ܥܣܪܝܢ ܠܝ ܫܢܝ̈ܢ ܒܒܝܬܟ *behold twenty years have I been in thy house* (Gen. 31:41).

ܗܘܐ ܡܐܐ ܫܢܝ̈ܢ *he was one hundred years old* (Aphr. 235:20).

ܐܪܒܥܡܐܐ ܐܢܘܢ ܠܝܛܪ̈ܐ *there are four hundred pounds* (Gen. 23:15).

1. Cardinals are generally in apposition with the substantive.
(1) The numeral is generally first in order and in the absolute state; the substantive following is in the absolute or emphatic state.

Rem.—ܐܠܦ and ܡܐܐ follow their limiting numeral.

(2) The numeral follows in the absolute state, the noun precedes in the emphatic state.

Rem.—Sometimes, even when the noun precedes, it is in the absolute state.

(3) When two or more numerals are used the highest stands first, the lowest last.

(4) With numbers from 2 to 9 ܐܠܦ and ܪܒܘ are treated like anyother substantive.

(5) A short word may come in between a numeral and its substantive, as also between the parts of a number.

B. ORDINALS.

ܝܘܡܐ ܫܒܝܥܝܐ *the seventh day* (Heb. 4:4).

ܚܝܘܬܐ ܬܠܝܬܝܬܐ *the third beast* (Rev. 6:5).

[§ 111] ELEMENTS OF SYRIAC. 141

ܝܘܡܐ ܕܬܪܝܢ *the second day* (Gen. 1:8).

ܠܫܢܬ ܐܪܒܥܡܐܐ *to the year* 400 (Aphr. 475:2).

ܫܢܬ ܬܡܢܡܐܐ ܘܥܣܪ *the year* 810 (Jos. Sty. 27:11).

ܒܝܘܡܐ ܚܡܝܫܝܐ *on the fifth day* (Jos. Sty. 27:1).

1. (1) ܫܒܥܐ ܫܒܥܐ *seven by seven* (Gen. 7:2).

(2) ܚܕ ܒܝܬ ܬܪܝܢ ܡܢܗܘܢ *between each two of them* (Jos. Sty. 85:10).

2. (1) ܥܕܡܐ ܠܫܒܥܐ ܙܒܢܝܢ *until seven times* (Matt. 18:21, also Luke 17:4).

(2) ܫܒܥܝܢ ܘܫܒܥܐ *seventy-seven times* (Gen. 4:24).

As to order and agreement they are like any other adjectives, see § 99.
By putting the noun in the genetive relation (either by construction or by ܕ) with a following cardinal, the ordinal may be superseded.
1. The distributive sense is denoted:
(1) By the repetition of the numeral.
(2) By the preposition ܠ before ܙܒܢ.
2. For multiplication the cardinal number
(1) Can be followed by ܙܒܢܝܢ *time*;
(2) Or may be used alone.

§ 111. The Verb.

1. ܗܘܐ (Gen. 1:2); ܗܘܐ (Gen. 1:1); ܗܘܘ (Gen. 2:25); ܢܗܘܐ (Gen. 1:2); ܐܚܬܡ (Gen. 2:18); ܬܐܟܘܠ (Gen. 2:17); ܫܡܥܬ (Gen. 3:10); ܐܟܠܬ (Gen. 3:12); ܬܐܠܕܝܢ (Gen. 3:16).

2. ܡܩܪܒܝܢ ܐܢܬܘܢ (Mal. 1:8); ܨܒܐ ܐܢܐ (Mal. 1:10); ܢܣܒ (Mal. 1:8); ܠܝܛ ܗܘ ܢܟܝܠܐ ܘܐܝܬ (Mal. 1:14); ܥܒܕܝ ܥܘܠܐ (Mal. 3:15); ܡܠܦܝܢ ܠܗ *we are learning Him* (Overbeck 22:5).

3. ܟܕ (Mat. 26:1); ܐܡܪ (Matt. 26:1); ܝܕܥܝܢ (Mat. 26:2); ܗܘܐ (Mat. 26:2); ܡܬܕܒܪ (Mat. 26:2); ܐܬܟܢܫܘ (Mat. 26:3).

1. Genders, numbers and persons are distinguished in the Perfect and Imperfect by means of preformatives and sufformatives.

2. In the participles, the first and second person require the personal pronoun, but the third needs none.

3. In general, it may be said, that the Perfect denotes a completed action, and the Imperfect an incomplete or dependent action; while the Participles denote states or continuous or frequentative actions. As to order of time, the Perfect and Participles may be past, present, or future; as is determined from the context, or the nature of the verb. The Imperfect is perhaps always absolutely or relatively future.

§ 112. The Perfect.

1. (1) ܒܪܐ *he created* (Gen. 1:1).

ܗܘܬ *it was* (Gen. 1:2).

(2) ܩܒܠܬ ܟܬܝ̈ܒܬܐ *I have received the letters* (Jos. Sty. 1:1).

ܡܛܠ ܕܣܠܩܬ ܒܝܫܘܬܗܘܢ ܩܕܡܝ *because their iniquity has come up before me* (Jon. 1:2).

(3) ܒ̈ܬܐ ܙܥܘܪ̈ܐ ܒܢܘ ܠܗܘܢ *they had built small houses for themselves* (Jos. Sty. 69:20).

ܕܥܒܕ *which he had made* (Gen. 2:8, so Gen. 2:1, 2:22, 3:10; Matt. 27:35).

2. (1) ܚܢܢ ܕܝܢ ܝܕܥܝܢ ܕܚܕ ܗܘ ܐܠܗܐ *for we know that there is one God* (Aphr. 497:17).

ܣܡܩ ܫܡܝܐ *the sky is red* (Matt. 16:2).

ܠܡܢܐ ܐܬܚܡܬ ܠܟ *why art thou angry* (Gen. 4:6).

ܟܪܝܐ ܠܝ ܥܕܡܐ ܠܡܘܬܐ *it grieves me unto death* (Jon. 4:9).

(2) ܕܠܐ ܗܠܟ *who hath not walked* (Ps. 1:1).

ܡܪܝܐ ܐܕܝܩ *the Lord looks down* (Ps. 14:2).

3. (1) *a.* ܗܐ ܒܪܟܬܗ ܘܐܣܓܝܬܗ *behold I shall bless him and multiply him* (Gen. 17:20).

§ 112.] ELEMENTS OF SYRIAC. 143

ܐܡܪ ܕܢܬܠ *he said that he would give* (Bar Heb. 80:1 [Uhl.]).

b. ܡܚܪ ܢܬܛܠܩ ܘܐܦ ܠܐ ܢܗܘܐ ܘܢܐܒܕ ܘܢܬܥܛܐ ܕܘܟܪܢܗ *to-morrow he shall disappear and shall not be and the memory of him shall perish and be effaced* (Jul. 9:6).

ܢܚܙܐ ܢܘܗܪܐ ܪܒܐ *shall see a great light* (Is. 9:2).

(2) a. ܥܠ ܫܘܚܠܦܐ ܪܒܐ ܕܗܘܐ ܒܥܠܡܐ *over the great change which shall have been in the world* (Jos. Sty. 92:4).

b. ܡܐ ܕܐܬܐ ܗܘ *when he shall have come* (John. 4:25).

ܡܐ ܕܩܒܠ ܙܘܙܐ *when he shall have received the money* (Jos. Sty. 61:15).

ܘܐܢ ܐܫܬܡܥܬ ܗܕܐ ܩܕܡ ܗܓܡܘܢܐ *and if this shall have been reported before the governor* (Mt. 28:14).

ܐܢ ܐܫܟܚܢ *if we shall have been able* (Spic. Syr. 13:2).

ܐܢ ܐܫܟܚܬܘܢ ܐܘ ܠܐ *whether thou shalt have found him or not* (Aphr. 144:22).

Rem. 1.—ܨܒܐ ܐܢܐ ܗܟܝܠ ܕܗܘܘ ܡܨܠܝܢ ܓܒܪܐ *I will therefore that men pray* (1 Tim. 2:8).

ܐܠܘܨ ܢܦܫܟ ܕܗܘܐ ܡܟܝܟ *constrain thyself to be humble* (Anal. Syr. p. 8. 1. 6 [Duv.]).

Rem. 2. a.—ܠܐ ܗܘܐ ܠܐܢ ܠܢ *let it not be wearisome to us* (Gal. 6:9).

ܗܘܝܬܘܢ ܥܝܪܝܢ *be watchful* (Mark. 13:37).

b.—ܠܘܝ ܩܪܝܪ ܗܘܝܬ *I would thou wast cold* (Rev. 3:15; Aphr. 221:22).

ܐܬܕܟܝܬܘܢ ܕܝܢ ܐܡܠܟܬܘܢ *O that ye did reign* (1 Cor. 4:8).

The Perfect denotes a completed action.

1. It is used for past time

(1) As the true historical tense, in the narration of events viewed as completed.

(2) Of events viewed as completed in the past.

(3) When the action expressed by the Perfect precedes another action already completed, then it corresponds to our Pluperfect.

2. It is used for present time

(1) In verbs which denote a mental or physical state or quality.

(2) In imitation of the Hebrew, in the statement of general truths.

3. It is used for future time.

(1) When the event is looked upon as certain.

a. In promises.

b. In prophecies.

Note.—This usage is mostly biblical.

(2) It may denote our future perfect, see *a*.

b. In this sense the Perfect is usually preceded by the hypothetical particle such as ܐܢ, ܐܘ and ܡܐ ?.

Rem. 1.—The perfect of ܗܘܐ is used with the participle in clauses denoting a purpose or result which is looked upon as certain of fulfilment.

Rem. 2.—The perfect of ܗܘܐ is used with an adjective or participle to express a wish or exhortation.

a. Absolutely.

b. After ܟܠ or ܐܝܬܘܗܝ.

Rem. 3.—For the auxiliary uses of ܗܘܐ, see § 127.

§ 113. The Imperfect.

1. (1) ܥܕܠܐ ܢܙܕܩܦ ܝܗܒ ܕܡܗ ܠܚܡܫܐ *and before he was crucified he gave his blood to drink* (Aph. 222:5).

ܥܕܠܐ ܢܬܬܣܝܡ ܢܡܘܣܐ *before the law was established* (Aph. 25:5), see also 2 King 6:32; Jer. 1:5; John 1:48.

Rem.—ܥܕܠܐ ܬܫܐܠܘܢܝܗܝ *before ye asked (or shall have asked) him* (Matt. 6:8), is probably meant for a literal translation of the Greek Aorist.

(2) ܥܡ ܕܢܡܠܠ ܟܬܒܗ ܐܠܗܐ *before God spake with him* (Aph. 2:35 ult.).

ܥܡ ܕܢܬܒܛܢ ܒܟܪܣܐ *before he was conceived in the womb* (Lk. 2:21).

(3) ܥܕ ܡܢ ܕܢܗܘܐ ܥܠܡܐ *before the world was* (John. 17:5).

§ 113.] ELEMENTS OF SYRIAC. 145

ܥܕ ܕܠܐ ܢܣܒ ܦܓܪܐ *before he had taken a body to himself* (St. Eph. Ov. 198:1 [Nöld.]).

2. ܣܝܦܐ ܘܪܘܡܚܐ ܠܐ ܡܬܚܙܐ *neither sword nor spear is seen* (Jud. 5:8).

ܠܡܠܐܟܘܗܝ ܣܟܠܘܬܐ ܡܚܝܒ *his angels he accuses of folly* (Joh. 4:18).

ܟܠ ܕܢܫܬܐ ܡܢ ܗܠܝܢ ܡܝܐ *whosoever drinks of this water* (John. 4:13).

ܟܘܪܣܘܬܐ ܕܐܝܩܪܐ ܢܘܪܬ ܐܢܘܢ *thrones of honor he causes them to inherit* (1 Sam. 2:8).

ܢܕܥܟܘܢ *they are quenched* (Is. 43:17).

3. ܠܐ ܢܗܘܐ ܬܘܒ ܛܘܦܢܐ *there will not again be a flood* (Gen. 9:11).

ܡܢ ܒܬܪ ܕܣܠܩܢܐ ܠܫܡܝܐ ܐܫܕܪ ܠܟ *after that I shall have gone to heaven I will send thee* (Ad. 5:22).

ܘܢܚܕܐ ܒܗܕܐ *and we shall rejoice in this* (Ad. 30:10).

ܢܒܣܡ ܠܟ ܛܒ *it will be very pleasant to thee* (Spic. Syr. 43:13).

ܐܟܬܘܒ ܠܟ *I shall write to thee* (Aphr. 6:8).

Note.—ܐܢ ܢܐܡܪ ܢܚܣܪ *if we shall speak we shall want* (Aphr. 496:8).

The Imperfect denotes an action as incomplete, either because future or because dependent on another action or state.

It is used:—

1. For past events after certain temporal participles such as ܥܕ ܕ, and ܥܕ ܠܐ in relation to which the action denoted by the verb was viewed as incomplete, or incipient.

This corresponds to the use of the Imperfect with טֶרֶם and אָז in Hebrew (see Harper's Syntax § 20. 1b; Driver's Use of the Tenses in Hebrew § 27. 1β; Ges. Heb. Gram. § 127. 4a) and to the Jussive in Arabic after لَمْ or لَمَّا (see Wright Ar. Gr. Vol. II § 12) and to the Subjunctive in Ethiopic after ቅድመ *kedma* (see Dill. Aeth. Gram. §§ 90, 120. In solchen Sätzen liegt der Sinn:—es sei etwas zu kommen oder zu werden bestimmt, nur sei es noch nicht verwirklicht, vid. p. 140).

Note.—Some claim a Perfect in other cases, *e. g.* Philips p. 163, Uhlemann § 61. 2c. Compare § 206. Philips mentions Hab. 2:1 (ܐܡܪ=Heb. אֲמַרְדָה a regular cohortative; see Driver § 49B and § 54). Judges 5:8 ܠܐ ܢܬܚܙܐ *cannot be seen*.

T

2. The use of the Imperfect for the present indicative is doubtful, except as an occasional imitation of the Hebrew.

Duval gives as examples Jud. 5:8 and Job. 4:18; Uhlemann gives John. 4:13; Philips 1 Sam. 2:8 (=Subjunct (?) comp. Uhl. 181 *Rem.* 2) and Is. 43:17 (which last Uhlemann and Cowper make Perfect or Preterite).

3. The Imperfect is sometimes used for the future Indicative.

Note.—This use of the Imperfect is especially common in conditional and hypothetical sentences. See § 138.

§ 114. The Imperfect (continued).

1. (1) ܠܐ ܐܢܫ ܢܟܠܐ ܐܢܘܢ *let no man forbid them* (Ad. 12:3).

   ܬܚܐ ܗܕܐ ܒܪܬܝ *let this my daughter live* (Ad. 14:5).

   ܢܗܘܐ ܢܘܗܪܐ *let there be light* (Gen. 1:3).

   (2) ܠܐ ܬܗܘܘܢ ܐܝܟ ܕܪܐ ܩܕܡܝܐ ܕܥܒܪܘ *be not as former generations which have passed away* (Ad. 22 ult.).

   ܠܐ ܬܐܨܦܘܢ *take no thought* (Matt. 6:31).

Rem.—ܢܣܒ ܐܚܘܗܝ ܐܢܬܬܗ *his brother shall take his wife* (Matt. 22:24).

   ܟܠ ܕܒܚܐ ܒܡܠܚܐ ܢܬܡܠܚ *every sacrifice should be salted with salt* (Mk. 9:49).

   ܟܠ ܕܬܫܐܠ ܡܢܝ ܗܒ ܠܝ *thou shalt give to me whatsoever I shall ask of thee* (Sindban 1:17).

2. (1) ܬܐܟܘܠ *thou mayest eat* (Gen. 2:16).

   ܐܠܐ ܢܐܡܪ ܐܢܫ *but one may say* (Spic. Syr. 6:21).

   ܘܡܕܝܢ ܢܬܕܡܪ ܐܢܫ *now one may wonder* (Spic. Syr. 47:6).

   (2) ܡܢ ܢܐܡܪ *who can say?* (Rev. 20:9).

   ܥܠ ܟܠ ܐܝܢܐ ܡܢ ܩܢܝܢܐ ܢܬܬܟܠ ܓܒܪܐ *on which of possessions can a man rely* (Spic. Syr. 45·6).

§ 114.]   ELEMENTS OF SYRIAC.   147

Most of the variations for mood are expressed by the Imperfect.
1. The Imperfect is used for the Imperative.
(1) Always for the third person, except in the cases mentioned under § 112. 3 (2), *Rem.* 2.
(2) Always for the negative, except in the cases mentioned in § 112. 3 (2), *Rem.* 2.
Rem.—The Imperative expressed in English by "*shall*", "*should*", "*is to*", "*has to*" &c. may be classed here.
2. The Imperfect is used for the Potential
(1) To express permission.
(2) To express possibility.

3. (1) ܐܫܒܘܩ ܥܡܟ ܡܢ ܥܡܐ ܕܥܡܝ *I wish to leave with thee some of the people who are with me* (Gen. 33:15).

ܢܓܡܪ ܣܢܝܐ *might the evil cease* (Ps. 7:9).

ܗܫܐ ܕܝܢ ܢܐܙܠ ܡܐܪܚܐ ܬܠܬܐ ܝܘܡܝܢ ܒܡܕܒܪܐ *now we would go a journey of three days into the wilderness* (Ex. 3:18).

(2) ܢܡܠܠ ܥܒܕܟ ܡܠܬܐ ܩܕܡܝܟ ܡܪܝ *let thy servant speak a word before thee, my Lord* (Gen. 44:18).

ܬܗܦܘܟ ܢܦܫܗ ܕܛܠܝܐ ܗܢܐ ܠܓܘܗ *restore the soul of this youth to his body* (1 King. 17:21).

(3) ܘܐܥܒܕܟ ܠܥܡܐ ܪܒܐ *and I will make thee a great people* (Gen. 12:2).

ܐܚܘܬ ܐܚܙܐ ܐܢ ܐܝܟ ܓܥܬܐ ܕܣܠܩܬ ܥܡܕܝ ܥܒܕܘ *I will go down and see if they have done according to the cry which has come up before me* (Gen. 18:21).

ܐܚܘܐ ܐܢܐ ܠܟ ܕܡܠܦ ܐܢܐ *I will show thee, that I shall teach* (Sindban 1:16).

(4) ܢܦܣܩ ܐܣܘܪܝܗܘܢ *let us break their bonds* (Ps. 2:3).

ܢܬܚܙܐ ܐܦܝܢ ܕܣܡ *let us look at each other* (2 King. 14:8).

ܐܕܘܨ ܘܐܣܬܕ ܒܛܝܒܘܬܟ *let me be glad and rejoice in thy grace* (Ps. 31:7).

Rem. 1 (1)—ܐܫܬܘܦ ܕܡܝܬܢ *Oh that we had died* (Num. 14:2).

ܐܠܘ ܕܝܢ ܐܝܫܡܥܝܠ ܢܐܚܐ ܩܕܡܝܟ *Oh that Ishmael might live before thee* (Gen. 17:18).

(2)—ܡܢ ܕܝܢ ܕܫܬܩ ܕܫܬܩܝܬܘܢ ܫܬܩܝܢ ܗܘܝܬܘܢ *Oh that ye had altogether held your peace* (Job. 13:5).

ܡܢ ܕܝܢ ܕܟܠܗ ܟܠܗ ܥܡܐ ܕܡܪܝܐ ܢܒܝܐ *Would that all of the Lord's people were prophets* (Num. 11:27).

(3)—ܐܠܘ ܥܡܝ ܫܡܥܢܝ *O that my people had heard me* (Ps. 81:14).

(4)—ܡܢ ܕܝܢ ܢܗܒ ܡܢ ܕܫܡܥ ܠܝ *Oh that one would hear me* (Job. 31:35).

ܡܢ ܕܝܢ ܢܗܒ ܠܝ ܓܦܐ ܐܝܟ ܕܝܘܢܐ *Oh that I had wings like a dove* (Ps. 55:7).

(5)—ܡܢܘ ܢܬܠ ܕܟܝܐ ܡܢ ܛܡܐܐ *Oh that a clean thing could come out of an unclean* (Job. 14:4).

ܡܢܘ ܢܬܠ ܠܝ ܕܬܐܬܐ ܫܐܠܬܝ *Oh that I might have my request* (Job. 6:8).

(6)—ܡܢ ܕܝܢ ܐܫܠܡܗ ܠܥܡܐ ܗܢܐ ܒܐܝܕܝ *Would that one had delivered this people into my hands* (Jud. 9:29).

ܡܢ ܕܝܢ ܠܡܣܡܢܝ ܕܝܢܐ ܒܐܪܥܐ *Would that they had made me judge in the land* (2 Sam. 15:4).

(7)—ܠܘܝ ܩܪܝܪܐ ܗܘܝܬ *Oh that thou wast cold* (Rev. 3:15).

ܠܘܝ ܕܝܢ ܐܠܘ ܐܢܬ ܦܘܩܕܢܝ *Oh that thou wast hearkening to my commandments* (Is. 48:18).

Rem. 2.—ܠܘ ܡܝܬܝܢ ܗܘܝܢ ܕܝܢ ܕܡܝܬܢ *would that we had died* (Ex. 16:3).

ܐܢ ܗܫܐ ܐܢܬ ܫܡܥܬܢܝ *O that thou wouldst hear me* (Gen. 23:13).

3. The Imperfect is used for the Optative

(1) To express a wish.

(2) To express a prayer.

(3) To express determination, or intention.

(4) To express "a self excitement toward a certain line of conduct."

Rem.—The Optative is often denoted by such particles and phrases

as ܐܬܡܠܟܘܢ, ܟܠܗ, ܡܢ ܢܗܘܢ, ܠܘܝ, ܡܢܘ ܢܬܠ (מִי יִתֵּן), ܡܢ and ܡܢ ܠܗܘ.
As the examples show, the Perfect, Imperfect or Participle may be used, according as the kind of action varies.

Rem. 2.—The auxiliary verb ܨܒܐ may be used to express a wish, see § 129:3.

4. (1) ܨܒܐ ܐܢܐ ܕܐܦܝܣܟ *I would persuade thee* (Aphr. 345:1).

ܐܢ ܕܬܙܕܕܩ ܠܐ ܡܫܟܚ ܐܢܬ *if thou canst justify thyself* (Aphr. 270:5; John. 3:3. 4. 5, 15:4).

(2) ܐܬܝܬ ܕܐܫܪܐ *I am come to destroy* (Matt. 5:17).

ܕܐܬܝܢ ܗܘܘ ܡܢ ܪܘܚܩܐ ܕܢܚܙܘܢ ܠܡܫܝܚܐ *who are coming from afar to see the Messiah* (Add. 2:6).

Rem. 1.—ܕܢܕܥܘܢ *that they might know* (Ez. 20:26).

ܘܢܕܒܚܘܢ *that they may sacrifice* (Ex. 8:8).

ܡܛܠ ܕܢܬܟܠܘܢ ܡܢ ܣܟܠܘܬܗܘܢ *on this account, that they may be restrained from their sins* (Jos. Sty. 6:2. See also Gen. 27:7; Aphr. 217:2, 20:18).

Rem. 2.—ܫܒܘܩܝܢܝ ܐܫܕܪ *permit me to send* (Jos. Sty. 76:5).

ܐܦܩ ܒܪܟ ܢܡܘܬ *bring out thy son that he may die* (Jud. 6:30).

ܠܐ ܐܢܫ ܡܫܟܚ ܢܥܒܪ *no man could pass* (Matt. 8:28).

Rem. 3.—ܫܪܝ ܠܡܟܪܙܘ *he began to preach* (Matt. 4:17, 11:7).

ܫܪܝ ܕܢܦܩ *he began to drive out* (Mk. 14:15).

ܠܐ ܐܢܫ ܡܫܟܚ ܠܡܦܠܚܘ *no man can serve* (Matt. 6:24).

ܠܐ ܡܫܟܚ ܕܢܚܙܐ *he cannot see* (John. 3:3).

Rem. 4.—ܠܐ ܡܫܟܚܐ ܕܬܬܠ *it is not able to give* (John. 15:4).

ܕܡܚܝܠ ܡܢ ܕܠܐ ܢܓܢܘܒ *who is too weak to avoid stealing* (Spic. Syr. 5:7).

4. The Subjunctive.

The Imperfect is the form generally used to express the Subjunctive or dependent mood. It is used especially:—

(1) When the first verb may be translated by one of our modal auxiliaries.

(2) When the second verb expresses the purpose or result of the action of the first, see § 137:4.

Rem. 1.—Waw and occasionally ܐܝܟܢܐ ܕ may be used to introduce the Subjunctive.

Rem. 2.—The conjunction before the Subjunctive may be omitted. Comp. Ges. Heb. Gr. § 142c.

Rem. 3.—After many verbs the Subjunctive or Infinitive may be used indifferently.

Rem. 4.—The Subjunctive may be used after adjectives.

§ 115. The Imperative.

1. ܥܒܕ ܟܠ ܡܕܡ ܕܐܡܪ ܐܢܐ ܠܟ *do whatever I say to thee* (Sind. 3:11).

   ܩܨܐ ܩܪܒܐ *take war* (Jos. Sty. 16:15).

   ܐܡܪ ܠܝ ܒܪܝ *tell me my son* (Spic. Syr. 1:11).

2. ܢܗܘܐ ܦܪܫ *let it be dividing* (Gen. 1:7).

   ܢܚܘܘܢ ܪܒܘܬܗܘܢ *let them show their greatness* (Spic. Syr. 48:13).

   ܢܫܬܡܥ ܠܫܘܠܛܢܐ *let us be obedient to the dominion* (Spic. Syr. 48:14).

   ܢܐܡܪ . . . ܘܢܚܘܐ *let us say and show* (Spic. Syr. 10·21).

3. ܠܐ ܢܩܫܐ *let him not harden* (Addai 22:3).

   ܠܐ ܬܫܬܒܘܢ *be ye not led captive* (Addai 22:4).

   ܠܐ ܬܩܛܘܠ *thou shalt not kill* (Matt. 5:21).

   ܠܐ ܬܐܡܐ ܣܟ *swear not at all* (Matt. 5:34).

   ܠܐ ܢܕܡܟ ܐܝܟ ܐܚܪܢܐ *let us not sleep as others* (1 Thess. 5:6).

4. ܗܘܝ ܫܠܡ *farewell* (Acts 23:30).

   ܗܘܝ ܡܗܝܡܢܐ *be faithful* (Rev. 2:10).

   ܗܘܘ ܡܛܝܒܝܢ *be ye ready* (Matt. 5:48).

5. ܗܘܝ ܥܡܝ ܐܝܟ ܚܒܪܝ *enter with me* (Addai 32:19).

ܠܳܐ ܗܘܳܐ ܛܳܥܢܰܢ ܠܰܢ *let it not be burdensome to us* (Gal. 6:9).

ܗܘܰܝܬܘܢ ܡܩܰܘܶܝܢ *be ye abiding* (Addai 41:16).

ܠܳܐ ܗܘܰܝܬܘܢ ܚܳܝܪܺܝܢ ܠܐܢܳܫ *be ye not looking* (Addai 42:15).

6. ܩܘܡ ܢܶܐܙܰܠ ܘܢܒܘܬ *get up and let us go and let us pass the night* (Jos. Sty 29:11). ܐܶܫܬܰܝ ܐܰܕܺܝ *be still* (Mk. 4:39).

1. The form of the verb called Imperative, see § 48, is used only for the second person, and then in positive commands only.

2. For commands or admonitions in the first and third persons, the Imperfect is used, see § 114. 1.

The Imperfect may be used also for commands in the second person, see § 114. 1.

3. All negative commands are in the Imperfect, (except those coming under 5 below).

4. The Imperative of ܗܘܳܐ may be used with participles or adjectives, instead of the Imperative from the root of the participle or adjective, § 112. 3 (2), *Rem.* 2.

5. A form of the Imperative is expressed by means of the Perfect of ܗܘܳܐ and the participle of a verb, see § 127. 4 (1).

6. The context sometimes compels us to translate a Syriac participle by our *"let"*. See § 116. 5. See Agrell's Supp. Syn. p. 25.

§ 116. The Participle Active.

The Active Participle is used to denote:—

1. A state, or an action viewed as continuing.
2. A series of actions or states (corresponding to the Hebrew frequentative Imperfect).
3. A state conditioning another verb.

1. (1) a. ܡܚܰܝܪܺܝܢܰܢ *are we to look?* (Matt. 11:3).

ܥܳܠܡܶܐ ܡܩܰܘܶܝܢ *worlds exist* (Ad. Sp. 14:11).

ܡܶܕܶܡ ܕܶܐܡܪܶܬ ܘܳܐܡܰܪ ܐܢܳܐ ܩܕܳܡܰܝܟܘܢ *anything that I have said and am saying before you* (Ad. Sp. 26:3).

ܟܽܠܡܶܕܶܡ ܕܠܳܐ ܪܳܚܶܡ ܐܰܢܬ *whatsoever thou dost not love* (Sind. 1:18).

b. ܐܦ ܗܫܐ ܡܩܒܠ ܐܢܐ ܦܘܩܕܢܗ *now also I receive his commandment* (Over. 172:5).

ܗܕܐ ܠܡܕܡ ܗܫܐ ܡܛܬ *this has come unto the present* (Over. 215:14).

ܗܫܐ ܐܡܪ ܐܢܐ ܠܟܘܢ *now I say to you* (Acts 5:38).

(2) *a.* ܩܐܡ ܐܚܘܟܝ *thy brother shall rise* (John. 11:23).

ܣܠܩ ܐܢܐ . . . . . . ܘܡܐ ܕܣܠܩܬ ܡܫܕܪ ܐܢܐ ܠܟ *I am about to ascend and after I have ascended I shall send to thee* (Ad. Ap. 4:15).

ܗܘܐ ܐܢܬ ܡܠܟܐ ܚܠܦܘܗܝ *thou shalt be king instead of him* (Sind. 3:12).

b. ܡܐ ܕܚܙܝܢ ܐܢܬܘܢ ܐܬܐ *when ye shall see the sign* (Matt. 24:15).

ܠܥܠܡ ܠܐ ܡܫܝܓ ܐܢܬ *thou shalt never wash* (John. 13:8).

ܗܐ ܐܢܐ ܡܫܕܪ ܐܢܐ *behold I shall send* (Mal. 3:1).

ܠܡܕܡ ܕܥܒܪܝܢ ܫܬܐ ܝܘܡܝܢ *until six days be passing away* (Sind. 2:20).

ܠܡܚܪ ܡܝܬܐ ܐܢܐ ܠܗ ܠܛܠܝܐ *to-morrow I shall bring the youth* (Sindban 2:9).

ܥܕ ܗܘܐ ܙܒܢܐ ܕܩܪܒܐ *until the time of war should come* (Jos. Sty. 64:11).

(3) *a.* ܡܠܦ ܗܘܐ ܠܗ *was teaching him* (Sind. 2:4).

ܗܘܘ ܓܝܪ ܐܟܠܝܢ *for they were eating* (Sind. 27:4).

ܠܕܘܟܬܐ ܗܝ ܕܒܗ ܡܩܛܠܝܢ ܗܘܘ *at the place where they were to be killed* (Mart. 1:91, 3:99.1).

ܘܫܪܝ ܗܘܐ ܚܙܐ ܟܠ ܢܗܝܪܐܝܬ *and began and continued to see* (Greek Imperfect) *everything clearly* (Mk. 8:25).

b. ܐܫܬܡܥܘ ܟܕ ܡܨܠܝܢ *were heard when they prayed* (Aph. 454:18).

ܡܢ ܙܒܢܐ ܣܓܝܐܐ ܡܗܝܡܢܐ ܗܘܬ *for a long time it was firmly believed* (Over. 225:15).

ܗܢܘܢ ܕܡܙܒܢܝܢ *those who were selling* (John. 2:14).

§ 116.]   ELEMENTS OF SYRIAC.   153

ܘܟܕ ܢܦܩܝܢ ܐܫܟܚܘ ܓܒܪܐ *and as they were going out, they found a man* (Matt. 27:32).

2. (1) *a.* ܐܪܝܐ ܓܝܪ ܒܣܪܐ ܐܟܠ ܟܝܢܐܝܬ *for the lion eateth flesh naturally* (Spic. Syr. 7:14).

ܘܐܝܢܐ ܕܝܗܒ ܦܐܪ̈ܐ ܕܟܐ ܠܗ *and whichever beareth fruits, he purgeth it* (John. 15:2. See also Mal. 3:17).

b. ܐܡܬܝ ܕܡܨܠܐ ܐܢܬ *whenever thou prayest* (Matt. 6:6).

ܡܐ ܕܡܨܠܐ ܐܢܬ *when thou prayest* (Matt. 6:5).

(2) ܝܕܥ ܐܢܐ ܕܡܦܩܕ ܠܒܢ̈ܘܗܝ ܡܢ ܒܬܪܗ *I know him that he will command his sons after him* (Aphr. 25:14. Compare Gen. 18:19).

(3) ܡܬܟܪܟܝܢ ܗܘܘ ܐܚ̈ܐ *the brethren used to go about* (Jos. Sty. 37:20).

ܡܫܓܪ ܗܘܐ ܢܘܪܐ *he used to kindle fire* (Sind. 269:9).

ܘܥܢܢܐ ܣܠܩܐ ܗܘܐ *and a mist used to go up* (Gen. 2:6. Comp. Matt. 27:30).

1. The participle denoting a state or continuous action.
(1) *a.* When the time is not defined by the context the participle generally denotes the present.
b. The present may be emphasized by a particle.
(2) *a.* For the sake of vividness or certainty the simple participle may be used for the future.
b. The future may be emphasized by particles and phrases denoting futurity; with some of which, it can scarcely be distinguished from our future perfect.
(3) *a.* When the participle refers to past time it is usually accompanied by the verb ܗܘܐ *"to be"*.
b. Without ܗܘܐ the past time is sometimes determined by the context.
2. The participle denoting a series of actions or states.
(1) In present time.
a. Especially in proverbial clauses.
b. After particles.
(2) In future time.
(3) In past time. Here the participle is accompanied by the verb ܗܘܐ.

3. (1) ܟܕ ܗܘ ܡܡܠܠ *while he was speaking* (Gen. 29:9).

ܘܐܣܩܗ ܠܘܬ ܐܒܓܪ ܟܕ ܗܘ ܗܘ ܐܕܝ ܝܕܥ *and brought him to Abgar, Addai himself knowing* (Add. 6:3).

ܘܟܠ ܕܐܬܐ ܗܘܐ ܣܓܕܝܢ ܗܘܘ ܩܕܡܘܗܝ ܟܕ ܠܐ ܨܒܝܢ *and all who came bowed before him unwillingly* (L'omilia di Giacomo di Saruq. 150).

ܘܢܦܩܘ ܟܕ ܡܫܒܚܝܢ ܠܐܠܗܐ *and they went out praising God* (Jos. Sty. 26:14).

(2) *a.* ܚܙܐ ܠܠܘܝ ܟܕ ܝܬܒ *he saw Levi (who was) sitting* (Mark 2:14).

ܐܝܢܐ ܕܡܬܬܚܕ ܟܕ ܓܢܒ *whosoever is taken (who is) stealing* (Prov. 6:30).

b. . . . . ܘܚܙܐ ܠܡܠܐܟܗ . . . ܟܕ ܩܐܡ *and he saw the angel of the Lord standing* (Num. 22:31).

c. ܥܒܕܬܟܘܢ ܠܝܛܐ *I have made you accursed* (Mal. 2:9).

4. ܐܫܒܩ ܐܙܠ *I will let him go* (Sind. 8:13).

ܫܪܝܘ ܕܝܢܝܢ ܠܗ *they have begun to judge him* (Aphr. 220:14).

ܫܒܘܩܘ ܪܒܝܢ ܬܪ̈ܝܗܘܢ *let both grow together* (Matt. 13:30).

ܫܒܘܩ ܢܥܩܒܘܢ ܦܪ̈ܣܝܐ *let the Persians go* (Jos. Sty. 77:6).

5. ܠܡܐ ܢܡܘܬ *why would he die?* (1 Sam. 20:32); ܡܣܬܟܝܢ *must we look* (Lk. 7:20).

   3. A participle may denote a state.

   (1) Conditioning another verb. The participle is usually preceded by ܟܕ or ܕ and forms an adverbial clause of time, see § 137:2.

   (2) Limiting a noun or pronoun, when:—

   a. It may be preceded by ܕ and form an adjective clause.

   b. Or the participle may be used as an accusative of state or condition. (Compare in Arabic مَرَرْتُ بِزَيْدٍ جَالِسًا *I passed by Zaid, (as he was) sitting down* (see Wright Arabic Gram. Vol. II, p. 122, sq.).

   c. Or it may be an objective complement.

   4. The Participle is frequently used as the objective complement of another verb.

   5. The Participle may be used to denote the various moods. Compare § 114. 3, *Rem.* 1 and § 115. 6.

§ 117. The Passive Participle.

1. ܐܰܝܟ݁ܰܢ ܕ݁ܰܟ݂ܬ݂ܺܝܒ݂ ܕ݁ܰܠܟ݂ܺܐܢܶܐ ܢܳܡܽܘܣܳܐ ܠܳܐ ܣܺܝܡ *as it is written: the law was not given for the righteous* (1 Tim. 1:9).

   ܗܳܐ ܕ݁ܰܠܺܝܚ ܝܰܡܳܐ *behold the sea is disturbed* (Overbeck 384:16).

   ܢܰܦ݂ܫܳܐ ܚܢܺܝܩܳܐ *the soul is strangled* (id. 385:8).

2. ܡܶܛܽܠ ܕ݁ܠܳܐ ܡܚܰܬ݁ܰܡ ܗ݈ܘܳܐ ܕ݁ܺܝܰܬ݂ܺܝܩܺܐ *for the covenant was not sealed* (Aphr. 28:8).

   ܐܰܝܟ݂ܳܐ ܕ݁ܰܟ݂ܬ݂ܺܝܒ݂ ܗ݈ܘܳܐ ܗܳܟ݂ܰܢܳܐ *which had been written thus* (Ad. 3:16).

3. (1) ܙܡܺܝܪܳܬ݂ܳܐ ܕ݁ܰܥܒ݂ܺܝܕ݂ܳܢ ܠܶܗ *hymns were made by him* (Jos. Sty. 52:1).

   ܡܶܕ݁ܶܡ ܕ݁ܰܥܒ݂ܺܝܕ݂ ܠܶܗ *whatsoever shall have been done by him* (2 Cor. 5:10).

   (2) ܟ݁ܬ݂ܳܒ݂ܶܐ ܕ݁ܰܩܪܶܝܢ ܠܳܟ݂ *books were read by thee* (Spic. Syr. 13:8).

   ܐܰܝܟ݁ܰܢ ܕ݁ܰܫܡܺܝܥ ܠܰܢ *as we have heard* (Spic. Syr. 16:22).

4. ܐܶܢܳܐ ܐܰܚܺܝܕ݂ *I possess* (Ad. 4:7).

   ܕ݁ܰܬ݂ܟ݂ܺܝܠܺܝܢ *who trust* (Ps. II. 12).

   ܬ݁ܟ݂ܺܝܠܺܝܢ ܐܢ݈ܬ݁ܽܘܢ *ye trust* (Ad. 23 ult.).

   ܡܟ݂ܰܢܫܺܝܢ ܡܰܝܳܐ *having gathered water* (Lk. 14:2).

   Rem.—ܚܕ݂ܺܝܪܺܝܢ ܠܳܗ̇ *surrounding it* (Lk. 21:20).

   ܛܥܺܝܢܺܝܢ ܠܗܽܘܢ *bearing them* (Mk. 6:55).

   ܡܙܺܝܥ ܗ݈ܘܳܐ ܠܡܰܝܳܐ *he troubled the water* (John. 5:4).

5. ܕ݁ܟ݂ܺܝܪ ܐ݈ܢܳܐ ܟ݁ܽܠ ܡܶܕ݁ܶܡ ܕ݁ܰܥܒ݂ܰܕ݂ *I remember all that he has done* (1 Sam. 15:2).

   ܕ݁ܟ݂ܺܝܪܺܝܢ ܐܢ݈ܬ݁ܽܘܢ *ye are mindful* (Spic. Syr. 18:17).

6. ܠܳܐ ܡܶܕ݁ܶܡ ܕ݁ܰܡܣܰܠܰܝ *nothing to be blamed* (1 Tim. 4:4).

   ܕ݁ܰܡܪܰܫܰܝ *to be blamed* (Ad. 26:18).

   ܕ݁ܰܡܗܰܝܡܰܢ *to be believed* (Overbeck 54:9).

   Rem.—ܡܶܬ݂ܦ݁ܰܬ݁ܰܚ *to be opened* (Ad. 14:18).

7. ܚܒܝܫ ܒܘܨܐ clothed in Byssus (Ez. 9:2).

8. ܟܡܝܗ ܐܝܕܐ wounded in the hand (Barh. 170:19 [Uhl.]).

   1. The passive participle represents the result of an action as continuing.
   2. With ܗܘܐ this participle forms a kind of pluperfect. See § 127. 1 (2).
   3. (1) The logical subject preceded by ܠ is often put after the passive participle.
   (2) A logical object may be used as the grammatical subject.
   4. Some particles of the form ܩܛܝܠ are used in an active sense as well as a passive.
   Rem.—The passive participle so used governs an accusative.
   5. Peculiar is the use of the passive participle of verbs like ܪܚܡ and ܕܟܪ "to remember".
   6. Sometimes the passive participle is used like a gerundive.
   Rem.—Reflexive participles are used in this sense.
   7. Passive participles of verbs which take two accusatives, take the second accusative after them.
   8. Passive participles may take after them an accusative of specification.

§ 118. Participles as Nouns.

1. ܪܚܡܐ *friend.*

   ܥܡܘܕܐ *pillar.*

   ܨܦܪܐ *bird.*

   ܪܥܝܐ *shepherd.*

2. ܐܟܠ ܠܚܡܝ *eating of my bread* (Ps. 41:9).

   ܕܚܠܝ ܫܡܟ *fearers of thy name* (Ps. 61:5).

   ܒܪܝܟ ܕܡܪܝܐ *blessed be the Lord* (Ps. 37:22).

   ܐܟܠܝ ܒܣܪܐ ܐܢܘܢ *they are flesh eaters* (Spic. 7:15).

   ܒܪܝܟܗ ܕܡܪܝܐ *blessed of the Lord* (Gen. 24:31, 26:29).

3. ܟܦܪܝ ܒܛܝܒܘܬܐ *deniers of beneficence (unthankful)* (2 Tim. 3:2).

   ܫܟܒܝ ܥܡ ܕܟܪܐ *lyring with males* (1 Tim. 1:10).

4. ܪܽܘܚܳܐ ܛܳܥܝܳܬܳܐ *a wandering spirit* (Is. 19:14).

ܕܰܒܨܠܽܘܬܶܗ ܡܩܰܒܰܠܬܳܐ *by whose accepted prayer* (Aphr. 454:19).

ܚܰܢܦܶܐ ܛܳܥܝܶܐ *erring heathen* (Addai 42 ult.).

1. Some participles have become real substantives.
2. Participles are used in construction before nouns.
3. Some participles receive a preposition between them and the noun, though the participle itself remains in construction.
4. The participle is sometimes used as an attribute.

§ 119. The Infinitive Absolute.

1. (1) *a.* ܡܡܳܬ ܬܡܽܘܬ *thou shalt surely die* (Gen. 3:2).

ܡܶܬܪܕܳܝܽܘ ܡܶܬܪܕܶܝܢܰܢ *we are chastened* (1 Cor. 11:32).

ܥܰܠ ܐܰܠܳܗܳܐ ܡܶܬܦܠܳܓܽܘ ܡܶܬܦܰܠܓܺܝܢ *concerning God they are doubting* (Spic. Syr. 2:25).

b. ܗܰܝܡܶܢ ܒܰܠܚܽܘܕ ܡܗܰܝܡܳܢܽܘ *only believe* (Spic. Syr. 2:13).

ܦܪܰܚ ܡܦܪܰܚ *flew swiftly* (Dan. 9:21).

(2) ܡܰܠܦܳܢܶܐ ܓܶܝܪ ܡܶܫܬܰܐܠܽܘ ܡܶܢ ܡܶܫܬܰܐܠܺܝܢ ܠܳܐ ܗܘܳܐ ܡܫܰܐܠܺܝܢ ܠܗܽܘܢ *for teachers are asked questions they do not ask them.*

2. ܦܰܘܠܳܘܣ ܙܒܰܢܺܝܢ ܡܶܐܣܰܪ ܘܙܒܰܢܺܝܢ ܡܶܪܓܰܡ *Paul was at times imprisoned and at times stoned* (Aphr. 300:20).

Rem. 1. (1)—ܠܡܶܩܛܰܠ ܩܛܳܠܳܐ *to kill at all* (Spic. Syr. 17:20).

ܡܳܐ ܕܕܳܡܟܺܝܢ ܒܢܰܝ ܐ̱ܢܳܫܳܐ ܗܳܕܶܐ ܫܶܢܬܳܐ *when the sons of men sleep this sleep* (Aphr. 170:12).

(2)—ܨܰܘܡܳܐ ܕܨܳܡܽܘܗܝ *the fast that they fasted* (Aphr. 49:12).

ܣܰܟܠܽܘܬܳܐ ܕܚܛܰܘ ܒܳܗ *the folly with which they have sinned* (Sim. Sty. 295:24 [Nöld.]).

1. The infinitive is used absolutely in order to intensify the meaning of the verb.

(1) *a.* Before the verb.
  b. Sometimes after the verb.
(2) In contrasted statements.
2. Without the finite verb the infinitive is occasionally found.

Rem. 1. (1)—Instead of the Infinitive Absolute an abstract noun from the same or a cognate root is sometimes used, especially when the idea of the root is to be further modified or when two infinitives would stand together.

(2) This abstract noun can precede and be connected with the verb by ܕ.

§ 120. The Infinitive Construct.

1. (1) ܐܢ ܠܡܫܬܒܗܪܘ ܘܠܐ *if to glory is necessary* (2 Corr. 11:30).

ܠܐ ܡܟܝܠ ܕܥܘܒ ܠܐܝܣܪܝܠ ܠܡܬܟܢܫܘ *it belongeth not to Israel again to be assembled* (Aphr. 359:7).

(2) ܫܪܝ ܠܡܒܢܐ *he began to build* (Jos. Sty. 24:11).

ܠܐ ܡܫܟܚ ܠܡܬܐܣܝܘ *he cannot be healed* (Aphr. 136:4).

(3) ܠܡܐܡܪ *saying* (Jon. 3:1).

ܥܬܝܕܝܢܢ ܠܡܩܡ *we are ready to stand* (2 Cor. 5:10).

(4) ܡܦܣܩ ܒܡܚܛܐ *cut off by sinning* (Jos. Sty. 20:15).

ܒܡܥܒܕ *by making* (Gen. 2:3).

(5) ܐܝܟ ܚܠܡܐ ܠܡܫܬܪܝܘ *as a dream are to be dissolved.*

ܐܢ ܢܗܘܐ ܠܝ ܕܝܢ ܠܡܡܬ ܥܡܟ *though I shall have to die with thee* (Matt. 26:35).

ܐܠܐ ܗܕܐ ܠܐ ܡܬܐܡܪܐ *but this cannot be said* (Jos. Sty. 5:20).

(6) ܕܕܠܝܠ ܗܘ ܠܡܥܒܕ ܛܒܬܐ ܛܒ ܡܢ ܕܠܡܛܪ ܢܦܫܗ ܡܢ ܒܝܫܬܐ *easier is it to do good than to keep oneself from evil* (Spic. Syr. 6:10).

ܪܒܐ ܗܝ ܣܟܠܘܬܝ ܡܢ ܕܠܡܫܬܒܩܘ *my sin is too great to forgive* (Gen. 4:13. Compare Jon. 4:3).

2. (1) ܠܡܩܡܘ ܒܢܝܐ *to raise up children* (Matt. 3:9).

ܢܰܦ̮ܫܝ ܠܡܶܩܛܰܠ *to kill my soul* (Ps. 40:14).

ܠܡܶܬܟܰܬܳܫܘ ܕܰܥܬܺܝܕ ܗܘܳܐ *that he was ready to deliver battle* (Jos. Sty. 18:10).

ܠܡܶܠܛ ܠܰܐܪܥܳܐ *to curse the earth* (Gen. 8:21).

(2) ܠܡܶܥܒܕܗܽܘܢ *to make them* (lit. *for the making of them*) (Aphr. 319:5).

1. The infinitive construct always takes ܠ before it. It may be used:—
(1) As the subject of a verb.
(2) As the object of a verb.
(3) To denote the purpose or result or manner of an action. Compare § 137. 3, 4.
(4) As a gerundive.
(5) With ܐܺܝܬ and ܗܘܳܐ, but sometimes without to denote "*can*", "*must*", "*have to*" &c.
(6) After the comparative ܡܶܢ, in which case the infinitive clause is preceded by the relative ܕ. § 100, *Rem.* 2.

2. (1) Like any finite verb, the infinitive can govern an object.
(2) Like any noun, it can take a pronominal suffix in the genitive.

§ 121. The Subject of the Verb.

1. ܒܪܳܐ ܐܰܠܳܗܳܐ *God created* (Gen. 1:1).

ܘܰܐܪܥܳܐ ܗܘܳܬ *and the earth was* (Gen. 1:2).

ܘܶܐܡܪܰܬ ܐܰܢܬܬܳܐ *and the woman said* (Gen. 3:2).

2. (1) ܚܙܳܐ ܥܰܡܳܐ *the people saw* (Ex. 32:1; John. 5:3).

ܐܶܣܛܪܰܛܺܝܰܐ ܕܪܽܗ̱ܘܡܳܝܶܐ ܕܥܰܡܗܽܘܢ ܗܘܰܘ ܗܳܠܶܝܢ *the troops of Romans who were with them had dispersed themselves* (Jos. Sty. 47:20)

ܩܳܡ ܟܽܠܶܗ ܟܶܢܫܗܽܘܢ *the whole assembly rose* (Lk. 23:1).

ܚܙܳܐ ܫܰܪܟܶܗ ܕܚܰܝܠܳܐ *the rest of the army saw* (Jos. Sty. 54:18, see also Mt. 27:49; Acts 26:13). ܟܽܠ ܐܢܳܫ ܩܥܳܐ *each cried* (Jonah 1:5).

(2) ܐܶܬܟܰܢܫܰܬ ܟܽܠܳܗ ܡܕܺܝܢ̱ܬܳܐ *the whole city assembled* (Acts 13:44).

ܐܶܢ ܬܶܬܟܰܢܰܫ ܟܽܠܳܗ ܥܺܕܬܳܐ *if the whole church be assembled* (1 Cor. 14:23).

121. ܗܘܐ ܓܝܪ ܥܡܐ ܣܓܝܐܐ ܕܥܡܐ ܢܩܝܦ ܗܘܘ ܘܩܥܝܢ *for the multitude of the people were following after him and crying* (Acts 21:36).

(4) ܫܪܝܘ ܚܕ ܚܕ ܠܡܐܡܪ ܠܗ *one after another began to say to him* (Matt. 26:22).

ܐܡܪܝܢ ܠܗ ܚܕ ܚܕ *they say to him one by one* (Mk. 14:19).

(5) ܚܕ ܡܢ ܗܠܝܢ ܠܐ ܗܘܐ *not one of these things happens* (Spic. Syr. 14:5).

ܕܠܐ ܢܚܙܐ ܚܕ ܡܢ ܓܒܪ̈ܐ ܗܠܝܢ ܐܪܥܐ *that not one of these men should see the land* (Deut. 1:35).

3. (1) ܡܐ ܕܡܙܕܥܙܥܝܢ ܡܝ̈ܐ *when the waters are troubled* (John. 5:7).

ܫܡܝܐ ܝܗܒܘ ܡܛܪܐ *the heavens gave rain* (Jos. 5:18).

(2) ܒܗ ܚܝ̈ܐ ܗܘܐ *in him was life* (John. 1:4).

ܘܠܐ ܢܗܘܐ ܬܘܒ ܓܢܣܐ ܡܪܝܪܐ *and there shall not be bitter absinthe* (?) (Ezek. 28:24).

4. ܘܬܫܒ̈ܚܬܐ ܘܙܡܝܪ̈ܬܐ ܥܒܝܕܢ ܠܗ *and psalms and hymms were made by him* (Jos. Sty. 52:1).

ܟܬܝܒܝܢ ܗܘܘ ܒܗ ܟܬ̈ܒܐ ܝܘ̈ܢܝܐ *Greek letters were written on it* (Jos. Sty. 66:10).

5. (1) ܘܦܛܪܝܩܣ ܘܗܘܦܛܘܣ ܨܪܘ ܠܐܡܝܕ *Patricius and Hypatius beseiged Amid* (Jos. Sty. 52:14).

ܦܘܠܘܣ ܕܝܢ ܘܒܪܢܒܐ ܩܘܝܘ ܗܘܘ ܒܐܢܛܝܟܝܐ *But Paul and Barnabas abode in Antioch* (Acts 15:35).

(2) ܐܬܬ ܡܪܝܡ ܡܓܕܠܝܬܐ ܘܡܪܝܡ ܐܚܪܬܐ *Mary Magdalene and the other Mary came* (Mk. 28:1).

ܘܐܡܬܝ ܗܘܐ ܪܥܠܐ ܘܟܦܢܐ ܘܡܘܬܢܐ ܘܩܪܒܐ *and when were the earthquake and the famine and the pestilence and the war* (Jos. Sty. 1:4).

6. ܘܩܝܡܝܢܢ ܐܢܐ ܘܗܘ *and we arise, I and he* (Jos. Sty. 29:13. 17).

ܐܢܬܝ ܘܝܘܣܦ ܛܫܝܬܘܢ ܝܘܡܐ *thou and Joseph have concealed the day* (Legends of St. Mary 25:3. See also J. S. 92:3; Lk. 2:48; S. S. 31:1).

§ 121.]   ELEMENTS OF SYRIAC.   161

Rem. 1.—ܐܢܐ ܘܡܫܝܚܐ ܚܕ ܐܝܬܝܢ *I and Messiah are of one nature* (Assem. 1:347. 28 [Uhl.]).

ܥܘܠ ܐܢܬ ܘܟܠ ܒܝܬܟ *enter thou and all thy house* (Gen. 7:1).

Rem. 2.—ܐܙܠܝܢ ܗܘܘ ܗܘ ܘܡܪܝܡ *he and Mary were going* (Legends of St. Mary 26:10).

ܥܠܬ ܣܒܬܐ ܘܝܘܣܦ *the old woman and Joseph went in* (Legends of St. Mary 27:10).

7. ܫܐܠܝܢ *they are asking* (Mal. 2:7); ܠܡܢܐ ܡܕܓܠܝܢ *why do we lie?* (Mal. 2:10); ܘܐܢ ܐܡܪܝܬܘܢ *and if ye say* (Mal. 2:14).

1. Regularly, the verb conforms in gender and number with the subject.

2. (1) Collectives, or other words when denoting more than one individual, take a verb in the plural. Compare § 90. 4.

(2) But a collective noun conveying the idea of unity requires a verb in the 3rd person singular. Compare § 90. 4.

(3) Hence arises the peculiar construction when in the same sentence two verbs agreeing with one subject are put one in the plural and the other in the singular.

(4) ܫܡ ܫܡ "one another" takes a verb in the plural.

(5) ܡܢ ܫܡ before a negative takes a verb in the plural.

3. Nouns plural in form but singular in signification

(1) Generally take a verb in the plural.

(2) Sometimes they take a verb in the singular.

4. The passive participle followed by a ܠ denoting the agent sometimes is uninflected.

5. (1) When a verb has for its subject two or more distinct nouns, it is generally in the plural number.

(2) It may be put in the singular number.

6. When the subjects are of different persons the first is preferred to the second or third and the second to the third.

Rem. 1.—With two subjects, one of the first or second, the other of the third person, the verb is sometimes put in the first or second person singular as if there were but one subject.

Rem. 2.—When the subjects are of different gender, the verb prefers the masculine.

x

§ 122. Impersonal Verbs.

1. ܘܰܗܘܳܐ *and it happened* (Lk. 10:13).

   ܕܢܺܛܰܐܒ ܠܰܢ *and that it may be well with us* (Deut. 6:24).

2. ܟܐܶܒ ܠܶܗ ܠܝܰܘܢܳܢ ܘܰܟܡܰܪ ܠܶܗ *it was painful to Jonah and it was grievous to him* (Jon. 4:1).

   ܘܠܳܐ ܬܶܐܐ ܠܗܽܘܢ *and it should not be weary to them* (Lk. 18:1).

   ܡܶܐܢܰܬ݂ ܠܺܝ ܒܕܳܪܐ ܗܰܘ *I was grieved with that generation* (Heb. 3:10, see also Gal. 1:9; 2 Thess. 3:13; Ephr. 3:13).

3. ܣܰܒܰܪܘ ܠܝܰܥܩܽܘܒ *they announced to Jacob* (Gen. 48:2).

   ܢܶܟܬܒܽܘܢ ܠܺܝ ܐܶܓܪ̈ܬܳܐ *let them write for me letters* (Neh. 2:7).

4. (1) ܠܺܝ ܠܳܐ ܡܳܐܢܳܐ *to me it is not irksome* (Phil. 3:1).

   ܟܰܪܝܳܐ ܗܝ ܠܳܗ ܠܢܰܦܫܝ ܥܕܰܡܳܐ ܠܡܰܘܬܳܐ *my soul is sorrowful even unto death* (Matt. 26:38).

   ܠܳܐ ܡܨܶܝܐ *it is not possible* (Jos. Sty. 46:6).

   ܠܳܐ ܛܥܳܐ ܠܝܺܕܰܥܬܳܟ *it has not escaped thy knowledge* (Jos. Sty. 15:16).

   (2) ܫܰܠܺܝܛ ܥܰܠ ܚܰܝܠܶܗ *it is in his power* (Spic. Syr. 5:13).

   ܘܳܠܶܐ ܗܘܳܐ ܕܢܶܗܘܶܐ *so it is necessary that it should be* (Matt. 26:54).

   Rem.—ܦܰܩܳܚ ܠܺܝ ܕܶܐܡܽܘܬ *it is better for me to die* (Jon. 4:3).

5. ܡܶܬܝܰܕܥܳܐ ܗܝ ܓܶܝܪ ܐܰܣܺܝܪܳܐܺܝܬ *for certainly it has been manifested* (Jos. Sty. 2:2).

   ܐܶܬܦܰܩܰܕ ܠܺܝ ܡܶܢܳܟ *it has been commanded me by thee* (Jos. Sty. 3:21).

   ܐܰܝܟ ܕܰܫܡܺܝܥ ܠܰܢ *as we have heard* (Spic. Syr. 16:22).

   Rem.—ܕܳܫܘ ܐܶܢܽܘܢ ܕܳܝ̈ܫܶܐ *tramplers have trampled them* (Nah. 2:3).

ܠܐ ܢܕܘܫ ܕܝܫܐ *the treader shall not tread out* (Is. 16:10).

ܘܐܢ ܢܡܘܬ ܡܝܬܐ *if a man die* (Num. 6:9).

ܐܬܦܩܕ ܦܘܩܕܢܐ *a command has been issued* (Jos. Sty. 49:8).

The following forms of the verb are used impersonally. Compare § 64. 9—11.

1. The third masculine singular.
2. The third feminine singular.
3. The third plural.
4. The participles.
(1) The feminine singular.
(2) The masculine singular.

Rem.—Adjectives, also, may be used in this impersonal sense.

5. Frequently the passive is used in an impersonal verb.

Rem.—Instead of the impersonal construction we meet occasionally with a subject from the same root.

Note—Generally this is a literal translation of the Hebrew; oftener, however, the Hebrew participle is dropped in the Peshito and the subject is unexpressed or expressed by ܐܢܫܐ as in Deut. 22:8.

§ 123. The Object of the Verb.

1. (1) ܢܣܒ ܛܠܝܐ *he took a child* (Luke. 9:47).

ܚܙܐ ܐܢܬܬܐ ܫܦܝܪܬܐ *he saw a beautiful woman* (Sind. 4:9).

(2) ܐܝܕܥܬܐ ܡܢ ܚܟܡܬܐ ܕܫܪܪܐ ܠܐ ܩܒܠܘ *knowledge from the true wisdom they have not received* (Spic. Syr. 2:22).

(3) ܕܢܓܢܐ ܠܐܢܫ *who would blame a man* (Spic. Syr. 6:1).

ܘܠܐ ܫܒܩ ܠܐܢܫ *and suffered not a man* (Lk. 8:51).

(4) ܘܠܬܠܬܐ ܡܢ ܦܪܣܝܐ ܗܠܝܢ ܕܩܪ *and three of these Persians he pierced* (Jos. Sty. 68:4).

2. (1) ܕܢܚܙܐ ܚܪܬܐ *that he might see the end* (Matt. 26:58).

ܩܒܠܬ ܐܓܪܬܐ *I have received letters* (Jos. Sty. 1:1, see also 3:15, 4:11, et al.).

(2) ܐܠܗܐ ܠܐ ܐܢܫ ܚܙܐ *God, no man hath seen* (John. 1:18).

ܣܢܝܩܘܬܝ ܡܡܠܐ ܗܘܝܬ *my deficiency thou wast supplying* (Jos. Sty. 3:9. See also 3:12, and Matt. 27:42).

(3) ܐܦܝܣܘ ܠܟܢܫܐ *they persuaded the multitudes* (Matt. 27:20).

ܟܕ ܚܙܐ ܗܘܝܬ ܠܐܬܘܬܐ *when I saw the signs* (Jos. Sty. 3:17. See also Jos. Sty. 3:14, 18:5, and Matt. 26:72, 27:30).

(4) ܠܝܫܘܥ ܒܥܝܢ ܐܢܬܝܢ *Jesus, ye are seeking* (Matt. 28:5).

ܘܠܝ ܫܐܠܬ *and me hast thou begged* (Jos. Sty. 3:12. See also Mt. 26:48, 27:32).

Rem.— ܠܝܫܘܥ ܕܝܢ ܕܢܘܒܕܘܢ *but that they should destroy Jesus* (Matt. 27:20).

(5) ܘܫܕܐ ܣܐܡܐ *and he threw down the silver* (Mt. 27:5).

ܟܕ ܐܡܪ ܗܘܐ ܗܕܐ ܡܠܬܐ *when he told this word* (Aphr. 520:18).

(6) ܗܕܐ ܒܛܢܢܟ ܐܡܪܬ *in thy zeal thou hast said this* (Jos. Sty. 5:5).

ܘܕܡܗ ܕܝܠܗ ܟܠܒܐ ܠܥܣܘ *his own blood the dogs licked* (Aphr. 183:16).

ܚܝܐ ܘܫܠܡܐ ܝܗܒܬ ܐܢܐ *life and peace have I given* (Mal. 2:5).

Rem.— ܕܠܐ ܝܕܥܝܢ ܚܪܝܢܐ *they know not stubbornness* (Aphr. 177 end).

(7) ܫܩܠܘܗܝ ܠܣܐܡܐ *they took the silver* (Matt. 27:6).

ܘܣܟܪܘܗܝ ܠܡܥܝܢܐ *and they closed the mine* (Jos. Sty. 68:13. See also Jos. Sty. 21:18, 5:17; Matt. 26:51, 57:69, 27:59).

Rem.— ܚܙܝܬ ܗܘܝܬ ܠܗ ܠܣܛܢܐ *I beheld Satan* (Lk. 10:10).

ܘܟܕ ܓܪ ܠܗ ܠܫܠܕܐ *and as he was dragging away the corpse* (Jos. Sty. 68:9, see also Jos. Sty. 4:11; Syr. Spic. 6:13).

(8) ܢܫܩܠܝܗ ܥܡܗ ܠܫܠܕܐ *he would take with him the dead body* (Jos. Sty. 68:7).

ܘܠܝ ܦܩܕܬ *and me thou didst command* (Deut. 4:14).

1. When the object is indefinite, it may be with or without ܠ and may be before or after the verb, that is the following constructions all meaning „*he built a house*" may occur.

(1) ܒܢܐ ܒܝܬܐ.

(2) ܒܝܬܐ ܒܢܐ.

(3) ܒܢܐ ܠܒܝܬܐ.

(4) ܠܒܝܬܐ ܒܢܐ.

2. When the object is definite and direct the following cases arise meaning "he built the house".

(1) ܒܢܐ ܒܝܬܐ.

(2) ܒܝܬܐ ܒܢܐ.

(3) ܒܢܝ ܠܒܝܬܐ.

(4) ܠܒܝܬܐ ܒܢܝ.

Rem.—The object with ܠ may be put before the particles which connect the sentence with that which precedes.

(5) ܒܢܝܗܝ ܒܝܬܐ.

(6) ܒܝܬܐ ܒܢܝܗܝ.

Rem.—The participle does not take the pronominal suffix directly but governs it by means of ܠ. See (7) Remark.

(7) ܒܢܝܗܝ ܠܒܝܬܐ.

Rem.—The participle takes the pronominal suffix just as in the construction (6). See (6) Remark.

(8) ܠܒܝܬܐ ܒܢܝܗܝ.

§ 124. The Verb with an Indirect Object.

1. ܗܢܘܢ ܕܝܢ ܐܡܪܝܢ ܠܗ *but they said to him* (Matt. 27:4).

ܚܢܢ ܕܝܢ ܐܡܪܝܢ ܠܗ *but we said to him* (Spic. Syr. 1:5).

ܕܡܬܚܝܒ ܗܘܐ ܠܗ *that was due to him* (Jos. Sty. 3:1).

2. ܠܟܘܢ ܐܫܬܕܪܬ݀ ܡܠܬܐ *to you is the word sent* (Acts 13:26).

3. ܘܠܝܫܘܥ ܡܢܐ ܐܥܒܕ *And to Jesus what shall I do* (Matt. 27:22).

4. ܐܡܪܘ ܥܒܕܘܗܝ ܠܗ ܠܡܪܐ *his servants said to the Lord* (Jos. Sty. 4:10).

2. ܢܚܬ ܠܗ *he went down for himself;* ܐܙܠ ܐܢܐ *I am going* (Ad. 4:15).

The Indirect object is preceded by ܠ. The following constructions occur.

1. ܐܡܪ ܠܗ *he said to him.*

2. ܠܗ ܐܡܪ *to him he said.*

3. ܐܡܪ ܠܡܪܝܐ *to the Lord he said.*

4. ܐܡܪ ܠܗ ܠܡܪܝܐ *he said to him i. e. the Lord.*

5. The so-called ethical dative is of frequent occurrence in Syriac; but it can scarcely ever be translated into English. See § 101 B, 1 (1), *Rem.* 3.

§ 125. The Verb with Two or More Objects.

Four cases occur. The verb may govern
1. Two direct objects.
2. Two indirect objects.
3. Two objects, one direct, the other indirect.
4. Three objects, one direct, two indirect.

1. (1) ܫܐܠܘܗܝ ܐܬܐ *they asked of him a sign* (Aphr. 460:20).

ܫܐܠܬܗ ܡܠܐ *I asked him words* (questions) (Aphr. 395:2).

ܐܠܦܬܟܘܢ ܢܡܘܣܐ ܘܕܝܢܐ *I taught you laws and judgements* (Deut. 4:5).

ܐܠܦܗ ܐܘܪܚܐ ܕܕܝܢܐ *he has taught him the way of judgment* (Is. 40:14. See also Lk. 11:5, 15:22; Ex. 27:2; Lk. 23:11; John. 14:26).

ܘܡܠܝܗ ܚܠܐ *and filled it with vinegar* (Matt. 27:48).

ܢܦܪܘܥ ܐܢܘܢ ܪܘܓܙܐ ܘܚܡܬܐ *he will reward them indignation and wrath* (Rom. 2:8).

(2) ܐܠܒܫܘܗܝ ܟܠܡܝܕܐ *they clothed him with a robe* (Matt. 27:28).

ܐܥܒܪ ܐܢܘܢ ܝܘܪܕܢܢ *he caused them to pass over Jordan* (Aphr. 357:8).

Rem.—ܐܘܪܬ݂ܶܬ݂ ܐܶܢܘܢ ܠܰܒ݂ܢܰܝ̈ ܐܺܝܣܪܳܝܶܠ *I caused the children of Israel to inherit the land* (Aphr. 20:4).

ܘܰܢܣܰܒ݂ܘ ܡܶܢܝ ܠܒ݂ܽܘܫܰܝ̈ܗܘܢ *and they took from me their glittering robe* (Apost. Apoc. 274:16).

(3) ܚܰܘܝ ܐܶܢܘܢ ܐܪܳܙܳܐ ܕܡܰܥܡܘܕ݂ܺܝܬ݂ܳܐ *he showed them the mystery of baptism* (Aphr. 226:11).

ܟܰܦܢ̈ܐ ܣܰܒܰܥ ܛܳܒ݂ܳܬ݂ܳܐ *the hungry he fills with good things* (Lk. 1:53).

ܚܰܘܳܢ ܐܰܒ݂ܳܐ *show us the father* (John. 14:8).

2. ܕܢܶܗܘܶܐ ܠܗܘܢ ܠܡܶܐܟ݂ܘܠܬܳܐ *that it might be to them for food* (Jos. Sty. 69:4).

ܡܶܛܽܠ ܕܰܠܒܶܢܝܳܢܟ݂ܘܢ ܗܘ ܝܰܗܒܶܗ ܠܘܳܬ݂ܰܢ *because that for your edification he hath given it to us* (2 Cor. 10:8).

3. (1) ܐܰܫܠܡܶܗ ܠܛܰܠܝܐ ܠܣܶܢܕܒܰܢ *he delivered the lad to Sindban* (Sindb. 1 ult.).

ܘܝܰܗܒ݂ ܚܶܛ̈ܐ ܠܐܘܪܗܳܝ̈ܐ *and he gave wheat to the Edesenes* (Jos. Sty. 67:14).

ܘܰܐܫܠܡܽܘܗܝ ܠܦܺܝܠܰܛܘܣ *and he delivered him to Pilate* (Matt. 27:2).

(2) ܘܝܰܗܒ݂ ܠܶܗ ܚܰܝ̈ܐ *and he gave him life* (Jos. Sty. 3:2).

ܥܒܰܕ ܠܶܗ ܡܶܫܬܽܘܬ݂ܳܐ *he made for him a feast* (Sindb. 2:23, see also Acts 13. 14. 20. 21. 32 and Matt. 26:15).

(3) ܗܘ ܬܘܒ݂ ܫܰܕܰܪ ܠܰܡܫܺܝܚܶܗ ܠܥܳܠܡܳܐ *he again sent his Messiah into the world* (Aphr. 5:1).

ܦܪܘܫܘ ܠܫܳܐܘܳܠ ܠܰܥܒ݂ܳܕܳܐ *set apart Saul for the work* (Acts 13:2).

ܘܶܐܢܳܐ ܡܰܫܠܶܡ ܐ݈ܢܳܐ ܠܶܗ ܠܟ݂ܘܢ *and I will deliver him to you* (Matt. 26:15).

ܕܠܳܐ ܢܶܗܘܘܢ ܡܩܰܒܠܺܝܢ ܠܗܶܪ̈ܛܝܩܘ ܠܡܰܥܡܘܕ݂ܺܝܬ݂ܳܐ *they should not be receiving heretics to baptism* (Overbeck 220:19).

(4) ܕܢܰܫܠܶܡ ܠܗܘܢ ܠܒܰܪܐܰܒܳܐ *that he should deliver to them Barabbas* (Matt. 27:20).

4. ܩܪܘܫܘ ܠܝ ܠܫܐܘܠ ܘܠܒܪܢܒܐ ܠܥܒܕܐ *set apart for me Saul and Barnabas for the work* (Acts 13:2).

ܠܐ ܢܒܗܬ ܠܡܥܠܘ ܠܢܫܐ ܗܕܐ ܠܘܬܢ ܐܘ ܠܝܘܠܦܢܐ *we should not be ashamed to take this woman to us for instruction* (Overb. 102:15).

5. ܫܡܥܬ ܩܠܝ *thou didst hear my voice* (Jon. 2:3); ܐܫܬܠܛ ܒܢܘܢܝ ܝܡܐ *rule over the fish of the sea* (Gen. 2:28); ܩܪܐ ܐܠܗܐ ܠܪܩܝܥܐ ܫܡܝܐ *God called the firmament heaven* (Gen. 1:8).

 1. (1) Verbs of asking, teaching, filling, rewarding &c., may take two direct objects.

 (2) Any causative (Aph'el or Shaph'el) may take two direct objects. *Rem.*—Either accusative may have ܠ.

 (3) Sometimes the Intensive Species governs two direct objects.

 2. Occasionally we meet with verbs having two indirect objects.

 3. Many verbs take both a direct and an indirect object; the indirect object always taking ܠ, the direct object being either with or without it. We have the following cases.

 (1) ܒܢܐ ܒܝܬܐ ܠܗ *he built a house for him*.

 (2) ܒܢܐ ܠܗ ܒܝܬܐ *a house for him he built*.

 (3) ܒܢܐ ܒܝܬܐ ܠܗ *a house he built for him*.

 (4) ܒܢܐ ܠܗ ܒܝܬܐ *a house for him he built*.

 4. Sometimes we have a verb having one direct and two indirect objects, all three preceded by ܠ.

 5. By means of a preposition before their object, some verbs have their meaning supplemented, or modified.

§ 126. Passives &c., with the Object.

1. ܐܬܦܪܥܬ ܒܝܫܬܟ *thou hast been repaid thy evil* (2 Sam. 16:8).

ܐܬܦܪܥܘ ܕܝܢܐ ܟܐܢܐ *they have been repaid a just judgment* (Aphr. 49:3).

ܗܝܕܝܢ ܫܡܥܘܢ ܟܐܦܐ ܐܬܡܠܝ ܪܘܚܐ ܕܩܘܕܫܐ *then Simon Peter was filled with the Holy Ghost* (Acts 4:8).

[§ 126.] ELEMENTS OF SYRIAC.

ܐܳܝܠܶܝܢ ܕܶܐܬܬܰܠܡܰܕܬ ܠܗܶܝܢ *which thou hast been taught* (Lk. 1:4).

Rem.—ܐܶܬܡܠܺܝ ܢܶܟܠܳܐ ܗܘܳܐ *he was full of cunning* (Aphr. 61:11).

ܠܒܺܝܫ ܐܰܢܬ ܐܺܝܩܳܪܳܐ *thou art clothed with glory* (Aphr. 494:12).

ܡܟܰܣܰܝ ܡܰܨܢܰܦܬܳܐ *wearing (covered with) turbans* (Jos. Sty. 25:1).

2. (1) ܐܶܫܬܰܘܕܥܽܘܗܝ *they knew him* (Mk. 6:54).

ܘܶܐܫܬܰܘܕܥܽܘܗܝ *and they knew him* (Lk. 24:31).

ܐܶܬܕܰܟܪܶܬ ܚܰܕ ܡܶܢ ܚܰܒܪ̈ܰܝ *I thought about one of my companions* (Sindb. 9:5).

ܡܰܕܟܰܪ ܐܢܳܐ ܫܡܶܗ ܕܰܡܫܺܝܚܳܐ *I make mention of the name of the Messiah* (Addai 20:19).

Rem.—ܐܶܬܟܰܣܺܝܘ ܣܰܩܶܐ *they clothed themselves with sackcloth* (Jon. 3:5). Compare Jon. 3:8 ܕܰܡܟܰܣܶܝܢ ܣܰܩܶܐ *they covered themselves with sackcloht.*

(2) ܐܶܬܟܰܣܳܐ ܒܰܡܨܺܝܬܳܟ *cover thyself with thy garment* (Acts 12:8).

ܐܶܬܟܰܣܺܝܬ ܢܘܗܪܳܐ *thou coverest thyself with light* (Ps. 104:2).

3. (1) ܕܠܳܐ ܓܕ̈ܰܫܘ ܠܶܗ ܒܺܝܫ̈ܳܬܳܐ *to whom some evils have not happened* (Jos. Sty. 81:4).

ܠܳܐ ܝܳܕܥܺܝܢܰܢ ܡܳܢܳܐ ܗܘܳܝܗܝ *we know not what has happened to him* (Acts 7:40).

ܟܽܠ ܕܰܗܘܰܝ̈ *all which happened to her* (Addai 12 ult.).

(2) ܪܶܓܬܳܐ ܪܶܓܬ *with desire the desire has come to me* (Lk. 22:15).

ܗܳܕܶܐ ܪܶܓܬܳܐ ܓܕܶܫܰܬ ܠܺܝ ܕܶܐܙܰܠ ܠܐܘܪܺܫܠܶܡ *this desire has come to me that I may go to Jerusalem* (Overbeck 164:23).

4. (1) ܐܳܣܘ̈ܳܬܳܐ ܪܰܘܪ̈ܒܳܬܳܐ ܣܳܥܰܪ ܗܘܳܐ *great cures he was working* (Ad. Apos. 7:14).

ܐܰܠܶܦ ܗܘܳܐ ܠܥܰܡܳܐ ܝܺܕܰܥܬܳܐ *he taught the people knowledge* (Eccles. 12:9).

ܥܒܰܕ ܥܰܡܗܽܘܢ ܩܝܳܡܳܐ *he made a covenant with them* (Jos. Sty. 90:5).

ܢܕܰܪ ܢܶܕܪܳܐ *he vowed a vow* (Sindb. 1:3).

Y

ܢܪܚܫܘܢ ܡܝܐ ܪܚܫܐ *let the waters swarm with swarms* (Gen. 1:20).

(2) ܐܬܐܠܨܬ ܐܘܠܨܢܐ ܪܒܐ *he experienced great agony* (Sindb. 3:14).

ܐܬܦܩܕ ܦܘܩܕܢܐ *he was commanded a command* (Jos. Sty. 49:8. See § 122. 5 Rem.).

1. (1) Verbs which in the active govern two direct objects may govern one in the passive, the other becoming the subject.

Rem.—Passive participles of such verbs may also govern an object.

2. (1) The reflexives of many *verba mentis*, in the derived forms, govern an object additional to that involved in the verbal form.

Rem.—Verbs which in the P⁶ʾal involve a reflexive action come under this same rule.

(2) Verbs which in the active govern two direct objects, may in the reflexive govern one additional to that involved in the verbal form.

3. (1) Verbs signifying "*to happen to*" take a direct object.

(2) The impersonal verb ܓܕܫ (3rd fem. sing.), see § 122. 2, sometimes takes a direct object.

4. (1) Some verbs take a cognate accusative from the same or a cognate root.

(2) Reflexives and Passives sometimes take a cognate accusative: but only those of such verbs as in the active would take two direct objects (see 1. 2 (2)), or such reflexives as would come under 2 (1).

§ 127. Uses of ܗܘܐ.

1. (1) ܣܠܩ ܗܘܐ *was going up* (Gen. 2:6).

ܚܪܥ ܗܘܐ *was cunning* (Gen. 3:1).

ܗܘ ܟܗܢܐ ܗܘܐ *he was the priest* (Gen. 14:18).

ܕܥܡܟܘܢ ܗܘܝܬ *because I was with thee* (John. 16:4).

ܒܥܠܡܐ ܗܘܐ *he was in the world* (John. 1:14).

(2) ܐܝܬܘܗܝ ܗܘܐ ܠܒܘܫܗ *his clothing was* (Matt. 3:4).

ܗܘܐ ܗܘܐ ܕܝܢ ܥܩܬܐ *now there was a question* (Jon. 3:25).

ܠܝܬ ܗܘܐ ܠܗܘܢ ܕܘܟܬܐ *they had not a place* (Lk. 2:7).

[§ 127.] ELEMENTS OF SYRIAC.

ܠܐ ܗܘܐ ܗܟܢ ܐܡܪ ܐܢܐ *but I am not thus saying* (Jos. Sty. 42:23).

ܝܗܒ ܗܘܐ *he had given* (Matt. 26:48).

2. (1) ܘܐܪܥܐ ܗܘܬ ܬܘܗ *and the earth was waste* (Gen. 1:2).

ܘܩܐܝܢ ܗܘܐ ܦܠܚ ܐܪܥܐ *Cain was a tiller of the ground* (Gen. 4:2).

ܒܗ ܚܝܐ ܗܘܐ *in him was life* (John. 1:4).

(2) ܗܘܐ ܥܠܡܐ ܒܐܝܕܗ *the world was made with him* (John. 1:10).

ܗܠܝܢ ܒܒܝܬܥܢܝܐ ܗܘܝ *these things were done in Bethany* (John. 8:28. Comp. Matt. 27:54).

1. (1) When ܗܘܐ stands after a predicate participle, adjective, noun, or even a clause, it takes the enclitic form ܗܘܐ and has the meaning "*was*".

(2) It is often so used to strengthen the past sense of ܐܝܬ or of the finite verb. Sometimes, also, it emphasizes the negative particle ܠܐ.

2. (1) When ܗܘܐ stands before the predicate the ܗ is pronounced and is written without linea occultans. This is true also when a word occurs between the predicate and ܗܘܐ.

(2) When ܗܘܐ is used in the sense of "*was made*", "*came into beeing*", "*happened*" &c., the ܗ is always pronounced.

3. (1) a. ܣܚܘ̈ܘܗܝ ܗܘܘ ܠܡܫܝܚܐ *they saw the Messiah* (Addai. 2:10).

ܘܐܫܬܠܡܬ ܗܘܬ ܣܘܪܝܐ ܟܠܗ ܒܐܝܕܝܗܘܢ *and all Syria was delivered into their hands* (Spic. Syr. 18:8).

ܓܒܪܐ ܚܕ ܐܝܬ ܗܘܐ *there was a certain man* (Matt. 21:28).

b. ܗܘ ܓܝܪ ܗܪܘܕܣ ܐܚܕ ܗܘܐ ܠܝܘܚܢܢ *for Herod had seized John* (Matt. 14:3).

ܕܐܬܝ ܗܘܝ ܒܬܪܗ *who had come after* (Matt. 27:55).

ܕܐܬܝܗܒ ܗܘܐ ܠܗ ܡܢ ܡܠܟܐ ܕܦܪܣܝܐ *who had been given to him by the Persian King* (Jos. Sty. 70:10).

(2) ܕܙܕܩ ܗܘܐ ܕܢܦܩ ܗܘܐ ܠܗ *it was right that he should let it well forth* (Aphr. 314:4).

ܘܘܠܐ ܗܘܐ ܕܬܬܝܗܒ ܗܘܬ *it was necessary that she should have been given* (Aphr. 234:2).

ܨܒܐ ܗܘܐ ܓܝܪ ܐܒܓܪ ܕܗܘ ܩܢܘܡܗ ܢܥܒܪ ܗܘܐ *Abgar wished that he himself might pass over* (Addai 3:6).

ܕܠܡܐ ܥܠܬܐ ܗܕܐ ܬܥܝܪ ܗܘܬ ܠܒܥܠܕܒܒܘܬܐ ܡܪܝܪܬܐ *lest this cause should call forth bitter enmity* (Ad. 3:9).

ܕܠܐ ܢܫܟܚܘܢ ܗܘܘ ܠܚܡܐ ܠܡܐܟܠ *that they could not eat bread* (Mk. 3:20).

(3) *a.* ܕܩܝܡܝܢ ܗܘܘ ܦܠܝܓܝܢ ܦܠܝܓܝܢ *who were standing in crowds* (Ad. 2:12).

ܝܘܩܪܐ ܣܓܐ ܗܘܐ *the dearness was increasing* (Jos. Sty. 35:2).

ܕܗܘܝܢ ܗܘܘ ܐܝܟ ܥܣܪܐ ܐܠܦܝܢ ܓܒܪܝܢ *which consisted of about ten thousand men* (Jos. Sty. 74:15).

ܒܥܝܢ ܗܘܘ ܥܠ ܝܫܘܥ ܣܗܕܐ *they were seeking, against Jesus, witnesses* (Matt. 26:59).

b. ܕܠܟܪ ܕܢܦܩܝܢ ܗܘܘ *withersoever they were going* (Jos. Sty. 34:10).

ܘܕܡܟܝܢ ܗܘܘ ܒܐܣܛܘܐ ܘܒܫܘܩܐ *they were in the habit of sleeping on the porches and streets* (Jos. Sty. 36:19).

ܘܡܒܘܥܐ ܣܠܩ ܗܘܐ ܡܢ ܐܪܥܐ *and a mist used to go up from the earth* (Gen. 2:6).

(4) ܠܐ ܓܝܪ ܡܫܠܡܐ ܗܘܬ ܗܝ ܕܝܬܩܐ *for the testament had not been completed* (Aphr. 28:8).

ܐܝܟܐ ܕܣܦܪܐ ܘܩܫܝܫܐ ܟܢܝܫܝܢ ܗܘܘ *when the scribes and elders were assembled* (Matt. 26:57).

ܡܫܕܪܐ ܗܘܐ ܠܗ *It had been sent to him* (Jos. Sty. 17:16).

3. (1) The Perfect ܗܘܐ is used to render more emphatic the past sense of the Perfect. It may express

a. The past.
b. The pluperfect.
(2) The perfect of ܗܘܐ is used after the imperfect to emphasize a past subjunctive.
(3) The perfect of ܗܘܐ is used after an active participle to express,—
a. A state, or continuous action in the past.
b. A state, or action as having occurred frequently in the past.
Rem.—For the subjunctive of (*a*) and (*b*), see 4 (2).
(4) The perfect of ܗܘܐ is used after a passive participle to denote the result of a past completed action. This is true of the participles of the reflexive forms, when they are used as the passive.

4. (1) ܗܘܐ ܦܩܝܕ ܗܘܐ ܠܟܘܢ ܒܗܢܐ ܥܠܡܐ *so be it reckoned by you in this world* (Addai 44 ult.).

ܠܐ ܗܘܐ ܡܐܢ ܠܢ *let it not be wearisome to us* (Gal. 6:9).

ܗܘܝܬܘܢ ܥܗܕܝܢ ܠܡܕܒܪܢܝܟܘܢ *remember your guides* (Heb. 13:7).

ܗܘܝ ܚܠܝܡܐ ܡܢ ܡܚܘܬܟܝ *be whole from thy plague* (Matt. 3:4).

(2) ܕܢܗܘܘܢ ܡܬܬܣܝܡܝܢ ܒܗ *that they might be put in it* (Jos. Sty. 23:14).

ܨܒܝܢ ܗܘܘ ܕܢܗܘܘܢ ܫܩܠܝܢ ܠܗ *they were willing to keep carrying it* (Aphr. 264:6).

ܥܝܕܗ ܗܘܐ ܕܢܩܒܠ ܐܟܣܢܝܐ *it was his custom to receive strangers* (Aphr. 391:8).

5. *a.* ܘܦܣܩܘ ܘܐܫܪܘ ܕܢܗܘܘܢ ܢܛܪܝܢ ܠܗ ܠܗܢܐ ܥܐܕܐ ܟܠ ܫܢܐ *and they determined that they would be keeping this festival every year* (Jos. Sty. 26:17).

ܠܐ ܢܗܘܘܢ ܥܐܠܝܢ ܠܕܝܪܬܗܘܢ *(they) shall not be entering into their cloisters* (Overbeck 212:5).

ܦܩܕ ܓܝܪ ܥܠ ܝܗܘܕܝܐ ܕܠܐ ܢܗܘܘܢ ܓܙܪܝܢ *for he commanded concerning the Jews that they should not keep circumcision* (Aphr. 95:14).

b. ܢܗܘܐ ܦܪܫ *let it be separating* (Gen. 1:6).

ܘܐܠܐ ܢܗܘܐ ܗܘܐ ܩܪܒܐ ܡܬܡܬܚ ܒܝܢܬܗܘܢ *and, if not, war should be continuing between them* (Jos. Sty. 77:12).

ܕܐܢܫ ܢܗܘܐ ܛܥܐ ܥܡ ܣܓܝܐܐ *that a man be erring with the many* (Spic. Syr. 22:13).

Rem.—ܘܢܬܢܛܪ ܠܗܘܢ ܥܕܡܐ ܠܐܪܒܥܣܪܐ ܒܗ ܒܝܪܚܐ *and it should be kept by them until the* 14th *of the same month* (Aphr. 217:7).

6. ܟܠܢܫ ܢܗܘܐ ܩܪܐ ܕܟܬܝܒܬܐ ܕܣܦܪܗ ܒܗܘ ܝܘܡܐ *every one will be reading the writings of his book in that day* (Ad. 23:10).

7. (1) ܟܕ ܚܙܬܗ ܗܘܬ ܩܒܠܬܗ ܗܘܬ *when she saw him she received him* (Addai 11:8).

ܫܒܩܗ ܗܘܐ *he left him* (Jos. Sty. 76:11).

(2) ܘܣܡܝܟܝܢ ܗܘܘ ܘܡܬܒܣܡܝܢ ܟܠܗܘܢ *they all were reclining and enjoying themselves* (Jos. Sty. 26:18).

ܝܬܒ ܗܘܝܬ ܘܡܠܦ *I was sitting and teaching* (Matt. 26:55).

ܘܡܨܠܐ ܗܘܐ ܘܐܡܪ *and he was praying and saying* (Matt. 26:39).

ܡܣܟܝܢ ܗܘܝܢ ܘܡܣܒܪܝܢ *we were expecting and hoping* (Jos. Sty. 41:15).

Rem.—ܕܠܐ ܢܗܘܘܢ ܢܟܝܢ ܠܓܡܪ ܘܠܐ ܡܬܢܟܝܢ ܠܓܡܪ *that they should not be altogether injurious nor altogether injured* (Spic. Syr. 21.4).

8. ܡܪܕܘܬܢ ܣܓܝܐܬܐ ܗܘܬ *our chastisement was abundant* (Jos. Sty. 4:14).

ܘܠܐ ܗܘܐ ܣܪܝܩܐ ܗܘܬ ܡܐܬܝܬܗ *and his coming was not in vain* (Aphr. 150:15).

ܗܘܘ ܒܝܫܐܝܬ ܠܚܪܬܐ *they were evil to the end* (Aphr. 293:5).

9. ܘܠܐ ܢܗܘܐ ܠܗܘܢ ܣܢܝܩܘ *and they should have no need* (Rev. 22:5).

ܐܝܬ ܗܘܐ ܠܗܘܢ *they had a prisoner* (Matt. 27:16).

ܗܘܐ ܠܗ ܡܢܗ ܒܪܬܐ *he had by her a daughter* (Jos. Sty. 19:7).

4. (1) The perfect of ܗܘܐ is used before adjectives and participles to express a wish, a command, or an admonition § 112. 3. (2), Rem. 2.

(2) When the frequentative expressed by means of ܗܘܐ with the

§ 128.]   ELEMENTS OF SYRIAC.   175

participle (see 3. (3) *b*.) is put in the subjunctive, ܗܘܐ precedes instead of following the participle.

5. When a frequentative action or a state is looked upon as future, or contingent, it is expressed by means of the imperfect of ܗܘܐ and a following participle.

6. The futurity of a state, or continuous action, may be emphasized by placing the participle of ܗܘܐ before the participle of another verb.

7. (1) The pronominal suffix is placed after the principal verb.

(2) Where two, or more, participles occur, ܗܘܐ is usually formed with the first only.

Rem.—For special emphasis, especially in contrasted statements, it may be repeated.

8. An adverb may be used with ܗܘܐ.

9. ܗܘܐ accompanied by ܠ expresses our verb *"to have"*.

§ 128. Uses of ܐܝܬ.

1. (1) ܐܝܬ ܕܡ ܥܠ ܐܘܪܚܐ ܢܦܠ *there were some that fell on the wayside* (Matt. 13:4).

ܥܡܠܐ ܕܐܢܫܐ ܠܝܬ ܐܢܘܢ *in the trouble of men are they not* (Ps. 73:5).

ܟܡܐ ܠܚܡܝܢ ܐܝܬ ܠܟܘܢ *how many loaves have ye?* (Matt. 15:34).

ܠܝܬ ܐܢܫ *there is not a man* (Jos. Sty. 77:19).

ܐܝܬ ܕܝܢ ܐܚܪܢܐ ܕܐܡܪܝܢ *there are others who say* (Spic. Syr. 9:7).

(2) ܐܝܬܘܗܝ ܓܠܝܠܝܐ ܒܛܘܗܡܗ *who was a Galilean by race* (Jos. Sty. 69:6).

ܐܘ ܚܠܩܐ ܡܕܡ ܠܐ ܐܝܬܘܗܝ *or fortune itself does not exist* (Spic. Syr. 9:9).

ܩܕܡ ܕܠܐ ܐܝܬܘܗܝ ܐܕܡ *when Adam did not exist* (Spic. Syr. 4:15).

2. (1) ܕܠܝܬ ܗܘܐ ܥܡܗܘܢ *who was not with them* (Jos. Sty. 76:10).

ܐܝܬܝܗܘܢ ܗܘܘ ܓܝܪ ܨܝܕܐ *for they were fishers* (Acts. 22:3).

(2) ܕܐܝܬܘܗܝ ܗܘܐ ܣܡܝܐ *who had been blind* (John. 9:24).

Rem.—ܘܠܐܝܠܝܢ ܕܐܝܬ ܗܘܐ ܥܡܗܘܢ ܩܛܠ *and them who were with them he killed* (Jos. Sty. 76:15).

ܐܺܝܬ݂ ܗܘܰܝ̈ ܬܰܡܳܢ ܢܶܫ̈ܶܐ *and now there were there women* (Matt. 27:55. See also the examples under (1) and (2)).

3. (1) ܐܺܝܬ݂ ܠܰܢ ܐܰܒ݂ܪܳܗܳܡ *we have Abraham* (Matt. 3:9).

ܐܺܝܬ݂ ܠܗܽܘܢ ܠܐܘܪ̈ܗܳܝܶܐ ܣܺܝܡܬܳܐ *the Edessians have care* (Jos. Sty. 38:15).

ܕ݁ܠܰܝܬ݁ ܗ̱ܘܳܐ ܠܶܗ ܒ݁ܢܰܝ̈ܳܐ *because he had no sons* (Matt. 22:25).

Rem.— ܡܶܣ̈ܟ݁ܺܢܶܐ ܐܺܝܬ݂ ܠܟ݂ܽܘܢ *ye have the poor* (John. 12:8).

(2) ܕ݁ܰܚܛܳܗ̈ܶܐ ܚܕܳܢܳܝܐܺܝܬ݂ ܐܺܝܬ݂ ܒ݁ܶܗ *that he had all possible vices* (Sind. 3:21).

ܘܺܐܝܬ݂ ܠܳܟ݂ ܫܽܘܠܛܳܢܳܐ *and thou hast power* (Jos. Sty. 76:19).

ܐܺܝܬ݂ ܠܰܢ *we have* (Kirsch Chrest. p. 80 ult.).

4. ܐܶܢ ܫܰܪܺܝܪܳܐ ܐܺܝܬܰܘܗ̱ܝ ܦܶܬ݂ܓ݂ܳܡܳܐ *if the word be true* (Deut. 13:14).

ܐܶܢ ܐ̱ܢܳܫ ܢܶܫܒ݁ܽܘܩ ܡܶܕ݁ܶܡ ܕ݁ܫܰܪܺܝܪܳܐܺܝܬ݂ ܐܺܝܬ݂ܰܘܗ̱ܝ *if one should leave something that really exists* (Spic. Syr. 22:15).

5. ܠܐ ܗܳܘܝܳܐ ܠܡܶܬ݂ܐܡܳܪܽܘ *but this cannot be said* (Jos. Sty. 5:20).

ܘܠܰܝܬ݁ ܗ̱ܘܳܐ ܠܡܶܫܬ݁ܡܰܥ *nothing could be heard* (Jos. Sty. 39:14).

ܠܰܝܬ݁ ܠܡܶܬ݂ܐܡܳܪܽܘ *It cannot be said* (Aphr. 496:3).

1. ܐܺܝܬ݂ is employed impersonally in the sense of *"there is"*, *"there exists"*; ܠܰܝܬ݁ in the sense of *"there is not"*, *"there exists not"*. They are used (Compare § 130. 1. (3)):—

(1) Uninflectedly.

(2) With pronominal suffixes. § 65.

2. ܐܺܝܬ݂ or ܠܰܝܬ݁ followed by ܗܘܳܐ is used to express, or emphasize, the past or pluperfect of *"to be"*, *"to exist"*.

Rem.—When ܗܘܳܐ is used with ܐܺܝܬ݂, either one or both may be either inflected or uninflected. See all the examples under 2. (1), (2) and Rem.

3. (1) The verb *"to have"* is generally expressed by means of ܐܺܝܬ݂ followed by the preposition ܠ and a pronominal suffix. But see also § 127. 9.

(2) ܐܺܝܬ݂ followed by ܒ or ܠܘܳܬ݂ with a pronominal suffix may also express our verb *"to have"*.

4. ܐܺܝܬ݂ is occasionally followed by an adverb. Compare § 127:8.

5. ܐܺܝܬ݂ followed by ܠ with an infinitive may be translated by *"can"*.

§ 129. ܥܬܝܕ and Other Auxiliaries.

1. ܕܝܢܐ ܕܥܠܡܐ ܕܥܬܝܕ *the judgment of the world which is to come* (Jos. Sty. 6:4).

ܗܟܢܐ ܥܬܝܕܐ ܕܬܬܒܥ ܟܐܢܘܬܗ ܡܢ ܟܦܘܪܐ ܠܬܡܢ *so shall her righteousness be avenged on the unbeliever there* (Addai 24:12).

ܐܠܝܐ ܕܥܬܝܕ ܠܡܐܬܐ *Elias who was to come* (Matt. 11:14).

2. (1) *a*. ܘܠܐ ܕܢܣܓܕܘܢ *must they worship* (John. 4:24).

ܘܠܐ ܗܘ ܕܝܢ ܕܢܗܘܐ ܩܫܝܫܐ *for the elder must be* (1 Tim. 3:2).

ܐܢ ܗܘ ܕܝܢ ܥܡܟ ܠܡܡܬ *though I should have to die* (Matt. 26:35).

b. ܠܐ ܚܝܒ ܕܢܟܣܐ ܪܫܗ *ought not to cover his head* (1 Cor. 11:7).

(2) *a*. ܡܫܟܚ ܐܠܗܐ ܠܡܩܡܘ *God can raise up* (Matt. 3:7).

ܠܐ ܐܢܫ ܡܫܟܚ ܢܥܒܪ *no one could pass* (Matt. 8:28, see also Mt. 26:9).

b. ܗܕܐ ܠܐ ܡܨܝܐ ܐܢܐ ܕܐܥܒܕ *this I cannot do* (Jos. Sty. 5:16).

c. ܠܐ ܐܢܫ ܡܕܡ ܟܒܫܗ *no man could quell* (Spic. Syr. 44:16).

(3) ܠܐ ܨܒܐ ܠܡܩܒܠ ܐܢܘܢ *he would not receive them* (Jos. Sty. 17:13).

Rem. 1.—ܛܝܒܘ ܕܝܢ ܠܐܠܗܐ *thanks be to God* (1 Cor. 15:57).

2.—ܐܒܘܢ ܕܝܠܢ ܐܒܪܗܡ ܗܘ *our own father is Abraham* (John. 8:39).

ܢܛܘܪܗ ܐܢܐ ܓܝܪ ܕܐܚܝ *for am I my brother's keeper?* (Gen. 4:9).

(3) ܚܙܐ ...... ܥܡܐ ...... ܕܠܝܬ ܠܗ ܡܢܝܢ *he saw people who were numberless* (Sim. Sty. 271).

ܚܘܝܘ .... ܕܬܠܡܝܕܐ ܐܢܘܢ ܕܡܫܝܚܐ *they showed that they were disciples of Christ* (Overbeck 177:3).

1. The futurity of an action or state is emphasized by the use of ܥܬܝܕ *futurus* ($=\mu\acute{\epsilon}\lambda\lambda\omega\nu$).

2. In regard to mood

(1) The Imperative is strengthened by the use of ܩ̇ܕܶܐ "*it is necessary*", ܣܢܝܩ "*it is due*" and ܗܘܐ ܠܗ "*one has to*".

(2) The Potential is strengthened by the use of ܡܨܶܐ "*is able*", ܡܛܝ "*is possible*" and ܡܕܶܩ "*is sufficient*".

(3) The Voluntativ is strengthened by means of ܨܒܳܐ "*to will*", "*to wish*".

Rem.—The Optative (1), Indicative (2) and Subjunctive (3) moods are all found in simple nominal sentences.

§ 130. Verbal and Nominal Sentences.

1. (1) ܐܢܐ ܥܒܕܟ *I am thy servant* (Overbeck 383:2).

ܕܫܦܝܪ *that it was good* (Gen. 1:3).

ܘܕܗܒܗ ܕܐܪܥܐ ܗܘ ܛܒ *the gold of that land is good* (Gen. 2:12).

ܩܠܝܠ ܗܘ ܚܘܒܐ *love is light* (Aphr. 257:22).

Rem.—ܢܒܘܬ ܥܡܪܐ ܐܢ ܩܪܝܒ *let him lodge in the cloister if it be near* (Overbeck 212:9).

(2) ܐܢ ܗܘ ܕܐܝܬ ܠܟ *if it be that thou hast* (Spic. Syr. 2:3).

ܪܒ ܗܘ ܚܛܗܗ *his sin is great* (Aphr. 45:10).

(3) ܟܠ ܡܐ ܕܐܝܬ ܠܥܠ ܡܢܝ *all that is above me* (Spic. Syr. 3:21).

ܘܣܘܟܬܐ ܐܢܬ ܕܡܚܘܬܐ *and thou art a branch of the plague* (Aphr. 82:4).

ܕܐܝܬ ܒܗ ܐܝܕܥܬܐ *in which is knowledge* (Spic. Syr. 8:11).

Rem.—ܡܢܘ ܐܝܬ ܒܟܘܢ *whom have you i. e. who is existing among you?* (Mal. 1:10).

2. ܠܐ ܓܝܪ ܦܩܝܕܝܢ ܐܢܘܢ ܒܢܝ ܐܢܫܐ *for the sons of man are not commanded* (Spic. Syr. 5:2).

ܫܠܚ ܗܘܐ ܠܗ *he sent to him* (Addai 37:11).

ܥܢܐ ܩܕܝܫܐ *the saint answered* (Apec. Acts. 25:4).

ܥܪܩ ܡܢ ܩܕܡܝܗܘܢ *he fled from them* (Jos. Sty. 70:9).

Simple sentences, and the parts of compound and complex sentences, may be either nominal 1. or verbal 2.

1. A nominal sentence is one in which there is no verb, but in which the predicate is a noun substantive or adjective or a pronoun. In nominal sentences, the subject and predicate may be

(1) Simply placed in juxtaposition.

Rem.—The subject, as well as copula, is sometimes omitted.

(2) Connected by the pronoun used as a copula, see § 101. 2.

(3) Connected by ܐܺܝܬ, in which case the idea of existence is emphasized. See § 128. 1.

Rem.—Occasionally both ܗܘ and ܐܺܝܬ are used.

§ 131. Simple Sentences.

1. ܚܙܳܐ ܗܘܳܐ ܡܰܠܟܳܐ *the king saw* (L'omelia di Giacomo 157).

   ܗܘ ܕܺܐܝܬ ܐܺܝܠܳܢܳܐ *that there is the tree* (Overbeck 348:20).

   ܢܣܰܒܘ ܡܶܠܟܳܐ *they took counsel* (Matt. 27:1).

   ܛܺܝܡܰܝ ܕܰܕܡܳܐ ܗܘ *it is the price of blood* (Matt. 27:6).

2. (1) ܘܠܳܐ ܥܢܳܝܗܝ ܟܰܕ ܚܕܳܐ ܡܶܠܳܐ *he answered him not a word* (Matt. 27:14).

   ܐܶܫܟܰܚ ܠܳܐ ܗܘܳܐ *he could not* (Add. 3:8).

   ܠܳܐ ܨܒܺܝܬ ܓܶܝܪ ܗܘܺܝܬ *for I did not wish* (Jos. Sty. 34:17).

   ܘܐܰܢܬܬܳܐ ܠܳܐ ܪܓܺܝܫܳܐ *the woman did not perceive* (Sindb. 16:8).

   Rem.—ܠܳܐ ܣܳܦܶܩ ܠܰܢ ܬܶܕܡܘܪܬܳܐ *the miracle is not sufficient for us* (Jos. Sty. 23:6).

   ܠܳܐ ܗܳܟܺܝܠ ܢܶܣܬܰܪܗܰܒ ܒܢܰܝ *let us not hasten then my sons* (Jul. 28:23).

   ܠܳܐ ܓܶܝܪ ܗܳܘܶܐ ܗܘܳܐ ܐܰܒܳܐ *for a man does not become a father* (Spic. Syr. 11:3).

(2) ܠܳܐ ܗܘܳܐ ܡܶܢ ܟܝܳܢܶܗ ܡܰܣܟܶܠ ܒܰܪܢܳܫܳܐ *it is not from his nature a man doeth wrong* (Spic. Syr. 12:21).

   ܐܰܝܠܶܝܢ ܕܠܳܐ ܡܶܢ ܕܡܳܐ ܐܶܬܺܝܠܶܕܘ *those who were not born of the blood* (John. 1:13).

180   ELEMENTS OF SYRIAC.   [§ 131.

(3) ܠܐ *it has not pleased him to be seen by any one* (Spic. Syr. 6:19).

ܠܐ *not as I will* (Matt. 26:39).

ܠܐ *not carnivorous* (Spic. Syr. 7:21).

(4) ܠܐ ... ܘܠܐ *and the body is neither restrained nor assisted* (Spic. Syr. 11:2).

ܕܠܐ ... ܘܠܐ ... ܘܠܐ *that neither death nor life nor angels* (Rom. 8:38).

Rem.—ܠܐ ... ܘܠܐ ... ܘܠܐ *For neither sun nor moon nor one of the stars* (Spic. Syr. 3:17).

ܠܐ ... ܘܠܐ *neither Joseph nor another* (Legends of St. Mary 25:7).

ܠܐ ... ܘܠܐ *nor height nor depth* (Rom. 8:38. 24).

I am not envious against thee and I do (not) excuse myself (Jos. Sty. 3:15).

(5) ܠܐ *not a little* (=*much*) (Matt. 28:12).

ܕܠܐ *without care* (Matt. 28:14).

ܠܐ *incorruptibility* (Rom. 2:7).

(6) ܠܐ *it is not good* (Gen. 2:18).

and in some things they are not powerful (Spic. Syr. 9:23).

Simple sentences are declarative, negative, optative, and interrogative. For optative sentences, see § 114. 3. For interrogative sentences, see § 132.

1. The declarative sentence may be either nominal or verbal.

2. (1) The negative ܠܐ precedes the verb to which it relates.

Rem.—A particle may intervene between ܠܐ and the verb.

(2) Generally, when the negative is separated from the verb which it modifies, it is reïnforced by the copula ܗܘ (which contracts into ܠܘ) or by ܗܘܐ.

[§ 132.] ELEMENTS OF SYRIAC. 181

(3) When the negative relates to a phrase, or to a part of speech other than a verb, it immediately precedes it.

(4) When the negative is repeated and has the sense of *"neither"*, *"nor"*, it comes at the beginning of the sentence.

Rem.—The negative must be repeated before each noun; but it may be omitted from before each verb after the first.

(5) ܠܐ݁ is used before substantives and adjectives in a privative sense. (*"un"*, *"in"*, *"a"*, *"without"* &c.)

(6) ܠܐ may be used, also, when the predicate is an adjective.

§ 132. The Interrogative Sentence.

1. ܡܰܢܽܘ ܚܰܘܝܳܟ *who showed thee?* (Gen. 3:11).

ܡܳܢܳܐ ܗܳܢܳܐ ܕܰܥܒܰܕܬ݁ *what is this that thou hast done?* (Gen. 3:13).

ܠܡܳܢܳܐ ܐܶܬܒ݁ܐܶܫ ܠܳܟ݂ *why art thou displeased?* (Gen. 4:6).

ܡܳܢܳܐ ܡܰܠܐܶܝܢ ܐܢܬ݁ܽܘܢ ܠܳܗ݀ ܠܐܰܢܬ݁ܬ݂ܳܐ *why trouble ye the woman?* (Matt. 26:10).

ܐܰܝܟ݁ܳܐ ܨܳܒܶܐ ܐܰܢܬ݁ *where wilt thou?* (Matt. 26:17).

ܐܰܝܟ݁ܰܢܳܐ ܗܳܟ݂ܺܝܠ ܢܶܬ݂ܡܰܠܽܘܢ ܟܬ݂ܳܒܶܐ *how then should the scriptures be fulfilled?* (Matt. 26:54).

ܡܳܐ ܠܰܢ ܠܳܟ݂ *what is that to us?* (Matt. 27:4).

ܘܡܶܢ ܐܰܝܢܳܐ ܐܰܢܬ݁ ܥܰܡܳܐ *from what people art thou?* (Jon. 1:8).

ܡܳܢܳܐ ܥܒܳܕܳܟ݂ ܘܡܶܢ ܐܰܝܡܶܟ݁ܳܐ ܐܳܬ݂ܶܐ ܐܰܢܬ݁ ܘܐܰܝܕ݂ܳܐ ܗܺܝ ܐܰܪܥܳܟ݂ ܘܡܶܢ ܐܰܝܢܳܐ ܥܰܡܳܐ ܐܰܢܬ݁ *what is thy business, whence art thou, what is thy country and of what people?* (Jon. 1:8).

2. ܠܳܐ ܫܳܡܰܥ ܐܰܢܬ݁ *thou hearest not?* (Matt. 27:13).

ܥܰܦܪܳܐ ܐܰܝܬܺܝܬ ܠܰܢ *hast thou brought dust to us?* (Sind. 10:13).

ܡܶܢܝ ܠܳܟ݂ ܣܶܦܪܶܐ *have you read the books* (Spic. Syr. 13:8).

ܡܶܢ ܗܳܕ݂ܶܐ ܐܶܬ݁ܛܦܺܝܣܬ *from this art thou persuaded?* (Spic. Syr. 12 ult.).

ܦܳܩܶܕ݂ ܐܰܢܬ݁ ܕ݁ܢܶܬ݂ܩܰܛܰܠ *art thou going to command that he shall be killed* (Sindb. 6:9).

ܠܳܐ ܝܳܕ݂ܥܺܝܢ ܐܢܬ݁ܽܘܢ ܕ݁ܡܰܥܡܽܘܕ݂ܺܝܬ݂ܳܐ ܚܰܝܠܳܐ ܣܳܥܪܳܐ *Do you not know that baptism works miracles?* (L'omelia di Giacomo 729).

‎ܐܢܬ ܗܘ ܡܠܟܐ ܕܝܗܘܕܝܐ *art thou the king of the Jews?* (Matt. 27:11).

‎ܗܐ ܡܢ ܐܝܠܢܐ ܐܟܠܬ *behold from the tree hast thou then eaten?* (Gen. 3:11).

3. (1) ‎ܠܐ ܠܢܡܘܣܐ ܫܡܥܝܢ ܐܢܬܘܢ *are ye not obeying the law?* (Gal. 4:21).

‎ܠܐ ܥܗܕܝܢ ܐܢܬܘܢ ܠܚܡܫܐ ܠܚܡܝܢ *do you not remember the five loaves?* (Matt. 16:9).

(2) ‎ܠܐ ܗܘܐ ܢܦܫܐ ܝܬܝܪܐ ܡܢ ܣܝܒܪܬܐ *is not the life more than the meat?* (Matt. 6:25).

‎ܘܐܦ ܠܐ ܐܢܬ ܡܠܟܐ *also art thou not king?* (Sindb. 3:9).

(3) ‎ܠܐ ܡܦܢܐ ܐܢܬ ܦܬܓܡܐ *answerest thou not a word?* (Mk. 14:60).

‎ܠܐ ܗܘܝܬ ܐܢܬ ܗܘ ܡܨܪܝܐ *art thou not that Egyptian?* (Acts. 21:38).

4. (1) ‎ܠܡܐ ܐܢܫ ܐܝܬܝ ܠܗ ܡܕܡ *has a man brought him something?* (John. 4:33).

‎ܠܡܐ ܩܛܠ ܗܘ ܢܦܫܗ ܡܢܗ *will he then kill himself?* (John. 8:22).

(2) ‎ܠܡܐ ܐܢܐ ܡܪܝ *is it I Lord?* (Matt. 26:22).

‎ܕܠܡܐ ܢܟܒܫ ܐܢܫ ܠܐܠܗܐ *will a man rob God?* (Matt. 3:8).

5. ‎ܕܠܡܐ ܠܐ ܗܘܐ ܥܣܘ ܐܚܘܗܝ ܕܝܥܩܘܒ *was not Esau the brother of Jacob?* (Mal. 1:2).

‎ܕܠܡܐ ܠܐ ܒܝܫ *is it not evil?* (Mal. 1:8).

‎ܕܠܡܐ ܠܐ ܗܘܐ ܚܕ ܐܒܐ ܕܟܠܢ *have we not all one father?* (Mal. 2:10).

Rem.—‎ܐܢ ܐܝܬ ܥܡܟ ܚܝܠܐ ܕܬܕܟܢܝ ܐܘ ܕܠܡܐ ܠܐ *have you power to purify me or not?* (L'omelia de Giacomo 211. See also Mt. 22:17).

6. (1) ‎ܐܢ ܐܢܬ ܗܘ ܡܫܝܚܐ *if thou be the Messiah?* (Matt. 26:63).

‎ܐܢ ܐܩܝܡܬ ܟܠ ܡܢܡ ܕܫܡܠܢ ܚܕ ܥܡ ܚܕ ܐܘ ܠܐ *if thou hast kept the agreement which we made with one another or not?* (Sindb. 13:18).

(2) ‎ܟܡܐ ܡܦܘܩܬܐ ܘܢܦܩܬܐ ܐܝܬ ܠܡܠܟܐ *how great expenses and outlays kings have?* (Jos. Sty. 15:16).

ܐܰܝܟܳܐ ܡܶܬܺܝܠܶܕ ܡܫܺܝܚܳܐ؟ *where Christ should be born?* (Matt. 2:4).

Rem.—ܢܓܰܠܽܘܢ ܠܰܢ ܡܳܢܰܘ ܪܶܥܝܳܢܗܽܘܢ *let them reveal to us what their mind is* (Add. 21:4). ܢܶܚܙܶܐ ܠܡܰܢ ܬܶܗܘܶܐ *let us see to whom she shall belong* (Legends of St. Mary 14:4).

7. ܐܰܢܬ ܗܽܘ ܒܰܠܚܽܘܕܰܝܟ ܢܽܘܟܪܳܝܳܐ *art thou then only a stranger?* (Luke 24:18).

ܠܡܳܐ ܢܶܫܟܰܚ ܗܰܝܡܳܢܽܘܬܳܐ *shall he then find faith* (Lk. 18:8).

1. Interrogative sentences are often denoted by interrogative pronouns or adverbs.
2. Generally, the interrogative is denoted by the inflection or connection without any particle.
3. The negative ܠܐ may be used in interrogative sentences, without showing whether the answer expected is dubious, positive, or negative; but always the answer *"yes"* is hoped for or at least desired.
4. The negative ܠܡܳܐ is used to express doubt in the questioner as to the answer.
    (1) When the answer *"yes"*, though half expected, is deemed scarcely possible.
    (2) When the answer *"surely, not"* is hoped for.
5. The double negative ܠܐ ܠܡܳܐ is used, when the answer *"surely, yes"* is hoped for, or expected.
    Rem.—In a double question, ܘܰܠܡܳܐ ܠܐ is often used elliptically for the alternative.
6. The indirect question is introduced by ܐܶܢ or ܕ.
    Rem.—The indirect question is sometimes introduced directly, without any connecting particle.
7. The particle ܟܰܝ is often used for the purpose of strengthening the interrogative.

§ 133. Compound Sentences: Conjunctive.

1. ܗܦܰܟ ܠܘܳܬ ܪܰܒܰܝ ܟܳܗܢܶܐ ܘܩܰܫܺܝܫܶܐ *he returned to the chief priests and elders* (Matt. 27:3).

ܡܶܛܽܠ ܒܰܣܺܝܡܽܘܬܶܗ ܘܛܰܝܒܽܘܬܶܗ ܘܢܰܓܺܝܪܽܘܬ ܪܽܘܚܶܗ ܕܰܐܠܳܗܳܐ *because of the kindness and grace and longsuffering of God* (Jos. Sty. 6:7).

Rem. 1.—ܐܰܪ̈ܥܳܬܳܐ ܪܰܘܪ̈ܒܳܬܳܐ ܘܣܽܘܚܳܦܳܐ ܕܰܡܕ̈ܝܳܢܳܬܳܐ *terrible earthquakes, overturnings of cities* (Jos. Sty. 4:21).

ܘܶܐܙܰܠ ܘܰܗܦܰܟ *and he went and returned* (Matt. 27:3).

Rem. 2.—ܐܽܘܠܨܳܢ̈ܐ ܕܩܰܡ̈ܨܐ ܘܕܟܰܦ̈ܢܐ ܘܕܡܰܘܬܳܢܐ *afflictions of locusts, and of famines, and of pestilence* (Jos. Sty. 40:16).

ܚܽܘܛܖ̈ܐ ܕܠܽܘܙܳܐ ܘܕܕܽܠܒܳܐ *rods of the hazel and of the poplar* (Gen. 30:37).

ܘܠܐ ܣܳܦܩܳܐ ܥܰܝܢܳܐ ܕܡܰܕ̈ܥܰܝ ܠܡܶܚܳܪ ܘܠܡܶܚܙܳܐ *but the eye of my understanding is unable to examine and to see* (Jos. Sty. 1:10).

ܠܐ ܐܶܬܡܨܺܝܘ ܠܡܶܥܰܠ ܘܠܡܰܗܳܪܽܘ *they were not able to enter and to harm* (Jos. Sty. 63:1).

ܫܰܕܰܪ ... ܕܢܰܝܬܶܐ ... ܘܢܶܫܐܰܠ *he sent ... to bring ... and to ask ...* (Jos. Sty. 78:8).

2. ܚܨܺܝܗ̇ ܘܫܕܺܝܗ̇ ܡܶܢܳܟ *pluck it out and cast it from thee* (Matt. 5:29).

ܒܰܙܘ ܘܰܚܪܶܒܘ ܘܰܫܒܰܘ ܘܰܐܘܩܶܕܘ ܟܽܠ ܕܶܐܫܟܰܚܘ *they plundered and destroyed and took captive and burned all which they found* (Jos. Sty. 63:12).

3. ܐܰܦܺܝܣܘܗܝ ܩܠܺܝܪ̈ܝܩܐ ܠܦܰܛܪܝܰܪܟܳܐ ܘܥܰܒܕܶܗ ܐܶܦܣܩܽܘܦܐ *The clergy persuaded the Patriarch and he made him their bishop* (Jos. Sty. 78:7).

ܨܳܪ ܘܚܳܙܶܐ *he foresaw* (Aphr. 12:3).

Rem.—ܕܢܺܐܙܰܠ ܢܶܩܘܶܐ ܒܰܐܪܥܳܐ *that he might go and stay in the land* (Jos. Sty. 57:15).

ܩܳܡ ܘܶܐܙܰܠ ܒܳܬܪܶܗ *and he arose and went after him* (Mk. 2:14).

Compound sentences, or phrases, may be conjunctive, alternative, or adversative. In conjunctive sentences, or phrases:

1. One word may govern two, or more, connected by ܘ.

Rem. 1.—The ܘ may be omitted.

Rem. 2.—The ܕ of the genitive and ܠ before the Infinitive cannot be omitted from before a second, or third word in the same government as the first.

2. Several verbs connected by ܘ may govern a common object.

3. Of two verbs connected by ܘ and in the same tense, one may be in dependence upon the other, often as an adverb or complement.

Rem.—In such cases the ܘ may be omitted.

§ 134. Alternative and Adversative Sentences.

1. ܢܨܡܐ ܐܘ ܢܚܕܫܐ *the law or the prophets* (Matt. 5:17).

ܐܘ ܠܡܐܡܪ ܠܡܠܟܐ ܕܥܒܕ ܩܪܒܐ *or to say to the king: "Take war."* (J. S. 16:15).

Rem. 1.—ܐܠܐ ܐܘ ܚܡܬܐ ܕܒܟܐ ܥܠ ܡܝܬܐ ܐܘ ܝܠܠܬܐ ܕܐܠܝܠܝܢ *but either the weeping over the dead or the lamentable cries of those in pain* (Jos. Sty. 39:15).

Rem. 2.—ܐܘ ܣܒܪ ܐܢܬ *or thinkest thou?* (Matt. 26:53).

ܐܘ ܕܠܡܐ ܚܛܗܐ ܣܥܪܬ *or did I commit a sin* (2 Cor. 11:7).

2. ܐܘ ܠܓܪܒܝܐ ܐܘ ܠܬܝܡܢܐ *either to the north or to the south* (Spic. Syr. 19:15).

ܐܘ ܐܒܘܒܐ ܐܘ ܩܝܬܪܐ *either flute or cithara* (1 Corr. 14:7).

3. ܠܐ ܐܝܟ ܕܨܒܐ ܐܢܐ ܐܠܐ ܐܝܟ ܕܐܢܬ *not as I will but as thou* (Matt. 26:39).

ܠܐ ܕܐܫܪܐ ܐܠܐ ܕܐܡܠܐ *not to destroy but to fulfil* (Matt. 5:17).

ܕܠܐ ܢܡܨܘܢ ܠܡܥܒܕ ܥܘܠܐ ܐܠܐ ܕܥܒܕܝܢ ܢܗܘܘܢ ܟܠܫܥ *that they should not be able to do wrong but that always they should be doing what is good* (Spic. Syr. 1:9).

ܗܢܘܢ ܢܒܢܘܢ ܘܐܢܐ ܐܣܚܘܦ *they shall build but I will destroy* (Mal. 1:4).

1. Alternative sentences are usually connected by ܐܘ.

Rem. 1.—ܐܘ may stand at the head of each clause.

Rem. 2.—In the Peshito New Testament, ܐܘ translates ἤ "used in an interrogative sentence which refers to a preceding categorical sentence".

2. Alternative sentences are sometimes introduced with ܐܘ or ܐܝܢ.

3. Adversative sentences are generally introduced with ܐܠܐ; but occasionally by Waw.

§ 135. Complex Sentences.

These may be divided into substantive, adjective and adverbial sentences. Substantive sentences are those in which the sentence takes the place of a noun, as subject or object of a verb, or in apposition to a noun.

1. ܠܐ ܝܐܐ ܠܟ ܕܢܫܬܘܢ ܥܒܕܝܟ ܟܦܢܐ *for that thy slaves should die of hunger does not become thee* (Jos. Sty. 76:6).

   ܕܐܬܦܩܕ ܠܗ ܕܢܚܬ ܒܥܘܡܩܐ ܕܡܝܐ *to whom it has been commanded to go down in the depth of the waters* (Jos. Sty. 4:1).

   ܦܩܚ ܠܟ ܕܢܐܒܕ ܚܕ ܡܢ ܗܕܡܝܟ *it is better for thee that one of thy members perish* (Matt. 5:29).

   ܡܢ ܕܠܝܬ ܒܗ ܕܚܠܬܗ ܕܐܠܗܐ ܗܘ ܡܫܥܒܕ ܠܟܠܗܝܢ ܕܚܠܬܐ *for whosoever has not the fear of God in him is subject to all fears* (Spic. Syr. 2:26).

2. ܗܕܐ—ܕܬܕܥ *this is that thou mayest know* (Aphr. 213:15).

   ܥܠܬܐ—ܗܘܐ ܐܝܟ ܕܙܒܢܐ *the reason was its being (it was) the time of fruitage* (Jos. Sty. 48:18).

   ܐܚܪܢܐ ܗܝ ܕܐܢܫ ܢܟܬܘܒ ܒܠܝܒܘܬܐ *it is one thing for a man to write sadly* (Jos. Sty. 5:7).

3. (1) ܗܢܘܢ ܕܩܪܝܢ ܗܘܘ ܟܬܒܐ ܗܘ ܡܠܦ ܒܗܘܢ *those who should read the Scriptures, he taught in them* (Add. 40:13).

   ܟܕ ܚܙܐ ܕܐܬܚܝܒ ܝܫܘܥ *when he saw that Jesus had been condemned* (Matt. 27:3).

   (2) ܘܢܕܥܘܢ ܡܢܐ ܨܒܝܢܗ *and they may know what his desire is* (Spic. Syr. 1:19).

ܕܢܚܘܝܟ ܡܛܠ ܡܢܐ ܠܐ ܫܦܪ ܠܢ *to show thee why it does not please us* (Spic. Syr. 2:5).

ܐܦܠܐ ܕܝܕܥܬ ܡܫܘܚܬܝ ܐܝܟܢܐ *also thou knowest not what my measure is* (Jos. Sty. 3:7).

(3) ܐܡܪ ܓܝܪ ܕܒܪܗ ܐܢܐ ܐܠܗܐ *for he saith: "I am the son of God"* (Matt. 27:43).

ܐܡܪ ܠܗܘܢ ܕܠܐ *he said to them "Nay"* (Jos. Sty. 4:11).

(4) ܐܠܨܗ ܕܢܣܒ *he pressed him to take* (Overbeck 167:17).

ܒܡܕܡ ܕܫܡܥܢ *to that which we have heard* (Heb. 2:1).

ܢܚܙܐ ܠܡܢ ܡܛܝܐ ܬܗܘܐ *let us see to whom she shall belong* (Legends of St. Mary 14:4).

4. ܘܗܘܐ ܙܗܝܪ ܕܠܡܐ ܐܦ ܐܢܬܘܢ ܬܬܢܣܘܢ *and be mindful lest ye also be tempted* (Gal. 6:1).

ܣܦܩܢ ܐܠܝܢ ܡܪܕܘܬܐ ܕܢܪܕܝܢܢ ܠܢ *these chastisements are sufficient to rebuke us* (Jos. Sty. 5:16).

5. ܐܠܐ ܗܕܐ ܘܠܐ ܠܡܐܡܪ ܕܐܝܟ ܕܘܝܕ *but this it is necessary to say that like David etc.*

ܗܕܐ ܕܟܬܒܬ ܠܟ *this that I have written thee* (Aphr. 359:1).

ܘܒܥܐ ܗܘܝܬ ܗܕܐ ܠܡܐܠܦ ܡܢ ܐܝܠܝܢ ܥܠܠܬܐ ܐܬܚܪܝܗ *and thou art desiring to learn this, by what causes it was provoked* (Jos. Sty. 7:22).

ܘܚܙܐ ܐܠܗܐ ܥܒܕܝܗܘܢ ܕܗܦܟܘ ܡܢ ܐܘܪܚܬܗܘܢ *and God saw their works that they turned from their ways* (Jon. 3:10).

1. Subject substantive sentences are such as are the subject of a verbal, or nominal sentence. A dependent question may constitute such a sentence.

2. A predicate sentence is one which corresponds to the predicate noun in nominal sentences.

3. An object sentence is one which is the object of a verb or preposition.

(1) It may be a direct object of the verb.

(2) It may be a dependent question.
(3) It may be a quotation.
(4) It may be an indirect object of a verb, or the object of a preposition.

4. Object clauses are sometimes found after adjectives and after the participles of intransitive verbs.

5. Substantive clauses may be in apposition with a preceding word.

§ 136. Adjectival or Relative Sentences.

1. (1) ܫܸܡ̈ܥܹܐ ܐܵܦ ܕܡܸܢ ܪܘܼܚܩܵܐ ܘܕܩܘܼܪܒܵܐ *reports also from far and near have terrified us* (Jos. Sty. 4:20).

   ܟܠ ܐܝܠܵܢ ܕܪܓܝܓ ܠܚܸܙܬܵܐ *every tree which was pleasant to the sight* (Gen. 2:9).

   (2) ܘܣܘܼܓܐܵܐ ܕܐܘܼܠܨܵܢܹ̈ܐ ܣܲܓܝܹ̈ܐܐ ܕܗܘܘ *and calamities that befell in many places* (Jos. Sty. 4:21).

   ܐܵܕܵܡ ܕܓܒܲܠ *the man that he had formed* (Gen. 2:8).

   ܒܝܘܡܵܐ ܕܬܐܟܘܼܠ ܡܸܢܹܗ *in the day wherein thou eatest of it* (Gen. 2:17).

2. ܡܕܝܼܢܬܵܐ ܕܦܬܘܿܠܡܐܘܿܣ ܕܗܝ ܥܟܘ *the city of Ptolmæus, that is Akka* (J. S. 44:8).

   ܐܢܫ ܕܠܐ ܩܲܒܹܠ ܡܸܢܗܘܿܢ ܢܸܟܝܵܢܵܐ *a man who did not suffer some harm from them* (Jos. Sty. 81:4).

3. ܘܠܡܲܢ ܕܫܲܕܪܹܗ *and him who had sent him* (Jos. Sty. 91:11).

   ܕܘܼܟܬܵܐ ܕܣܝܼܡ ܗܘܵܐ ܒܵܗ ܡܵܪܲܢ *the place in which the Lord was placed* (Matt. 28:6).

   ܡܫܲܡܠܝܵܢܹܗ ܕܢܡܘܿܣܵܐ *fulfilling the law* (Jos. Sty. 2:2).

   ܠܐ ܣܓܕܘ ܠܨܲܠܡܵܐ ܕܲܥܒܲܕ *they worshipped not the image which he had made.*

Rem.—ܥܠ ܦܝܠܘܿܣܘܿܦܲܝܟ ܕܡܲܠܟܝܼܢ ܠܵܟ *over thy philosophers who are counselling thee* (Sindb. 17:18).

   ܥܲܠ ܗܵܘ ܕܐܸܡܲܪ *because of that which he said* (Jos. Sty. 42:5).

4. ܕܛܝܡܗ ܕܝܩܝܪܐ *the price of him who is precious* (Matt. 27:9).

ܥܝܢܟ ܕܝܡܝܢܐ *thy right eye* (Matt. 5:29).

5. ܓܘܬܝܐ ܕܫܡܗ ܐܝܠܘܕ *a Goth whose name was Illod* (Jos. Sty. 68:3).

ܕܡܠܝܢ ܐܝܕܝܗܘܢ *whose hands are full* (Addai 43:13).

6. ܥܕܢܐ ܕܥܐܕܐ ܗܘ ܕܚܢܦܘܬܐ ܬܫܥܝܬܐ ܡܬܙܡܪܢ ܒܗ *the time of that festival in which heathen tales were sung* (Jos. Sty. 24:16).

ܥܡܡܐ ܐܚܪܢܐ ܕܠܘܬܗܘܢ ܡܫܕܪ ܐܢܐ ܠܟ *the other peoples to whom I send thee* (Acts 26:17).

Rem. 1.—ܕܐܡܪܬܘܢ ܠܝ *of whom ye spake to me* (Gen. 43:27).

ܒܝܘܡܐ ܠܬܡܝܢܝܐ ܕܡܬܓܙܪܝܢ *on the eighth day when they were circumcised* (Spic. Syr. 19:17).

Rem. 2.—ܘܠܐܝܟܐ ܕܡܬܦܢܐ ܗܘܐ ܙܟܐ ܗܘܐ *whithersoever he turned he was victorious.*

ܠܟܠܡ ܕܡܬܐܬܝܢ *whithersoever they came* (Aphr. 339:9).

ܬܡܢ ܡܢ ܕܫܩܠ ܐܢܬ ܘܡܕܠܩ ܐܢܬ ܠܐ ܚܣܝܪܐ *It is not wanting there, when thou takest and kindlest.*

7. ܘܕܥܡܗ ܒܩܒܘܬܐ *and those who were with him in the ark* (Gen. 7:23).

ܘܕܢܨܠܐ ܕܫܦܝܪ *and to pray for that which is good* (Spic. Syr. 5:12).

ܠܢܚܬ *to him who descends* (Overbeck 385:6).

8. ܕܢܚܙܐ ܠܕܘܡܪܬܐ ܗܕܐ ܘܢܟܠܐ ܦܘܡܗ ܡܢ ܬܫܒܘܚܬܐ *who might see this miracle that could restrain his mouth from praise* (Jos. Sty. 66:18.)

ܓܘܬܝܐ ܕܫܡܗ ܐܝܠܘܕ ܘܡܩܝܡ ܗܘܐ ܛܪܝܒܘܢܐ *a Goth whose name was Illod and who had been made tribune* (Jos. Sty. 68:3).

Rem.—ܘܠܝܬ ܗܘܐ ܐܢܫ ܕܡܙܗܪ ܘܠܐ ܕܡܟܣ ܘܠܐ ܕܡܪܬܐ *and there was no one who warned nor who rebuked, nor who admonished* (Jos. Sty. 25:10).

9. ܬܨܒܥ ܐܢܘܢ *whom it immerses* (Overbeck 384:17).

ܠܐ ܓܝܪ ܫܬܐܣܬܐ ܕܗܝܡܢܘܬܐ ܐܝܬ ܠܗܘܢ ܢܒܢܘܢ ܥܠܝܗ *for they have not the foundation of the faith upon which to built* (Spic. Syr. 2:23).

10. ܘܠܐ ܗܘ ܓܝܪ ܕܬܠܬܝܗܘܢ ܨܒܘܬܐ ܕܢܗܘܘܢ ܢܛܝܪܝܢ *for it is necessary that three things [that of nature, and that of fortune, and that of purity] that they should be maintained.*

11. *a.* ܘܐܢܬܝ ܟܦܪܢܚܘܡ ܗܝ ܕܥܕܡܐ ܠܫܡܝܐ ܐܬܬܪܝܡܬܝ *and thou Capernaum which art exalted unto heaven* (Matt. 11:23).

ܐܘ ܐܠܗܐ ܐܢܬ ܕܢܚܬܬ ܡܢ ܫܡܝܐ ܘܥܒܕܬ ܗܠܝܢ *or thou art God who hast come down from heaven and hast done these things* (Addai 3 ult).

ܠܟܘܢ ܕܡܗܝܡܢܝܢ ܐܢܬܘܢ *you who believe* (Spic. Syr. 2:19).

ܐܦ ܐܢܐ ܕܚܙܝܢ ܐܢܬܘܢ ܠܝ *I also whom you see* (Addai Apost. 21:18).

b. ܘܐܝܠܝܢ ܕܨܒܝܢ ܕܢܫܬܡܥܘܢ ܠܡܫܝܚܐ ܢܕܥܝܢ ܐܢܬܘܢ *and ye who wish to be to the Messiah obedient know* (Addai the Ap. 30:7).

ܐܢܬܘܢ ܐܝܠܝܢ ܕܨܒܝܢ ܕܢܗܘܘܢ ܬܚܝܬ ܢܡܘܣܐ *ye who wish to be under the law* (Gal. 4:21).

Adjective sentences are introduced by the relative particle ܕ and may limit any noun.

1. Adjective sentences may be

(1) Nominal.

(2) Verbal.

2. It may limit the subject.

3. It may limit the object.

Rem. 1.—It may limit a noun or pronoun, which is the object of a preposition.

4. The relative ܕ when it follows a noun with a pronominal suffix may refer to either.

5. When the relative is in the genitive relation with the noun following it, the noun must take the pronominal suffix.

6. When the relative clause is to be governed by a preposition, the

relative appears at the head of the clause and the preposition with its appropriate pronominal suffix follows, either immediately or with intervening words.

Rem. 1.—The relative sometimes stands alone where we would expect the preposition and pronominal suffix to follow; especially is this the case where it may be construed as an adverbial accusative of place or time.

Rem. 2.—The preposition is sometimes placed before the antecedent to which the relative belongs.

7. The relative may stand without an antecedent, provided that it involves a demonstrative conception. It may then be regarded as a substantive clause, see § 135.

8. When several relative phrases are joined by the copula, ؟ is often found but once, even when the relative is used in different constructions.

Rem.—It may, however, be repeated.

9. The relative is sometimes omitted, especially in servile imitation of the Hebrew.

10. When the subordinate phrase has been separated from the Dolath to which it belongs, the relative is sometimes repeated pleonastically.

11. When the antecedent is a pronoun in the first or second person, two constructions are possible in the relative phrase.

(1) The verb, or pronoun, of the relative phrase is in the person of the antecedent.

(2) The verb of the relative phrase is in the third person, although the antecedent is of the first or second.

137. Adverbial Clauses and Sentences.

1. ܘܟܪ ܕܚܛܝܼܬܐ ܣܓܝܐܬ *and where sin abounded* (Rem. 5:20).

   ܩܡ ܠܥܠ ܡܢ ܐܬܪܐ ܕܐܝܬܘܗܝ ܛܠܝܐ *he stood over the place where the young child was* (Matt. 2:9).

2. (1) ܐܚܕܘ ܐܬܐ ܩܡܨܐ *when the locusts came* (Jos. Sty. 1:3).

   ܟܕ ܚܙܝܬ ܗܠܝܢ ܐܬܘܬܐ *when I saw the signs* (Jos. Sty. 3:17).

   ܡܢ ܒܬܪ ܕܩܐܡ ܐܢܐ *after that I am risen* (Matt. 26:32).

ܟܰܕ ܠܳܐ ܩܪܳܟ ܦܺܝܠܺܝܦܳܘܣ *before Philip called thee* (Jud. 1:48).

ܟܰܕ ܢܰܣܝܽܘܢܝ ܐܰܒܳܗܰܝܟܽܘܢ, *when your fathers tempted me* (Heb. 3:9).

ܗܳܐ ܝܰܘܡܳܬܳܐ ܐܳܬܶܝܢ ܐܳܡܰܪ ܡܳܪܝܳܐ ܘܢܺܐܩܰܕ *the days are coming when my wrath shall burn like a furnace* (Mal. 4:1).

(2) ܟܰܕ ܐܳܟܠܺܝܢ ܗܘܰܘ ܩܰܪܨܰܘ̈ܗܝ *while they were calumniating him* (Matt. 27:12).

ܟܰܕ ܥܳܐܶܠ ܐܢܳܐ *as I was entering* (Spic. Syr. 1:3).

ܟܰܕ ܡܢܰܣܶܝܢ ܠܗܽܘܢ *while they are proving them* (Jos. Sty. 5:13).

ܥܕܰܡܳܐ ܕܝܺܠܶܕܬܶܗ ܠܰܒܪܳܗ̇ ܒܽܘܟܪܳܐ *until she had borne her first born son* (Matt. 1:25).

ܟܰܕ ܐܶܙܰܠ ܐܶܨܰܠܶܐ *until I go and pray* (Matt. 26:36).

ܡܶܢ ܗܳܝܕܶܝܢ ܡܰܠܟܽܘܬܶܗ ܕܰܐܠܳܗܳܐ ܡܶܣܬܰܒܪܳܐ *since then the kingdom of God has been preached* (Lk. 16:16).

ܕܣܶܠܩܶܬ ܠܐܽܘܪܺܫܠܶܡ ܕܶܐܣܓܽܘܕ *since I went up to Jerusalem to worship* (Acts 24:11).

(3) ܟܽܠ ܐܶܡܰܬܝ ܕܰܒܣܽܘܛܡܶܐ ܘܫܺܫܠܳܬܳܐ ܡܶܬܐܣܰܪ ܗܘܳܐ *as often as with fetters and chains he was bound* (Mk. 5:4).

ܟܽܠ ܐܶܡܰܬܝ ܕܫܳܬܶܝܢ ܐܢܬܽܘܢ *as often as ye drink* (1 Cor. 11:25).

3. ܟܰܕ ܠܳܐ ܨܳܒܶܐ *unwillingly* (L'omelia di Giacomo 150).

ܐܰܝܟ ܕܘܳܠܶܐ *as is necessary* (Jos. Sty. 4:6).

ܐܰܝܟ ܕܶܐܡܪܶܬ *as I said* (Inedita Syr. 18:1).

ܐܰܝܟ ܕܺܐܝܬܰܝܗܽܘܢ *as they are* (Jos. Sty. 4:12).

ܐܰܝܟ ܕܢܰܘܒܕܽܘܢܳܝܗܝ *how they might put him to death* (Matt. 27:1).

ܥܕܰܡܳܐ ܕܡܶܢ ܚܽܘܡܶܗ ܕܫܽܘܦܪܶܟܝ ܐܳܦܠܳܐ ܒܪܶܟܝ *until that from the warmth of thy love thou dost not know* (Jos. Sty. 3:7).

ܐܰܝܟܰܢܳܐ ܕܳܐܡܪܺܝܢ ܐܢܬܽܘܢ *as ye say* (Spic. Syr. 1:6).

ܐܰܝܟܰܢܳܐ ܕܝܳܕܥܺܝܢ ܐܢܬܽܘܢ *as ye know* (Matt. 27:65).

4. (1) ܡܘܡܐ ܐܢܐ ܠܟ ... ܕܬܐܡܪ ܠܢ *I adjure that thou tell us* (Matt. 26:63).

ܘܝܕܥܢܐ ܕܗܕܐ ܐܡܪܬܗ ܕܬܗܘܐ ܬܘܝܐ *and I knew that this thou hast said in order that there may be contrition* (Jos. Sty. 5:7).

ܘܢܫܠܐ ܝܡܐ *that the sea may rest* (Jon. 1:11).

ܕܠܡܐ ܐܬܐ *lest I come* (Mal. 4:6).

(2) ܐܝܟܢܐ ܕܡܝܬܪܐܝܬ ܠܐ ܬܦܪܘܩ ܡܢ ܠܘܬܢ *in order that thou mayest not depart from us without profit* (Spic. Syr. 2:7).

ܐܝܟ ܡܢ ܕܢܗܝܪܐܝܬ ܬܗܘܐ ܡܣܟܠ ܐܢܬ *or that thou mayest know clearly* (Jos. Sty. 8:6).

Rem.—ܫܕܪܬ ܠܝ ܐܟܬܘܒ ܐܢܝܢ *thou hast sent me* [*that*] *I should write them* (Jos. Sty. 5:3).

ܟܠܗ ܓܝܪ ܕܡܬܪܕܝܢ ܒܢܝܢܫܐ ܒܥܠܡܐ ܗܢܐ ܡܛܠ ܕܢܬܟܠܘܢ ܡܢ ܚܛܗܝܗܘܢ *for the whole (purpose) of it, (to wit) that men are persecuted in this world (is) on account of (this) that they may be restrained from their sins* (Jos. Sty. 6:2).

ܥܕ ܐܙܠ ܐܨܠܐ *until I go to pray* (Matt. 26:36).

ܗܕܐ ܕܟܬܒܬ ܠܟ ܚܒܝܒܝ ܕܐܢܫ ܢܥܒܕܘܢ ܨܒܝܢܗ ܕܐܠܗܐ *this that I have written to thee, my beloved, (I have written) in order that men may do the will of God* (Aphr. 75:6).

Adverbial sentences are such as modify the verb as to place, time, manner, condition and so forth. The most common forms of adverbial sentences are as follows.

1. Local.

2. Temporal. These are:—

(1) Those answering to the question "*where*".

(2) Those answering to the question "*how long*".

(3) Those answering to the question "*how often*".

3. Modal or Comparative clauses are introduced with some combination with ܐܝܟ or ܟܡ or ܡܢ.

4. Final or consecutive. (Purpose or result).

These are (1) generally preceded by ܕ (=*ut*), but sometimes by ܘ.

(2) Sometimes after combinations of particles.

Rem.—Sometimes we meet with elliptical sentences from which ܕ or some other word has been omitted.

Rem. 2.—The Infinitive with Lomadh sometimes takes the place of the Imperfect with Dolath § 120. 1 (3).

5. (1) ܕܗܝܡܢ ܠܐܢܬܬܐ *because he believed the woman* (Sindb. 4:2).

ܕܐܫܠܡܬ ܕܡܐ ܙܟܝܐ *because I betrayed the innocent blood* (Matt. 27:4).

(2) ܘܒܗܝ ܣܡܬ ܕܘܝܘܬ ܚܘܫܒܝ ܘܕܚܠܬ *and in that I considered the weakness of my mind* (Jos. Sty. 3:20).

ܡܛܠ ܕܬܟܝܠ ܐܢܐ ܥܠ ܨܠܘܬܟ *because I trust upon thy prayers* (Jos. Sty. 4:2).

ܡܛܠ ܕܛܝܡܝ ܕܡܐ ܗܘ *because it is the prise of blood* (Matt. 27:6).

ܡܛܠ ܕܐܝܟ ܚܝܠܝ ܡܣܚܐ ܐܢܐ *since according to my strength I shall swim* (Jos. Sty. 4:4).

ܡܛܠ ܗܘܐ ܓܝܪ *for he was accustomed* (Spic. Syr. 1:3).

ܣܓܝ ܓܝܪ ܚܫܬ *for I have suffered much* (Matt. 27:19).

ܘܡܛܠ ܕܐܢܫܐ ܗܘܐ ܡܘܬܐ *and since through man was death* (1 Cor. 15:21).

ܥܠ ܕܡܩܪܒܝܢ ܐܢܬܘܢ *because ye are offering* (Mal. 1:7).

ܠܐ ܗܘܐ ܡܛܠ ܕܩܒܝܥܝܢ ܐܠܐ ܥܠ ܕܡܫܠܛܝܢ *not because they are fixed but because they have power* (Spic. Syr. 4:21).

ܥܠ ܕܠܐ ܗܘܐ ܗܘܐ ܫܘܝܐܝܬ ܡܬܕܒܪܝܢ ܐܢܫܐ *because men are not equally governed* (Spic. Syr. 12 ult.).

6. ܘܥܡ ܕܐܦ ܕܐܟܘܬܗ ܡܕܡ ܠܐ ܐܣܬܥܪ *and although nothing like this has been done by me to thee* (Jos. Sty. 3:3).

ܥܡ ܕܡܕܡ ܥܠ ܥܠܬܗܘܢ ܠܐ ܐܬܗܢܝܘ *although they have been profited nothing by their sons* (Jos. Sty. 3:10).

ܐܦܢ ܟܠܗܘܢ ܢܬܟܫܠܘܢ ܒܟ *though all men should be offended at thee* (Matt. 26:33).

7. ܘܲܚܙܵܐ ܠܡܲܠܲܐܟܹܗ ܕܡܵܪܝܵܐ ܩܵܐܹܡ *and he saw the angel of the Lord standing* (Num. 22:31).

ܡܗܲܠܸܟ *as he was walking* (Gen. 3:8).

5. Causal adverbial clauses are introduced:—
(1) By the relative ܕ.

(2) By ܕܲܒ *in that*, ܕܥܲܠ *because that*, ܡܸܢ *since*, ܓܹܝܪ *for*, ܐܲܝܟܲܢ ܕ *as that*, ܒܗܵܕܹܐ ܕ *in this that*, and ܡܸܢ ܗܵܕܹܐ ܕ *from this that*, ܥܲܠ ܕ *on account of this*.

6. Concessive adverbial clauses are introduced by ܕܲܒ and ܐܵܦܹܢ.
7. The adverbial accusative belongs here.

138. Conditional Sentences.

1. (1) ܐܸܢ ܐܹܢܵܐ ܣܹܪܚܹܬ . . ܡܵܢܵܐ ܣܪܲܚܘ *if I have sinned, wherein have they sinned?* (Jos. Sty. 40:2).

ܐܸܢ ܕܹܝܢ ܫܲܦܝܪ [ܥܲܕܟܹܝܠ] ܕܡܲܠܠܹܬ ܡܵܢܵܐ ܡܚܸܐ ܐܲܢ̄ܬ ܠܝ *but if well have I spoken, why smitest thou me* (John. 18:23).

ܐܸܢ ܗܵܢܵܐ ܟܹܐܦܵܐ ܣܝܼܡ ܗ̄ܘܵܐ ܐܲܝܟ ܫܹܬܐܸܣܬܵܐ ܐܲܝܟܲܢܵܐ ܗܘܵܐ ܪܹܫܵܐ ܐܵܦ ܕܙܵܘܝܼܬܵܐ *if this stone had been placed as foundation, how was it head also of the corner?* (Aphr. 11:13. See also Overbeck 62:6).

(2) ܐܸܢ ܠܝ ܪܕܲܦܘ ܐܵܦ ܠܟܘܿܢ ܢܸܪܕܦܘܿܢ *if they have persecuted me they will also persecute you* (John. 15:20).

ܘܐܸܢ ܡܝܼܬܢ ܥܲܡ ܡܫܝܼܚܵܐ ܡܗܲܝܡܢܝܼܢܲܢ *if then we have died with Christ we believe* (Rom. 6:8).

(3) ܐܸܢ ܕܡܸܟ ܡܬܚܠܸܡ *if he is fallen asleep, he will be saved* (John. 11:12).

ܐܸܢ ܗܘܼ ܪܕܲܦܘܗܝ ܐܲܝܟܲܢܵܐ ܠܵܐ ܢܸܪܕܦܘܿܢܢ *if they persecuted him, how shall they not persecute us?* (Overbeck 228:14. See also Overbeck 67:8).

(4) ܐܸܢ ܕܹܝܢ ܪܘܼܚܵܐ ܐܵܘ ܡܲܠܲܐܟܵܐ ܡܲܠܸܠ ܥܲܡܹܗ ܡܵܢܵܐ ܐܝܼܬ ܒܹܗ ܨܸܒܘܼܬܵܐ *if then a spirit or angel has spoken with him what is there in that?* (Acts. 23:9).

ܐܸܢ ܐܲܡܬܲܢ ܒܸܪܵܬܹܗ ܕܲܫܡܝܼܫ ܐܲܦܼܵܡܹܗ ܕܢܸܪܘܵܙ . . ܐܸܠܵܐ ܗܘܼ ܕܲܡܚܲܣܸܡ ܠܹܗ

if his will has been able to quench the violence of fire, it is to be believed (Overbeck 54:7).

2. (1) ܘܗܘ ܐܢ ܗܘܐ ܕ . . . . ܬܘܒ ܐܢ *if again it happen etc., they had to endure great fatigue* (Jos. Sty. 83:13).

ܐܬܚܙܝ . . . ܢܐܡܪܘܢ ܐܢ *if they shall say . . . it has been seen* (Overbeck 54:27. Comp. also 48:27).

(2) ܐܢ ܕܝܢ ܢܗܘܘܢ ܡܢ ܒܢܝ ܚܝܠܗ ܢܥܠܘܢ *if they would be members of his army they should enter* (Jos. Sty. 19:5).

ܐܢ ܐܫܬܝܘܗܝ ܢܗܘܐ ܨܒܝܢܟ *if I must drink it let thy will be done* (Matt. 26:42).

ܐܢ ܢܦܘܩ ܠܘܬܗܘܢ ܢܟܡܢܘܢ ܠܗ *if he shall go forth to them they should lie in ambush for him* (Jos. Sty. 58:4).

(3) ܐܢ ܕܝܢ ܢܬܠ ܡܪܢ . . . ܡܡܠܠܝܢܢ ܥܡܟ *if then our Lord will grant, we will speak with thee* (Jos. Sty. 43:16).

ܠܐ ܐܢܫ ܡܚܐ ܠܟ ܐܦܠܐ ܐܢ ܟܚܕܘܪܝܟ ܬܦܘܩ *no man will harm thee even if thou comest out alone* (Jos. Sty. 89:21).

(4) ܘܐܢ ܕܝܢ ܗܢܘܢ ܢܥܫܢܘܢ ܕܟܝ ܦܩܚ *if then they be too strong for us it is better* (Jos. Sty. 65:12).

ܘܐܢ ܢܐܬܐ ܛܘܒܝܗܘܢ ܠܥܒܕܐ ܗܢܘܢ *and if he come blessed are those servants* (Lk. 12:38).

3. (1) ܐܢ ܒܪܘܚܐ ܕܐܠܗܐ ܐܢܐ ܡܦܩ ܐܢܐ ܕܝܘܐ ܡܛܬ ܠܗ ܥܠܝܟܘܢ ܡܠܟܘܬܗ ܕܐܠܗܐ *if by the spirit of God I cast out demons, the kingdom of God is nigh unto you* (Matt. 12:28).

ܐܢ ܡܛܠ ܕܢܦܫܐ ܒܦܓܪܐ ܥܠܬ ܚܒܝܫ ܐܢܐ ܡܕܝܢ ܐܝܟܐ ܣܝܟ ܗܘ ܘܠܐ ܚܒܝܫ ܗܘܐ *if, because the soul has entered into the body, I am enclosed, that which was not enclosed, has been enclosed* (Overbeck 63:7).

(2) ܐܢ ܐܝܬ ܗܘܐ ܡܘܡܬܐ ܥܒܝܕ ܠܐ ܡܫܬܟܚ ܗܘܐ ܒܗ *if there should be any oath he would not be found by it* (Jos. Sty. 76:12).

[§ 138.]

ܐܹܢ ܫܒܼܿܩ ܐܼܪܗܒܘܿܢܕܘܿܣ ... ܢܗܦܟܘܿܢ *if Areobindus allowed, they should turn* (Jos. Sty. 58:9).

ܐܹܢ ܗܘܼ ܕܨܒܝܢܐ ܗܢܐ ... ܡܨܐ .. ܡܗܝܡܢܝܢܢ *if this will were able to separate evil, we would believe* (Overbeck 50:8).

(3) ܐܹܢ ܗܟܝܠ ܐܢܬ ܝܕܥ ܐܢܬ ܡܢܘ ܐܢܐ ܠܐ ܟܠܐ *if then thou knowest who he is I shall not hinder thee* (Jos. Sty. 76:19).

ܐܹܢ ܐܢܐ ܒܒܥܠܙܒܘܒ ܡܦܩ ܐܢܐ ܕܝܘ̈ܐ ܒܢܝܟܘܢ ܒܡܢܐ ܡܦܩܝܢ ܠܗܘܢ *if I by Beelzebub cast out demons, by whom do your sons?* (Matt. 12:27).

(4) ܐܢ ܗܟܝܠ ܕܘܝܕ ܩܪܐ ܠܗ ܡܪܝܐ ܐܝܟܢܐ ܒܪܗ ܗܘ *if David then call him Lord, how is he his son* (Matt. 22:45).

ܐܹܢ ܗܘܼ ܕܡܕܓܠ ܠܐ ܗܘܐ ܡܠܟܐ ܗܘ *if he deceives he is no king* (Jos. Sty. 61:19).

4. (1) ܗܘ ܕܐܠܗܐ ܗܘܐ ܫܦܝܪ ܗܘ ܐܦܢ ܗܘܼ ܕܫܦܝܪ *if it were right God himself would have put it in his heart* (Jos. Sty. 74:4).

ܘܐܢ ܠܝܬ ܩܝܡܬܐ ܐܦ ܠܐ ܡܫܝܚܐ ܩܡ *and if there be no resurrection Christ also is not risen* (1 Cor. 15:13).

(2) ܐܠܘ ܗܘܘ ܡܫܟܚܝܢ ܢܐܪܥܘܢܝܗܝ ܒܩܪܒܐ *if they were able, they should meet (him) in battle* (Jos. Sty. 14:4).

ܐܠܘ ܗܘ ܕܨܒܐ ܐܢܬ ܕܢܥܒܕ ܥܡܟ ܫܠܡܐ ܗܒ ܠܢ *if thou desirest us to make peace give us etc.* (Jos. Sty. 58:17).

ܐܹܢ ܐܝܬ ܐܢܫ̈ܝܢ ܕܠܐ ܨܒܝܢ .. ܢܬܩܪܒܘܢ ܠܘܬܢ *if there be those who are not willing .. let them draw near to us* (Addai 21:2).

ܐܹܢ ܡܠܟܗ ܗܘ ܕܐܝܣܪܐܝܠ ܢܚܘܬ ܗܫܐ ܡܢ ܙܩܝܦܐ *if he be the king of Israel let him come down now from the cross* (Matt. 27:42).

(3) ܐܹܢ ܗܘ ܕܒܥܐ ܐܢܬ ܒܫܐܠܐ ܡܫܕܪ ܐܢܐ ܠܟ *if thou askest it as a loan I will send it to thee* (Jos. Sty. 18:15).

ܡܢܐ ܗܟܝܠ ܡܥܡܕ ܐܢܬ ܐܢ ܐܢܬ ܠܐ ܐܝܬܝܟ ܡܫܝܚܐ *why then baptizest thou, if thou art not the Messiah* (John 1:25).

(4) ܗܟܢܐ ܐܡܪܘܢܢ ܐܢ ܐܢܬ .. ܐܹܢ ܗܘ ܕܡܬܚܙܝܐ ܠܐ ܗܘܐ ܣܓܝܐܐ

what profit is there from them if it be that admonition be not mingled? (Jos. Sty. 5:14).

ܐ݂ ܗܳܟܰܢܐ ܐܺܝܬ ܟܰܪܟܳܐ ܥܰܡ ܐܰܢ̱ܬܬܳܐ ܠܐ ܦܰܩܳܚ ܠܡܶܫܩܰܠ ܐܰܢ̱ܬܬܳܐ *if the case between a man and his wife be so, it is not expedient to marry* (Matt. 19:10).

5. ܐܶܠܳܐ ܕܪܶܢ ܗܳܐ ܐܶܠܘܳܐ ܠܐ ܡܰܠܦܺܝܢ ܗܘܰܘ ܠܰܢ ܗܳܠܶܝܢ ܐܳܦ ܐܶܢ ܡܶܕܶܡ ܐ̱ܚܪܺܝܢ ܐܶܬܚܰܫܰܒܘ ܗܘܰܘ ܠܰܢ *if they did not teach us this, they would be quite useless to us* (Jos. Sty. 5:19).

ܐܶܠܘܳܐ ܐܶܬܟܬܶܒ ܬܰܫ̈ܥܝܳܬܳܐ ܪܰܘ̈ܪܒܳܬܳܐ ܗܘ̈ܰܝ ܗܘ̈ܰܝ *if they were written great histories would they form* (Jos. Sty. 80:6).

ܐܶܠܘܳܐ ܠܺܝ ܝܳܕܥܺܝܢ ܗܘܰܝܬܘܢ ܐܳܦ ܠܐܒܝ ܝܳܕܥܺܝܢ ܗܘܰܝܬܘܢ *if ye were knowing me, ye would be knowing my father also* (John. 14:7).

ܐܶܠܘܳܐ ܪܳܚܡܺܝܢ ܗܘܰܝܬܘܢ ܠܺܝ ܚܳܕܶܝܢ ܗܘܰܝܬܘܢ *if ye had loved me ye would have rejoiced* (John. 14:28).

ܐܶܠܘܳܐ ܗܳܕܶܐ ܠܐ ܗܘܳܬ ܝܰܘܡܳܢܳܐ ܗܘܳܬ *if this had not happend to-day, it had happened* (Addai 15:7).

ܐܶܠܘܳܐ ܠܐ ܨܒܳܐ ܠܐ ܡܺܝܬ ܗܘܳܐ *if he had not wished, he had not died* (Addai 19:16).

ܐܶܠܘܳܐ ܠܐ ܝܺܕܰܥܘ ܗܘܰܘ ܐܳܦ ܠܐ... ܠܐ ܗܘܳܐ ܚܽܘܪܒܳܐ *if they had not known, there had not been the desolation* (Addai 27:21).

ܐܶܠܘܳܐ ܨܒܰܘ ܗܘܰܘ ... ܠܐ ܫܰܒܩܘ ܗܘܰܘ ܠܗܘܢ ܫܓܘ̈ܫܝܶܐ *if they had wished, the commotions had not permitted them* (Addai 28:2).

ܐܶܠܘܳܐ ܐܺܝܬ ܗܘܳܐ ܒܗܘܢ ... ܪܶܓܫܳܬܐ ܙܳܕܶܩ ܗܘܳܐ ܠܗܘܢ *if there were in them feeling, it would be right for them* (Addai 24:1).

Adverbial sentences of condition are of two kinds, those which express a possible and those which express an impossible condition. Of sentences expressing a possible condition, there are sixteen constructions according to the form of the verb, or copula, that is employed.

1. When there is a Perfect in the protasis, there may be in the apodosis:—
(1) A Perfect.
(2) An Imperfect.

(3) A Participle.
(4) A nominal sentence.

2. When there is an Imperfect in the protasis, there may be in the apodosis:—

(1) A Perfect.
(2) An Imperfect.
(3) A Participle.
(4) A nominal sentence.

3. When there is a Participle in the protasis, there may be in the apodosis:—

(1) A Perfect.
(2) An Imperfect.
(3) A Participle.
(4) A nominal sentence.

4. When there is a nominal sentence in the protasis, there may be in the apodosis:—

(1) A Perfect.
(2) An Imperfect.
(3) A Participle.
(4) A nominal sentence.

5. The impossible condition is expressed by ܐܠܘ or ܐܢ ܐܠܘ. In the protasis is found the Perfect, with or without ܗܘܐ, or the Participle with ܗܘܐ, or a nominal sentence; in the apodosis, the Perfect, or the Participle with ܗܘܐ.

INDEX.

a-class vowels, 29. 1, 5.
ă-ă, nouns with, 68.
ă-â, nouns with, 69.
â-ă, nouns with, 70. 1.
ă changed to e in nouns, 67. 1.
ă changed to e in verbs, 41. 2.
ă-e, nouns with, 68. 3.
ă-î, nouns with, 69. 4.
ă-û, nouns with, 69. 5.
â-î, nouns with, 70. 2.
â-î, nouns with, 71. 2.
â-û, nouns with, 71. 1.
â becomes o, 29. 5. (1).
ă, when found, 29. 1.
ă obscured to e, 29. 2.
ă contracted with w into ô, 29. 5. (3).
ă contracted with 'a into ô, 29. 5. (4).
ă contracted with y into ê, 29. 3.
ă contracted with y into î, 29. 4. (4).
â becomes û through ô, 29. 7. (3).
ă volatilized, 30, 31, 42. 1, 69.
Absolute state, masculine singular, 76. 1.
Absolute state, feminine singular, 76. 2. (1).
Absolute state, masculine plural, 76. 3.
Absolute state, feminine plural, 76. 4.
Absolute state dual, 76. 5.
Absolute state often definite, 93. 1.
Absolute state generally indefinite, 93. 2.
Absolute infinitive, 49.
Absolute infinitive used to intensify the meaning of the verb, 119. 1.
Absolute infinitive used alone, 119. 2.
Abstract nouns, 75. 4.
Abstract ideas sometimes denoted by the plural, 92. 2. (2).
Accent, 14.
Accents, system of, 15.
Accusative, position of, 123. 1, 2.
Accusative, different ways of denoting it, 123. 1, 2.
Accusative cognate, 126. 4.
Accusative of specification, 117. 8.
Accusative of condition, 116. 3. (2) b.
Accusative of the pronoun, 36. 1, 51.
Active stems, 41. 1, 2, 3.

Active stems, how made passive or reflexive, 41. 4.
Active signification of passive forms of intransitive verbs, 41. 5. Rem. 2.
Active participles, how formed, 50.
Active participle of simple stem, 50. 1, 70. 2.
Active participles of guttural verbs, 52. 3. Rem. 1.
Active participle of Ê Ê verbs, 54. 3.
Active participle of Ê Wau verbs, 59. 4.
Active participle of Ê Olaph verbs, 56. 4.
Active participle of Lomadh Olaph verbs, 60. 5.
Active participle, syntax of, 116.
Addition, 20.
Addition of Olaph, Nem, Mim, Rish, Gomal, and Hê, 20. 2. of Tau, 20. 3.
Addition for stem, 41. 3–5.
Additions for inflection of perfect, 43. 1.
Additions for inflection of imperfect, 45. 2.
Additions for noun formations, 74, 75.
Adjective, verbal, 72. 2. (4).
Adjective, agreement of, 99. 1.
Adjective, definiteness of, 93. II. 3.
Adjective, position of, 94. 5, 99. 1.
Adjective clauses, 97. B. Rem. 1.
Adjective predicate, 93. II. 3. (2), 99. 2.
Adjectives with two short vowels, 68. 2.
Adjectives ending in ôn, 75. 1. (2).
Adjectives ending in ôy, 75. 3.
Adjective, syntax of, 99.
Adjective, comparison of, 100.
Adjective sentences, 136. (See under relative sentences.)
Adverb, 88. II. Rem. 2, 89. A. 1–4.
Adverb with the substantive verb, 127. 8.
Adverb with '*Ith*, 128. 4.
Adverbial accusative. (See under Accusative.)
Adverbial sentences, 137, 138.
Adversative sentences, 134. 3.
Affix. (See sufformative and suffix.)
Agency expressed. (See Nomina agentis, and 121. 4.)
Agreement, 121.
Alphabet, 1.–4.

202   INDEX.

Alternative sentences, 134. 1, 2. 132. 5. Rem.
Annexion, 96.
Annexion, to express the superlative degree, 100. 2. (1).
Annexion, periphrasis for, 98.
Anomalous nouns, 86, 87.
Anomalous verbs, 64.
Aph'el stem, 41. 3, 42, 44.
Apocopation. (See Rejection.)
Apocopation of the Tau of the feminine, 76. 2. (1).
Apodosis, 137, 138.
Apposition, 94.
Apposition of a noun with a pronominal suffix, 94. 6.
Apposition of substantive clauses, 135. 5.
Aspirates, 2. 2.
Aspiration, how denoted, 10.
Aspiration of the Tau in the first person singular of Lomadh Olaph verbs, 60. 2, Rem. 3.
Assimilation, 18, 53. 2.
Asyndeton, 133. 1, Rem. 1.

Bêth, 1, 2. 2, 4. 3. (2), 5. 1, 10.

Cardinals, 88. I, 110. A.
Causative verb-stem, 41. 3, 42, 44.
Changeable vowel sounds, 7. 3.
Changes of vowels in the inflection of the verb, 42, 45. 1, 3, 52. 3, 58. 2, 59, 60.
Changes of vowels in the inflection of the noun, 28. 3. (1), 67. 1, 2. (5), 68. 5, 76. 2. (1), 79. 8. 1, 82. Rem. 2.
Characteristic of the stems, 42.
Classification of nouns, 66. B.
Closed syllables, 17. 2.
Cognate accusative, 126. 4.
Collective, 90.
Collective with suffixes, 77. 7.
Collective nouns, agreement of, 90. 4, 121. 2.
Command, how expressed, 114. 1, 115.
Commutation. (See Permutation.)
Comparative degree, how expressed, 100. 1.
Compound words drop letters, 23. 4.
Compound nouns, gender of, 91. 4.
Compound sentences, 133.
Conditional sentences expressing possibility have sixteen constructions, 138. 1-4.
Conditional sentences expressing an impossible condition have six constructions, 138. 5.
Conjunctions, 89. 5.
Conjunctive sentences, 133.
Conjunctions with adverbial clauses, 137, 138.
Consonants, 1.-5, 9-12.
Consonants, euphony of, 18-27.
Consonantal character of Olaph lost, 25. 1.

Consonantal character of Wau and Yudh lost, 25. 1, 2.
Construct state of nouns, 76. 1-5.
Construct state of numerals, 88. I Rem. 3.
Construct state of participles, 96. 4 Rem. 2.
Construct state of prepositions, 89. B.
Construct infinitive, 49.
Construct infinitive with suffixes, 51. F. 74. 2, 85 Rem. 2.
Construct infinitive, syntax of, 120.
Construct infinitive always takes the preposition l before it, 120. 1.
Construct infinitive as a gerundive, 120. 1. (4).
Construct infinitive to denote "can," "must," "have to," etc., 120. 1. (4).
Construct infinitive after the comparative, 120. 1. (6).
Contraction of Wau and Yudh to form a long vowel, 29. 3. (1), 4. (4), 5. (3) (4), 7 (1) (2).
Contract nouns, 67. (5) (7), 68. 5.
Contraction of personal and demonstrative pronoun, 57. 3.
Contract verbs, 54, 56-61.

Dative ethical, 124. 5.
Declension of nouns, 78. *sq.*
Defective verbs, 64.
Definiteness of nouns, how expressed, 93.
Demonstrative pronoun, 37.
Demonstrative contracted with personal pronoun, 37. 3.
Demonstrative pronoun, syntax of, 102.
Demonstrative pronoun as an article, 102. 2.
Denominatives, 63. 2.
Dentals, 5. 1.
Dependent question, 135. 1, 3. (2).
Desire, how expressed, 114. 3. (1).
Determination of nouns, 93.
Determination of adjectives, 93. II.
Diacritical points, 6. 6.
Diminutives, how formed, 69. 6, 75. 2.
Diphthongs, 8.
Diphthong in iu, 60. 2. Rem. 1.
Direct object, 123, 125. 1, 3, 4.
Direct objective sentence, 135. 3.
Distribution, how denoted, 92. 3.
Dolath, 2. 2, 4. 3. (3), 4. 4, 5. 1, 10, 18. 3, 19. 5, 21. 1, 22. 4.
Dolath as the inseparable relative, 34.
Doubling of consonants, 10. 2. (4).
Doubly weak verbs, 62.
Dropping of Olaph et al. (See Rejection.)
Dual, 76. 5, 77. 3.

e, how written, 6. 1. Note, 4, 5. (1)-(8).
e, how pronounced, 6. 3. (2).
e, quantity of, 7. 1.
e, origin of, 7. 2.

INDEX.   203

e, value of in inflection, 7. 3.
e followed by u, 8. 1. (2).
e anomalous in certain forms, 28. 3. Rem.
e before doubled radical, 28. 3. (3).
ĕ, where found, 29. 2.
ê, how formed, 29. 3.
e heard, but not written, 31. 3. Rem. 1.
e as helping vowel, 33.
Ê, 3, 4. 1, 3. (6), 5. 1, 11. 4, 22. 5, 23. 4, 26. 3.
Ê Ê verbs, 54.
Ê Ê nouns, 79. B. Rem. 2, 80. Rems. 1. 2.
Ê Olaph verbs, 55.
Ê Olaph nouns, 79. B. Rem. 2.
Ê Olaph verbs which are also Lomadh Olaph, 62. 4.
Ê Wau verbs, 59.
Ê Wau nouns, 79. B. 1, Rem. 1, 80. Rems. 2. 3, 82. Rem. 2.
Ê Wau verbs which are also Lomadh Olaph, 62. 3.
Ê Yudh verbs, 59.
Ê Yudh nouns, 79. B. Rem. 1. 80. Rem. 2.
Elision. (See Rejection.)
Emphatic state, 76. 1–4.
Emphatic state, syntax of, 93.
Enclitics, 23. 4, 35. 2.
Endings for gender, number, and state of noun, 76.
Endings to denote person, gender, and number of the verb, 43, 45.
Endings for forming noun-stems, 66. A. 1, B. 4, 75.
Eshtaph'al, 41. 5.
Ethical dative, 124. 5.
'*Ethidh* used to emphasize the future, 129. 1.
Ethpa'al, 41. 4, 42, 44.
Ethpe'el, 41. 4, 42, 44.
Ettaph'al, 41. 4, 42, 44.
Etymology, 34–89.
Euphony of consonants, 18–27.
Euphony of vowels, 29.
Exhortation or excitement, 114. 3. (4). 112. 3. Rem. 2.

Feminine ending, 76. 2.
Feminine ending dropped, 76. 2. (1).
Feminine ending retained in the construct and emphatic states, and before suffixes, 76. 2. (2).
Feminine nouns, 78. II.
Feminine nouns, declension of, 82–85.
Feminine nouns, anomalies of, 86. 6–10, 13.
Feminine nouns, syntax of, 91. 2.
Fractional numbers, how formed, 88. II. Rem. 3.
Frequentative action denoted by the participle, 116. 2.

Future, sometimes denoted by the imperfect, 113. 3.
Future may be denoted by the perfect, 112. 3.
Future often denoted by the active participle, 116. 1. (2), 2. (2).
Future, emphasized by '*Ethidh*, 129. 1.
Future perfect denoted by the perfect, 112. 3. (2).

Gender of noun, 76, 78.
Gender, anomalies of, 86. 7, 8, 10, 12.
Gender, syntax of, 91.
Gender, neuter, how denoted, 91. 5.
Gender of compound nouns, 91. 4.
Gender of plural follows that of the singular, 91. 5.
Gender of nouns used figuratively often that of the thing which they represent, 91. 6.
Gender of verb, 43, 111. 1.
Gender of verb having two subjects of different genders is masculine, 121. 6. Rem. 2.
Genitive relation expressed in four ways, 96.
Genitive expressed by annexion. (See Annexion.)
Genitive expressed by the relative, 97. A. (Used when there are two or more genitives, or with indeclinable nouns, or when words intervene.)
Genitive expressed by means of the pronominal suffix and the relative, 97. B.
Genitive expressed by means of prepositions, 98.
Genitive subjective and objective, 96. 4.
Gomal, 2. 2, 5. 1, 10, 20. 2.
Gutturals, 4. 5, 5. 1, 26, 52, 57, 68. 5. (2). 40. 3, 41. 2.

Half-open syllables, 17. 4.
Half-vowel, 7. 1. (3), 9.
Hê, 1, 3, 4. 4, 4. 5, 5. 1, 11. 1, 18. 1 Rem. 19. 1, 20. 2, 21. 3, 22. 5, 25. 4.
Heightened vowel-sounds, 7. 2. (4).
Heightening of vowels, 20. 4. (3), 29. 5. (2).
Helping vowels, 33, 34. 3, 4.
Hêth, 3, 4. 5, 5. 1, 19. 4.
Hewo, as enclitic, 127. 1.
Hewo before the predicate, 127. 2.
Hewo used in the perfect to emphasize the past tense, 127. 3. (1).
Hewo used in the perfect after an imperfect to emphasize a past subjunctive, 127. 3. (2).
Hewo used in the perfect after an active participle to express a past state, 127. 3. (3).
Hewo used in the perfect before adjectives or participles to express a wish, command, or admonition, 127. 4. (1). 112. 3. (2) Rem. 2.
Hewo used in the perfect before a participle to express the frequentative subjunctive, 127. 4. (2).

Hᵉwo used in the perfect after an active participle to express frequentative action in the past, 127. 3. (3) b.
Hᵉwo used in the imperfect with a following participle to express a future frequentative action or state, 127. 5.
Hᵉwo used in the active participle before an active participle to emphasize the future of a state, 127. 6.

i, how written, 6. 1. Note, 4, 5, 29. 4.
i, how pronounced, 6. 3. (3).
i, quantity of, 7. 1. (2), 29. 4.
i, origin of, 7. 2.
i, euphony of, 29. 4.
ỉ found in the Nestorian, 7. 2 Note.
ỉ, class segholates, 67. 1, 2 (5).
î derived from ê, how written, 6. 5. (1).
I as first vowel in nouns, 69, 72. 2. (2) (6), 74. 2. (6) (7), 3. (7) (8).
î as second vowel in nouns, 69. 4, 71. 2, 72. 2. (4), 74. 2. (2), 3 (2) (5).
Imperative, sufformatives of, 48. Note 2.
Imperative, stem of, 48.
Imperative with suffixes, 51. E.
Imperative of guttural verbs, 52. 4.
Imperative of Pê Nun verbs, 53. 1.
Imperative of Ê Ê verbs, 54. 1.
Imperative of Pê Olaph verbs, 55. 1. Note 2.
Imperative of Pê Yudh verbs, 58. Rem. 2. (2).
Imperative of Ê Wau verbs, 59. 2.
Imperative of Lomadh Olaph verbs, 60. 4.
Imperative of Lomadh Olaph verbs with suffixes, 61. 3.
Imperative, syntax of, 115.
Imperative expressed sometimes by means of *hᵉwo* and a participle, 115. 5, 127. 4. (1).
Imperative denoted by participle, 115. 6, 116. 5.
Imperative expressed by imperfect, 114. 1, 115. 2.
Imperative emphasized by means of auxiliary verbs, 120. 1. (5), 129. 2. (1).
Imperfect, formation of, 43.
Imperfects in A and E, 46.
Imperfect of derived forms, 47.
Imperfect with suffixes, 51. C. D.
Imperfect of guttural verbs, 52. 4.
Imperfect of Pê Nun verbs, 53. 2.
Imperfect of Ê Ê verbs, 54. 2.
Imperfect of Pê Olaph verbs, 55. 2, 3.
Imperfect of Ê Olaph verbs, 56. 3.
Imperfect of Pê Yudh verbs, 58. 2.
Imperfect of Lomadh Olaph verbs, 60. 2, 3.
Imperfect of Lomadh Olaph verbs with suffixes, 61. 2.
Imperfect, person, gender, and number of denoted by preformatives and sufformatives, 111. 1.

Imperfect denotes incomplete or dependent action, 111. 3, 113.
Imperfect used for past events after certain temporal particles, 113. 1.
Imperfect, use of in present time doubtful, 113. 2.
Imperfect sometimes used for the future indicative, 113. 3.
Imperfect denotes future, especially in conditional clauses, 138.
Imperfect denotes most of the variations for mood, 114.
Imperfect as imperative, 114. 1.
Imperfect as potential, 114. 2.
Imperfect as optative, 114. 3.
Imperfect as subjunctive, 114. 4.
Imperfect in conditional sentences, 138.
Impersonal verb, 122.
Impersonal use of adjectives, 122. 4. Rem.
Impersonal verbs with a direct object, 126. 3. (2).
Impersonal use of 'Ith, 128. 1.
Impersonal use of the passive, 122. 5.
Impersonal use of participles, 122. 4.
Indeclinable nouns, 86. 6.
Indeclinable nouns use the absolute state for the emphatic, 93. 1. (4).
Indeclinable nouns use the construction with the relative, 97. A. Rem. 3.
Indefinite pronouns, adjectives, and nouns, 107, 108. 2, 109.
Indirect object, 124, 125. 2, 3, 4.
Indirect object a substantive sentence, 135. 3. (4).
Indirect question, 132. 6.
Infinitive construct. (See Construct Infinitive.)
Infinitive absolute. (See Absolute Infinitive.)
Inflection of nouns, 66. A. sq.
Inflection of verbs, 43. sq.
Inseparable particles, 34.
Insertion of Olaph, Nun, Mim, Rish, Gomal, Hê, and Tau, 20. 2, 3.
Insertion of vowels, 33. 3, 4.
Intensive stem, 41. 2, 63. 2.
Intensive of Ê Ê verbs, 54. 4.
Interrogative particle, 89. A. 4, 132. 1, 7.
Interrogative pronouns, 39, 132. 1, 103.
Interrogative adjective, 39, 103. 2.
Interrogative contracted with personal pronoun, 39. Rem. 4.
Interrogative sentence, 132.
Irregular nouns, 86, 87.
Irregular verbs, 64.
'Ith, inflection of, 65.
'Ith, syntax of, 128.
'Ith used impersonally, 128. 1.
'Ith followed by *hᵉwo* emphasizes the past of "to be," 128. 2.

'Ith followed by *l* expresses "to have," 128. 3. (1).
'Ith followed by *b* or *l*woth expresses "to have," 128. 3. (2).
'Ith followed by an adverb, 128. 4.
'Ith followed by the infinitive construct expresses "*can.*"

Kaph, 2. 2, 4. 1, 4. 3. (2), 5. 1, 10.
Kul, uses of, 108.
Kushoy, 10. 1, 44. Rem. 1, 47. Rem. 1.

Labials, 5. 1.
Lengthening, 28. 3.
Letters at beginning of syllable, 16. 2.
Letters at end of syllable, 16. 3.
Letters, peculiar forms of, 4. 1–4.
Letters, distinction of, 4. 3, 4.
Letters, classification of, 5.
Letters, doubling of, 10. 2.
Linea occultans, 11, 19.
Linguals, 5. 1.
Linguo-dentals, 5. 1.
Lomadh, 41, 2, 3. (1), 5. 1, 18. 4, 19. 6, 23. 2. (3).
Lomadh as inseparable preposition, 34.
Lomadh with pronominal suffixes, 36. 3.
Lomadh Olaph verbs, 60.
Lomadh Olaph verbs with suffixes, 61.
Lomadh Olaph verbs which are also Ê Olaph, 62. 4.
Lomadh Olaph segholates, 79 B. 2.–4.
Lomadh Olaph nouns of two syllables ending in *e'* or *ay*, 81.
Lomadh Olaph feminine segholates, 82. Rems. 3, 4, 5.
Lomadh Olaph feminine participles, 83. Rems.
Long and short vowel nouns, 70.
Long vowels, 7. 1. (2).
Long *e*, 29. 3.
Long *i*, 29. 4.
Long *o*, 29. 5.
Long *u*, 29. 7.
Long vowels in nouns, 67. 2. (5), 69, 70, 71, 72. 2, 74. 2. (4) (5) (7) (9), 74. 3. (1) (2) (3) (6), 75.

Man, who ? 39.
Marhitono, 12. 2.
Masculine gender, 76. 1, 3, 78.
Masculine gender preferred, 126. 6. Rem. 2.
Medhem, 109.
Mehagyono, 12. 1.
Middle A verbs, 41. 1. (1).
Middle E verbs, 41. 1. (2), 43. 5, Note 2, 59. 6. Rem. 1.
Middle U verbs, 41. 1. (3).
Monosyllabic nouns, 67, 68, 69, 79, 80.
Mood, generally denoted by the imperfect, 114.
Mood sometimes denoted by the participle, 116. 5.

Mood sometimes denoted by the perfect, 112. 3, Remarks.
Mood emphasized by auxiliary verbs, 120. 1. (5), 120. 2. (1).

Names of letters, 1.
Names of vowel signs, 6. 2.
Naturally long vowels, 7. 3. (2). 29. 3, 4, 5, 7.
Negative commands, 115. 3.
Negative interrogative sentences, 132. 3.
Negative sentences, 131. 2.
Negative double, 132. 5.
Neuter, 91. 5.
New vowels, 33.
Nomina agentis, 70. 2, 71. 1, 72. 2. (1), 75. 1.
Nominal inflection, 66. A.
Nominative of the pronoun, 35.
Nominative absolute, 95.
Noun, inflection of, 66. A.
Nouns, classification of, 66 B.
Nouns with one short vowel, 67, 79, 80, Rems. 1, 2.
Nouns formed with two short vowels, 68, 79, Rem. 3, 79. B. 3, 4, 80. Rem. 3.
Nouns with one short and one long vowel, 69, 80, Rem. 4.
Nouns with one long and one short vowel, 70, 81.
Nouns with two long vowels, 71, 80, Rem. 5.
Nouns with second radical doubled, 72, 80, Rem. 5, 81.
Nouns with third radical doubled, 73. 1, 81.
Nouns with two radicals doubled, 73. 2.
Nouns with preformative, 74.
Nouns with sufformative, 75.
Nouns, anomalies of, 86, 87.
Nouns, gender of, 76, 86.
Nouns, number of, 76, 92, 121. B.
Nouns, declension of, 78–85.
Nouns indeclinable, 86. 6.
Nouns, state of, 76, 86. 17, 93.
Nouns, dual of, 76. 5, 77. 3.
Nouns as adverbs, 89. 1, 2.
Noun-stems classified, 66 B.
Nouns plural in form but singular in signification take verb in singular, 121. B.
Number of noun, 76.
Number, anomalies in, 86. 1–5, 9, 11, 14, 92. 6, 7.
Number in verb, 43, 111. 1.
Number of verb and adjective agreeing with collective, 90. 4.
Number of nouns denoted in four ways, 92. 1.
Number, grammatical, sometimes different from logical, 92. 2.
Numerals, the, 88.
Numeral cardinal in construction, 88. I. Rem. 3.

Numeral cardinal in emphatic, 88. I. Rem. 4.
Numeral cardinal with suffixes, 88. I. Rem. 6.
Numeral cardinal in dual, 96. 5.
Numeral ordinal. (See Ordinal.)
Nun, 4. 1, 5. 1, 11. 1, 18, 19. 6, 20. 2, 23. 1. (3), 23. 2. (3), 3. (2), 53, 62. 1, 67. 2. (3) (6).

Object of the verb, 123.
Object indirect, 124.
Objects, two or more, 125.
Object with passive or reflexive, 126.
Object, various positions and ways of uniting it when indefinite and direct, 123. 1.
Object, when definite and direct, how written, 123. 2.
Object after impersonal verbs, 126. 3.
Object as cognate accusative, 126. 4.
Objective pronoun, 36. 1, 51.
Obscured vowels, 7. 2. (2).
Occultation, 11, 18.
Olaph, orthography of, 2, 4. 1, 4. 2, 4. 3, 4. 4, 4. 5, 5. 1, 5. 2, C. 5, 11. 2, 13. 1, 20. 1, 21. 2, 22. 1, 2, 3, 5, 23. 1, 2, 3, 24. 1, 25. 1, 26. 2.
Olaph as sign of causative stem, 41. 3.
Olaph, for the second radical in participle of Ê Ê verbs, 54. 3. a.
Olaph falls away in some forms of Pê Olaph verbs, 55. 1. Rem. 2. 55. 2. Rem. 55. 3. Rems. 1, 2, 3.
Olaph as third radical in verbs, 57.
Olaph written for Yudh in the participle of Ê Wau verbs, 59. 4.
Olaph as vowel letter in Lomadh Olaph verbs, 60.
Olaph as first radical of segholates, 67. 2. (1).
Olaph as third radical of nouns with two short vowels, 68. 5. (2).
Olaph in nouns with one short and one long vowel retains the original vowel, 69.
Omission. (See Rejection.)
Open syllable, 17. 1.
Optative, 112. 3, Rem. 2, 114. 3, 115. 6, 116. 5, 127. 4. (1), 129. 2. (3).
Ordinal, 88. II.
Ordinal, formation of adverbs from, 88. II. Rem. 2.
Ordinal, formation of fractional numbers from, 88. Rem. 3.
Ordinal, syntax of, 110. B.
Ordinal used for distribution, 110. B. 1.
Ordinal used for multiplication, 110. B. 2.
Origin of vowels, 7. 2.
Origin of vowel signs, 6. 1.
Original vowels in verb-stems, 42.
Original vowels of noun-stems, 67-74.
Orthography, 1–33.
Otiose letters, 24.

Pa'el stem, how formed, 41. 2, 42. 2.
Pa'el, inflection of, 44.
Pa'el, of guttural verbs, 52. 3. Rem. 1.
Pa'el of Pê Nun verbs, 53.
Pa'el of Ê Ê verbs, 54. 4.
Pa'el of Pê Yudh verbs, 55. 3.
Pa'el of Ê Olaph verbs, 56. 4.
Pa'el of Lomadh Olaph guttural verbs, 57.
Pa'el of Pê Yudh verbs, 58. 4.
Pa'el of Ê Wau verbs, 59. 5.
Pa'el participle of Lomadh Olaph verbs, 60. 5.
Palatals, 5. 1.
Participles with enclitic subject, 35. 2.
Participles, how formed, 50. 1, 2, 69. 4. 70. 2, 72. 2. (4), 74. 2.
Participles, how inflected, 50. 3, 81, 83, 84.
Participles with suffixes, 77. 6, 36. 1, 50. 3, 51. F.
Participles of guttural verbs, 52. 3. Rem. 1.
Participles of Pê Nun verbs, 53.
Participles of Ê Ê verbs, 54. 3.
Participles of Pê Olaph verbs, 55. 1. Rem. 3, 55. 3.
Participles of Ê Olaph verbs, 56. 4.
Participles of Ê Wau verbs, 59. 4.
Participles of Lomadh Olaph verbs, 60. 5.
Participle as predicate, 93. II. 3. (2).
Participle in construction, 96, 4. Rem. 2.
Participle, person of denoted by the personal pronoun, 111. 2.
Participle, active, use of, 116.
Participle as objective complement, 116. 3, 4.
Participle denoting mood, 116. 5.
Participle as accusative of condition, 116. 3. b.
Participle as noun, 118.
Participle as adjective, 118. 4.
Participle with direct object, 123. 2. Rems.
Participle in conditional sentences, 138.
Participle, passive, 117.
Participle, passive, used with *hewo* to denote the pluperfect, 117. 2.
Participle, passive, used in an active sense, 117. 4.
Participle, passive, used like the gerundive, 117. 6.
Participle, passive, with accusative of specification, 117. 7.
Particles, inseparable, 34.
Particles, 89.
Particles between nouns in construction, 96. 2. Rem., 97. B. Rem. 2.
Passive stems, 41. 4, 41. 5.
Passive participle. (See Participle, Passive.)
Passive with object, 126.
Passive, followed by *l* denoting the agent, 121. 4.
Passive with cognate accusative, 126. 4. (2).
Passive used impersonally, 122. 5.

Pê, 2. 2, 5. 1, 10.
Pê Nun verbs, 53.
Pê Nun verbs which are also Lomadh Olaph, 62. 1.
Pê Nun verbs which are also Ê Wau or Ê Ê, 62. 2.
Pê Nun noun forms which have the Nun dropped or assimilated, 67. 2. (3), 71. 1, 2.
Pê Olaph verbs, 55.
Pê Olaph nouns, 79. A. Rem. 1.
Pê Olaph verbs in causative stems, like Pê Wau verbs, 65. 3, 58. 3.
Pê Olaph verbs sometimes like Pê Yudh verbs, 58. 4. Rem. 2.
Pê Olaph verbs which are also Lomadh Olaph, 62. 1.
Pê Yudh verbs, 58.
Pê Yudh nouns, 79. A. Rem. 2, 82 Rem. 1.
Pê Wau verbs, 58.
Pe'al stem, 41. 1, 42.
Pe'al perfect, 43.
Pe'al of guttural verbs, 52.
Pe'al of Pê Nun verbs, 53.
Pe'al of Ê Ê verbs, 54. 1-3.
Pe'al of Pê Olaph verbs, 55. 1, 2.
Pe'al of Pê Wau and Pê Yudh verbs, 58. 1, 2.
Pe'al of Ê Wau verbs, 59. 1-4.
Pe'al of Ê Yudh verbs, 59. 5. Rem. 2.
Pe'al of Lomadh Olaph verbs, 60. 1-4.
Peculiarities of gutturals and of Wau and Yudh, 26, 27.
Perfect, inflection of, 43, 44.
Perfect with suffixes, 51. A, B.
Perfect of Lomadh Olaph verbs, 60.
Perfect, persons, genders, and numbers of denoted by sufformatives, 43, 111. 1.
Perfect denotes completed action, 111. 3.
Perfect may be used for past, present, or future time, 111. 3, 112.
Perfect in promise or prophecy, 112. 3. (1).
Perfect to express wish or exhortation, 112. 3. Rem. 2.
Perfect with *hewo* to denote purpose or result, 112. 3. Rem. 1.
Perfect in conditional sentences, 138.
Permutation, 22, 44 Rem. 2. 47. Rem. 3.
Person in verb, 43, 111. 1.
Person in participles denoted by the personal pronouns, 111. 2, 121. 7.
Person, first preferred to second or third, and the second to the third, 121. 6.
Personal pronoun, 35.
Personal pronoun, syntax of, 101.
Personal pronoun used independently, 35. 1.
Personal pronoun, enclitic, 35. 2.
Personal pronoun contracted with participle or adjective, 35. 2.
Personal pronoun used as suffix, 36.

Personal pronoun used as a possessive, 36. 1, 77.
Personal pronoun as suffix of nouns, adjectives and participles ending in Yudh, 77. 5, 6.
P*thoḫo*, 6.
Phrases. (See Sentences.)
Place, sentences of, 137. 1.
Pluperfect, 112. 1. (3), 117. 2, 127. 3 (1) *b*.
Plural, sign of, 13.
Plural. (See Number.)
Plural of paucity, 92. 3.
Plural of majesty, 92. 4.
Plural of compound ideas, 92. 5.
Possessive, 36. 1, 38. 2, 101. 2, 104, 3. Rem. 106.
Potential mood, 114. 2, 120. 1. (5), 128. 5, 129. 2. (2).
Precative perfect, 112. 3. Rem. 2.
Predicate, participle as, 93. II. 3. (2).
Predicate adjective, agreement of, 99. 2.
Predicate adjective, definiteness of, 93. II. 3. (2).
Predicate in adjective clauses after the relative, 97. B. Rem. 1.
Predicative accusative, 94. 4.
Prefix. (See Preformative.)
Preformative of stem, 41.
Preformative of imperfect, 45. 2, 3, 47. Rem. 4, 5.
Preformatives in formation of nouns, 74.
Prepositions, 89. B.
Prepositions with pronominal suffixes, 77. 4, 36. 3.
Prepositions inseparable, 34.
Prepositions between nouns in construction, 96. 2. Rem.
Prepositions before a relative clause, 97. B. Rem. 3.
Prepositions denoting the genitive relation, 98.
Present, 112. 2, 113. 2, 116. 1. (1), 116. 2. (1).
Primitive adverbs, 89. A. 4.
Prohibition, how denoted, 115. 3, 5.
Pronominal fragments, 35. 2, 36, 45. 2, 43. 5. Rem. 1.
Pronoun, personal, 35, 36. (See Personal Pronouns.)
Pronoun, possessive. (See Possessive Pronoun.)
Pronoun, demonstrative. (See Demonstrative Pronoun.)
Pronoun, relative, 34, 38. 1.
Pronoun, interrogative, 39, 103. (See Interrogative Pronoun.)
Pronoun, indefinite, 39. Rem. 1, 107, 108. 2, 109.
Pronoun, reflexive, 105.
Pronominal suffix, 36, 77.
Pronunciation of letters, 2, 3.

208 INDEX.

Prophetic perfect, 112. 3. (1).
Prosthetic Olaph, 20. 1.
Protasis, 137, 138.
Pure vowels, 7, 2. (1).

Quadriliterals, 63.
Quiescence, 25.

Rebbuy, 13, 77. 7.
Reflexive stems, 41. 4, 5.
Reflexive with object, 126. 2.
Reflexive with cognate accusative, 126. 4. (2).
Rejection, 23, 53, 55, 3. Rem. 3, 58. 1. (2). Rem. 2. (2), 60. 3, 4, 67. 2. 64. 1, 2.
Relative pronoun, 34, 38. 1.
Relative pronoun used to denote the genitive relation, 97.
Relative sentences, 136.
Resh, 4. 3. (3), 4. 4, 5. 1, 11. 5, 13. 2, 19. 6, 20, 2, 21. 3, 23. 2. (3), 26. 1.
Roots, 40.
Rukhokh, 10. 1, 44. Rem. 1, 47. Rem. 1, 68. 1.

Segholates, 67.
Sentences, verbal and nominal, 130.
Sentences, simple, 131.
Sentences, declarative, 131. 1.
Sentences, negative, 131. 2.
Sentences, interrogative, 132.
Sentences, compound conjunctive, 133.
Sentences, alternative and adversative, 134.
Sentences, complex, 135-138.
Sentences, substantive, 135.
Sentences, adjective or relative, 136.
Sentences, adverbial, 137.
Sentences, conditional, 138.
Shaph'el, 41. 5.
Shin, 3, 4. 3. (5), 5. 1, 20. 1. Rem. 1.
Sh°wa, 7. 1. (3), 9, 31.
Sharpened syllables, 17. 3.
Shifting of vowels, 32.
Short vowels, 7. 1. (1).
Sibilants, 5. 1, 21. 1.
Sign, vowel. (See Vowel.)
Sign, consonant. (See Alphabet.)
Signs, orthographic, 10 sq.
Sign of definite object, 89. C.
State of noun, 76.
State, anomalies of, 86. 17.
State. (See Absolute, Emphatic and Construct.)
Stative perfect, 41. 1. (2), 43. 5. Rem. 2.
Stems, verb, 41.
Stem, simple verb, 41. 1.
Stem, intensive, 41. 2.
Stem, causative, 41. 3.
Stem, reflexive or passive, 41. 4.
Stem, Shaph'el, 41. 5.
Stem, Taph'el, 41. 5. Rem. 1.

Stems, verb, general view of, 42.
Stems, original forms of, 42.
Stems, first forms of, 42, 43. 4, 43. Rem. 2.
Stems, names of, 42.
Stems, force of, 42.
Stems, characteristics of, 42.
Strong verbs, 40. 2.
Subject of the verb, 121.
Subject when a collective, 121. 2.
Subject when plural in form and singular in signification, 121. 3.
Subject when the predicate is a participle, 121. 7.
Subject from cognate root, 122. 5. Rem.
Subject, substantive sentence used for, 135. 1.
Subject and predicate in nominal sentences, 130. 1.
Subjects, two or more, 121. 5, 6.
Subjunctive, 112. 3. Rem. 1, 114. 4, 127. 3. (2), 127. 4. (2), 129. 2. (3). Rem.
Substantive clause in apposition, 135. 5.
Substantive sentences, 135.
Substantive sentences used as subject, 135. 1.
Substantive sentences used as object, 135. 3.
Substantive sentences used as predicate, 135. 2.
Substantive sentence used as dependent question, 135. 3. (2).
Substantive sentence used as a quotation, 135. 3. (3).
Substantive sentence used as an indirect object, 135. 3. (4).
Substantive object clauses after adjectives or participles, 135. 4.
Suffix, 36, 77, 51, 61.
Sufformative of perfect, 43. 1, 4.
Sufformative of imperative, 48. Rem. 2.
Sufformative of imperfect, 45. 2, 3, 47. Rems. 4, 5.
Sufformatives of perfect, peculiar forms of, 43. 5.
Superlative, 100. 2.
Syllable, how formed, 16.
Syllables, kinds of, 17.

Table showing classification of letters, 5.
Table showing personal pronouns, 35.
Table showing pronominal suffixes, 36.
Table giving general view of the verb-stems, 42.
Table giving the formation of the perfect p°'al, 43.
Table giving the first forms of the perfects of the derived stems, 44.
Table giving the p°'al imperfect, 45.
Table giving a summary of the pronominal fragments used in the perfect, 43. 5. Rem. 1.
Table giving the pronominal fragments used in forming the imperfect, 45. 2, 47. Rem. 5.

INDEX.

Table showing the pe'al imperfects in A and E, 46.
Table giving the first forms of the imperfects of the derived stems, 47.
Table giving the preformative of stem and the vowels of the stem, 47. Rem. 4.
Table showing the formation of the imperative, 48.
Table showing the infinitive, 49.
Table showing the participles, 50.
Tables giving the verb with suffixes, 51.
Table giving the first forms of Ê Ê verbs, 54.
Table giving the first forms of Pê Yudh verbs, 58.
Table giving the first forms of Ê Wau verbs, 59.
Table giving the first forms of Lomadh Olaph verbs, 60.
Table giving the Lomadh Olaph verbs with suffixes, 61.
Table giving 'Ith with suffixes, 65.
Table showing the classification of nouns, 66. B.
Table showing the changes of the noun for gender, number and state, 76.
Table of nouns with suffixes, 77.
Table showing the declension of the noun, 79-85.
Tables of anomalous nouns, 86.
Tables of numerals, 88. I.
Taph'el stem, 41. 5. Rem. 1.
Tau, 2. 2, 4. 4, 5. 1, 10, 18. 3, 19. 5, 20. 3, 21. 1, 22. 4, 23. 2. (4), 23. 3. (3). 41. 4, 47. Rem. 2, 60. 2. Rem. 3.
Tense, 111. 3.
Teth, 5. 1, 18. 3, 21. 1, 22. 4.
Time, how expressed, 111. 3.
Transposition, 21, 44. Rem. 2, 47. Rem. 3.

u, how written, 6. 1, 6. 4, 6. 5. (6).
u, how pronounced, 6. 3. (3).
u, quantity of, 7. 1.
u, origin of, 7, 2.
u, value of, 7. 3.
$ŭ$, in an open syllable always dropped, 28. 3.
u, euphony of, 29. 6, 7.
Unchangeable vowels, 7. 3.
Union of subject and predicate, 130. 1.

Verb, strong, 40. 2.
Verb, sorts of, 40. 1.

Verb, weak, 40. 3.
Verb stems, 41.
Verb stems, general view of, 42.
Verb, quadriliteral, 63.
Verb, anomalous, 64.
Verb, defective, 64.
Verb, syntax of, 111 sq.
Verb, subject of, 121.
Verb, impersonal, 122.
Verb, direct object of, 123.
Verb, indirect object of, 124.
Verb with two or more objects, 125.
Verb, passive or reflexive, with object, 126.
Verb, substantive, 127.
Verbs in e, 43. Rem. 2.
Verbs in u, 41. 1. (3).
Verbal adjective, 72. 2. (4).
Voluntative. (See Optative.)
Vowel letters, 4. 5, 5. 2.
Vowel signs, 6.
Vowel sounds, 6. 3.
Vowels, names of, 6, 2.
Vowels, changes of, 7. 3, 29-33, 42, Rems. 45. 1, 3.
Vowels, defectively or fully written, 6. 5.
Vowels, quantity of, 7. 1, 28.
Vowels, quality of, 7. 2, 3.
Vowel-half, 7. 1, 16. 1, 31.
Vowel, position of, 6. 4.
Vowel-helping, 9. 2 Rem. 32.
Vowels, euphony of, 29.
Vowels, loss of, 30.
Vowels, shifting of, 32.
Vowels, new, 33, 77. 2, 82. Rems. 1-3.

Wau, 4. 3 (4), 4. 4, 4. 5, 5. 2, 6. 5. (6) (7) (8) (9), 8, 11. 3, 16. 2, 19. 7, 22. 1, 2, 23. 1 (2), 2, (2), 3 (1), 24. 2, 25. 2, 27. 2, 40. 2. (4). 58, 59. 60, 67. 2. (2) (5), 79. B.
Wau, before unvowelled consonants, 34.
Weak verb, 40. 3.
Weakness of Wau and Yudh, 27.
Wish, how expressed. (See Optative.)

Yoth, 89. C.
Yudh, 4. 3. (5), 4. 5, 5. 1, 5. 2, 6. 5. (4), (5), (8), 8, 11. 3, 16. 2. Rem. 2, 19. 7, 20. 1. Rem. 2, 22. 1.-3, 22. 5, 23. 1. (2), 2. (2), 3. (1), 24. 3, 25. 3, 26. 2. (2), 27. 1, 3, 30. 2. (5), 58, 59. 6. Rems. 1, 2, 60, 67. 2. (2) (4) (5), 75. 5, 6, 7, 77. 5, 6, 79. A. Rem. 2, 79. B.

www.ingramcontent.com/pod-product-compliance
Lightning Source LLC
Chambersburg PA
CBHW071439150426
43191CB00008B/1183